Copyright © 2005 by Roger Steffens and Leroy Jodie Pierson

Published by Rounder Books

an imprint of:
Rounder Records Corp.
One Camp Street
Cambridge, MA 02140

Published per agreement with LMH Publishing, Ltd., Kingston, Jamaica.
Special thanks to Mike Henry.

All rights reserved. No part of this book may be reproduced in whole or in part without written permission from the publisher, except by reviewers who may quote brief excerpts in connection with a review in a newspaper, magazine, or electronic publication; nor may any part of this book be reproduced, stored in a retrieval system, or transmitted in any form or by any means electronic, mechanical, photocopying, recording, or other, without written permission from the publisher.

ISBN: 1-57940-120-1

Cover design and book layout by Geoff Gans

Steffens, Roger
Bob Marley and the Wailers: The Definitive Discography
1. Reggae music. Jamaica. Discography. 2. Marley, Bob 3. Wailers (Reggae group)
I Pierson, Leroy Jodie II T.

First Edition
2005926918
781.646'092
ISBN 1-57940-120-1

9 8 7 6 5 4 3 2 1

PRINTED IN CANADA

OTHER BOOKS BY ROGER STEFFENS:

as author:
The World of Reggae featuring Bob Marley: Treasures
  from Roger Steffens' Reggae Archives

as co-author:
Bob Marley: Spirit Dancer
One Love: Life with Bob Marley and the Wailers

as contributing writer:
Dictionnarie des chansons de Bob Marley (France)
Reggae International
Rebel Music: Bob Marley & Roots Reggae (UK)
Every Little Thing Gonna Be Alright: The Bob Marley Reader
Chanting Down Babylon
New Grove Dictionary of Music & Musicians
All Music Guide
A Magia Do Reggae (Brazil)
Rolling Stone Illustrated History of Rock
The Rolling Stone Book of the Seventies
Jimi Hendrix: The Ultimate Experience
Hollywood Shack Job
Smokestack El Ropo's Bedside Reader
Rastafari: The Mysticism of Bob Marley (Argentina)

as contributing photographer:
Bob Marley: Le Reggae & Les Rastas (France)
Coleur Reggae (France)
Lonely Planet: Jamaica

BOB MARLEY And The WAILERS

THE DEFINITIVE DISCOGRAPHY

By Roger Steffens and Leroy Jodie Pierson

Table of Contents

How to Use This Book (LJP)   I

Bob Marley Biography   III

Peter Tosh Biography   VII

Bunny Wailer Biography   XI

My Romance with Record Collecting (RS)   XIV

The Definitive Discography   1

Acknowledgements   162

Appendices   164

Index   168

How to use this book

In 1990 Roger Steffens and I traveled to Jamaica at the request of Bunny Wailer who wanted our help in writing a book detailing the history of the Wailers, Jamaica's most important vocal group, and a group that launched the careers of international superstars Bob Marley, Peter Tosh, and Bunny Wailer. I asked Bunny if we could simultaneously prepare a complete and definitive discography of the group. With his agreement, we subsequently listened to the entire catalogue of material the Wailers had recorded as a group, and he patiently shared his recollections of each song and session. This book could not have been produced without his help and support. Quite often his memories are the only reliable source available. Bob Marley, Peter Tosh, Junior Braithwaite, Joe Higgs, Carly Barrett, Clement Dodd, Leslie Kong, Tommy McCook, Roland Alphonso, and many others important to the group's history have passed away. Lee Perry, who could offer much insight, is seldom willing to engage the topic in interview. When Bunny was occasionally unable to identify horn players, he brought in "Dizzy" Johnny Moore and Bobby Ellis for help.

The music created by the Wailers, collectively and individually during the formative years of Jamaican blues, ska, rock steady, and reggae is hard-hitting funky folk music of the Trench Town ghetto of Kingston, Jamaica. Their music was written and performed for the people of the Jamaican ghettos, often using patois that made their messages impenetrable to the uninitiated. Even in later years when their audience was world wide, and they were selling the vast majority of their records overseas, they all continued to write primarily for their original constituency. Their large body of work, their preeminence in their field, and the enduring influence their legacy has had on not only musical but political, religious, and philosophical thought, demands a more serious work of discography than the mere listing of titles and labels.

A good discography not only answers questions but often introduces them. Detail and chronology is of great importance, and exact detail is often difficult to come by in the chaotic world of Jamaican music. We have done the best job we could, but recognize that the work will change as new detail is revealed by time. So then, this is a work in progress and revisions and additions are welcome.

Material is deemed worthy of inclusion in this text if Bob Marley, Bunny Wailer, or Peter Tosh vocalizes on the song as either lead or harmony singer. There are very few exceptions to this rule. The Wailers made a few instrumental titles that are included. The book includes all issued recordings, unreleased studio recordings, well-recorded rehearsals, sound system specials, informal composing tapes, well-recorded live shows, live shows of historic interest, live performances on radio, and live performances on television programs. The selection of live shows is admittedly arbitrary. We originally planned to include all live shows, but found that it slowed down the flow of the book with material of interest to a very small number of collectors. Both Bob and Peter kept up intensive touring schedules, often performing the same songs on virtually every show of a given tour. Sample shows from each tour are included to indicate the scope of the material performed. Also included are live shows that were historic events and well-recorded live shows in the vaults of Island, Solomonic, Tuff Gong, EMI, or Columbia Records.

LAYOUT

The first line of each section displays the original record label artist credit or credits in large capital letters followed by the date of the recording session. The next line in a smaller font begins a listing of the participants in the session including vocalists, musicians, engineers, and producers, along with the name of the recording studio, the number of tracks on the original tape, and details of later overdubs. The next line lists the original titles recorded at the session. Matrix numbers are given before the title if that title saw issue as a single.

These numbers are especially useful to the collector of Jamaican music because so many records were issued with only a blank label and sold as pre-release items. Song titles are followed by the name of the original label for the first Jamaican single release, followed by original foreign single issues, and then original record album and CD issues. If the next line of text uses a ditto mark under the title, the song is the same recording listed above, but with an alternate matrix number, alternate mix or later overdubs. If the title is repeated in full, it is an alternate recording of the song. Ditto marks appearing under label issues mean that the listed title appears on the same record or CD listed above. Reissues and bootlegs are not included in this text. Reissues are of little interest to the true collector, and bootlegs are illegitimate issues on which no royalties are paid to the original artists. Finally, most sections have an indented note with additional information on songs from that session, including composition, conflicting information, alternate titles, first issue details, identification of album titles, biographical or historical observations, explanations of patois used, etc. If no other composer is noted after the first listing of a title, it may be assumed that the vocalist wrote the song.

Appendix A: Album Title Index presents a listing of album titles otherwise referred to in the text by label name and issue number only. This appendix is not a listing of all Wailers albums.

- Leroy Jodie Pierson

Bob Marley, San Diego, Nov. 1979. Photo by Roger Steffens.

BOB MARLEY

Considered by many to be the Musical Artist of the 20th Century, Bob Marley planted the seeds of a local recording career in Jamaica and saw its fruits appear throughout every continent before his untimely death at 36 in 1981. He was totally unafraid of experimenting in the studio, and indeed his catalog of early records indicates an interest in straight-ahead pop, gospel, Latin, rhythm and blues, rock and roll, doo-wop, country and western, and of course ska, rock steady, and reggae. In the latter three categories of island music, Marley was an influential innovator, working alongside historic producers like Leslie Kong, for whom he cut four songs prior to the formation of his group, the Wailers; Coxson Dodd, who almost single-handedly created the Jamaican music business as we now know it; and the irrepressible dub genius Lee "Scratch" Perry.

Among the least recognized influences, however, was the American pop singer Johnny Nash, who "discovered" Bob in 1968 at a grounation (a Rasta religious gathering) in Kingston, and immediately signed him to his label, JAD Records, as both songwriter and performer. Nash had several American hits with songs penned by Marley, but his label was never able to achieve air-play for the Wailers' own recordings of those songs. For four years, JAD gave Marley a weekly salary and royalties once the Nash covers started to chart. It enabled him to finance his own labels, beginning with Wail 'N' Soul M which was transformed into Tuff Gong, taken from Marley's nick-name in the ghettos of Western Kingston. "We originally wanted to call it Tuff Gang," Bunny Wailer said in 1990 during extensive weeks-long interviews with us for a now-aborted autobiography. "But people felt that was too aggressive. Bob was already being called the Gong, the Don, so we just adapted it."

The Wailers group rehearsed for a couple of years in the yard of the legendary singer Joe Higgs, called, legitimately, the "Father of Reggae Music," because of the great influence he had on so many of the form's early adherents. Joe's yard in Trench Town, an area of government housing, became a kind of informal "college of musical knowledge." Singers like Alton Ellis and groups like the Wailing Souls were often found there, sometimes singing through the night. Joe took these informal sessions quite seriously, and would coach the youngsters in voice control, harmony, mic technique, and stagecraft. The initial Wailers group was composed of five members: Junior Braithwaite, who everyone thought had the best voice; a young woman named Beverley Kelso, who joined the night before the Wailers' first recording session, replacing Cherry Green (aka Ermine Bramwell) who had rehearsed with the group for almost two years, but had a real job and couldn't get time off to join them in the studio; as well as the core trio of Peter Tosh, Bunny Livingston, and Bob. Following a successful audition for Coxson, they succeeded beyond their wildest dreams with their very first recording for him in 1964, "Simmer Down," a plea to cool things down in the ghetto. During the next two years they were never off the charts. They covered the Beatles' "And I Love Her," the Bronx, New York, Italian doo-wop group Dion and the Belmonts' "Teenager in Love," even Tom Jones' "What's New Pussycat." Gospel songs that Bob and Peter sang in church in their youth were added to their repetoire like "Let the Lord Be Seen in You," and "Just in Time." Their own songwriting skills were being honed, resulting in songs like Bob's emotional ballad "It Hurts to Be Alone," which Junior sang the day before he quit the group and moved to America in 1965.

Occassionally others were called in to help on the sessions when the Wailers just couldn't get their harmonies right. This occurred with "Lonesome Feelings," for example, on which the group was joined on record by Joe Higgs and his companion Sylvia Richards. Although their time with Coxson at Studio One produced a multitude of local hits, the Wailers were unhappy with the lack of financial rewards, receiving, according to Bunny, "only three pounds a week each, no matter how many thousands of records we were selling at the time." Frustrated, Bob took a temporary leave from the Wailers and moved to America in February 1966, joining his mother who had moved to Delaware in 1962. He took a job sweeping floors in the Dupont Hotel in Wilmington, trying to save enough money to start his own label and gain control of the profits of his own work. When the American Army asked him to register for the draft eight months later, he returned quickly to Jamaica. The small amount of money he had accumulated allowed him to press the Wailers' first single on their own, "Freedom Time," a cry of liberation from Coxson, and its flip side, "Bend Down Low," done in the new rock steady style that had superseded ska.

During this late '60s period, the Wailers had but one overriding goal - to make enough money so they could buy a house where they could all live together with their families, and establish a private studio, where they could go whenever inspiration struck. A year later, JAD bought the foreign rights to their music, allowing the Wailers to keep the Caribbean rights. The group continued to have minor local hits, but they could never get enough money behind them to achieve their goals and, in fact, quit the business for a while. This was due in part to a case of writer's block that Bob suffered. To clear his head, Bob and Bunny moved back to the little northern village of Nine Mile where Bob had been born. Peter came too, but only lasted a week, as the silence drove him back to Kingston. Eventually Bob returned too, opening a record shop staffed in part by his wife Rita. Peter, always the best musician in the group, began to cut solo records and play on others' studio sessions, doing vocals like "Funeral," and organ and melodica instrumentals for producers like Joe Gibbs. Always a fan of American soul music, Bob even covered James Brown's "I'm Black and I'm Proud," giving it a decidedly Caribbean twist and titling his version, "Black Progress." In a blatant attempt to get a hit, the Wailers covered the sacharrine American hit by the Archies, "Sugar Sugar," for Randy's, the label owned by the folks whose studio they were then often using for their own compositions. "The Letter," a number one U.S. hit by the Box Tops, was covered on a blank label single, and retitled "Give Me A Ticket."

Finally, in May 1970, the Wailers recorded for less than a month for Leslie Kong, Bob's original producer seven years earlier. This was, in fact, the first real album cut in Jamaica - as opposed to a collection of singles. Inspired by the thematic experiments of rock and roll, such as the Rolling Stones' *Their Satanic Majesties Request*, and the Beatles' *Sgt. Pepper's Lonely Hearts Club Band*, the Wailers recorded an album-length pep-talk to themselves to get a firm hold of their career, recording tracks like "Go Tell It On the Mountain," "Caution," "Do It Twice," "Soul Captives," and "Soul Shakedown Party," lifted from a James Brown song. There was even a nod to the current acid-inspired pop world, an unreleased track called "Sophisticated Pyschedelication." Kong wanted to called the album *The Best of the Wailers*, but the Wailers warned him that they had a long career in front of them, and if this were their best in his opinion, it meant that he was going to die soon. Kong laughed, and shortly after he released the album, dropped dead at 38. The album was stillborn, but the Wailers' legend had begun.

Next they turned to a former colleague of theirs at Studio One, a nascent producer/songwriter/performer named Lee "Scratch" Perry, a diminutive wild-man known also as "The Upsetter," and "Scratch," because "all things start from Scratch!" Their collaboration produced about four dozen songs, and was entered into optimistically with an agreement that would give the Perry and the Wailers an equal 50-50 split on everything they made. Sadly, this was not to be. Bunny claimed, "Perry sold a bunch of our songs to Trojan Records in England and when he came back he told us he was not going to split the advance with us, but would pay us royalties instead." Bunny attacked him physically, and the collaboration wound down after a mere eight months. Many critics consider this the finest period of the Wailers' trio, and many of the songs created with Perry would be redone on solo albums by each of the three members in years to come. Although Bunny and Peter had bitter feelings toward Perry, Bob forgave him in later years, and collaborated on several notable songs such as "Jah Live" and "Punky Reggae Party."

The major turning point in the Wailers' lives came at the end of 1972, when JAD Records sold their contract to a white Jamaican millionaire, Chris Blackwell, founder of Island Records. The label had started a decade earlier in order to reissue Jamaican music to overseas Jamaicans who had migrated to Britain. Blackwell gave the group a small amount of money to record an album, and the result was the magnificent *Catch A Fire*, with pop overdubs on keyboards and guitar by a pair of American musicians. Critics hailed it as a masterpiece, but initial sales were only about 15,000 copies. Blackwell promised to underwrite a tour of England, but at its conclusion he sent them a bill for the tour's expenses instead, and Bunny quit the group on the spot. The final album by the Wailers trio, *Burnin'*, came out at the end of 1973, just as Peter left to go solo. A recently released live album of Bob and Peter in November of that year, *Live at Leeds*, showcases the ferocious power of the group as it closed out a decade's work. Their reputation as "the Jamaican Beatles" became apparent immediately, as Peter released his debut, *Legalize It,* and Bunny recorded *Blackheart Man,* two monuments in reggae's international breakthrough in the mid-70s.

After their breakup with Perry, the Wailers had teamed up with the rhythm section of Perry's studio band, the Upsetters. On bass was Aston "Family Man" Barrett and on drums was his brother, Carly. "They were the best vocal group," recalled Fams, "and we were the best backing band, so we decided to come together and mosh up the world." The prophecy was fulfilled when Marley's first solo album, the dark, minimalist classic, *Natty Dread*, was released at the end of 1974. Fans in England hailed him as reggae's first true superstar, and sold out crowds greeted every stop of Bob's first tour without his old friends in 1975. That year's *Live* album, recorded at London's Lyceum, documented Bob's triumph.

A year later, *Rastaman Vibration*, hit the American charts' top ten (his only record to do so). By the end of the year, an ominous event turned Bob from showman to shaman. Gunmen invaded his home studio at Tuff Gong headquarters in uptown Kingston, and shot him, his wife, and his manager (and one other man) in an attempt to keep him from performing two nights later at the "Smile Jamaica" concert. He narrowly escaped with his life, and an aura of blessed immortality descended upon him. Some saw the inscription on the album he had released a few months earlier as a prophecy. It was "The Blessing of Joseph," whom Bob believed he was the reincarnation of. "Joseph is a fruitful bough...the archers have sorely grieved him, and shot at him, and hated him." *Rastaman Vibration* contained an anti-CIA track called "Rat Race," which had been banned in Jamaica, and - more importantly - a speech of Haile Selassie's set to music, called "War." Derided at first, the track has gone on to become one of his most important accomplishments, insisting that "until the color of a man's skin is of no more significance than the color of his eyes, everywhere is war."

Following the assassination attempt, Bob went into a self-imposed exile for fourteen months. Much of the time was spent in England, where his inspiration was at an all-time high. In a few brief months, he recorded enough tracks to fill his next two albums. *Exodus* came out in late spring of 1977, and went on to be declared the "Best Album of the 20th Century" by *Time* magazine. The following year, *Kaya* received an initially tepid response from many who thought he had gone soft because of the light love songs contained on it. Bob was in love, and it showed. His paramour was Cindy Breakspeare, newly crowned Miss World, and their cohabitation in London in '77 drew screamingly derisive headlines in England's tabloids ("Miss World and Her Wild Man") and much consternation at home in Jamaica.

Eventually Bob returned to Kingston to headline a giant One Love Peace Concert in the National Stadium. At the end of the eight-hour show, Bob summoned the Prime Minister and leader of the opposition to shake hands in front of 40,000 people, to "show the people that you love them right, show the people that you're gonna unite!" Under a full moon, on the 12th anniversary of the visit of Haile Selassie, the god of the Rastafarian faith, Michael Manley and Edward Seaga bracketed Bob as he held their hands aloft in a benediction to Jah Rastafari. The Peace Truce between the warring factions in Kingston's contentious ghettos did not last, however. When asked if anything had changed since the Peace Truce, Bob's former partner Peter Tosh exclaimed angrily, "Yes. More dead." But Bob's peace-keeping attempts were recognized by no less a body than the United Nations, and two months after the concert, Bob received the U.N. Peace Medal in New York "on behalf of 500 million Africans."

It was in 1978 that Bob finally fulfilled his dream of having his own studio. The first album to be cut there was *Black Woman*, by Judy Mowatt, a member of Bob's backing trio, the I Three, and an established solo star in her own right. Bob's first project there was *Survival*. A private visit to Ethiopia in the latter part of 1978 opened Bob's eyes to the reality of the political situation in Africa, and he came back home sobered by the experience. Orginally intended to be titled *Black Survival*, the album contained songs relating to the ongoing struggles in Angola, South Africa, and especially Rhodesia. A track called "Zimbabwe" became the anthem for the freedom fighters in that country in the final days of their struggle against the colonialist oppressors. When the country achieved its long-sought independence in April of 1980, Bob was invited to headline the celebrations in Harare. He spent a quarter of a million dollars to bring lights, sound equipment, and a stage to that country which hadn't seen a live concert in more than twenty years. Today, *Survival* is considered one of his paramount efforts, filled with tunes that will be sung as long as people are denied their rights, like "Top Ranking" ("are you skanking?") and "Africa Unite."

By 1980 Bob was as big a star as anyone in popular music. He set out on the most successful reggae tour in history across Europe that summer. In Milan he played in a stadium where the Pope had appeared shortly before, and he outdrew the Pope! One hundred thousand people came to sing along with his songs of freedom. That fall, he came back to America for a tour that was to include stops with Stevie Wonder, a dear friend with whom he had performed at events in Kingston and the U.S. It was Bob's deepest wish to reach the black American audience, who, in the cocaine-fueled '70s, had seemed largely impervious to Bob's music. But after only five shows in late September, Bob collapsed while jogging in New York's Central Park. Doctors gave him a few weeks to live. The melanoma cancer which had been diagnosed in 1977 and prevented him from finishing the world tour he had begun that summer in Europe, had now spread to his lungs and brain. The last show of his life took place in Pittsburgh, Pennsylvania. Tapes of the concert show no sign of debilitation, and he did two tumultuous sets of encores, ending with a medley of "Work" ("five days to go, four days to go...") and "Get Up Stand Up," the anthem that some of the music world's greatest stars would use to open and close a globe-spanning Amnesty International tour a few years later.

Bob's final album, *Uprising*, maintained a prophetic tone, foreseeing the imminence of his life's end in tracks like "Zion Train" ("...is coming our way"), "Coming in from the Cold," and the final, acoustic, "Redemption Song" ("all I ever had, these songs of freedom"). He passed on May 11, 1981, and was given the biggest funeral in the history of the Caribbean ten days later.

Politicians paid him honor, now that he was safely out of the way. But his prophecy about reggae ("it will go on and on until it meets its rightful people") could just as easily be applied to him. Each year his stature has grown. At the millenium, the *New York Times* declared that "Around the world Bob Marley may be the most influential musician of the second half of the [20th] century," and built a time capsule to be opened in the year 3000, containing Marley's video *Live at the Rainbow 1977*, to represent the finest musical moments of the century. He became the first (and still only) Third World star to be inducted into the Rock and Roll Hall of Fame and Museum; won a Lifetime Achievement from the Grammys; and a star on Hollywood Boulevard.

But the real proof of his power can be seen in the ongoing two decades' success of *Legend*, an album of his greatest hits, that has been number one on the catalog charts of Billboard magazine longer than any other album in pop music history. It can also be seen in the continuing affection of young people for his rebel image, and the fact that there is virtually nowhere on earth where you won't encounter his image on t-shirts, banners, and posters, as ubiquitous as his fellow revolutionary, Che Guevara.

Let the final word come from the head of Amnesty International, Jack Healey, who said, "Everywhere I go in the world today, Bob Marley is the symbol of freedom."

Peter Tosh, L.A., Sept. 1979. Photo by Roger Steffens.

PETER TOSH

"All we had was nothing, but because of the divine spirit that we were born and raised with, it teaches us to multiply nothing with nothing and get something." – Peter Tosh.

Peter Tosh was born on October 19, 1944. His musical training began in the church, and his mother recalls him singing "Christian songs" with accompaniment on his own home-made sardine pan guitar as early as age five. Elders would often encourage him with gifts of a shilling or two, given in appreciation of the amusement or entertainment he provided. Participation in his church's choir taught Peter the rudiments of vocal harmony and introduced him to the piano, an instrument on which Peter would gain proficiency by his middle teenage years, a period in which Peter ultimately rejected Christian teachings as expressed by the church. Cut off from the piano, Peter shifted his attention back to the guitar. He would later say, "If I only had the opportunity of having my own professional instrument, I would play the songs that angels sing."

In his late teens, attracted by musical opportunity, Tosh moved from the rural parish of Westmoreland into the city of Kingston on Jamaica's south coast. He experienced profound culture shock. "It was a new era in my life, a whole new page turned over because this was totally different from what I grew up with in the country. The most dangerous things I ever heard or seen in my life was when I find myself in Trench Town."

The Rasta elders say, "You will find your food more time in a desolate place," and so it was that Peter would meet Bob Marley and Bunny Livingston in the heart of one of the most notorious ghettoes in the Western Hemisphere. Bob and Bunny had decided to form a vocal group and they were looking for a third voice that would complement their own singing. Bunny recalls that he and Bob first saw Peter walking the street as he played his guitar and sang "Go Tell It On The Mountain" and "Sinner Man," two church songs that he would later record with the Wailers. Bob and Bunny were both impressed with Peter's full baritone voice which could slide easily both into the bass register and into high falsetto. They were also impressed with his skill on the guitar, an instrument they both hoped to learn, and soon asked Peter to join them in the formation of the Wailers. Peter was not only delighted to find serious musical compatriots, but happy to gain the friendship of these two brothers who knew the runnings of the ghetto and who had established street credentials in Trench Town.

As the group began their rehearsals in the tenement yards of Trench Town, Peter would play guitar to supply the key and rhythm for the songs, and he patiently taught Bob the rudiments of the instrument. He also played guitar when they eventually auditioned successfully for Clement "Coxson" Dodd's Studio One company. For the innovative producer, the Wailers would record over one hundred titles in less than two years, many with Peter singing lead. Songs like "Maga Dog," "The Toughest," "Jumbie Jamboree," and "Don't Look Back" (recorded 12 years before his duet on the same tune with Mick Jagger) helped establish Peter as a major force on the Jamaican music scene. It was also around this mid-60s period that Tosh got a nickname that clung to him to the end of his days, based partly on the Jamaican pronunciation of his last name as "Touch." But he was notorious, too, for touching girls, pinching them on their arms and other existential areas. Thus he became Peter Touch on record labels and on the sweaty back streets of Jamdung.

Years later when naive journalists would interview Peter and compare him to Bob, Peter would kiss his teeth and say, "Bob Marley was my student." This was true to a certain extent, but one must never underestimate the years of private tutelage Bob received from Joe Higgs, prior to ever laying eyes on Peter. Under Tosh's tutelage, Bob eventually developed into a competent rhythm guitarist, but was never able to approach the complete rhythmic mastery of the instrument ultimately achieved by Tosh. By the late sixties Peter was in demand as a session musician and he played guitar or keyboard on countless recording dates for Randy's, Joe Gibbs, and especially for Duke Reid, who regularly employed Peter during the early seventies. Thus Peter's rhythm guitar work appeared on many of Reid's Treasure Isle releases during this period, including classic recordings of the Paragons, the Melodians, and Justin Hinds and the Dominoes. Peter's guitar work on the Wailers records of the same period recalls the playing of Jamaica's master percussionists. Never content with playing repetitively simple ska or reggae rhythm guitar cliches, the best of Peter's work is full of invention with complex, ever-changing rhythmic variations effortlessly executed throughout a piece while never losing sight of, or letting the listener forget, the "one drop" at the core of the music. In addition, Peter mastered two electronic effects, wah-wah pedal and phase shifter, which he cleverly used to create additional rhythmic tension and counterpoint in his performance. Peter's keyboard talents were modest, but informal sessions at Randy's Studio yielded several keyboard-led instrumentals credited to Tosh and released in both Jamaica and England. Peter's ability with keyboards was perhaps best expressed in his playing of the melodica, a cheap, hand-held instrument combining a short keyboard with a mouthpiece blown in a similar fashion to a saxophone. His keyboard work also appeared on dozens of early seventies Wailers recordings.

Peter had grown up without a father figure, and over the years had developed a deep distrust and even contempt for figures of authority, like the woman he called Queen 'Ere-lies-a-bitch. A master of deconstructing language to find its secret meanings, he was especially contemptuous of the police who were on the front line protecting the status quo of Babylon and its savage shitstem which downpressed black people in poverty while preserving the wealth and privileges of the ruling class in Western shrivelization. He spat his disgust at the Crime Minister and the politricksters who shit in the House of represent-a-thief. His first clash with the police (whom he also called Babylon) occurred after he was arrested and abused during a highly destructive 1968 demonstration protesting the current regime in Rhodesia. He would later record rants against the constabulary in songs like "No Mercy" and the excoriating "Mark Of The Beast," songs that delighted Kingston ghetto sufferers, but enraged the authorities who made sure that these and others of their ilk were banned from Jamaican radio. Despite their efforts at suppression, Peter's records sold well, especially in the western ghettoes of the city. Also banned was Peter's "Legalize It," a mid-seventies plea to legalize ganja which went on to become one of the biggest hits in Jamaican history as well as the title song of Peter's first solo album for Columbia. For two years it sang from every rum bar juke box in shanty town. He followed it in 1977 with the peerless *Equal Rights* which contained "Apartheid," his demand for an end to the illegal regime in South Africa, one of the first such popular songs of its kind; "African," which spoke directly of the mother continent, to whose soil Peter longed to return; and "Stepping Razor," one of his signature songs, written by his early coach, Joe Higgs.

Peter had linked up with the emergent Sly & Robbie in the earliest stages of their partnership, and toured throughout the seventies with them as his backing rhythm section, Word Sound and Power. They were with him at the One Love Peace Concert in April of 1978, as Tosh astonished the sold-out crowd at the National Stadium with his filthy-sounding language and bombastic harangue of the Prime Minister and Opposition Leader, delivered ferociously right to their faces as they sat stunned before him in the second row. He told them that until ganja was legalized they were just doing the work of the slave masters, and nothing in 400 years had changed. The performance was released almost a quarter of a century later, with a booklet containing transcripts of everything he had said that night in its original patois, and with facing "translations" into standard English. A few months after the tense event, police arrested Peter on a trumped-up ganja charge, and he was dragged to a cell and beaten with batons ceaselessly by seven cops for an hour and a half. Peter's hands and wrists were savaged by the authorities while Tosh tried to fend off blows which ultimately required dozens of stitches in the center of his scalp, where his skull had burst open. His instrumental work was directly impacted by this assault and he never regained his former manual dexterity.

Also as a direct result of his intense and fiercely political performance at One Love, Peter was signed to a recording and touring contract by the Rolling Stones' Mick Jagger and Keith Richards, who had witnessed Peter's explosive outbursts that night. Alongside Tina Turner, he opened the Stones' North American tour of 1978, touring at the same time as Bob Marley, and overlapping in Burbank, California's Starlite Amphitheater with his former partner. Bob came onstage for his encore set singing "Get Up Stand Up," the anthem he co-wrote with Peter. At the place in the song where Peter comes in on the record, he stepped out of the wings with a mighty stride, reaching Bob just as his part came, and took the mic from his hand, never missing a beat. Bob was beside himself leaping in wide-eyed joy and surprise. It would be the last time they would ever share a stage.

The first single from the Rolling Stones collaboration was "Don't Look Back" with Jagger, sung in a famous performance by the duo on an early Saturday Night Live broadcast. The debut album, *Bush Doctor*, contained another of Tosh's signature songs dating back to Coxsone days, "I'm the Toughest," based on James and Bobby Purify's "I'm Your Puppet." In 1979, *Mystic Man* followed, with nine songs divided between those which encouraged acts of rebellion, and others that mined a more spiritual vein of forbearance.

Although their relationship with Tosh was checkered, the Rolling Stones' alliance with him provided him the chance to record some fine albums and gained him a high visibility, propelling him to the forefront of the reggae explosion, an obvious heir apparent. But Tosh's contentious spirit would have side effects. After a two year break, Peter returned to the world's stages, and in the sad aftermath of Bob's passing in May of '81, he announced to all who would listen, "I am not the New King of Reggae." Then, pausing for effect, he would say, "There is nothing new about me!" Cutting his final album for the Stones,1981's *Wanted: Dread and Alive*, Peter sang "Coming in Hot," about relief from a fever, though many thought it was his answer to one of Bob's final compositions, "Coming in from the Cold." Peter lost many fans because of his acerbic attitude to his former comrade's death, and in fact during the final two years of Bob's life, Peter never spoke to him and, like Bunny, refused to attend his funeral.

At Thanksgiving time in 1982, Peter headlined an international array of pop stars and reggae greats at the opening event of the Bob Marley Performing Arts Center in Montego Bay. Another lengthy speech, caused by a long power outage, stirred the sunrise crowd, as Peter lamented the fact that there was no reggae radio in the country of its birth. The following year, an all-reggae format was introduced on a new station, IRIE-FM, and today one wonders how Peter would react to the news that there are now 17 broadcast stations, most of them reggae-oriented, on his home island. Peter's stirring performance was released posthumously as *Live at the Jamaica World Music Festival* on Danny Sims' revived JAD label.

Mama Africa came out in 1983, with Peter backed by a new band, composed of key members of the studio giants Soul Syndicate, including drummer Carlton "Santa" Davis and bassist George "Fully" Fullwood. They played the Greek Theater in Hollywood for an album and a video, and accompanied Tosh at a controversial concert in Swaziland, where the crowd broke down the fences and the promoter had to flee for his life. Peter's final performance came on December 30, 1983 at SuperJam in Kingston.

For the next four years, Peter sought help from various healers in Jamaica, Nigeria, the States, and other places, trying to find surcease from the constant pains caused by the numerous police beatings he had been subjected to. Finally, in late 1987, he prepared a return to touring and released his first album in four years, *No Nuclear War*. A few days later, on September 11, thieves invaded his home. Of the seven people present, three were killed at point black range, including Peter. Santa Davis, his drummer, was shot at his side, and to this day carries a bullet lodged between his lung and his heart. Tosh's murderer languishes on death row, but his two accomplices, rumored to be off-duty cops, have never been caught. The tragedy was compounded with the seizure by police of Peter's property from his New York apartment, including master tapes of unissued songs that were damaged beyond repair while in improper storage in police custody.

Peter Tosh's accomplishments as both a Wailer and as a solo artist will forever resonate in reggae music like the heartbeat at its core. His persona contained the fiery commitment of a Malcolm X or even a Che Guevara. Like those revolutionary leaders, Peter recoiled from poverty. He was enraged by official indifference and police brutality. He preached against racial injustice, imperialism, and colonialism. His songs convey a philosophy that, combined with his life story, was to form the basis of his uncompleted autobiography *Red X*. Tapes on which he dictated the book were used in a film called *Stepping Razor: Red X*, an early nineties biographical documentary film that is now in release as a DVD. Peter's murder has also been the subject of a VH1 documentary in their Behind the Music series.

"I don't want no peace," sang Peter with a snarl, "I want equal rights and justice!" – a plea echoed in the cries of the L.A. revolt after the Rodney King verdict was announced: "No justice, no peace!" Wherever there are oppressors, Tosh's music will continue to ring out and identify them, calling them to task before the Almighty Jah Rastafari.

Roger Steffens' Reggae Archiives.

Bunny Wailer, Kingston, JA., Nov. 1979. Photo by Kate Simon.

BUNNY WAILER

If Peter Tosh was the firebrand radical John Lennon of the Wailers, the group that became known as the Jamaican Beatles, and if Bob Marley was the more melodic and revolutionary version of Paul McCartney, then Bunny Wailer was certainly the George Harrison figure. Able to write and sing lead on major songs of his own, the youngster of the group was forever in the shadows of his two more aggressive older bredren until his first solo album, *Blackheart Man*, in 1975. That record, often cited as one of roots reggae's all-time top ten, established him immediately as a figure to be reckoned with.

"We were all basically motherless children," Bunny revealed during our conversations in 1990. Like Bob, Bunny's family had roots in the rural village of Nine Mile in St. Ann's. Born Neville O'Reilly Livingston on April 10, 1947, Bunny was eight when he moved there from Kingston with his father, "Toddy" Livingston. Toddy subsequently fell in love with Bob's mother, Cedella, and not long after, they moved to Kingston with their sons who, from that day forward, would be raised alongside each other. Two years behind his "brother" Bob, Bunny began writing songs by the age of fifteen. One of his first compositions was "Pass It On," and he would have recorded it for Leslie Kong in 1962 if he could have got out of school in time to make the scheduled session. (It would take another eleven years before he would actually record it.)

Following Bob's unsuccessful solo attempts in that same year, Bunny joined Bob and Junior Braithwaite, Peter Tosh and Cherry Green for a couple of years of rehearsals in Joe Higgs' yard. After a successful group audition for Coxson Dodd, Bunny contributed harmony on nearly one hundred songs, and took the leads on tunes like the enchanting doo-wop ballad "I Need You," the plaintive "Where is My Mother," the 1920s gospel treat, "This Train," and its spiritual companion, sung with Peter, "Sinnerman." Around June '66, Bunny hit a trifecta, utilizing Rasta champion Count Ossie on percussion, the great Nyahbinghi drummer who had just played for Emperor Haile Selassie I of Ethiopia a few weeks before. Recording on Studio One's new four-track machine, Bunny laid down the ineffable "Sunday Morning," and "He Who Feels It Knows It," along with the rude boy anthem, "Let Him Go." He was beginning to hit his stride because Bob had left for the States, and Bunny finally had the space to develop some of his own ideas in Bob's absence. Coxson gave him other songs to try, including an early '60s American release called "My Dream Island" written by Al Johnson for a group called El Tempos. He dropped a few letters from the title and cut "Dreamland," which went on to become one of his signature songs, covered by many other reggae greats such as Marcia Griffiths and Third World.

Bunny's career took an unexpected turn in the summer of 1967, when he was busted for herb dealing. He had the misfortune to be in a friend's yard in Trench Town, a man who actually did sell the ubiquitous weed, and he was sentenced to fourteen months in prison, including an initial period in the hellish depths of the General Penetentiary. His composition, "Battering Down Sentence," released in 1974, reflected this grave experience. Eventually Bunny went to a work farm, returning to the group with renewed strength, and the desire to help establish their new self-owned Wail 'N' Soul M label. He had embraced the Rasta faith following Selassie's visit, and the group's music began to reflect that philosophy more overtly, particularly on Peter's "Rasta Shook Them Up," and Bob's celestial "Selassie Is the Chapel," written for him by his Rasta mentor, Mortimo Planno.

Album sessions with Leslie Kong and Lee "Scratch" Perry found Bunny mainly in the background, offering low-end broop-broops, angelic falsettos, and other smooth harmonic underpinnings. But it was something that happened as a result of Kong's lethal intransigence that made Bunny an early legend in Western Kingston. As Kong prepared to release an album's worth of their collaborations, he told them he was going to call it *The Best of the Wailers*. Bunny was furious and warned him that no one knows the best of their works until their lives are at an end and, since the Wailers were all young men, that must mean that Kong was about to die, so he better not do that. Kong laughed. Shortly after the album's release, he dropped dead. "Because he saw the last of the Wailers," Bunny laughed, twenty years after the sessions, "so to him it was really the best of the Wailers, for it ended for him. He heard the best." Bunny's reputation as a wrathful prophet had begun.

For the next several years, Bunny remained content with his role as a harmony vocalist creating smooth and sweet contrast to the rougher singing styles of Bob, who sang almost all the leads, and Peter, who sang the rest. Bunny was also learning to play bass, an instrument he subsequently played on classic recordings like "Trench Town Rock," "Redder Than Red," "Guava Jelly," and the original cut of "Concrete Jungle."

There was so much energy in the group, other outlets were needed. Peter turned to instrumental backup work in different studios. In 1972 two new labels were born. "I created both labels," Bunny says, "Solomonic and Intel-Diplo, and I brought the two of them to Peter and just say pick one, and he picked Intel-Diplo. So Solomonic Production was destined to be my label." Asked whether he would have chosen it if he had first pick, he hesitated. "Yeah, maybe. Maybe, maybe, maybe. Because, you see, Intel-Diplo is very deep. Solomon was an intelligent diplomat, so that's the meaning of Intel-Diplo, it means Intelligent Diplomat. I only shortened it." Both meant King Solomon? "Yeah, either one of them would mean just the same, because King Selassie I say we have to live as intelligent diplomats among men, so you have to be wise, wiser than the serpent and more harmless than the dove: that's to be an intelligent diplomat. That's how you are wise, to survive. You have to be very highly intelligent to be a diplomat."

By 1972, Bunny released his first solo single, under the name Heat Air and Water, "Searching for Love," followed quickly by "Life Line" and "Bide Up." His prophetic heralding of the impending world oil crisis a year later was titled "Arab Oil Weapon." Work on the Wailers' first two albums for Chris Blackwell's Island label began to take up much of the band's time in Jamaica and the UK. "Pass It On" finally saw the light of day during the group's final sessions together, a decade after Bunny missed out laying the track for Leslie Kong. It was one of the emotional highlights of the Wailers' swan song, *Burnin'*. Bunny had become angered by the long months of touring and recording in England in the winter and spring of 1973, and when Chris Blackwell gave them a bill for some $80,000 at the end of their spring tour, Bunny quit on the spot, vowing never to trade one part of white man's Babylon for another. In fact, it would be 13 years before he left Jamaica again.

Despite his bitter feeling toward the man Peter Tosh called "Whiteworst" ("Because if him black show me how him black, and if him well, show me one t'ing dat is well with him! No mon, him Whiteworst."), Bunny signed a two-album deal with Island Records and received an unprecedented $42,000 advance. Bunny used it to spend weeks touring the entire country of Jamaica with his wife, Jean Watt, looking for an appropriate piece of land that he could shape into his own "Dreamland." They finally found a sprawling 142-acre hilltop spread overlooking the easternmost tip of the island. The owner quoted a price, and Bunny calmly opened the trunk of his car, into which a large number of shopping bags had been stuffed, each overflowing with low-denomination Jamaican banknotes. Stunned, the man asked Bunny suspiciously why he was driving around like that. Bunny locked him in his most penetrating and mystic stare and said, "Would you accept a check from a man who look like me?"

In 1976, Bunny's universally-acclaimed debut, *Blackheart Man*, took the world by storm. It contained backing from Family Man and Carly Barrett, coming over from the Wailers' band to help out alongside Robbie Shakespeare, a youth-man bass sensation whom Family Man was training, and Earl "Chinna" Smith, another prodigy who had been called Melchisidek the High Priest from the time he was a teen studio sensation. With arrangements that were generous, imaginative, and lush, the album was a virtual catechism of the Rastafari faith, a mellow meditation on truth and rights from the viewpoint of some of the most disenfranchised people on earth, secure in their I-nity with the Creator. With Peter's *Legalize It* album making a similar impression, and achieving major-label release in the U.S. on Columbia Records, the Wailers were now seen as one of the most inventive supergroups that hardly anyone ever saw, discovered by the world after their ten year career had been brought to an abrupt conclusion. For a couple more years, after they finished recording together, the trio made infrequent appearances together at major Jamaican events, in concerts with Marvin Gaye, the Jackson Five, and finally, Stevie Wonder at the "Dream Concert" on October 14, 1975. It would be the only time that the I Three, Marley's new backing trio, and the original Wailers ever played together.

Bunny issued a regular stream of vocal and dub albums and 7" and 12" singles throughout the rest of the '70s, but made no live appearances, preferring to tend to what he termed generally as "cultivation." The cover of his late '70s album *In I Father's House* even pictures him seated aboard a tractor. As the decade ended, he composed and sang the title song for a rollicking reggae film called *Rockers*, but demurred when asked to perform on screen. In 1980 he recorded *Bunny Sings the Wailers*, which touched a nerve with the public due to the recurring rumors of Bob's ill health at the time. It was Bunny singing of his respect and love for the person he considered his older brother. Following Bob's passing, he began to produce another Wailers retrospective he called *Tribute*.

The early '80s belonged to Bunny Wailer in Jamaica. For two years, everywhere one trod on the island, the sounds of Bunny's era-defining dancehall collection, *Rock and Groove*, were bouncing from bayside shack to shanty town to the ballrooms of the poshest hotels. It was like the Beatles emerging from the funk of JFK's murder, Bunny bringing us light from the incomprehensible downer of Marley's cruel and untimely death. It would turn out to be one of the final major moments before the music turned sick and slack, awash in decadence and degeneracy and leaving the past behind. It was a path that Bunny would find himself increasingly running toward, to the dismay of his original audience.

The trend toward his trans-genre experiments began with a nod toward the second line sounds of New Orleans on an album called *Hook Line and Sinker*, intended to capture a wider audience but basically befuddling buyers as Bunny was caught rapping on a jazzy riff called "The Monkey Speaks."

By the end of 1982, Bunny was ready to make a comeback after a seven year absence from the stage. He planned a giant concert in the National Stadium in Kingston, with himself as the headliner, and performances from friends including Jimmy Cliff, Judy Mowatt, and his former partner, Peter Tosh. But the event itself was a failure, partly because of its ill-timing on Boxing Day, a National Holiday the day after Christmas that is a time of family gatherings for Jamaicans, and partly due to near constant rain that fell throughout the night. Only a couple of thousand people came, making the stadium appear almost empty. The show was recorded and released as an album.

One of Bunny's greatest successes came the following year, albeit not with his voice. He had composed a track that became a local hit for Marcia Griffiths on a Solomonic 12" called "Electric Boogie," a kind of throw-away tune for the dancehalls that metamorphosed into a gigantic international smash. Diplomatic parties in swank Washington Embassies rocked to the riddim of the new dance, dubbed the Electric Slide. Half-time ceremonies at football games presented thousands of dancers filling the field doing the lock-step motions. And Marcia had her biggest hit since her British Top five duet with Bob Andy on "Young, Gifted and Black," more than a dozen years earlier.

The Reggae Consciousness concert that took place on Christmas Day, 1984 drew a larger crowd than the paltry few who had come out for Bunny's come-back show two years earlier. Eventually it was time for his first foreign solo show, and Bunny planned a massive extravaganza for July 12, 1986, featuring Ras Michael and the Sons of Negus, Leroy Sibbles, and others. To back his 3 1/2 hour non-stop set he brought some of the finest musicians in Jamaican musical history, dating to the original Skatalites, and working his way up through Sly & Robbie and the current studio heavies, Roots Radics Band. The concert was presented in Long Beach, California on a sun-kissed Saturday afternoon, attended by thousands of people, many of whom had traveled thousands of miles to see this historic event. Bunny seemed truly energized on our Reggae Beat radio program the following day, and you could hear the deep emotion in his voice as he acknowledged the adulatory reception he had been accorded. With Peter in seclusion and Bob dead five years already, in 1986 Bunny was poised to retake his crown with a strong one-two punch that found him on stage three months later in Madison Square Garden before an ecstatic 14,000. The show reunited Bunny (for a scant two minutes at least) with Junior Braithwaite and "Vision" Walker of the original Wailers, singing the optimistic title song they had just recorded for a reunion album to be called *Together Again*. A concert video was released, celebrating Bunny's triumphant return to international touring.

For more than a decade, Bunny's fans had been eager for him to return to the rootical commitments of his *Blackheart Man* period. He finally answered them with 1988's brilliant album, *Liberation*. "Botha the Mosquito," "Food," "Serious Thing," and the title track were mini-masterpieces. Bunny seemed the obvious standard bearer for Rasta music at a time when pure slackness was ruling the local charts and major roots artists were left without labels.

But rather than continuing the battle, Bunny subtly surrendered and released dancehall albums like *Dance Massive*, *Gumption*, and *Just Be Nice*. He headlined the Sunsplash 1990 tour of Europe and played many of the major reggae festivals in North America. His usual show is a fairly elaborate stage review, with dancers and a backup trio which includes one of the founding members of the Gaylads. Called Psalms, these aging brethren are the epitome of old school innocence and charm. They were singing behind him during another failed attempt of Bunny's to reach the youth market. At an annual dancehall festival called Sting in Kingston, Bunny found himself bottled off the stage by angry youngsters crying for Ninja Man and Beenie Man, the harder-edged heroes of that moment in the early '90s. It was, without question, a rude awakening for one who had helped create the original dancehall scene thirty years before. The Jamaican papers were filled with shocked editorials, ruing the decline in behavior 'mongst de yout'-dem, who seemed to show no respect for the door openers who had pioneered their culture. Bunny, perversely, continued to make records with youngsters and their continually degrading tastes as his target audience.

Perhaps the brightest Wailers moment from the '90s was the long-awaited *Together Again* project, involving a studio reunion of Peter Tosh, Bunny Wailer, Junior Braithwaite, "Vision" Walker, and Peter's son, Andrew Tosh. Several master tapes of unreleased Bob Marley vocals were joined together with the voices of the newly dubbed "Original Wailers." Then new backing tracks were laid which retained the flavor of the originals, but laid with much better technical equipment. Musicians such as Sly & Robbie and Tosh Drummer Carlton "Santa" Davis added strength to the arrangements, and the harmonies of the reunited veterans soared and swooped. When the album was finally released in 1993, the skin crawled as listeners heard Peter sing these lines in the title song recorded back in the 1986 over-dubbing sessions: "Some will rise and some will fall/but who will be the survivors/only Jah Jah will know." The collection of old and new songs was released by RAS Records under the title *The Never Ending Wailers*, and brought the hope that we would actually see the new lineup – sans Peter and Bob of course – on stage. Sadly, this was never to manifest. Junior Braithwaite was murdered and "Vision" is now in retirement.

Another mid-'90s undertaking was a salute to Marley's 50th birthday, for which Bunny cut a two cd, 50 track anthology of Marley covers. In 2000 he issued *Communication*, whose key track was titled "Millenium Rock." In true soon-come fashion it was not available until several months after the Millenium.

For the year 2005, a seven-cd box set called *Ark of the Covenant* or *The Wailers Legacy* was privately pressed by Bunny in a numbered collectors' edition of just 500 copies. Four albums' worth of previously available Coxson-through-Lee Perry tracks are coupled with three albums of Bunny reading a script about the Wailers' history from formation through breakup, the only such document from a Wailer insider ever. (We say this cognizant of Rita Marley's book, which unfortunately does not deal with the music from either her own or her husband Bob's career.)

Bunny has lived to see the timeless songs he co-created become worldwide anthems of freedom and liberation, soul-soothing chants that will help to heal generations yet to come. He is truly one of a trio of immortals.

MY ROMANCE WITH RECORD COLLECTING
by Roger Steffens

INTRODUCTION

If you were born in '33 you turned 45 in '78.

If you understand the significance of those numbers immediately – you're old. For those who don't quite get it, singles were the way we used to buy our favorite songs, big heavy things that spun really fast at 78 rpm (revolutions per minute). My first record was a 78, "Rock Around the Clock," on its initial pressing in 1954 on Decca, a year before it broke really big when featured over the opening credits for a rude bwoi school boy flick called *Blackboard Jungle*. Its thick vinyl weighed several ounces and, even when played today, though scratchy, it still sounds immediate and impressively present, pure sonic passion exploding from the box. It's no surprise that when NASA launched its extra-solar probe several years back, it contained songs by Chuck Berry and others on a gold-plated copper record, for some future E.T. to bop to. This was the best way, scientists decided, to hear music.

"The warmth of the vinyl sound (as opposed to digital) seems more suited to an art that is emotional and ephemeral. It's a fireplace to an electric heater," says Devon Steffens, my savvy 22-year-old, who like his older sister, is a vinyl hound. Kate used to work in one of those *High Fidelity*-type used record and collectors' shops called Rockaway Records, at the convergence of tragically hip Silver Lake and gentrifying Echo Park – here in the town Peter Tosh called Hellay. When people brought records she didn't like to the register, teenage Kate would refuse to ring them up, "That's crap! You don't want that. I won't let you buy that!" she'd rant.

My wife Mary, a fellow WWII baby, recalls that her first records were an album of Bozo's Adventures. Mine were Tex Ritter and Genie the Record ("That's who I am, the record."). "What I loved was the different colored vinyl," Mary remembers, "and the talking books that my blind grandmother used to listen to on records."

Alan Freed – Photo courtesy Roger Steffens' Reggae Archives.

For me as a '50s teen-acher, my love affair with records began at 11 with the constant barrage of "rock 'n' roll platters," a brand new music that was about to become the thrilling soundtrack to my life. This music inspired a new kind of adolescence. I was introduced to it in New Milford, New Jersey, around late 1953, when I was in the sixth grade, and home from school with some awful childhood malady for which bed rest was the only solution. Under the covers, so the radio dial's tiny light could not be seen under the crack in my bedroom door after ten o'clock at night, and listening at the lowest possible setting, I discovered Alan Freed's syndicated nighttime "Moondog Matinee" beamed from its home in Cleveland to a scratchy station in Newark. Each evening on "W.A.D.O. radio" it was Jocko Henderson's "Rocketship Show," my baptism in fast-talking, rhyme-spawning black hipster delight. Jocko played even blacker records than Freed, although Freed never let color enter into his eclectic playlist choices. Nor money, despite what his McCarthyite accusers later charged in the payola witch trials which abruptly ended his career.

Alan Freed was my hero, the uncle I wished I had. I used to hang around WINS in the summertime, and had several encounters with him. Once I even told him that I wanted to be Alan Freed when I grew up. I admired him as a white man who recognized great music, and fought the color bar every chance he could. I realized he was helping to ignite a movement that would ultimately draw the races closer together. In 1957 I saved up enough money to buy an enormous Pentron reel-to-reel tape recorder with its own separate microphone. This I would prop up in front of our beige 1948 Bendix table-model radio with its brown, light-up dial, and tape Alan Freed's frenetic speed-riddled raps and sweaty rhythm and blues.

The only time I ever heard my Puritanical Irish Catholic mother swear was when I played a 78 of Little Richard in 1955 singing "Keep A Knocking" at rather loud volume, several times in a row. BOOM! BOOM! came two sudden pounds on my door, and when I tore it open my red-faced mom screamed at me, "Turn off that goddamn bugga-wugga jungle music!" I told that story years later, in 1985, to Richard, and

XIV

he howled with laughter, "I still love that bugga-wugga jungle music!"

There were other discoveries made possible on the far right low-watt end of the AM dial. Also on WADO was a swing shift master, a white guy called Alan Fredricks. He could sit in for the gospel host (who was opposite Freed) or for Jocko himself from ten until midnight. He could even take over believably for Symphony Sid, who was avuncular in a whole lot more threatening way. Sid was the Voice of Jazz in New York City, and he spoke with a heavy whiskey bass voice, a lot like Tom Donohue, the visionary founder of underground radio in San Francisco a decade onward. Sid played records by Nina Simone, Mongo Santamaria, Miles Davis, Dizzy Gillespie, Herbie Mann, and Babatunde Olatunji, and many nights I stayed up way past midnight to catch his broadcasts. I didn't quite know what to make of most of this kind of music, but I was trying to broaden my taste, because a new writing muse of mine, Jack Kerouac, wrote so stirringly about it. Certain things brought me around, especially 'Tunji's pioneering in-studio African drumming, which moved me in an entirely different kind of way.

In 1960 I graduated from Bergen Catholic High School as the N. J. State Oratory Champion in the American Legion's annual competition, with a speech called "The Constitution: A Barrier Against Tyranny." As the payola scandals brought the first era of rock 'n' roll to an abrupt end, a new category of popular music, Oldies but Goodies, also championed by Freed, created a new kind of store. A block below street level in a subway station at a famous shop called Times Square Records, 45s from just a few years back were selling for huge bucks. A typical day on which I went wax spelunking there might also find me at the Village Gate catching Miriam Makeba, or Dave Brubeck at Birdland, or John Lee Hooker at Gerde's Folk City. What a time and place for an 18-year-old pimply-faced hipster wannabe, with ears to dig the hottest live sounds and the coolest cuts he could find. I was completely into lps and 45s, and except for clothes, my stereo and records were all that went away to college with me that fall.

I got a job as a page at ABC, and met "Cousin Brucie" Morrow, who had been tapped by WABC radio to fill Alan Freed's former slot, opposite Murray the K on WINS. I became an assistant stage manager at Palisades Park during all-star lip-synch festivals emceed by the affable Morrow. But he would never have the impact of the other two, and the demarcation of generations in my youth was laid out in whether you were into Alan Freed or Murray the K, who seemed as much about comic gimmickry, show bizzy bits, and submarine watching, as about the music. With Freed, it was always where's the next great sound coming from, back in the time when every single week brought a record that Freed proudly predicted with unerring accuracy would be a classic fifty years down the road. The records you played defined who you were, and they become icons of eras, aural Proustian madeleines. And I never threw any of mine away. When I went to Nam in '67, I taped my favorite discs onto a new format called a cassette. I carried them everywhere with me, throughout the Tet Offensive in Saigon and during the rest of my 26 months in-country, and made hundreds of copies for guys out in the field. Music as medicine.

THE DISCOGRAPHY AND THE BIRTH OF REGGAE

What does all this have to do with a Wailers discography? Most of the text of this massive discography is about records. To this day, well into the new millennium, there are vinyl releases of the Wailers, both new and reissues (counting recent Bunny and the Complete Wailers series on JAD). Bob died before cds were introduced, and therefore prior to the digitalization of music. So Bob, being Jamaican, was able to impishly push the politely set boundaries of the RIAA (Recording Industry Association of America) recording curve limits to doggy highs and squid-deep lows, way down where Family Man's bass anchored the riddim and the melody at the same time, the bass being the lead instrument of roots reggae. Quite simply, the best way to hear the music of the Wailers as they intended it to be heard, is on plastic. It is there that one hears "presence," the subtle ambient sound of reality, not the dead-air quality of gigabyte computer discs. (Tosh would have called them "poisonal confusers.")

CDs make great targets for a redneck pistol picnic or as opalescent tree ornaments for a hippie orchard, but, to many aging geezers like us, their very existence is offensive. This begins with the two-point type of their unreadable liner notes (we poor writers of same lament that our work often languishes in the land of the unread because one needs a magnifying glass to see the damn things), and extends to the tiny illustrations and unnatural sound created by the mathematical impingement of ones and zeros.

Back in the day, the marvelous, inventive foot square lp art work, sometimes adorning double, triple and quadruple sleeves, fostered a bounteous burst of creativity, most especially in the '60s and '70s, and in fact, helped alert the world to the specialness of the Wailers. Chris Blackwell, the shrewd head of England's Island Records who signed the group at the end of '72, released their first album with him, *Catch A Fire*, in a sleeve that was sliced horizontally down the middle, with a stud at one end that allowed it to be opened at a diagonal. The plain blue cover had the curved-corner shape of a Zippo lighter, and when pulled back, a lighter aflame in a die-cut attachment flipped into sight. The expense that obviously was taken to package the band indicated that this was not the usual anthology of sappy Jamaican pop rehashes such as those that the U.K.'s Trojan Records rolled out regularly like fast food. No, this was a group that someone was actually slapping real money on, as if they were some kind of Carib rock 'n' roll royalty with something absolutely crucial to say. Blackwell gave them a tiny advance to record the album, about the equivalent of a rock star's weekly cocaine budget, and the Wailers returned with a masterpiece.

In the middle of the summer of '73, about six months after the release of Catch A Fire, I read a cover story in Rolling Stone about a new kind of music coming out of Jamaica. Its author, an inventively humorous Australian gonzo journalist named Michael Thomas, said that reggae music "crawls into your bloodstream like some vampire amoeba from the psychic rapids of Upper Niger consciousness." Those mind-bending words catapulted me out of my Berkeley apartment in search of a copy of the Wailers' Island debut, which I found in a used record store on Shattuck Avenue for a couple of bucks. The next day I saw the breakthrough Jamaican movie by Perry Henzell, The Harder They Come. During its famous ganja pipe scene, everyone in the theater lighted a spliff, and the rest of the film was seen through a thick haze that at times threatened to obscure the screen. Without realizing it, the rest of the audience and I were in the middle of our first Rasta grounation; our thoughts and the smoke making for one I-nity.

On the way home from the tiny northside theater, I stopped at Leopold's Records and bought the film's soundtrack. Bummed out by the '70s takeover of music biz-mess by corporate swine who gutted the social consciousness from the American pop charts, I was starving for something new that combined the celestial harmonies of '50s doo-wop with the political and spiritual awareness of the best of the '60s. And so my life was forever changed by this triple lick of fortune. I put the Rolling Stone piece in a manila folder, and from that day forward, I began to save everything I ran across regarding the music and its culture. Little did I realize the enormous long-term impact of these formative encounters, which would lead to multi-media projects, round-the-world travel, and encounters with the genre's biggest stars.

Not only did Berkeley have some of the country's best import record stores, something it shared with Boston, that other bastion of early reggae discovery, but just across the Bay, in San Francisco on Fillmore Street, an old spar of Marley's named Ruel Mills had opened Trench Town Records. It was there that I bought my first Jamaican 45s, harmonic gems by Alton Ellis and the Flames, the Techniques, Slim Smith and, of course, the Wailers. I learned that Bob and company had been recording for ten years already, and that reggae was just part of a continuing flow of Jamaican musical creativity that had begun with the double-time ska of Independence time, morphed into the slower more sinuous and seductive rock steady for a brief two year period, and then, in 1968, became the rhythm of reggae, based on the beat of the healthy human heart at rest. It was also in Ruel's store that I first encountered Rastafari, the movement that underpinned the best of the art form.

A SEARCH FOR DADAWAH

In 1976, my new wife Mary and I decided to go to Jamaica, to see if we could find some of the rare records we had been reading about in the pages of Kingston's Swing magazine and Britain's Black Music and Black Echoes periodicals, plus New Musical Express and Melody Maker. We stayed with a Jamaican family on the northwestern coast of the island in the little rural town of Lucea (pronounced "Lucy") and discovered how hard it was going to be to find the music in its own home. The only record seller in the area was a barefoot Rasta man who had a tiny shack that opened at eccentric hours and on no fixed schedule. After three tries, we finally found him ready for business, although his stock consisted of just a few singles and no albums. I managed to score "The Best Dressed Chicken in Town" by Doctor Alimantado, with its frenetic squawking "dub" side, the instrumental accompaniment to the vocal side that was a feature of nearly all Jamaican 45s.

On one of our first nights in Lucea, we had been taken to a hillside shack in which a young Jamaican student, educated in a stateside college to be a CPA, had moved upon his return home. He could find no work anywhere on the island, and lived a solitary existence with but a single electrical outlet, into which was plugged a 25 watt bulb, a hot plate, and a cheap turntable/cassette/amp. "Do you know Nyahbinghi?" he asked. "I've heard the term," I said, "but I'm not sure what it means." "Death to black and white oppressors," he said, not in a threatening way. "But it's also the kind of music on this new record by Ras Michael and the Sons of Negus called Dadawah," an Amharic Ethiopian word for Peace and Love. As he lowered the needle, Mary and I experienced something completely new, haunting, and unutterably captivating. Under a moonless sky, on a steep palm-filled hillside, we skanked to the hypnotic riddims over and over, and determined that we would do whatever it took to bring a copy of the record back with us. State of Emergency or not, we'd even go to the frightening capital if we had to, to get this unique lp.

Eventually we met a young doctor, home on holiday from Brooklyn, who was headed for Ocho Rios on the northeastern coast from which we could get a minibus directly to Kingston, and he invited us along. During the ride, Dr. Paul's dashboard cassette machine blared a constant barrage of dub. For me, being a wordsmith who had made his living for the previous decade reading poetry, this was like eating a sandwich with only one slice of bread, or - as a reggae wag sang - "like a toilet without the paper." When queried as to why he liked these bare instrumentals so much, the good doctor replied by tapping his forehead and smiling knowingly, saying, "Psychological music." He stretched each syllable slowly and deliberately in a deep, baritone voice and it would take me several more years to fully penetrate the profound truth of his pronouncement.

Mary Steffens, Tuff Gong, Kingston 1976. Photo by Roger Steffens.

Everyone warned us not to go to Kingston because of the omnipresent violence and current, critical danger. At the end of our first week in Lucea, on a blistering Sunday afternoon, the JBC's mid-day broadcast had been interrupted by an emergency announcement from the Socialist Prime Minister, Michael Manley, alleging the threat of an imminent American invasion of the island, and declaring an immediate State of Emergency. Manley's friendship with Cuba, coupled with the massive exportation of marijuana into North America, presented an unacceptable threat to the States. We were fascinated to see that alongside nearly every straight stretch of roadway, tall steel poles had been placed, designed to rip the wings off light planes that would utilize the roads for improvised landing strips

In the days to come, Manley stationed army tanks at every significant crossroad, and dispatched troops throughout the island, itchy teenagers with machine guns and thousand-yard stares. Kingston itself was locked down tight "under heavy manners," as singer Derrick Morgan had sung a few years before about the frequent curfews that the political situation created. As a consequence, all live music seemed to have disappeared in fear, and the only group we were able to see during our three week sojourn turned out to be Light of Saba, with the elegant Cedric 'Im Brooks fresh from his years with Count Ossie and the Mystic Revelation of Rastafari, performing in Lucea High School.

After spending an amazing night in a hand-woven seaside house with a tiny Rasta artist named Bongo Sylly, we boarded an early morning minibus in Ochi, as the locals called it, and headed south to the capital city. As we entered Kingston, the streets seemed weirdly deserted, and there were soldiers and jeeps and even an occasional armored personnel carrier. Around noon we were dropped off on Orange Street, in front of a tiny shack about the width of three telephone booths over which hung a hand-painted sign that bore the imprints of Tuff Gong, Bob Marley's own label, and others associated with it. Our minibus driver summoned a young fellow on the street and asked him to keep an eye on us. As fate would have it, we needed him more quickly than we could imagine. We hadn't been on the ground for more than two minutes when, standing before the shop's counter, I suddenly felt a hand in my pocket and it wasn't mine. A slim young fellow in a three piece suit, whose pants ended about five inches above his battered shoes, was in the process of picking my pocket. Idiot that I was, I had all the money I'd saved for the trip, $400, in that pocket, so I grabbed his wrist as tightly as I could, and he withdrew his hand, empty. Glancing at an accomplice, bunched tightly beside him, he put his hand into his vest and pulled out a 45.

Record.

It had a reference to the Rasta god, Jah, in its title. I figured I got off pretty cheap, buying it directly from this duded-up hypocrite (who also happened to be one of the bigger names in reggae at that time, but it wouldn't be smart for me to identify him further) for a dollar and a quarter, instead of paying a "tourist tax" of 400 clams. DeBrucier, the passerby who had been entreated by our driver to watch out for us, came to our rescue as the pickpockets took their leave, exiting quickly down the deserted street. He asked us what we were looking for - records - and told us he'd take us to the best shops, many of which were just around the corner on the city's main square known as Parade. But first, we wanted to buy every Marley record in Tuff Gong. "No Marleys," said the kid behind the counter dismissively. "What about Peter Tosh?" I asked, incredulous. "No, mon, nuttin'." I stepped back out onto the street, and looked up at the sign advertising all the different labels supposedly on sale within. How could this be? Then asked, without much optimism, "Bunny?" The youth leaned under the wooden plank that separated us and withdrew two of Bunny Wailer's earliest Solomonic singles, "Search for Love" and "Arab Oil Weapon."

"Come with me to Randy's and JoGibbs," said DeBrucier, and we followed him around the block, crossing Idler's Corner, an alley that separated the two rather large record stores on the edge of Parade. A small group of familiar looking men was there, and we were introduced to Big Youth and Tinga Stewart, who politely posed for a picture with us, Youth flashing his four jewel-encrusted front teeth in a welcoming smile. "You must be careful," he cautioned, "times a go dread right now." Inside Randy's several clerks were filling orders for anxious youth who were obviously middle-men from other areas stocking rural shops with the latest shots from the overheated music studios during what we now know as the Golden Age of Reggae. But what an endless cacophony! Discs were sampled in ten second ear-shattering bursts, so that the opening lyrics were barely heard before another 45 was slapped on the turntable, imposing instant and most unscientific purchasing choices. We were able to buy some newly issued recordings by artists whose work I had already discovered, but it was really not the place to audition anything new, so we hustled next door to JoGibbs, only to find a similar situation.

Unfortuately, Randy's didn't have *Dadawah*, neither did JoGibbs. And no one else during our three weeks on the island seemed to be able to come up with a copy of it, even though it was a current release. We were learning a lot about the vagaries of the Jamaican music business, the randomness of it all, the sheer luck factor in finding anything. In fact, it wasn't until later that summer, when we returned to San Francisco and ventured down to Ruel's Trench Town Records, that we found three copies of the album on his sparse shelves on Fillmore Street.

Reggae is a music you have to meet half-way

It's got its own language – Rasta patois – and its own mythology, based in part on the prophecies of that great 20th century prophet of repatriation, Marcus Garvey (who was jailed by the colonial authorities, and once he was safely dead, his image was put on the Jamaican currency). A true comprehension of reggae's lyrical concerns leads one to the Bible; to Jamaica's history of slavery, rebellion, independence movements, and "politricks"; to Ethiopia and Haile Selassie, who Rasta believe is the reincarnated Christ, the Almighty God incarnate in this I-wah (time), come forward to lead His people home to Africa. A person versed in Greek mythology could probably find all of the gods in its pantheon among the hundreds of home-grown "Stars" striding the wicked streets of Kingston with their cock-of-the-walk gaits and their confident dreams of international success. The more you know about these things, the more you can appreciate the accomplishments of reggae's greatest adherents.

When we moved to Los Angeles in late 1975, we were tipped to Barton's Records, a pair of Jamaican record stores run by Bally Barton and his wife Yvonne. Yvonne held forth at the uptown branch. Located at the convergence of La Brea Avenue and Hollywood Boulevard, it sat just around the corner from where they laid Bob Marley's star in 2001. It was in Barton's one afternoon in 1978 that I ran into Josh Harris, the drummer from an early ska-revival band called the Untouchables. We began comparing notes on where we could find the music we both loved in a town that hadn't even a single reggae radio program on any of its 84 AM or FM stations. "There's this guy I met here a couple of weeks ago you should know," said Josh. "His name is Hank Holmes and he sells reggae singles out of his house over in the Fairfax district every Friday night. I'll give you his number. You won't believe his collection!"

Hank Holmes and Roger Steffens, at Hank's Archives in Los Angeles, 1981. Photo by Peter Simon.

Intrigued, I called Hank as soon as I got home. He told me that I was the first person he had encountered who had actually been to Jamaica looking for records and experiencing the culture first hand. I told him how we had landed in Montego Bay airport expecting to be greeted by the sounds of reggae, only to find that the passenger areas' loudspeakers were blasting out "California Dreaming" by Jose Feliciano, and the minibus that took us to Lucea played nothing but country and western music. Hank laughed knowingly, and when I told him about some of the singles I had found, he asked me to come over right away. He lived upstairs in a fourplex a half a block from CBS Television City in Hollywood. I was staggered when I walked into his dining room. Surrounding it on two walls were thousands of reggae albums and singles. Nothing we had seen in

Kingston, Jamaica's music capital, compared with this! In a back room there was even more, including piles of unopened international shipping crates with hundreds of singles in each, sent from record dealers in the north of England. On Friday nights, Hank opened Reggae Beat, his informal home-based business which sold Jamaican records to a select clientele who would gather around a thick wooden table to hear his latest batch of finds. Well, not actually the latest, because the boxes had backed up so much and his selection method was so meticulous, almost to the point of being fetishistic, that he was many months behind in opening his purchases.

A typical listening session at Hank's place went something like this: he would pry open a crate and find, perhaps, five copies of "Sweetie Come from America" by Well Pleased and Satisfied on a small hole UK 45 (a tune which, ten years onward, I would help place on the soundtrack of the film about Jamaica's Olympic bobsled team, *Cool Runnings*). Before each play he would take care to brush off even the tiniest speck of dust, using a chamois cloth or, more than occasionally (and inexplicably, considering his obvious concern for a record's impeccability) the hem of his t-shirt. He would audition both sides and make notes about the sound quality; then he'd play the second copy, both sides; and the third, fourth, and fifth. By now, the eight or nine folks seated around the table could sing along with every word. The obvious lesser quality discs would be put up for sale, and if Hank really liked a record, he would save the best two copies for himself; one to play, one to put away. But the pressings might have a great vocal side and a faulty dub side, or vice versa, so which do you keep? Sometimes he would keep three. His prices were more than fair (and highly profitable as it would turn out), usually about $3 a record, and these included my first U.K. pressings of the Wailers, on immaculate white and red Island labels and superior vinyl. Some evenings we went home with only three records following the laborious winnowing process, and many of these have become more valuable than computer stock.

It was some time later that Hank revealed his secret. In the back pages of British music mags there were small classified ads from dealers, primarily in the north of England, offering ten reggae records for a pound, their choice. Meantime, Hank was working in a record one-stop on Pico Boulevard, a wholesale-retail establishment that specialized in cut-outs, albums that had been overpressed and were basically unsaleable, which you could snap up for 25 cents each. Many of these contained '60s and '70s r&b music, revered among a certain hip cognoscenti up in the north of England as "Northern Soul," and highly collectible, as it turns out, worth ten pounds or more each. So Hank made a few calls and suggested that he could supply these albums on a regular basis for ten pounds apiece, but instead of sending him money, he asked for ten pounds' worth of reggae singles in return for each lp.

Babatunde Olatunji and Roger Steffens, 1961. Photo by Martin Clancy.

You got it – one hundred discs for a 25 cent investment!

Of course, there were many duplicates in the weekly shipments, but that's how he added to his income, and this sideline would lead directly to the founding of our "Reggae Beat" radio program. Frustrated by the lack of airplay for such appealing music, we decided to link up to try to find a station that would let us tap Hank's extraordinary resources. With my broadcasting background, beginning on WVOX in New York in 1961 with my first guest, the great Nigerian drummer Babatunde Olatunji, and with Hank's stunning collection of music and his great stories that regaled us weekly, we felt we could do a terrific show and fill a very obvious gap on L.A.'s airwaves. It took us a year before a small, west-side station called KCRW put us on. Located then in a junior high school classroom across the street from its license holder, Santa Monica College, the station was an NPR outlet with great plans to grow. As it turned out, the "Reggae Beat" show, initially broadcast on Sundays from noon to two, became the flagship of the station. In our first on-air subscription fund drive, we made in three hours of pitching what the entire station had made during its previous ten day drive. Our time was immediately doubled to four hours per week, and the audience grew exponentially. Back in October of 1979 when we began, our first guest was Jeff Walker, who had been Bob Marley's west coast promo chief at Island Records in the mid-'70s and had actually filmed the events surrounding the assassination attempts on the lives of Bob, his wife Rita, and manager Don Taylor in December of 1976. Our first guest from the performance world was none other than Bob himself. Island's publicist called us up and asked if we would "mind going on the road with Bob Marley for a couple of weeks" on his *Survival* tour. Twist my bleedin' arm.

Our first day together, Don Taylor, Bob's sour-faced, condescending manager, pulled us reporters aside and told us that on the bus trip with the band down south to San Diego, we were not to talk to Mr. Marley under any circumstances. And if he spoke to us, answer quickly and do not attempt to engage in conversation.

With these dire admonitions firmly absorbed, I felt a deep dismay. I had prepared for the three hour ride down by packing a bag of Bob's records, both singles and albums, in the hopes that he would sign them for me. So we get on the bus and sit about halfway back on the right, Hank and I, and on comes Bob, the first person aboard, and heads right down toward us, sitting one seat back across the aisle. And we're not supposed to even acknowledge his presence. Damn! Off we go, and about an hour south of town, near San Clemente, I look back and notice with great chagrin that Bob is reading a copy of *Reggae News*, a new paper founded by Warren Smith to bring the word of Jah Music to America. Hank and I were among its first writers, initial forays for each of us into the world of reggae journalism. (Our first print interview came in September of '79, when Peter Tosh came to Hank's house to check out his collection, finding several instrumentals released under his name that he had no knowledge of ever recording.) I can't stand it as I see this picture before me begging to be taken, knowing that I risk ostracism if the wrathful Taylor should catch me, but I ask politely, "Bob, my editor would kill me if I don't get a shot of you reading his magazine. Would you mind please?"

"Do it quick," he said, and I snapped off two blurry, but very moody pictures. As I sat down, I pointed out to a bluff, with a windswept helipad and giant intercontinental communications towers bestriding a slightly-gone-to-seed ocean front compound.

"See over there, Bob," I pointed. "That's Nixon's house."

Bob looked at me with a stony expression. All he said was, "What year him president?"

"Oh, Bob, he was in much more than a year, long enough to do some permanent damage."

A little while down the road, driving through the spookily militant confines of the Marines' training base at Camp Pendleton, I put the bag of rare Wailers records on my lap and pulled out the albums. After waiting a bit, I glanced at Bob. He motioned for me to hand them to him, and I passed the bag over nervously. Very much the awestruck fan, I was exultant that Bob was actually touching my records! But I didn't dare say anything or ask him to sign them. Not now. We would be together for several days, and I really didn't want to blow this opportunity, especially not in its first iteration.

As luck would have it, Bob was virtually never left alone in the hurly-burly of the days ahead, and I was never able to find that ten minute space in which to get the works signed. What the heck, I thought, Bob comes through every year, we're friends now, he'll sign them next year. Famous last words. I never saw him again. But that experience taught me to be firm when given the opportunity to have an artist bless their work with his or her signature. I became, I must admit, much more aggressive when artists of the stature of Peter Tosh came back to town, or when Bunny finally arrived in 1986 for his first foreign solo show, so virtually all their records bear their signatures.

Over the years, the "Reggae Beat," show was graced with visits from virtually every major figure in the music. It was like church. As the station grew and moved to much larger new facilities with a live music studio, we added live concerts, often with jam sessions involving several superstars at once. Free of commercial responsibilities, we were a mighty team, Hank with his incredibly obscure singles and off-air knowledge, me with interviews and the best of the new releases. Alton Ellis came through six weeks in a row, and whenever he appeared at the station, we just turned the show over to him for as long as he wished. He sang the history of the music for us. Others, like Johnny Osbourne, Eek-A-Mouse, and Rankin' Roger made repeat visits and performed every time.

In 1981, CC Smith, a woman we had met on the way to that year's Marley Memorial Sunsplash Festival in Montego Bay, began coming to the station every Sunday to answer phones and, eventually, do a weekly calendar of events as reggae began to kick into second gear, finally, in Southern California. Several regular events and visiting artists from Jamaica demanded another form of communication with the reggae community, and one Sunday CC suggested a newsletter of some kind, and we asked on the air for anyone who wanted to receive it to send us their address. The next week CC came running in yelling, "We got 300 letters! What should I do? Do you think I should start a magazine?"

"Sure, CC," I said encouragingly, "start a magazine." Thus began *The Beat*, now in its 23rd year of publication, considered the premier reggae and world beat magazine in North America. It is distinguished, I'm proud to say, by the fact that all its contributors are unpaid volunteers. Many of them, like best-selling music biographer Stephen Davis, are considered among the best in their fields, so *The Beat* is truly a labor of love. I edit the Bob Marley Memorial Edition in May of every year, and it's our annual best seller. Nearly a quarter of a century since his passing, Bob is still reggae's best selling artist, accounting in many quarters for 50% of the music's gross sales.

Another prominent spinoff of our fandom came when I was approached in 1980 by a Trinidadian drummer named Chili Charles, who

Bob on the bus to San Diego, November 1979. Photo by Roger Steffens.

wanted to do video documentation of artists as they came through town. Since many of them contacted the radio program, it was easy to arrange early video interviews with Black Uhuru and Sly & Robbie, Jimmy Cliff, Peter Tosh, Freddie McGregor, Judy Mowatt, and scores of others. Although the cable tv series that developed from them, *L.A. Reggae*, hasn't run in many years, to this day each video discussion I do is recorded as if it's an episode of an on-going series. Many are shot here at the "Ark-hives in Hellay," (as Peter would say), so artists can hold their various works and tell the stories behind them. Often Chili would bring his tiny son, Oliver, with him. Today Oliver Charles is the highly respected drummer of the Ben Harper Band, touring all over the world to enormous audiences, modernizing the reggae riddims.

In 1982 I was "drafted" into my first real music business job. In a stroke of great fortune, the first albums for which I was asked to do national promotion were Elektra's initial foray into reggae, a double album of live shots from the Marley memorial edition of Sunsplash in 1981, and Steel Pulse's best album ever, *True Democracy*. That was followed by a job that came about because I had been such a harsh critic of Island Records' dismal promotional record in America, which I felt had been holding the music back. I met Chris Blackwell at a party at which he was introducing some new discoveries of his that he predicted were going to be huge. Turned out he was right. The band was U2. At the party I expressed my dismay that, even though Hank and I had the only reggae program on the air in L.A., we never received any promotional copies of Island's releases. "Well," he said, "why don't you come aboard and help us fix that?"

Taken aback at first, I eventually agreed to be hired as the National Promotions Director of Island Records for Reggae and (at my insistence) African music. My first projects were the posthumous Marley album, *Confrontation*, as well as Nigerian superstar King Sunny Ade's first two releases and Gregory Isaacs' career-maker, *Night Nurse*. I was flown to London to work with Trevor Wyatt on a series called "Reggae Greats," that was originally intended to be Blackwell's swan song to reggae, summing up the best work of the major roots artists on his label. The job lasted a little less than a year, until the day when Blackwell marched into my office and announced that he could no longer "afford to promote reggae and African music in the U.S." The sojourn in Britain resulted in the acquisition of a great many UK-oriented items of historic interest that enriched the archives. While there, I attended the closing day sale of Rita King's R&B Record Shop, where I added dozens of British singles to the collection in the bustling final minutes of the store's existence. I was also allowed by the generous-spirited Wyatt to tape discs in the Island singles archive, which I believe had been assembled by Roger Dalke, Britain's premier discographer. Blackwell had been repressing Marley's efforts from the very start, and the virgin vinyl of which they were made gave crystal clear, though less bassy, readings of songs I had only known from their often shabbily pressed Jamaican versions.

In 1985 I was contacted by Mike Melvoin, one of the heads of NARAS, the Recording Academy folks who give out the Grammys each year. He told me he and several of the Hollywood-based board members had become regular listeners of the Reggae Beat and they realized that there was a serious gap resulting from the Grammys ignoring reggae. They wished to establish a category for the music and asked if I would be the chairman of that committee, a position I've retained for the past twenty years. It created greater recognition and respect for the music, although annually there is always controversy when a huge selling album is ignored among the nominees. I end up having to explain, over and over again, that the committee just "screens" the potential nominees to make sure they actually belong in the reggae category, and that the voters, in two separate ballots, decide what becomes nominated and who eventually wins. The results have nothing to do with sales, quality, or airplay, and the voters must be actual dues-paying members of NARAS. For a long time, anything with the words Marley or Wailers in an album's title or artist attribution meant that it was an almost automatic shoo-in, with Bunny Wailer, Ziggy Marley & the Melody Makers, and even Damian Marley carrying home the little gramophone trophies in recent years.

In 1987 I left the "Reggae Beat" show as dancehall slackness began to overshadow the roots music that had drawn Hank and me and so many others into reggae in the first place. I was succeeded by the estimable Chuck Foster, another veteran of the Friday night '70s listening sessions at Hank's home. As fate would have it, we each ended up doing 7 1/2 years with Hank before the show got cancelled on its 15th anniversary. The tirelessly devoted Foster also reviews every new reggae record released in America in *The Beat*, and today Chuck hosts his own program, "Reggae Central," on the Pacifica outlet in L.A., KPFK. This is the same left-wing station, ironically, that had originally rejected me and Hank doing a reggae show there because, they told us, "you're white." Curiously enough, we had almost called our show "Reggae Central" to avoid confusion with Hank's record business, but KCRW's publicity had already gone out using the "Reggae Beat" title. Much later Chuck came up with that same Central title on his own.

The week after I quit the "Reggae Beat," I was visited by the head of the Schomburg Center for Research in Black Culture of the New York Public Library. He had come to check out the collection and make me aware of the value of what I had, sometimes in strange ways. "What do you do with the fan mail?" he asked. "I read it, answer it if necessary, sometimes months later, and then throw it away." He grimaced, and insisted, "You must never throw anything like that away. It's first-hand documentation of the spread of a culture. A hundred years from now it will have important historic value." A few months later, he made a modest bid for the purchase of the collection, which by then contained a few thousand cassettes, many of which were live board tapes from concerts I had emceed throughout the '80s around L.A.

I began to think more seriously about preserving things better, their potential value becoming more apparent. A few years later Japanese bootleggers made a huge offer for the entire collection, which I flatly rejected for the obvious Karmic consequences. I hadn't assembled this stuff with money in mind anyway. The Marley family made a few passes, too, but it was apparent they were only interested in the Marley elements. I've always believed that in order to understand the great accomplishments of reggae's paramount figure, you must know the context in which Bob created - and that's what the other 90% of the archives cover. I don't ever want the collection to be broken up, and wherever its future home, I want everything to be made available to anyone who wants to make use of it. Those are my two non-negotiable bottom lines - it must be kept intact forever and made available to the public, while respecting all rights of the artists whose work it contains.

Other items joined the melange and threatened to burst our walls: posters and fliers, mounds of t-shirts, badges and buttons, sculptures, banners, books, magazines, stuff ad infinitum. Artists began to park "safety copies" of their composing demos and other works, knowing that there was a safe, neutral ground where they could store their personal histories.

In the late '80s an earthquake sent two thousand cassettes cascading off their wall-mounted racks, spawning a terrifying thirty-second tsunami of smashing cases. Miraculously, only protective boxes broke, and not one of the tapes was harmed. Shortly after, an itinerant British reggae-loving carpenter built the first of four massive cabinets that now house more than 12,000 hours of tapes in specially constructed drawers whose back hinges allow them to be pulled all the way out for easy access to everything. It would take a colossal tremor to dislodge them.

As the '90s dawned, Leroy Jodie Pierson, a fellow Wailers record researcher who I would call at his home in St. Louis when I had Wailers questions, was enlisted with me for a remarkable project. Cambridge, Massachusetts-based Rounder Records' boss Bill Nowlin and Chris Wilson were in the process of negotiating rights to Coxson Dodd's definitive reggae catalog, hoping to eventually release everything known to exist in his vaults from the Wailers' foundation years. This was a thrilling challenge, and from that time forward until Mr. Dodd's sudden passing in May of 2004, I had many conversations with him while co-writing liner notes for Heartbeat Records' *Wailers at Studio One* series. Coxson was behind so many thousands of productions, that it is no wonder his memory was somewhat fuzzy in later years, and getting specific information from him was often daunting. But one certainly got the flavor for the era and a genuine love for the youngster who went on to be his biggest success. The resulting notes, and many more by Chris and others on non-Wailers Heartbeat/Studio One albums, remain among the most important first person information ever revealed by Mr. Dodd.

It is here that I think we should hear Leroy's tale from his own pen:

LEROY'S STORY

I first became aware of reggae music in 1977, when a friend returned from Jamaica with a handful of local singles which included several Wailers records like Bob Marley's "Screwface," Bunny Wailer's "Life Line," and Peter Tosh's "Mark Of The Beast." I was deeply impressed with these records and captivated in a way reminiscent of my early days collecting old blues records and trying to learn everything I could about blues music. Most of the great blues recordings were not available on album when I began collecting in the mid-sixties. I found quite a few old blues 78s in St. Louis and surrounding locales, often guided by local blues legend Henry Townsend, or the pioneer of blues radio in St. Louis, "Gabriel." During the late sixties I traveled extensively throughout the Deep South, spending considerable time learning guitar licks from legendary bluesmen like Fred McDowell, Robert Wilkins, and Johnny Shines. I spent a lot of time on these trips looking for old records, often going door to door in promising neighborhoods. When I returned to St. Louis, cleaned up my finds and placed the needle to the wax, I would often experience pure musical bliss as I heard for the first time rare and obscure sides by artists like Robert Nighthawk, Frank Stokes, Baby Boy Warren, King Solomon Hill, Jesse Thomas, and Robert Lockwood.

After hearing those first Wailers records, I began buying stacks of reggae albums by artists like the Wailers, Justin Hinds, Burning Spear, Lee Perry, The Maytals, and Max Romeo. I soon realized that these great artists all had long and historic recording careers in Jamaica before gaining enough prominence to rate an international release on a foreign label. It became clear that the best way to find and hear the early classics of reggae was to go to the source, the notorious ghetto of Kingston, Jamaica.

In 1979 I went to Jamaica as a journalist and photographer to document Reggae Sunsplash II for the premier issue of a magazine covering all forms of music generally ignored by mainstream media. I witnessed fine sets by Burning Spear, Mighty Diamonds, Joe Higgs, Israel Vibration, and Bob Marley and the Wailers, who turned in a superb high-energy set to end the show. The day after Sunsplash I went to Kingston to buy records, take photographs and soak up the vibes of reggae's birthplace. The first stop was on Orange Street at the Cash & Carry shop owned by Bunny Wailer, Big Youth, and Gregory Isaacs. Bunny wasn't there, but I purchased all of his latest records and pushed on to Randy's Record Mart on Parade where I was able to buy a small stack of Bob Marley and Peter Tosh records. I then headed to 56 Hope Road, the home of Tuff Gong Records and Bob Marley, who happened to be sitting on a side porch enjoying his first spliff of the morning. I approached and extended my hand as I introduced myself. Bob shook my hand and for a few minutes we talked about his performance at Sunsplash. He then allowed me to take two photographs.

Before my second trip to Jamaica a few months later, I wrote a letter to Bunny Wailer asking for a meeting and telling him how impressed I was with the music and spirituality of his *Blackheart Man* album. The day I arrived I phoned the Cash & Carry shop. Bunny was not in, but the fellow I spoke to, one "Leggo Beast," told me that Bunny had received my letter and would meet with me later in the week. A few days passed before "Leggo" called back asking me to come to the shop early the next morning. When I arrived at Cash & Carry, "Leggo" ushered me into the back room and told me to wait for Bunny. The large back room had several chairs and a table. Four dreadlocks sat around the table smoking herb and speaking in a patois impenetrable to me at that time. They ignored me as I sat down to begin my wait. After nearly an hour had passed, one of the dreads, a skinny short muscular man with a penetrating stare, came over, sat down next to me, and asked my business. I said I was waiting to meet Bunny Wailer. He smiled and said, "I am Bunny Wailer." After a short conversation, he introduced me to his friends – Peter Tosh, Gregory Isaacs, and Cedric Myton.

Back in St. Louis, I was keeping up a heavy performance schedule playing blues in local clubs, and I was doing a blues radio show on a local NPR affiliate, KWMU. They agreed to let me do an additional show of reggae music, and my "Beat Down Babylon" program aired for seven years. I had sold my interest in Nighthawk Records a few years earlier, and now had the opportunity to again travel to Jamaica, this time doing studio production work for the label. From 1980 through 1983 I visited Jamaica frequently, producing works by the Gladiators, Justin Hinds and the Dominoes, the Itals, Wailing Souls, Junior Byles, Culture, the Ethiopian, the Morwells, and the Mighty Diamonds. One highlight of that period came when I sat in on a mixing session with Bunny Wailer and the famous engineer Sylvan Morris at the Harry J Studio as they remixed several early Bunny Wailer recordings for inclusion on two Nighthawk albums of classic older tracks. One of the tracks was "Life Line," the first Bunny Wailer recording I ever heard.

When not working in the studio, I spent most of the time in pursuit of old records. I bought discs from shops, distributors, sets, sound systems, juke box dealers, bars, and individuals. I traded or sold duplicate records to improve my collection and finance further excursions. Perhaps my best friend in Jamaica was a cab driver and ex-boxer named George Robinson. George loved the music as I did, and often spoke of the days when Duke Reid would send him out to pick up various members of the Skatalites for recording sessions.

Together we went places where Bruce Lee would have been afraid to go. I recall one day when we went to Matches Lane, a feared Kingston locale even avoided by police. George parked in front of a bar long out of business and covered by a pull-down metal garage-style door. He told me to stay in the car, then got out, opened the trunk and withdrew a long shining machete which he snapped through the air as he glared at a group of local rude bwois leaning on the walls surrounding a doorway down the lane. After making the desired impression, George tapped the machete on the metal door. When it opened, he motioned me to go inside. While he stood at the door brandishing his weapon, I met the owner of the property named Beanie who proceeded to show me a small storage room stacked high with records from the old days. That day I bought nearly four hundred records including four near mint copies of "Black Progress," an ultra-rare early Wailers item and two copies of "Give Me A Ticket," a scarce Peter Tosh rendition of the Boxtops' late '60s hit, "The Letter." Beanie told me that Mortimo Planno's brother lived in a tenement yard at the top of the lane. George and I went to see if he had any records. Planno had produced the very rare Marley single "Selassie Is The Chapel." His brother didn't have a copy of "Selassie," but he did sell me a copy of "Judge Not," Bob's very rare first record. George and I called it a day and went to lunch.

Often the best records came as gifts from friends made along the way. After I had shown a kindness to Lloyd "Matador" Daley's son, the "Matador" gave me a small box of singles from his legendary sound system. Included was a near mint copy of "White Christmas" by the Wailers and a copy of "Making Love" by Peter Tosh. Reggae journalist Carl Gayle gave me several very rare early Lee Perry albums after I had told him of my admiration of the Upsetter. Among these records were the ultra rare Jamaican albums *Good, Bad, And The Upsetters* and *Double Seven*, both featuring Wailers material. After suffering an assault and robbery one morning on Parade, I received a call from Carl, the counter man at Randy's Record Mart. He had heard of my misfortune and was anxious to let me know that most Jamaicans were good and generous people unlike the desperado who had attacked me. He asked me to come next morning to the store where he gave me a mint copy of the extremely rare "Feel Alright" by the Wailers. My good spar Jah Lloyd once brought me a mint copy of an Upsetter 12" disco mix called "Bad Weed" by Junior Murvin. This was a record I had searched after for several years. When I reached into my wallet to pay him a proper bounty, he motioned my hand away and said, "A good friend is better than pocket dunza."

In 1985 I toured Jamaica with my band playing blues, country music, rockabilly, and reggae. This tour was a cultural offering sponsored by the National Council of Traditional Arts and also included the Louisiana Zydeco band Rocking Dopsie and the Twisters, a New York based classical horn quartet, and a trio of champion break dancers from Philadelphia. Together we performed 56 shows in thirty days, playing the World Music Festival and venues throughout Kingston and around the countryside. Many of my Jamaican friends came to the shows and I was privileged to perform for the likes of "Chinna" Smith, Gregory Isaacs, Jah Lloyd, the Righteous Flames, Freddy McKay, Bernard Collins, and others. While performing one day at the Bank of Jamaica, a crazed youth with no shoes and torn pants and shirt jumped on stage and began a Dervish-like dance while the band played Burning Spear's classic "Ethiopians Live It Out." After the show the youth introduced himself as Johnny Scar and said, "From you perform the works of His Majesty, I muss a deh deh." It was easy to see how he got his name, as he was seemingly scarred head to foot by hundreds of straight short razor cuts. These scars, I later learned were received in retribution from gang posse members who accused Johnny of informing on them. Johnny Scar sang a song for me that he wanted to record, and I promised to mention him to some record people in America. I kept that promise but heard no more from Johnny Scar after the trip. In 1990 I told the story about Johnny Scar to Bunny Wailer. Bunny replied that he had recorded Johnny Scar and had issued on a Solomonic 12" disco in 1987 the very song Johnny had auditioned for me. But Bunny had killed the song when, a few weeks later, he found out that Johnny Scar had been involved as a getaway driver in the murder of Peter Tosh and that Johnny himself was now dead at the hands of unknown gunmen.

ROGER RESUMES

In 1995, two major things coincided that would bring some of the fruits unearthed by Leroy and other record hunters to a much wider public. Danny Sims, the controversial co-founder of JAD Records, with whom the Wailers had signed as performers and writers from 1968 - 1972, moved to L.A. from Southern Africa, where he had been living for several years. During that same period, I had met an extraordinary polymath from Paris named Bruno Blum. A professional musician, artist, producer, composer, editor, author, cartoonist, documentarian, and God knows what else, Bruno learned that I had been retained by Sims to help him identify everything that the Wailers did during the period they were signed to him, and help him find someone to release this vast body of work. He said he owned the foreign rights to the Beverley's and Upsetter periods as well, which had been confirmed when pieces from each catalog were issued as part of Island's 1992 million-selling Wailers box set, *Songs of Freedom*, licensed officially from Sims. Bruno found a label in France that was willing to put up the production money for a series of box sets to be called *The Complete Bob Marley and the Wailers 1967 - 1972*, to be compiled by Bruno and me. The bulk of the work was done by Bruno in Europe. Leroy and I had compiled an earlier draft of this book with notes regarding the collections we had access to, enabling us to initiate a plan to get the best known copies of rare Wailers records for which the master tapes no longer existed. Bruno spent many long nights at Abbey Road in London with the engineers who had done the Beatles' *Anthology* series. By vowing to be scrupulously legitimate, we could not include, unfortunately, the aforementioned Beverley's and Upsetters' tracks, which had been licensed exclusively by Island until 2003. Otherwise, for the first time, the fecund period that began at the end of the Coxson era and extended to the initiation of the Island releases, was issued in chronologically arranged sequence, with never-before-seen photographs, extensive fact-filled liner notes, and essays that were contributed by Bruno and me along with Leroy and Jeremy Collingwood, an employee of Sims' partner in the U.K. It was a massive international effort that documented in full the Wailers' intense five year growth spurt in that brief period of seismic musical shifts. And it was the first time that the estates of Bob and Peter, and the living Wailer, Bunny, ever received a penny for their work with Lee Perry, as the oft-maligned Sims actually paid out generous advances and royalties to each.

With this series, which eventually produced 15 separate discs, collectors at last had access to unheard gems like Bunny's weird "Tread Oh"; Bob's "Black Progress" (a take on James Brown's "I'm Black and I'm Proud," whose chorus had ironically contained almost all white and Asian backup singers); and the ineffable "Selassie Is the Chapel." Perhaps the most valuable of all the Marley releases, "Selassie" was reputed to have been privately pressed in an edition of 26 copies by its lyricist and producer, Mortimo Planno. I paid quite a bit for my mine, but it has a very significant "provenance," a museum word I'm learning to use these days. It's the actual record that was played on the Jamaican Broadcasting Company by its anchorman, Dermot Hussey, on the day Marley passed. Since then, it has been signed to that effect by Dermot, and also by Planno whose inscription reads, "I wrote this song and gave Bob Marley to sing 1968."

During the next couple of decades, we had to move three times due to the pressures of two growing children and the exponential growth of the collection, which today fills six rooms of our hillside home in Echo Park. A good deal of the key things are no longer here, however, but in storage at Curatorial Assistance, an exhibition company in Pasadena, following the display it designed for 6,000 objects in 2001 at the Queen Mary. For eight months, "The World of Reggae featuring Bob Marley: Treasures from Roger Steffens' Reggae Archives" saw thousands of visitors from around the world touring two buildings on the ship's dock in Long Beach, California, filled with autographed records, posters, photographs, films, priceless Selassie treasures loaned by famed Rasta collector Jim Marshall, and all kinds of artifacts from the fifty year history of Jamaican music. As I write in April of 2005, we are in the final stages of negotiations for this collection to go to Jamaica to become the foundation of the National Museum of Jamaican Popular Music. It's a heckuva long way from Ruel Mills on Fillmore Street, and those first precious few singles I hurried back to Berkeley to play.

"From fan to honoring the work of a legend," is how Mary describes the arc of my collecting life during the past 32 years, "but always essentially a fan." And when a fan gets an opportunity to etch his way into the saga, even in the tiniest way, chances must be grabbed. Bruno and I wrote secret messages cut into the matrix areas, just before the labels on the vinyl *Complete Wailers* releases. Check 'em out sometime, if you're lucky enough to come across these limited edition copies. They've become more valuable since the whole series was eliminated in 2004 after Universal/Island's English office bought a ten year exclusive lease on Sims' catalog, and existing pressings of the JAD series were ordered destroyed.

ABOUT THIS BOOK

This long-promised book is a product of the combined efforts of Leroy Jodie Pierson and yours truly, a total of 55 years of research between us and 15 years of active collaboration researching the arcana, years filled with the life-affirming joy of discovery and gracious thanksgiving for the aural transcendence of the Wailers' music.

That said, this book is not totally accurate. Any discographical study of the Wailers that purports to be the "definitive" or "final word" on the group's recording history, is just frontin'. I suspect we chose the "Definitive" title as a challenge to ourselves, aware that this was, from the start, a huge affair involving hundreds of people from all over the world. It's an ongoing discussion and this is the opening salvo, the first draft of many, as we add to the knowledge and debate the details.

A website will be set up for your comments and emendations on this book's contents, and will contain regular replies from Leroy and me, as part of the Rounder Records' website at: www.rounderbooks.com.

As Leroy has written elsewhere in this book, the true record of the Wailers in the studio will never be totally understood. Faulty memories and few written records, the twin nemeses of discographical detective work, make that an impossibility. Details of relatively recent history, like the release date of "Simmer Down," are subjects of rabid discussion, with several divergent viewpoints strongly defended by dozens of putative "experts," and original participants. The old saying that "an expert is just a guy from out of town," rings true, and neither Leroy nor I claim to be one, preferring to be thought of as fellow students and researchers. But we did have the distinct advantage of spending three weeks with Bunny Wailer and other early associates of the group, playing every song that they had recorded and attempting to get the full story of each. As other musicians passed through our lives, we cross-referenced various claims, and wherever possible, tried to decide which was the most probable. We have added notes that indicate particular disagreements, and who said what, so that history may decide ultimately the whos and whats of the Wailers' enormous oeuvre.

One of the most important things I learned from Leroy was the examination of matrixes. Having been only vaguely aware of them and their value, Leroy taught me to be alert to the many variations on Wailers' pressings, even though the record's label might be the same on all of them. The multitude of pressings of "Smile Jamaica" is a perfect example of that. There's a slow version, a faster reggae version, and then an extended version of that one, too. Numbers followed by dashes and 1, 2, 3, or 4, for example, usually indicate the take of the song on the master tape that was used to make the disc. Most of the time this can be helpful, but sometimes confusing as when different takes are indicated but there is no discernible difference among them, as on "Fire Fire."

While writing the first draft of this essay, Mary asked me at what point did I truly become a collector? Well, I pondered, when I was six my mother gave me her big Scott stamp album, and I have collected stamps, with various degrees of commitment, for the rest of my life. As a teenager, I spent hundred and hundreds of dollars on mint new issues, bought with the dollar-five-an-hour salary I was getting working 29 hours a week after high school at the local Acme super market in Westwood, New Jersey, where I grew up. But, although the kindly old man (who bore the unfortunate name of Rudolf Quirsfeld) who ran the Pascack Stamp Company out of his den had cautioned me against buying scattershot, I never specialized in anything other than nice looking stamps. No investment value there for the most part, I learned later. Had I heeded his wise instruction, I might have collected nothing but Vatican City, back then when you could have a full run of everything ever issued by the tiny principality for a relatively modest amount, and sailed around the world years later on what it would grow to be worth. Likewise, my record collection grew, but had no particular direction. As I matured, I learned from watching other people about how to add value to one's interests - if I had the patience to wait say, twenty years, which is the cycle of the nostalgia racket.

So from the start of my reggae odyssey, I decided to concentrate on the Wailers. I've met many obsessed people during the trod, and encountered attitudes that I found distasteful among people who would almost kill to beat someone out of something to which they attached great, if sometime subjective, value. An old spiritual aphorism would always spring to mind on those occasions: "I have given everything I see all the value it has for me." I was an aggressive collector, but I always figured that what came to me was what was meant to come, and if I really was meant to have something, it would eventually present itself. There was no sense losing friends over pieces of plastic. And as the word began to circulate in the reggae world that I was seriously thinking about a long term home for all of the things that were being shared with me, even more things began to arrive almost daily.

An early discussion concerning my ideas for some kind of Reggae Center in Jamaica, a place where people could actually buy classic records and hear performers play live when they came to Jamaica, developed at the Seawind in Montego Bay in 1983. I met then Prime Minister Edward Seaga's two sisters poolside. They introduced themselves by first names only, and I had no idea who they were. As the discussion turned to music, I complained vociferously about how Jamaica was blowing it by making it so hard for the thousands of music tourists who came in search of reggae to actually find reliable sources. Next thing I knew, I was in a Sunday brunch meeting with the head of the MoBay Chamber of Commerce. He brought elaborate maps of the city's waterfront, and pointed to several empty acres, offering them to me free for a reggae center. All I had to do, he said, was go back to America and raise the money to build it myself. It would take twenty more years to really get the idea back on track, well after the peak of the roots music explosion.

Peter at Hank Holmes' Archives, L.A., September 1979. Photo by Roger Steffens.

Regarding the music, no one had a more profound effect on my tastes than Hank Holmes. It is to him I pay tribute. Many of the records detailed in this book came initially from Hank, who let me borrow his Wailers singles to tape on the day we met - and act of profound generosity. He taught me how to tell the difference between Slim Smith and Cornell Campbell, and why Yabby You and the Prophets were among the greatest groups ever. When I brought Peter Tosh over to see Hank's collection in September 1979, Tosh was stunned. Hank had amassed a group of instrumentals released under the name Peter Touch on British singles, most of which were brand new to him. One of the pictures of Peter I treasure most is of him sitting under a chalk board notation for the record, "What A Shame" by Still Cool, a remnant of a "reggae clash" that Hank had hosted for a dozen collectors.

As far as serious record collecting goes, I have to thank one person in particular, Leroy Jodie Pierson. Without his fearless efforts to unearth ridiculously rare records, and his generosity in sharing them, my collection would be infinitely poorer. I am grateful for his selfless education in the nefarious underworld of record fanatics. The same obeisance goes, to a slightly lesser extent, to Charlie Morgan of Outernational Records in Washington State, and Dixie Diamond and Susan Stockstill of Crucial Riddims in Berkeley, as well as their Canadian counterpart Greg Lawson, whose countless trips to the bowels of the ghettoes in Jamaica have helped make certain that Jamaica's rich, though often disrespected, musical culture is preserved. These are folks whose auction lists, or set sale lists, of discs going back to the 1950s, helped establish the early standards for valuation of out of print Jamaican records. Among the first North Americans to develop such a business, these friends of ours have been unselfish with information and advice.

In Leroy's case, as he described above, he was taking a life-long love of blues, and a knowledge of the record business that goes along with it, and applying similar research techniques to reggae. A white boy from St. Louis, he was a blues prodigy who made his stage debut at 21 playing alongside Son House, Mississippi Fred McDowell, and Arthur "Big Boy" Crudup. As a mark of the respect that the young guitarist enjoyed, when McDowell died, he left his two guitars to Leroy. His love of the blues form took Leroy to remote Southern black hamlets, where he would go from shack to cardboard shack knocking on doors and asking if the occupants had any old records they might want to sell. His collection developed rapidly, and by 1980 had become the most comprehensive post-war blues library in the country, missing only six known singles to be totally complete.

In the mid-seventies Leroy began the reissue of the best of his blues finds, first on his Boogie Disease label and later on the Nighthawk label. Then he caught a chronic case of reggae mylitis. Traveling to Jamaica, Leroy began to penetrate some of Kingston's most lethal precincts, fetid quarters filled with rude bwois brandishing ratchet knives and Glocks and machettes, *weh dem naw check fi no outsidas*, especially white ones. But Leroy was blessed, his naivete and sheer dumb luck getting him out alive time after time, clutching some of the most overlooked and historic pieces of wax in Jamaica's multitudinous history. He kept the best of these for himself, of course, concentrating on first pressings. The rest he put up for sale. As he began the Nighthawk list, he called me and asked if I would share some addresses of potential customers with him. In return, he offered me first chance to buy any of the Wailers material that he would offer. That was how I wound up two decades ago with a mint copy of "White Christmas" by Bob Marley and the Wailers, the only record that I know of that has both Irving Berlin's and Bob Marley's names on the label. Today that record is worth more than 20 times what I paid for it. Dozens of other treasures, unearthed through increasingly hairy circumstances, found their way into what Timothy White, in his biography of Bob, called "Roger Steffens' reggae archives," the first time I'd heard that phrase, adding that he couldn't have done his book without access to them. I guess it was at that point that I was made to realize that all the things I had years ago thrown into a tiny walk-in closet were no longer just a pile of stuff, but an actual "archive."

A passion for record collecting has led down more pathways than I ever could have imagined. Since 1984, a multi-media presentation called "The Life of Bob Marley," initially commissioned for the National Video Festival, has brought me and my wife to Japan, the Smithsonian, Martinique, Hawaii, Toronto, Paris, Australia, the University of the West Indies in Kingston, the Rock and Roll Hall of Fame, and hundreds of other places. In the latter facility, I was the first speaker, and after I finished my talk about the Reggae King, I paid homage to the King of Rock and Roll, my childhood hero, by presenting the museum with copies of Freed's radio programs that I had taped off the air as a kid from 1957 through 1959. I brushed back a tear as I explained what Freed had meant to me during those impressionable teen years, and now at the Hall of Fame, built in Cleveland because that's where Freed threw the world's first "Rock and Roll Dance" in 1952, I was joining my two greatest musical heroes in one event, full circle, recognizing at once what Bob had sung: "What goes around comes around." On the way out, my old friend Bob Santelli, himself a noted reggae journalist and now the head of the Rock Hall, took me into the room in the museum devoted to Alan Freed. On a long shelf lined with '40s and '50s radios sat the very same beige and brown 1948 Bendix table model on which I had listened to Freed all those years ago.

Today, due largely to the double-edged assistance of eBay, the world of reggae collecting is getting broader by the minute. And it'll just get bigger and bigger, as more youngsters take up the Marley banner. For Bob has become, in the early 21st century, exactly what Amnesty International's head, Jack Healey, said a few years back: "Everywhere I go in the world today, Bob Marley is the symbol of freedom." It is our sincere hope that this book will provide a clearer path for all of the Wailers' fans and collectors through the immortal works of Jah's finest heralds.

– Roger Steffens, Echo Park, Los Angeles, April 2, 2005

Bob Marley, 1977. Photo by Kate Simon.

Bob Marley, Neville Livingston, Peter Tosh circa 1964.

BOB MARLEY And The WAILERS

THE DEFINITIVE DISCOGRAPHY

By Roger Steffens and Leroy Jodie Pierson

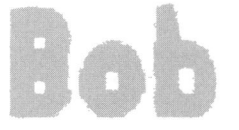

Bob Marley, Neville Livingston, Beverley Kelso, and Peter Tosh circa 1964, Kingston.

ROBERT MARLEY   BEVERLEY'S ALL STARS   ROBERT MARLEY (UK)   circa: **February 1962**

Bob Marley (Robert Nesta Marley), vocal; Arkland "Drumbago" Parks, drums; Lloyd Brevett, bass; Jerome "Jah Jerry" Haines, guitar; unknown piano; unknown electric piano (-1); Roland Alphonso, tenor sax; Charlie Organaire, harmonica (-1); unknown recorder or flute (-2); Buddy Davidson, engineer; recorded Federal Studio; one track; Leslie Kong, production.

Federal FLK 2338	Judge Not! (-2)	Beverley's LM 027, Island (UK) WI 088, Mango MLPS 9844, Tuff Gong (UK) CD TGCBX 1
Federal FLK 2339	Do You Still Love Me? (-1)	Beverley's LM 027, Island (UK) WI 088

Note: A myth, often repeated in print, incorrectly states that Beverley's original yellow and black label issue credits Robert Morley.

BOBBY MARTELL   BEVERLEY'S ALL STARS   ROBERT MARLEY (UK)   circa: **April 1962**

Bob Marley, vocal; Arkland "Drumbago" Parks, drums; Lloyd Brevett, bass; Jerome "Jah Jerry" Haines, guitar; unknown piano; Roland Alphonso, tenor sax; Don Drummond, trombone; Charlie Organaire, harmonica; unknown electric piano; unknown tenor sax; Buddy Davidson, engineer; recorded Federal Studio; one track; Leslie Kong, production.

FLK 2476	One Cup Of Coffee	Beverley's LM 052, Island (UK) WI 128, Tuff Gong (UK) CD TGCBX 1
	Terror	Beverley's (?)

Note: Bobby Martell was a pseudonym apparently chosen for Bob Marley by Leslie Kong. Bunny Wailer (Neville Livingston) remembers "Terror" having been issued on Beverley's, but the authors have been unable to document this independently. Bunny Wailer was scheduled to record "Pass It On" at this session but he was late getting out of school that day, which caused him to arrive late at the studio and earned him the enmity of Leslie Kong, who had already paid for the recording time. Although credited to R. Marley on the original yellow and black Beverley's label, Bob Marley is not the composer of "One Cup Of Coffee," which is an American song recorded by Claude Gray that entered the Billboard top ten country and western chart in April of 1961. Bunny recalls that between this session and the initial Wailers session at Studio One, he and Bob auditioned as a duo for local producers Prince Buster and Duke Reid, who both rejected them.

THE WAILERS   BOB AND THE WAILERS   BOB MARLEY & THE WAILERS   **July 6, 1964 (?)**

Bob Marley, vocal (-1) or harmony vocal (-2); Junior Braithwaite, vocal (-2) or harmony vocal (-1); Bunny Wailer (Neville Livingston), harmony vocal; Peter Tosh (Peter McIntosh), harmony vocal; Beverley Kelso, harmony vocal; Lloyd Knibbs, drums; Lloyd Brevett, bass; Jerome "Jah Jerry" Haines, guitar; Jackie Mittoo, piano; Don Drummond, trombone; Roland Alphonso, tenor sax; Tommy McCook, tenor sax; "Dizzy" Johnny Moore, trumpet; Dennis "Ska" Campbell, baritone sax; Clement Dodd, engineer and production; recorded Studio One; one track (Ampex 350). Overdubs c. 1975: unknown percussion (-3); unknown guitar (-4).

C-Dodd-II-13	Simmer Down (-1)	Coxsone C 111, Ska Beat (UK) JB 186, ND lp, Studio One lp, Tuff Gong (UK) CD TGCBX 1
C&N XX-X2	"	Coxsone
C-Dodd-II-12	I Don't Need Your Love (-1)	Coxsone C 110, Ska Beat (UK) JB 186, Heartbeat CD HB 251
	" (-3)	Calla lp 2 CAS-1240
CN-1	I Am Going Home (-1)	Coxsone, Coxsone lp, Heartbeat CD HB 111, Heartbeat CD HB 319
	" (-4)	Calla lp CAS-1240
Federal FC 6406	Do You Remember (-1)	Muzik City, Island (UK) WI 211, ND lp, Coxsone lp, Heartbeat CD HB 111, Heartbeat CD HB 319
	" (-3)	Calla lp CAS-1240
Federal FC 6157-1	Straight & Narrow Way (-2)	Coxsone, Coxsone lp

Note: The above titles are listed in the order in which Bunny Wailer remembers recording them. The original Coxsone issue of "Simmer Down"/ "I Don't Need Your Love" credits the Wailers and lists label numbers C 111/C 110 respectively. The Coxsone issue of the same coupling credited to Bob and The Wailers reverses the label numbers. Both of these early pressings were initially released with black and silver labels. Colored wax examples of this initial Wailers release were pressed. Labeled copies have been found with green or yellow wax. Blank pre-release copies have been found with green, red, yellow, or blue wax. Small quantities of the original black and silver label issue of "I Am Going Home"/ "Destiny" were pressed on blue wax. Federal FC 6157-1 was mastered on September 23, 1964. Federal FC 6406 was mastered on November 26, 1964. "Do You Remember" was coupled with "Hoot Nanny Hoot" on the original white and blue Muzik City issue. "Do You Remember" was re-titled as "How Many Times" when reissued on ND lp and Coxsone lp, *This Is Jamaican Ska*. "Straight

Coxson Dodd at Studio One, Kingston, 1976. Photo by Peter Simon.

& Narrow Way" was coupled with "Climb The Ladder" on the original red and black Coxsone label issue. Studio One lp is *The Wailing Wailers*. "I Am Going Home" and "Straight And Narrow Way" reissued on Coxsone lp, *The Best Of Bob Marley & The Wailers*. Bob wrote all the songs, but "I Am Going Home" used elements and lyrics of the traditional spiritual song, "Swing Low Sweet Chariot." The liner notes of Heartbeat CD HB 111 describe the included cut of "I Am Going Home" as a longer version than previously heard, but it is the same length as the original Coxsone single and album cuts. The overdubbed version of the song on Calla lp fades 24 seconds earlier. Ermine "Cherry Green" Bramwell says that she sang on "I Am Going Home" and that the track was recorded after Junior Braithwaite left the group, but both Bunny Wailer and Clement Dodd remember this track being recorded at the first session. There has been some dispute over "Simmer Down" being the first Wailers recording and release. Clement Dodd remembered "It Hurts To Be Alone"/ "Mr. Talkative" as being the first Jamaican single by the Wailers, but the label issue numbers (C 113/C 112 respectively) clearly contradict that memory. "Simmer Down"/ "I Don't Need Your Love" has the label issue numbers C11/C110. It is possible the two singles might have been released simultaneously. Also of interest is the fact that "I Am Going Home"/ "Destiny," with matrix numbers CN-1/CN-2 were mastered earlier or on the same date as "Mr. Talkative" with matrix number CN-3 and "It Hurts To Be Alone" with matrix number CN-4. "It Hurts To Be Alone"/"Mr. Talkative" was the first Wailers release in England, so Dodd may have been thinking of that. Dodd also believed that "It Hurts To Be Alone" was the first recording by the group. Bob, Bunny, Peter, Junior, and Beverley have all identified "Simmer Down" as their first recording. The session date was gleaned from the original Studio One tape box containing "Straight And Narrow Way." This date may be the date a copy was made or it may be the original recording date. Beverley Kelso thinks this session was done in December 1963. An informant reports the listing of "Simmer Down" on a chart from April 1964, but the authors have been unable to confirm this statement. Bunny places the session in June or July of 1964 and remembers "Simmer Down" as being a big hit during the early August Independence celebrations of that year. Bunny clearly recalls that the Skatalites backed the Wailers on their first session. The Skatalites were officially formed in June of 1964. "Doctor Kildare," a Skatalites title with the matrix number C-Dodd-II-16, appears to have been mastered on the same day as "Simmer Down" with the matrix number C-Dodd-II-13. "Russian Ska Fever," a Skatalites title with the matrix number CN-7, appears to have been mastered on the same day as "It Hurts To Be Alone" with the matrix number CN-4. These details appear to confirm Bunny Wailer's memory of the first session date. Bunny remembers that Peter was taking a shower in the evening after their initial session, when they began to hear "Simmer Down" being played on Dodd's sound system a few blocks away. He is definite that "Simmer Down" was both the first played and first issued Wailers recording. It should be noted here that Bunny says that alternate takes were routinely recorded at their Studio One sessions and that two or three takes of each song were recorded at their initial session. These takes may no longer exist as Clement Dodd often recorded over tapes that were not of immediate use to him.

LORD BRYNER   circa: early July 1964

Lord Bryner, vocal; Bob Marley, harmony vocal; Bunny Wailer, harmony vocal; Peter Tosh, harmony vocal; Junior Braithwaite, harmony vocal; Beverley Kelso, harmony vocal; Lloyd Knibbs, drums; Lloyd Brevett, bass; Jerome "Jah Jerry" Haines, guitar; Jackie Mittoo, piano; Roland Alphonso, tenor sax; Tommy McCook, tenor sax; Don Drummond, trombone; "Dizzy" Johnny Moore, trumpet; Clement Dodd, engineer and production; recorded Studio One; one track.

C-Dodd-II-7   Where Sammy's Gone   Rolando & Powie, Heartbeat CD HB 201

Note: Calypso artist Lord Bryner recorded extensively for Clement Dodd, and additional tracks with the Wailers may exist.

THE WAILERS   circa: mid July 1964

Bob Marley, vocal; Bunny Wailer, harmony vocal; Peter Tosh, harmony vocal (-1); Junior Braithwaite, harmony vocal; Beverley Kelso, harmony vocal (-2); Joe Higgs, harmony vocal (-3); Lloyd Knibbs, drums; Lloyd Brevett, bass; Jerome "Jah Jerry" Haines, guitar; Jackie Mittoo, piano; Roland Alphonso, tenor sax; Tommy McCook, tenor sax; Don Drummond, trombone; "Dizzy" Johnny Moore, trumpet; Clement Dodd, engineer and production; recorded Studio One; one track.

Federal FC 6159-1	Climb The Ladder (-1) (-2)	Coxsone, Heartbeat CD HB 251
CSD-41	Your Love (-2) (-3)	Studio One St. 28, Island (UK) WI 206, Heartbeat CD HB 191
CN-3	Mr. Talkative (-1)	Coxsone C 112, Island (UK) WI 188, Coxsone lp, Heartbeat CD HB 111, Heartbeat CD HB 319

Note: Federal FC 6159-1 was mastered on September 23, 1964. The Federal master matrix catalogue mistakenly assigns this matrix number to "Mr. Talkative" which may indicate that CN-3 was mastered at the same time. A limited quantity of both blank label pre-release and original maroon and silver labeled copies of "Mr. Talkative"/ "It Hurts To Be Alone" were pressed using colored plastic. Labeled copies have been found with green or yellow wax. Coxsone/Studio One lp is *The Best Of Bob Marley & The Wailers*. Joe Higgs was the Wailers' vocal coach and was often on hand at their recording sessions for Clement Dodd. "Climb The Ladder" was coupled with "Straight & Narrow Way" on the original red and black label Coxsone issue. "Your Love" was coupled with "Playboy" on the original white, red, and black Studio One issue.

THE WAILERS　　　　　　　　　　　　　　　　　　　　　　　　　　　　　　　　circa: mid July 1964

Bob Marley, vocal; Bunny Wailer, harmony vocal; Peter Tosh, harmony vocal; Junior Braithwaite, harmony vocal; Beverley Kelso, harmony vocal (-1); Blossom Johnson, harmony vocal (-1); Lloyd Knibbs, drums; Lloyd Brevett, bass; Jerome "Jah Jerry" Haines, guitar; Jackie Mittoo, piano; Roland Alphonso, tenor sax; Tommy McCook, tenor sax; Don Drummond, trombone; "Dizzy" Johnny Moore, trumpet; Clement Dodd, engineer and production; recorded Studio One; one track.

Federal FC 6407	Tell Them Lord (-1)	Muzik City, Heartbeat CD HB 201
Federal FC 6423	Christmas Is Here	", Studio One lp, Heartbeat CD HB 118
CN-2	Destiny (-1)	Coxsone, Studio One (US) lp SO 1106, Heartbeat CD HB 191

　Note: Federal FC 6407 was mastered on November 26, 1964. Federal FC 6423 was mastered on December 4, 1964. The original Muzik City issue of "Tell Them Lord"/ "Christmas Is Here" bears a white and red label. "Destiny" was coupled with "I Am Going Home" on the original black and silver Coxsone label issue. "Christmas Is Here" was re-titled as "Sound The Trumpet" when reissued on Studio One lp, *Christmas In Jamaica* and on Heartbeat CD HB 118. Small quantities of "Destiny"/ "I Am Going Home" were pressed with colored wax. Labeled examples have been found with blue wax. Blossom Johnson was Joe Higgs' girlfriend at this time.

PETER TOUCH　　PETER TOUCH & THE WAILERS　　PETER TOSH & THE WAILERS (UK)　　circa: mid July 1964

Peter Tosh, vocal; Bob Marley, harmony vocal; Bunny Wailer, harmony vocal; Junior Braithwaite, harmony vocal (-1); Beverley Kelso, harmony vocal (-1); Lloyd Knibbs, drums; Lloyd Brevett, bass; Jerome "Jah Jerry" Haines, guitar; Lyn Taitt, guitar; Jackie Mittoo, piano; Roland Alphonso, tenor sax; Tommy McCook, tenor sax; Don Drummond, trombone; Lester Sterling, alto sax; "Dizzy" Johnny Moore, trumpet; Clement Dodd, engineer and production; recorded Studio One; one track. Overdubs c. 1988: unknown percussion (-2); unknown bongos (-3).

Federal FC 6425	Hoot Nanny Hoot	Muzik City, Island (UK) WI 211
	" (-2)	Studio One lp, Heartbeat CD HB 150
CSD-46	Maga Dog (-1)	Studio One C. 41, Island (UK) WI 212,
		Calla lp 2CAS-1240
	" (-3)	Studio One lp, Heartbeat CD HB 150

　Note: Federal FC 6425 was mastered on December 4, 1964. "Hoot Nanny Hoot" was coupled with "Do You Remember" on the original white and blue or white and red Muzik City issue. "Maga Dog" was coupled with "Hooligans" on the original white, red, and black Studio One issue. Studio One lp is *Marley, Tosh, Livingston & Associates*. Bunny Wailer thinks "Hoot Nanny Hoot" was an American song. The original Studio One label credits R. Marley with the composition of "Maga Dog," but Bunny says Peter wrote the song. Ermine "Cherry Green" Bramwell says that she sang on "Maga Dog."

THE WAILERS　　PETER TOUCH & THE WAILERS (-1)　　　　　　　　　　　　　circa: mid July 1964

Peter Tosh, vocal and guitar (-1) or harmony vocal (-2); Junior Braithwaite, vocal (-2) or harmony vocal (-1); Bob Marley, harmony vocal; Bunny Wailer, harmony vocal; Beverley Kelso, harmony vocal; Clement Dodd, harmony vocal (-1); Lloyd Knibbs, drums; Lloyd Brevett, bass; Jerome "Jah Jerry" Haines, guitar; Jackie Mittoo, piano; Roland Alphonso, tenor sax; Tommy McCook, tenor sax; Don Drummond, trombone; "Dizzy" Johnny Moore, trumpet; Lester Sterling, alto sax; "Ska" Campbell, baritone sax; Clement Dodd, engineer and production; recorded Studio One; one track.

Federal FC 6477	Habits (-2)	Muzik City, Heartbeat CD HB 111, Heartbeat CD HB 319
Federal FC 6478	Amen (-1)	" , " , "

　Note: Both Federal FC 6477 and Federal FC 6478 were mastered on January 13, 1965. Bob Marley wrote "Habits." "Amen" was written by Johnny Pate and heard by the Wailers on a recording by the Impressions. "Habits"/ "Amen" was originally issued on a white and blue Muzik City label. Ermine "Cherry Green" Bramwell says that she sang on "Amen."

Junior Braithwaite, a still from a video shot by Neville Garrick in 1984, during the Original Wailers reunion session for "Together Again."

Beverley Kelso, who joined the Wailers the night before their first recording session for Coxson Dodd. Taken in N.Y.C. 2003. Photo by Roger Steffens.

THE WAILERS　　　　　　　　　　　　　　　　　　　　　　　　　　　　　　　　circa: late July 1964

Bob Marley, vocal; Bunny Wailer, harmony vocal; Peter Tosh, harmony vocal; Junior Braithwaite, harmony vocal; Beverley Kelso, harmony vocal; Lloyd Knibbs, drums; Lloyd Brevett, bass; Jerome "Jah Jerry" Haines, guitar; Jackie Mittoo, piano; Roland Alphonso, tenor sax; Tommy McCook, tenor sax; Don Drummond, trombone; "Dizzy" Johnny Moore, trumpet; Lester Sterling, alto sax; Dennis "Ska" Campbell, baritone sax; Clement Dodd, engineer and production; recorded Studio One; one track.

　　　　　　　　　　Go Jimmy Go　　　　　　　　Coxsone (?), ND lp, Coxsone lp, Heartbeat CD HB 111,
　　　　　　　　　　　　　　　　　　　　　　　　　Heartbeat CD HB 319

　Note: This title is said to have been issued in Jamaica as a Coxsone single, but the authors have been unable to confirm this. This song was originally recorded by American Jimmy Clanton. ND and Coxsone lps are titled *This Is Jamaican Ska*.

LEE PERRY　　　　　　　　　　　　　　　　　　　　　　　　　　　　　　　　　　circa: late July 1964

Lee Perry, vocal; Bob Marley, harmony vocal; Bunny Wailer, harmony vocal; Peter Tosh, harmony vocal; Junior Braithwaite, harmony vocal; Lloyd Knibbs, drums; Lloyd Brevett, bass; Jerome "Jah Jerry" Haines, guitar; Jackie Mittoo, piano; Roland Alphonso, tenor sax; Tommy McCook, tenor sax; Don Drummond, trombone; "Dizzy" Johnny Moore, trumpet; Lester Sterling, alto sax; Dennis "Ska" Campbell, baritone sax; Clement Dodd, engineer and production; recorded Studio One; one track.

C-Dod-22　　　　　　　Hand To Hand　　　　　　　C&N, Ska Beat (UK) JB 201, Heartbeat CD HB 53

　Note: C-Dod-22 re-titled "Man To Man" on Heartbeat CD issue. Also known as "One By One." A limited number of pre-release blank copies of this title were pressed with green wax.

THE WAILERS　　**BOB MARLEY & THE WAILERS**　　　　　　　　　　　　circa: early August 1964

Bob Marley, vocal; Bunny Wailer, harmony vocal; Peter Tosh, harmony vocal; Beverley Kelso, harmony vocal (-1); Lloyd Knibbs, drums; Lloyd Brevett, bass; Jerome "Jah Jerry" Haines, guitar; Jackie Mittoo, piano; Roland Alphonso, tenor sax; Tommy McCook, tenor sax; Lester Sterling, alto sax; "Dizzy" Johnny Moore, trumpet; Clement Dodd, engineer and production; recorded Studio One; one track. Overdubs c. 1975: unknown synthesizer (-2); unknown percussion (-3).

C-Dod-17　　　　　　　Dana (Donna) (-1)　　　　　　Coxsone, Island (UK) WI 216, Heartbeat CD HB 251
　　　　　　　　　　　　"　　　(-2)　　　　　　　　　Calla lp 2 CAS-1240
　　　　　　　　　　　Dance With Me　　　　　　　　Studio One lp, Heartbeat CD HB 191
　　　　　　　　　　　Wings Of A Dove　　　　　　　ND lp, Coxsone lp, Heartbeat CD HB 251
　　　　　　　　　　　　"　　　(-2, -3)　　　　　　　Calla lp 2 CAS-1240
　　　　　　　　　　　Nobody Knows (-1)　　　　　　Heartbeat CD HB 251
　　　　　　　　　　　　"　　　(-2)　　　　　　　　　Calla lp 2 CAS-1240

　Note: C-Dod-17 was correctly re-titled "Donna" when it appeared on Island (UK) single and later album releases. The Island (UK) single has been reported as an alternate mix, but this seems odd since the song was recorded on one track. Studio One lp is *Marley, Tosh, Livingston & Associates*. Coxsone lp is *The Best Of Bob Marley & The Wailers*. Both "Wings Of A Dove" and "Nobody Knows" are Wailers' arrangements of traditional songs. "Dance With Me," composed by Bob Marley, borrows heavily from "On Broadway," a Leiber and Stoller song first recorded by the Drifters. "Dana" was originally coupled with "Don't Ever Leave Me" on a yellow and black Coxsone label. ND lp is titled *Ska Au Go Go*. Coxsone lp is titled *The Best Of Bob Marley & The Wailers*.

JACKIE OPEL　　　　　　　　　　　　　　　　　　　　　　　　　　　　　　　　circa: early August 1964

Jackie Opel, vocal; Bob Marley, harmony vocal; Bunny Wailer, harmony vocal; Peter Tosh, harmony vocal; Lloyd Knibbs, drums; Lloyd Brevett, bass; Jerome "Jah Jerry" Haines, guitar; Lyn Taitt, guitar; Jackie Mittoo, piano; Roland Alphonso, tenor sax; Tommy McCook, tenor sax; Lester Sterling, alto sax; Don Drummond, trombone; "Dizzy" Johnny Moore, trumpet; Clement Dodd, engineer and production; recorded Studio One; one track.

CSD-43　　　　　　　　The Mill Man　　　　　　　　Studio One, Heartbeat CD HB 201

　Note: A small number of labeled copies of this title were pressed using red plastic. Bunny recalls the original title of this song as being "The Grinding Mill."

THE WAILERS   **BOB MARLEY & THE WAILERS**   circa: **early August 1964**

Bob Marley, vocal; Bunny Wailer, harmony vocal; Peter Tosh, harmony vocal; Junior Braithwaite, harmony vocal; Beverley Kelso, harmony vocal; Lloyd Knibbs, drums; Lloyd Brevett, bass; Lyn Taitt, guitar; Jackie Mittoo, piano; Tommy McCook, tenor sax (-1); Roland Alphonso, tenor sax (-2); "Dizzy" Johnny Moore, trumpet (-2); Clement Dodd, engineer and production; recorded Studio One; one track.

CSD-51	Teenager In Love (-1)	Coxsone, Ska Beat (UK) JB 228, Heartbeat CD HB 111, Heartbeat CD HB 319
WIRL CS 1119-1	Love Won't Be Mine This Way (-2)	Coxsone 512, Island (UK) WI 268, Coxsone lp
WIRL CS 1119-3	"	"
	Love Won't Be Mine This Way (-2)	Studio One (US) lp SO 1106, Heartbeat CD HB 251

   Note: Coxsone lp is *The Best Of Bob Marley & The Wailers*. "Love Won't Be Mine This Way" also known as "Follow Bad Company." "Teenager In Love" derives from the Dion and the Belmonts late fifties hit. "Teenage In Love" was coupled with "Love & Affection" on the original maroon and silver Coxsone issue. "Love Won't Be Mine This Way" was coupled with "I'm Gonna Put It On" on the original black and silver Coxsone issue.

DELROY WILSON   circa: **late August 1964**

Delroy Wilson, vocal; Bob Marley, harmony vocal; Bunny Wailer, harmony vocal; Peter Tosh, harmony vocal; Junior Braithwaite, harmony vocal; Lloyd Knibbs, drums; Lloyd Brevett, bass; Jerome "Jah Jerry" Haines, guitar; Lyn Taitt, guitar; Jackie Mittoo, piano; Roland Alphonso, tenor sax; Tommy McCook, tenor sax; Don Drummond, trombone; "Dizzy" Johnny Moore, trumpet; Lester Sterling, alto sax; Clement Dodd, engineer and production; recorded Studio One; one track.

Federal FC 6512	Low Minded Hypocrite	Studio One

   Note: Some blank label pre-release copies of this title paired with "I Want Justice" were pressed using colored plastic.

BOB MARLEY AND THE WAILERS   circa: **late August 1964**

Bob Marley, vocal; Bunny Wailer, harmony vocal; Peter Tosh, harmony vocal; Junior Braithwaite, harmony vocal; Beverley Kelso, harmony vocal; Carl McCloud, drums; Lloyd Spence, bass; Ernest Ranglin, guitar; Richard Ace, piano; Clement Dodd, engineer and production; recorded Studio One; one track.

Federal FC 6768-7	Where Will I Find	Supreme, Island (UK) WI 254

   Note: Bunny Wailer remembers this song's original title as "Lights In The Harbour." "Where Will I Find" was coupled with "What's New Pussy Cat?" on the original white and black Supreme label.

THE WAILERS   **BOB MARLEY AND THE WAILERS**   **August 28, 1964**

Junior Braithwaite, vocal (-1) or harmony vocal (-2); Bob Marley, vocal (-2) or harmony vocal (-1); Bunny Wailer, harmony vocal; Peter Tosh, harmony vocal; Beverley Kelso, harmony vocal; Carl McCloud, drums; Lloyd Spence, bass; Ernest Ranglin, guitar; Richard Ace, piano; Roy Richards, harmonica (-2); Clement Dodd, engineer and production; recorded Studio One; one track. Overdubs c. 1975: unknown guitar (-3).

CN-4	It Hurts To Be Alone (-1)	Coxsone C 113, Island (UK) WI 188, Studio One lp
	" (-3)	Calla lp 2 CAS-1240
	It Hurts To Be Alone (-1)	Heartbeat CD HB 111, Heartbeat CD HB 319
	It Hurts To Be Alone (-1)	unissued
	It Hurts To Be Alone (-1)	unissued
	Don't Ever Leave Me (-1)	Heartbeat CD HB 191
	Don't Ever Leave Me (-1)	"
C-Dod-16	Don't Ever Leave Me (-1)	Coxsone, Island (UK) WI 254
	True Confessions (-2)	Heartbeat CD HB 111, Heartbeat CD HB 319
	True Confessions (-2)	unissued
	True Confessions (-2)	unissued

Cherry Green, also known as Ermine Bramwell, rehearsed with the Wailers for a couple of years before they cut their first record. N.Y.C. 2003. Photo by Henry Eccleston.

Note: A limited quantity of both blank pre-release and original maroon and silver label Coxsone issues of "It Hurts To Be Alone"/ "Mr. Talkative" were pressed with colored plastic. Examples have been found in both green and yellow wax. "It Hurts To Be Alone" was a big hit in Coxsone's sound system before its public release in November. The song charted #24 on the RJR Radio chart of December 5 through December 12 of 1964, and was #2 on the chart for the week of December 19 through 26. "It Hurts To Be Alone" also appeared on WIRL (Canada) WLS 1045 paired with the early 1967 Wailers' production of "Nice Time." "Don't Ever Leave Me" was coupled with "Dana" on the original yellow and black Coxsone label. Within weeks of this session Junior Braithwaite immigrated to the United States. He would not appear or record again with the Wailers until 1984. Bob Marley wrote "It Hurts To Be Alone" and "Don't Ever Leave Me." The composition of "True Confessions" is in question.

BOB MARLEY AND THE WAILERS   SOULETES (-1)   SUMMERTAIRS (UK)   circa: September 1964

Bob Marley, vocal; Marcia Griffiths, vocal (-1); Bunny Wailer, harmony vocal (-2); Peter Tosh, harmony vocal (-2); Rita Anderson, harmony vocal (-2); Carl McCloud, drums; Lloyd Spence, bass; Ernest Ranglin, guitar; Richard Ace, piano; unknown percussion (-1); Clement Dodd, engineer and production; recorded Studio One; one track.

DIR CS 2007-B-1H	Oh My Darling (-1)	Muzik City, Coxsone (UK) CS 7021, Heartbeat CD HB 201
	I Need You (-2)	Studio One lp, Heartbeat CD HB 111, Heartbeat CD HB 319

Note: Coxsone (UK) CS 7021 is wrongly credited to the Summertairs. The Summertairs made several recordings for Dodd, but none feature the Wailers. The original Jamaican red and white Muzik City release of "Oh My Darling" wrongly credits the Souletes (sic). Rita Anderson was Rita Marley's maiden name. Originally thought to be a duet between Bob and Rita and identified as such by Bunny Wailer, the female vocalist on "Oh My Darling" proved to be Marcia Griffiths, who confirmed this identification in a quote from Reggae Calendar International SF 11/93. Both Coxsone (UK) and Jamaican Muzik City releases of "Oh My Darling" couple the song with "Trying To Keep A Good Man Down" by the Hamlins. Both English and Jamaican issues use the same English matrix number, and the English release may be the first. "I Need You" with Marley singing lead should not be confused with the 1966 Bunny Wailer led "I Need You" which is a different song. Studio One lp is *The Wailing Wailers*.

THE WAILERS   THE MIGHTY VIKINGS   circa: October 1964

Bob Marley, vocal; Bunny Wailer, harmony vocal; Peter Tosh, harmony vocal; Beverley Kelso, harmony vocal; Ermine "Cherry Green" Bramwell, harmony vocal; Joe Higgs, harmony vocal (-1); Sylvia Richards, harmony vocal (-1); Esmond Jarrett, drums; Desi Miles, bass; Hux Brown, guitar; Lloyd Delpratt, piano; Bobby Ellis, trumpet; "Trummie" Miles, trumpet; Tony Wilson, tenor sax; Seymour Walker, alto sax; Clement Dodd, engineer and production; recorded Studio One; one track. Overdubs c. 1991: probably Noel Alphonso, drum machine (-2).

WC 5	Lonesome Feelings (-1)	Wincox, Ska Beat (UK) JB 211, Studio One lp
FCD 7430-B	"	Coxsone
	" (-2)	Heartbeat CD HB 111, Heartbeat CD HB 319
WC 6	There She Goes	Wincox, Ska Beat (UK) JB 211, Heartbeat CD HB 111, Heartbeat CD HB 319

Note: Blank pre-release copies of this coupling have been found with red or green plastic. Studio One lp is *The Wailing Wailers*. "Lonesome Feelings" appeared at #39 on the RJR chart of December 12 through 19 in 1964, and was #19 on the next week's chart. Mighty Vikings is the name of the backing band. Sylvia Richards was Joe Higgs' first "baby mother." The label of the original Wincox issue is typically white and green, but some copies are yellow and green.

THE WAILERS   January 13, 1965

Bob Marley, vocal; Bunny Wailer, harmony vocal; Peter Tosh, harmony vocal; Beverley Kelso, harmony vocal; Lloyd Knibbs, drums; Lloyd Brevett, bass; Lyn Taitt, guitar; Jackie Mittoo, organ; Clement Dodd, engineer and production; recorded Studio One; one track.

Federal FC 6535	I Made A Mistake	Studio One, Ska Beat (UK) JB 226, Calla lp 2 CAS-1240, Heartbeat CD HB 251
	I Made A Mistake	unissued
	I Made A Mistake	unissued

Note: FC 6535 was mastered on February 23, 1965. The recording date was written on the tape box. This title was composed by Curtis Mayfield. "I Made A Mistake" was coupled with "The Vow" by Bonny & Rita on the original yellow and black Studio One issue.

BONNY & RITA   circa: January 1965

Bunny Wailer, vocal; Rita Anderson, vocal; Peter Tosh, harmony vocal; Lloyd Knibbs, drums; Lloyd Brevett, bass; Lyn Taitt, guitar; Jackie Mittoo, organ; Clement Dodd, engineer and production; recorded Studio One; one track.

Federal FC 6538   The Vow   Studio One

Note: This title was likely recorded at the same session that produced "I Made A Mistake." FC 6538 was mastered on February 23, 1965. The song derives from a mid-fifties recording by rhythm and blues duo Gene & Eunice. "The Vow" was coupled with "I Made A Mistake" on the original yellow and black Studio One issue.

SOULETTES   circa: January 1965

Rita Marley, vocal; Bob Marley, harmony vocal; Bunny Wailer, harmony vocal; Peter Tosh, harmony vocal; Constantine "Vision" Walker, harmony vocal; Marlene "Precious" Gifford, harmony vocal; Lloyd Knibbs, drums; Lloyd Brevett, bass; Jerome "Jah Jerry" Haines, guitar; Jackie Mittoo, piano; Roland Alphonso, tenor sax; Tommy McCook, tenor sax; Lester Sterling, alto sax; unknown trombone; "Dizzy" Johnny Moore, trumpet; Clement Dodd, engineer and production; recorded Studio One; one track.

CSD 54   One More Chance   Studio One, Heartbeat CD HB 201

Note: Pre-release blank label copies of "One More Chance"/ "Dick Tracy" (Skatalites) have been found with red wax. According to Clement Dodd, this song was written by Bob and Rita Marley. Constantine Walker's mother gave him the nickname "Dream," but that was changed when the Soulettes first began to rehearse with the Wailers in Trench Town. Walker was introduced to a tall dreadlocks who said that Walker should change his name to "Vision." He then spoke the proverb, "Old man get dream. Young man see vision." The Wailers immediately began referring to Walker by this new nickname.

DELROY WILSON   circa: January 1965

Delroy Wilson, vocal; Bob Marley, harmony vocal; Bunny Wailer, harmony vocal; Peter Tosh, harmony vocal; Lloyd Knibbs, drums; Lloyd Brevett, bass; Lyn Taitt, guitar; Jackie Mittoo, piano; Roland Alphonso, tenor sax; unknown trombone; "Dizzy" Johnny Moore, trumpet; Lester Sterling, alto sax; Clement Dodd, engineer and production; recorded Studio One; one track.

Federal FC 6567   I Want Justice   Studio One, Heartbeat CD HB 201

Note: Blank label pre-release copies of "I Want Justice"/ "Low Minded Hypocrite" have been found with colored plastic.

THE WAILERS   BOB MARLEY & THE WAILERS   circa: January 1965

Bob Marley, vocal (-1) or harmony vocal (-2); Peter Tosh, vocal (-2) or harmony vocal (-1); Bunny Wailer, harmony vocal; Lloyd Knibbs, drums; Lloyd Brevett, bass; Lyn Taitt, guitar; Jackie Mittoo, piano or organ (-3); Roland Alphonso, tenor sax (-4); Lester Sterling, alto sax (-4); unknown trombone (-4); "Dizzy" Johnny Moore, trumpet (-4); Clement Dodd, engineer and production; recorded Studio One; one track.

Federal FC 6570	Diamond Baby (-1) (-4)	Coxsone, Heartbeat CD HB 111, Heartbeat CD HB 319
Federal FC 6571	Playboy (-1) (-4)	Studio One blank, Heartbeat CD HB 111, Heartbeat CD HB 319
Federal FC 6589	Playboy (-1) (-4)	Studio One ST. 27, Island (UK) WI 206, Studio One (US) lp SO 1106
	Playboy (-1) (-4)	unissued
Federal FC 6573	Where's The Girl For Me (-1) (-3)	Coxsone, Heartbeat CD HB 111, Heartbeat CD HB 319
Federal FC 6574	Hooligans (-1) (-4)	Studio One C. 40, Island (UK) WI 212
CSD-53	Hooligan Ska (-1) (-4)	Studio One, Heartbeat CD HB 111, Heartbeat CD HB 319
CS 76	Jumbie Jamboree (-2) (-4)	Studio One ST 70, Island (UK) WI 260, Heartbeat CD HB 150

Note: "Playboy" (Federal FC 6571) was mastered on April 4, 1965. Heartbeat CD HB 111 lists their "Playboy" as a previously unreleased alternate take, but it is the take issued on blank label pre-release in Jamaica. "Hooligans" and "Hooligan Ska" are alternate takes of the same song. The Wailers played the Palace Theatre in Kingston in late December of 1964, and "Hooligans" and "Jumbie Jamboree" were written in response to a riot that broke out in the theatre that night. Bunny Wailer remembers recording these songs within weeks of that event. Bunny recalled that the three Wailers collaborated in the writing of "Jumbie Jamboree." The original Studio One label credits S. M. Burke with the composition of "Hooligans." "Diamond Baby" was coupled with "Where's The Girl For Me" on the original white and black label Coxsone issue. "Playboy" was coupled with "Your Love" on the original white, red, and black label Studio One issue. "Hooligans" was coupled with "Maga Dog" on the original white, red, and black label Studio One issue. "Hooligan Ska" was coupled with "Jerico Skank" by Jackie Mittoo on the original light blue and black label Studio One issue. "Jumbie Jamboree" was coupled with "I Should Have Known Better" by Roland Alphonso & the Soul Brothers on yellow and black label Studio One issue. All titles from this session were originally issued credited to the Wailers except "Where's The Girl For Me" which was credited to Bob Marley & The Wailers. Bunny recalled that Don Drummond played on this session, but this seems unlikely. Early in the morning of January 1, Drummond had murdered his lover, a famous rhumba dancer named Margarita Mahfoud. Within days, he was confined in the Bellevue sanitarium and, according to Roland Alphonso, Tommy McCook, and other Skatalites, Drummond never recorded again. Both Bunny Wailer and Vin Gordon say Drummond was occasionally released to work even after the murder.

JACK SPARROW   circa: March/April 1965

Leonard Dillon, vocal; Bob Marley, harmony vocal; Peter Tosh, harmony vocal; Lloyd Knibbs, drums; Lloyd Brevett, bass; Lyn Taitt, guitar; Jackie Mittoo, piano; Roland Alphonso, tenor sax; unknown trombone; "Dizzy" Johnny Moore, trumpet; Lester Sterling, alto sax; Clement Dodd, engineer and production; recorded Studio One; one track.

CS 70	Ice Water	Studio One, Heartbeat CD HB 201
	Bullwhip	Studio One
	Women Wine & Money	Studio One

Note: "Sparrow" was Leonard Dillon's street name in Port Antonio. He says the Wailers sang on the three titles listed above, and that all were issued on the Studio One label. Bunny Wailer remembers the Wailers singing three songs with Dillon, but could only recall one title, "Ice Water." Dillon has stated that his "Beggars Have No Choice" features Wailers harmony, but that song actually features harmony from Peter Austin of the Clarendonians. Dillon later became lead singer of the Ethiopians.

THE WAILERS   circa: April/May 1965

Bob Marley, vocal; Bunny Wailer, harmony vocal; Peter Tosh, harmony vocal; Beverley Kelso, harmony vocal (-1); Lloyd Knibbs, drums; Lloyd Brevett, bass; Lyn Taitt, guitar; Jackie Mittoo, piano; Roland Alphonso, tenor sax; Vin Gordon, trombone; "Dizzy" Johnny Moore, trumpet; Lester Sterling, alto sax; unknown percussion (-2); Sydney Bucknor, engineer; recorded Studio One; two track (Ampex 252); Clement Dodd, production. Overdubs c. 1975: unknown percussion (-3). Overdubs c. 1991: probably Noel Alphonso, drum machine (-4).

Federal FC 6649-1	Love & Affection	Coxsone, Ska Beat (UK) JB 228, Studio One lp
	" (-3)	Calla lp 2 CAS-1240
	" (-4)	Heartbeat CD HB 111, Heartbeat CD HB 319
Federal FC 6677	And I Love Her	Coxsone, Ska Beat (UK) JB 230
	And I Love Her	Heartbeat CD HB 112, Heartbeat CD HB 319
	And I Love Her	unissued
Federal FC 6680	Do It Right (-1, -2)	Coxsone, Ska Beat (UK) JN 230,
		Heartbeat CD HB 191

Note: FC 6649-1 was mastered on June 9, 1965. Studio One lp is *The Wailing Wailers*. Bunny recalls that Don Drummond played on this session, but this seems unlikely. Vin Gordon states that he played on this session. "And I Love Her" was written by John Lennon and Paul McCartney. People in Kingston were calling the Wailers "The Jamaican Beatles" because of the Wailers' knack for topping the local charts, and the group may have cut "And I Love Her" to reinforce this flattering identification. "Love & Affection" was coupled with "Teenager In Love" on the original maroon and silver label Coxsone issue. "And I Love Her" was coupled with "Do It Right" on the original maroon and silver label Coxsone issue.

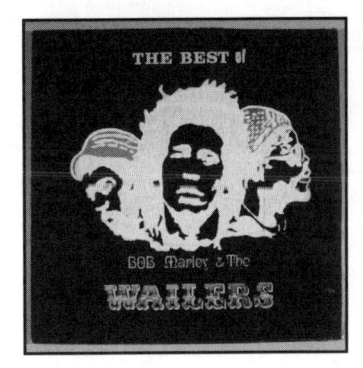

THE WAILERS   July 8, 1965

Bob Marley, vocal (-1) or harmony vocal (-2); Peter Tosh, vocal (-2) or harmony vocal (-1); Bunny Wailer, harmony vocal; Lloyd Knibbs, drums; Lloyd Brevett, bass; Lyn Taitt, guitar; Jackie Mittoo, piano; Roland Alphonso, tenor sax; Lester Sterling, alto sax; unknown trombone; "Dizzy" Johnny Moore, trumpet; Sydney Bucknor, engineer; recorded Studio One; two track; Clement Dodd, production. Overdubs c. 1975: unknown percussion (-3). Overdubs c. 1981: unknown percussion (-4); unknown bongos (-4); unknown guitar (-4). Overdubs c. 1991: probably Noel Alphonso, drum machine (-5).

CS 0022	One Love (-1)	Coxsone 505, ND lp, Studio One lp
FCD 743-A	"	Coxsone
	" (-3)	Calla lp 2 CAS-1240
	" (-5)	Heartbeat CD HB 111, Heartbeat CD HB 319
CD-1036 A	One Love (-4)	Studio One
CD-1036 B	One Love Version (-4)	Studio One
CS 0027	Do You Feel The Same Way Too (-1)	Coxsone 504, Calla lp 1 CAS-1240, Heartbeat CD HB 191
CS 0028	Shame And Scandal (-2)	Studio One ST 711, Island (UK) WI 215, ND lp, Studio One lp, Heartbeat CD HB 150
	The Jerk (-1)	Coxsone (?), Island (UK) WI 215, Heartbeat CD HB 251

Note: Blank label pre-release copies of "Shame And Scandal" have been found with red or multi-colored plastic. "One Love" is on ND lp, *Ska Au Go Go* and on Studio One lp *The Wailing Wailers*. "Shame And Scandal" is on ND lp, *Ska Au Go Go* and on Studio One lp *Ska Strictly For You*. The date given is from the original Studio One tape box containing "One Love" and "Do You Feel The Same Way Too." Bunny believes strongly that Don Drummond played on this session. "Shame And Scandal" is described by Bunny as a calypso song that Clement Dodd asked the Wailers to cover. It was written as "Shame And Scandal In The Family" by Donaldson and Brown and a recording of the song by Shawn Elliot was released in America and England in 1964 and was probably the model of the Wailers' version. "One Love" was coupled with "Do You Feel The Same Way Too" on the original blue and silver label Coxsone issue. This issue includes two horizontal silver lines with the number 505 between them on the right side of the label. Early purple, blue, and silver reissues do not have the lines or label number. "Shame And Scandal" was coupled with "Sca-Balena" by Roland Alphonso & The Soul Brothers and has been found on red and black label and on blue and silver label. It is uncertain which came first. "The Jerk" was probably issued in Jamaica, but the authors have not seen a copy.

BOB MARLEY AND THE WAILERS   circa: July/August 1965

Bob Marley, vocal; Bunny Wailer, harmony vocal; Peter Tosh, harmony vocal; Ermine "Cherry Green" Bramwell, harmony vocal; Lloyd Knibbs, drums; Lloyd Brevett, bass; Jerome "Jah Jerry" Haines, guitar; Jackie Mittoo, piano; Tommy McCook, tenor sax; unknown trombone; "Dizzy" Johnny Moore, trumpet; Lester Sterling, alto sax; Sydney Bucknor, engineer; recorded Studio One; two track; Clement Dodd, production.

Federal FC 6767-1	What's New Pussy Cat	Supreme, Island (UK) WI 254, Studio One lp, Heartbeat CD HB 191

Note: Federal FC 6767-1 was mastered on August 23, 1965. Studio One lp is *The Wailing Wailers*. Bunny Wailer recalls that Don Drummond played on this title. This seems unlikely. This song was written by Hal David and Burt Bacharach and was first recorded by Tom Jones. "What's New Pussy Cat" was coupled with "Where Will I Find" on the original white and black label Supreme issue.

THE WAILERS
circa: September 1965

Bob Marley, vocal; Bunny Wailer, harmony vocal; Peter Tosh, harmony vocal; Lloyd Knibbs, drums; Lloyd Brevett, bass; Jerome "Jah Jerry" Haines, guitar; Jackie Mittoo, piano; Roland Alphonso, tenor sax; Lester Sterling, alto sax; Sydney Bucknor, engineer; recorded Studio One; two track; Clement Dodd, production. Overdubs c. 1991: probably Noel Alphonso, drum machine (-1).

WIRL CS 1026-2	Rude Boy	Coxsone 509, Doctor Bird (UK) DB 1013, Studio One lp
WIRL CS 1026-4	"	" , Heartbeat CD HB 201
WIRL CS 1026-6	"	"
	" (-1)	Heartbeat CD HB 112, Heartbeat CD HB 319

Note: "Rude Boy" also known as "Rude Boy Ska" and "Rule Them Rudie." Studio One lp is *The Wailing Wailers*. Released in December, "Rude Boy" peaked at #4 on the RJR chart ending February 5, 1966. WIRL CS 1026-2 was used for a blank label pre-release. WIRL CS 1026-4 was originally released on a maroon and silver label Coxsone issue. WIRL CS 1026-6 was later released on a black and silver Coxsone label. The lyrics "Lick me belly 'pon the tamboreen" are taken from traditional Jamaican mento music.

KING PERRY
circa: September 1965

Lee Perry, vocal; Bunny Wailer, harmony vocal; Peter Tosh, harmony vocal; Lloyd Knibbs, drums; Lloyd Brevett, bass; Jerome "Jah Jerry" Haines, guitar; Jackie Mittoo, piano; Roland Alphonso, tenor sax; Lester Sterling, alto sax; Sydney Bucknor, engineer; recorded Studio One; two track; Clement Dodd, production.

Federal FC 6869	Pussy Galore	Studio One pre
Federal FC 6869	Pussy Galore	Studio One ST 714, Heartbeat CD HB 201

Note: "Pussy Galore" was voiced over the rhythm track of "Rude Boy." The alternate take of "Pussy Galore" which appears on blank label pre-release is also known as "Pussy Man." Both takes of this song share the same matrix number.

BOB MARLEY   THE WAILERS & SOUL BROTHERS ORCHESTRA
circa: October 1965

Bob Marley, vocal; Bunny Wailer, harmony vocal; Peter Tosh, harmony vocal; King Sporty, vocal effects (-1); Lloyd Knibbs, drums; Lloyd Brevett, bass; Lyn Taitt, guitar; Jackie Mittoo, piano; Roland Alphonso, tenor sax (-2); Lester Sterling, alto sax (-2); Carlton Samuels, baritone sax (-2); "Dizzy" Johnny Moore, trumpet (-2); Vin Gordon, trombone (-3); Sydney Bucknor, engineer; recorded Studio One; two track; Clement Dodd, production.

Federal FC 6908	I'm Still Waiting (-3)	Studio One, Studio One lp, Tuff Gong CD TGCBX 1
Federal FC 6924-I	"	Studio One
Federal FC 6924-II	"	Studio One
	I'm Still Waiting (-3)	Coxsone CD SOCD 1001, Heartbeat CD 261
	I'm Still Waiting (-3)	Heartbeat CD HB 112, Heartbeat CD HB 319
	Ska Jerk (-2)	Heartbeat CD HB 112, Heartbeat CD HB 319
Federal FC 6909	" (-1, -2)	Studio One

Note: "Ska Jerk" with no matrix is not an alternate take, but the basic track without the vocal effects by King Sporty overdubbed for FC 6909, the version of the tune originally issued on Jamaican single. "Ska Jerk" was re-titled "Ska Jam" and credited to the Skatalites on an early blue and silver Coxsone reissue. The two masterings of "I'm Still Waiting" numbered FC 6924 are not alternate takes, but louder masterings of the same tape used for FC 6908. "I'm Still Waiting" is on Studio One lp, *The Wailing Wailers*. Released in December 1965, "I'm Still Waiting" reached #14 on the RJR chart in early January 1966. The melody of "Ska Jerk" is borrowed from Junior Walker & the All Stars 1964 hit, "Shotgun." Bunny says that the inspiration for Bob's "I'm Still Waiting" was Billy Stewart's "Sitting In The Park." The original coupling of "I'm Still Waiting" and "Ska Jerk" appeared on a white, red, and black label Studio One issue.

BOB MARLEY & THE WAILERS (-1)   BOB MARLEY & THE SPIRITUAL SISTERS (-2)
circa: October 1965

Bob Marley, vocal; Bunny Wailer, harmony vocal (-1); Peter Tosh, harmony vocal (-1); Beverley Kelso, harmony vocal (-2); Ermine "Cherry Green" Bramwell, harmony vocal (-2); Bunny Williams, drums; Bryan "Bassie" Atkinson, bass; Lyn Taitt, guitar; Jackie Mittoo, piano; Sydney Bucknor, engineer; recorded Studio One; two track; Clement Dodd, production.

Federal FC 6935-II	White Christmas (-1)	Supreme 417, Heartbeat CD HB 191
Federal FC 6036-II	Let The Lord Be Seen In You (-2)	Supreme 416, "

Note: "Let The Lord Be Seen In You" was re-titled as "Let The Lord Be Seen In Me" on Heartbeat CD. Composition of this sacred title is credited to R. King on the original Supreme label. Irving Berlin wrote "White Christmas." The Wailers change the song a bit, singing, "I'm dreaming of a white Christmas, not like the ones I used to know." The original release is a blue and silver label Supreme issue.

THE WAILERS   circa: October 1965

Bob Marley, vocal; Bunny Wailer, harmony vocal; Peter Tosh, harmony vocal; Lloyd Knibbs, drums; Lloyd Brevett, bass; Lyn Taitt, guitar; Jackie Mittoo, piano; Roland Alphonso, tenor sax; "Dizzy" Johnny Moore, trumpet; Lester Sterling, alto sax; Carlton Samuels, baritone sax; Sydney Bucknor, engineer; recorded Studio One; two track; Clement Dodd, production. Overdubs c. 1988: unknown percussion (-1). Overdubs c. 1991: unknown drums (-2); unknown bass (-2); unknown percussion (-2).

Federal FC 6950	Another Dance	Coxsone, Heartbeat CD HB 191
Federal FC 6950-II	Another Dance	Studio One, Studio One lp
Federal 6951	Somewhere To Lay My Head	Coxsone
	" (-1)	Studio One lp
	" (-2)	Heartbeat CD HB 112, Heartbeat CD HB 319

Note: Studio One lp is *Marley, Tosh, Livingston & Associates*. "Another Dance" was written by Curtis Mayfield and was originally recorded by the Impressions. The authors have only seen the original coupling of FC 6950 and FC 6951 on blank label pre-release. Federal FC 6950-II was coupled with "Jack And Jill" by Theophilus Beckford on a white and blue hanging mic style label Studio One issue.

JACKIE OPEL   circa: October 1965

Jackie Opel, vocal; Bob Marley, harmony vocal; Bunny Wailer, harmony vocal; Peter Tosh, harmony vocal; King Sporty, vocal effects (-1); Lloyd Knibbs, drums; Lloyd Brevett, bass; Jerome "Jah Jerry" Haines, guitar; Jackie Mittoo, piano; Roland Alphonso, tenor sax; Lester Sterling, alto sax; Tommy McCook, flute (-1); Sydney Bucknor, engineer; recorded Studio One; two track; Clement Dodd, production.

WIRL CS 1045-1	Hairy Mango (-1)	Studio One
WIRL CS 1046-1	My Girl	"

Note: These titles originally appeared together on an early Studio One label.

JOANNE DENNIS AND THE WAILERS   circa: October 1965

Joanne "Joey" Dennis, vocal; Bob Marley, harmony vocal; Bunny Wailer, harmony vocal; Peter Tosh, harmony vocal; Lloyd Knibbs, drums; Lloyd Brevett, bass; Jerome "Jah Jerry" Haines, guitar; Jackie Mittoo, piano; Roland Alphonso, tenor sax; Lester Sterling, alto sax; Carlton Samuels, baritone sax; "Dizzy" Johnny Moore, trumpet; Sydney Bucknor, engineer; recorded Studio One; two track; Clement Dodd, production.

	Don't Cry Over Me	Heartbeat CD HB 201

Note: Trench Town resident Joanne Dennis was half of the successful recording duo, Andy & Joey. She was also sister to Garth Dennis who would become a member of both the Wailing Souls and Black Uhuru.

BOB MARLEY AND THE WAILERS   circa: October 1965

Bob Marley, vocal and guitar; Bunny Wailer, vocal and harmony vocal; Rita Anderson, harmony vocal (-1); Sydney Bucknor, engineer; recorded Studio One; two track; Clement Dodd, production. Overdubs c. 1975: unknown drums (-2); unknown bass (-2); unknown guitar (-2).

	Where Is My Mother	Heartbeat CD HB 191
	" (-2)	Studio One (US) lp SO 1106, Heartbeat CD HB 191

	This Train	Heartbeat CD HB 111, Heartbeat CD HB 319
	" (long splice mix)	unissued
	Wages Of Love Rehearsal (-1)	Heartbeat CD HB 112, Heartbeat CD HB 319

Note: The notes of Heartbeat CD incorrectly identify "This Train" as a duet between Bunny and Peter. Bunny sings lead on one verse of "This Train." The long splice mix of "This Train" cleverly lengthens the short piece by repeating the song with a seamless splice. The song was originally recorded in January of 1927 by the Biddleville Quintette as "This Train Is Bound For Glory." Bunny sings lead on one verse of "Where Is My Mother." Bunny's section incorporates part of the Curtis Mayfield song, "Little Boy Blue."

BOB MARLEY & THE WAILERS   circa: October 17, 1965

Bob Marley, vocal; Bunny Wailer, harmony vocal (-1); Rita Anderson, harmony vocal (-1); Lloyd Knibbs, drums; Lloyd Brevett, bass; Lyn Taitt, guitar; Jackie Mittoo, piano; Vin Gordon, trombone; Sydney Bucknor, engineer; recorded Studio One; two track; Clement Dodd, production. Overdubs c. 1975: unknown guitar (-2).

		Wages Of Love	Heartbeat CD HB 191
FC 7042		Wages Of Love (-1)	Coxsone, Heartbeat CD HB 112, Heartbeat CD HB 319
		" (-1) (-2)	Studio One (US) lp SO 1106
		Wages Of Love	unissued

Note: FC 7042 "Wages Of Love" was coupled with "Cry To Me" on the original maroon and silver label Coxsone issue.

BOB MARLEY & THE WAILERS (-2)   BOB MARLEY & SPIRITUAL SISTERS (-1)   circa: November 1965

Bob Marley, vocal; Bunny Wailer, harmony vocal; Peter Tosh, harmony vocal; Rita Anderson, harmony vocal (-1); Marlene Gifford, harmony vocal (-1); Lloyd Knibbs, drums (-2); Lloyd Brevett, bass; Lyn Taitt, guitar (-2); unknown guitar (-2); Jackie Mittoo, piano; Sydney Bucknor, engineer; recorded Studio One; two track; Clement Dodd, production. Overdubs c. 1985: unknown drums (-3); unknown percussion (-3); unknown guitar (-3).

WIRL CS 1066-2	I Left My Sins (-2)	Tabernacle
WIRL CS 1069-1	Just In Time (-1)	" , Studio One (US), Heartbeat CD HB 251
SOL 78A	" (-3)	Studio One (US) SOL 78
SOL 78B	Part Two (-3)	"

Note: "Just In time" is credited to Bob Marley & Spiritual Singers on the original blue and silver Tabernacle label, but credited to the Soul Harmonizers on black and white Tabernacle 7" reissue. Early reissues of "I Left My Sins"/ "Just In Time" featured red and black Tabernacle labels. Composition of both titles is credited to R. King on the original blue and silver Tabernacle issue.

B. MARLEY AND THE WAILERS   DELROY WILSON (-1)   circa: November 1965

Bob Marley, vocal or harmony vocal (-1); Delroy Wilson, vocal (-1); Bunny Wailer, harmony vocal; Peter Tosh, harmony vocal; King Sporty, vocal effects (-2); Lloyd Knibbs, drums; Lloyd Brevett, bass; Jerome "Jah Jerry" Haines, guitar; Jackie Mittoo, piano; Roland Alphonso, tenor sax; "Dizzy" Johnny Moore, trumpet; Sydney Bucknor, engineer; recorded Studio One; two track; Clement Dodd, production. Overdubs c. 1975: unknown percussion (-3). Overdubs c. 1988: unknown percussion (-4).

	Lonesome Track	Heartbeat CD HB 251
WIRL CS 1221-1	" (-2)	Coxsone 601
	" (-3)	Calla lp 2 CAS-1240
	" (-4)	Studio One lp
WIRL CS 1088-1	Jerk All Night (-1)	Studio One, Heartbeat CD HB 201

Note: King Sporty's vocal effects on "Lonesome Track" were overdubbed for the original maroon and silver label Coxsone release. Bob Marley is credited with the composition of "Jerk All Night" on the label of the original Jamaican single. Bunny agrees but says the song uses the melody of Lee Dorsey's "Ya Ya." Clement Dodd has claimed that he composed the track with Delroy Wilson. "Jerk All Night" was coupled with "Here Comes The Heart Aches" by Delroy Wilson on the original white, red and black Studio One issue.

Coxson Dodd at his headquarters in Brooklyn, with original master tapes of the Wailers, 1993. Photo by Roger Steffens.

BOB MARLEY AND THE WAILERS   circa: November 1965

Bob Marley, vocal; Bunny Wailer, harmony vocal; Peter Tosh, harmony vocal; Lloyd Robinson, drums; Fred Crossley, bass; Dwight Pinkney, guitar; Danny McFarlane, piano; Roland Alphonso, tenor sax; Sydney Bucknor, engineer; recorded Studio One; two track; Clement Dodd, production. Overdubs c. 1982: unknown drums (-1); unknown guitar (-1); unknown keyboard (-1); unknown percussion (-1). Overdubs c. 1991: unknown guitar (-2); unknown drums (-2); unknown percussion (-2).

WIRL CS 1118-1	I'm Gonna Put It On	Coxsone 511, Island (UK) WI 268, Studio One lp, Heartbeat CD HB 251
WIRL CS 1118-2	"	Coxsone 511
WIRL CS 1118-4	"	"
DSR 9095-A	" (-1)	Coxsone
	" (-2)	Heartbeat CD HB 112, Heartbeat CD HB 319
DSR 9096-B	Put It On Version (-1)	Coxsone

Note: Mis-titled as "Put It On" on Studio One lp, *The Wailing Wailers*. The recording of this tune on Heartbeat CD HB 112 is incorrectly termed a previously unreleased alternate take. In fact, it is the original take overdubbed with guitar. "Rub & Squeeze" by Lee "King" Perry & The Soulettes on Studio One uses the rhythm track of "I'm Gonna Put It On." "I'm Gonna Put It On" was #21 on the RJR chart of the last week of January 1966 and was at #4 the week of February 13 through 19. "I'm Gonna Put It On" was coupled with "Love Won't Be Mine This Way" on the original black and silver label Coxsone issue. The musicians on this session were collectively known as the Sharks. Clement Dodd maintains that the Sharks did record the song with the Wailers, but that he was not satisfied with the result and brought the Wailers back in to re-cut the tune with the Soul Brothers. He says that it was this second take of the song that was chosen for issue. Bunny Wailer remembers the details as given above and maintains that the Sharks played on this hit. When interviewed he did not remember recutting the song with the Soul Brothers. To date, no tape of any alternate take has been found.

BOB MARLEY AND THE WAILERS   circa: November 1965

Bob Marley, vocal; Bunny Wailer, harmony vocal; Peter Tosh, harmony vocal; Lloyd Knibbs, drums; Lloyd Brevett, bass; Lyn Taitt, guitar; Jackie Mittoo, piano; Sydney Bucknor, engineer; recorded Studio One; two track; Clement Dodd, production. Overdubs c. 1975: unknown guitar (-1).

	Ten Commandments Of Love	Studio One lp, Heartbeat CD HB 251
	Ten Commandments Of Love	unissued
	" (-1)	Calla lp 2 CAS-1240

Note: Studio One lp is *The Wailing Wailers*. This song was originally a US hit for the Moonglows.

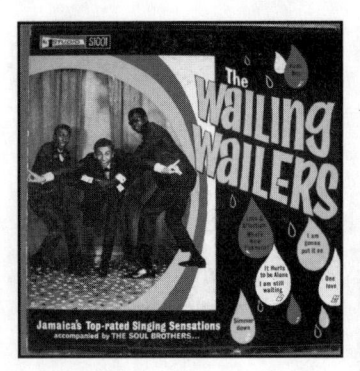

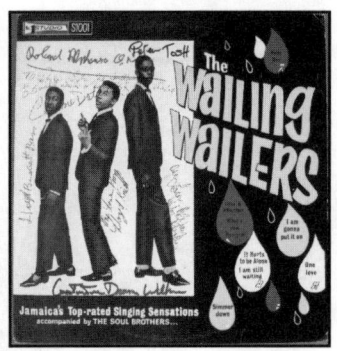

THE SOULETTES   circa: November 1965

Rita Marley, vocal; Peter Tosh, harmony vocal; Constantine "Vision" Walker, harmony vocal; Marlene Gifford, harmony vocal; Lloyd Knibbs, drums; Lloyd Brevett, bass; Jerome "Jah Jerry" Haines, guitar; Jackie Mittoo, piano; Roland Alphonso, tenor sax; Lester Sterling, alto sax; "Dizzy" Johnny Moore, trumpet; unknown trombone; Sydney Bucknor, engineer; recorded Studio One; two track; Clement Dodd, production.

Wirl CS 1143-1   Don't Care What The People Say   Studio One

THE WAILERS   BOB MARLEY AND THE WAILERS   circa: December 1965

Bob Marley, vocal; Bunny Wailer, harmony vocal; Peter Tosh, harmony vocal; Lloyd Knibbs, drums; Lloyd Brevett, bass; Jerome "Jah Jerry" Haines, guitar; Jackie Mittoo, piano; Roland Alphonso, tenor sax; Vin Gordon, trombone; Sydney Bucknor, engineer; recorded Studio One; two track; Clement Dodd, production. Overdubs c. 1981: unknown guitar (-1).

WIRL CS 1175-3	Cry To Me	Coxsone 23, Coxsone lp
	Cry To Me	Studio One (US) lp SO 1106, Heartbeat CD HB 112, Heartbeat CD HB 319
WIRL CS 1176-1	Good Good Rudie	Coxsone 509, Doctor Bird (US) DB 1021, Coxsone lp
	" (alt. mix)	Studio One (US) lp SO 1106, Heartbeat CD HB 112, Heartbeat CD HB 319
CN 3207-A	" (-1)	Coxsone
CN 3207-B	Rudie Part Two (-1)	"

   Note: "Good Good Rudie" was re-titled as "Jailhouse" or "Rudie Rudie" on subsequent 7" reissues on the Studio One label, "Rudie" on 7" Coxsone reissue (CN 3207-A), and "Ruddie" or "Ruddie Boy" on later album issues. This led to confusion in the compilation of Studio One (US) lp SO 1106, which included the title twice under the names "Ruddie Boy" and "Jailhouse," the latter being an alternate short mix. The Heartbeat issue of the short mix is also titled "Jailhouse." Coxsone lp is *The Best Of Bob Marley & The Wailers*. Bob sings "Dem peego a go lingua" in "Good Good Rudie." This is Jamaican patois meaning that rude girls will talk. These were Bob's last recordings produced by Clement Dodd. Bob left Jamaica for Delaware in February of 1966 and did not return until October. "Cry To Me" was coupled with "Wages Of Love" on the original maroon and silver label Coxsone issue. "Good Good Rudie" was coupled with "Ocean 11" by the City Slickers on the original blue and silver label Coxsone issue.

THE WAILERS   B. MARLEY AND THE WAILERS   circa: March 1966

Peter Tosh, vocal; Bunny Wailer, vocal; Lloyd Knibbs, drums; Bryan "Bassie" Atkinson, bass; Lyn Taitt, guitar; Jackie Mittoo, piano; Sydney Bucknor, engineer; recorded Studio One; two track; Clement Dodd, production.

	Sinner Man (take 1)	unissued
WIRL CS 1208-1	Sinner Man (take 2)	Coxsone 600, Ska Beat (UK) JB 249, Heartbeat CD HB 112, Heartbeat CD HB 319
WIRL CS 1208-2	"	Coxsone 64

   Note: The take listed as a previously unreleased alternate on Heartbeat CD is actually the same as that issued on the Jamaican single. CS 1499 has been reported as another matrix number for "Sinner Man" and might feature take one. Despite the artist credit of B. Marley And The Wailers on Coxsone 600, Bob does not appear on this title. "Sinner Man" was mis-titled as "Zimmerman" on Ska Beat (UK) release. "Sinner Man" is a traditional American song, which Peter recorded several times, recasting it as "Downpresser Man" or "Oppressor Man." WIRL CS 1208-1 was coupled with "Lonesome Track" and credited to B. Marley and the Wailers on the original maroon and silver label Coxsone issue. WIRL CS 1208-2 was coupled with "Let Him Go" on a later red and black Coxsone issue credited to the Wailers.

SOUL BROTHERS   BOB MARLEY & THE WAILERS   circa: early 1966

Bunny Wailer, vocal; Peter Tosh, vocal; unknown vocal; unknown vocal; Lloyd Knibbs, drums; Lloyd Brevett, bass; Jerome "Jah Jerry" Haines, guitar; Jackie Mittoo, piano; "Dizzy" Johnny Moore, trumpet; Roland Alphonso, tenor sax; Lester Sterling, alto sax; Carlton Samuels, baritone sax; Sydney Bucknor, engineer; recorded Studio One; two track; Clement Dodd, production.

WIRL CS 1253	Guajara Ska	Coxsone, Coxsone CD SOCD 1001
WIRL CS 1253-1	"	Coxsone
WIRL CS 1253-A	"	Money Disc

Constantine "Vision" Walker, 1990s publicity photo.

Note: Although the original Coxsone single issue credits this track to the Soul Brothers, Coxsone CD issue credits the track to Bob Marley & The Wailers. The performance is an instrumental with a repetitive vocal chorus. Clement Dodd identifies the vocalists as the Wailers. "Guajara Ska" WIRL CS 1253 was the original issue of the song and was coupled with "Forsaken Friend" by the Gaylads. The other Coxsone and Money Disc releases are reissues. On the *Wailing Wailers* Studio One CD the title is rendered as "Guajira Ska", which is the way the word is pronounced in the song.

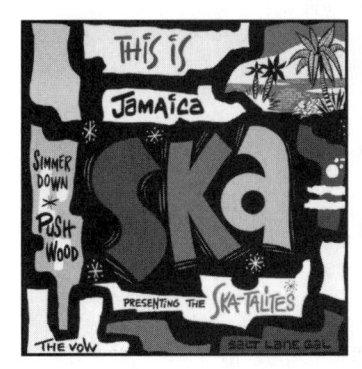

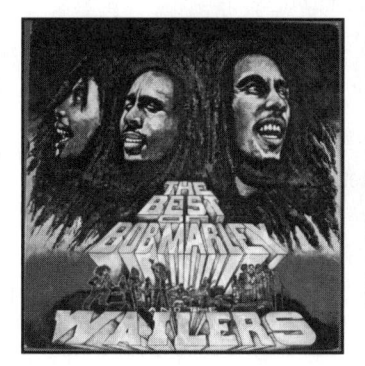

THE WAILERS   circa: late April 1966

Peter Tosh, vocal; Horace "Bibby" Seaton, harmony vocal; Winston Stewart, harmony vocal; Maurice Roberts, harmony vocal; Lloyd Knibbs, drums; Lloyd Brevett, bass; Jerome "Jah Jerry" Haines, guitar; Jackie Mittoo, piano; Sydney Bucknor, engineer; recorded Studio One; two track; Clement Dodd, production.

WIRL CS 1317-1	Rasta Shook Them Up	Coxsone 52, Doctor Bird (UK) DB 1039, Island lp IRSP 7, Heartbeat CD HB 150
WIRL CS 1317-2	"	Coxsone 52

Note: Bunny Wailer says Peter recorded this song within a few weeks time after the visit of Emperor Haile Selassie to Jamaica on April 21, 1966. In the lyric, Tosh refers to the event as having taken place "a few days ago." The harmony singers are collectively known as the Gaylads, who later changed their name to the Gailads and then to Psalms. Gaylads leader Horace "Bibby" Seaton was also commonly credited as B. B. Seaton. "Rasta Shook Them Up" was mis-titled on Island lp as "Rasta Put It On." Over the introductory instrumental passage, Peter speaks several words in the Amharic language of Ethiopia. Composition credit on the original label is to Peter Touch. "Rasta Shook Them Up" was coupled with "Ringo's Ska" by the Soul Brothers on the original maroon and silver label Coxsone issue and a red and black second issue.

PETER TOUCH   circa: May 1966

Peter Tosh, vocal and harmony vocal; Constantine "Vision" Walker, harmony vocal; Lloyd Knibbs, drums; Lloyd Brevett, bass; Jerome "Jah Jerry" Haines, guitar; Jackie Mittoo, piano; Roland Alphonso, tenor sax; "Deadly" Headley Bennett, alto sax; Sydney Bucknor, engineer; recorded Studio One; four track; Clement Dodd, production.

WIRL CS 1793-1	The Toughest	Studio One 7, Heartbeat CD HB 159
CD 1033A	"	Studio One
CD 1033B	Version	"

Note: Re-titled as "I'm The Toughest" on CD 1033A, a late seventies reissue. The label of the original Studio One 7" release credits C. Dodd & J. Mittoo with composition. Peter said that he wrote the song after Clement Dodd asked him to version a then popular American record called "I'm Your Puppet" by James & Bobby Purify. During the instrumental break and at the end of the song when Peter seems to be choking or belching out the words "Tough" and "Rough," he is imitating the then recently deceased Emmanuel Zachariah "Zackie" Palm, a notorious JLP gunman and the leader of the Phoenix street gang that ruled the Tivoli Gardens area of downtown Kingston. "Zackie" was also known as "the high priest." His name appeared in dozens of rock steady rude boy songs of the era. "The Toughest" is coupled with "No Faith" by Marcia Griffiths on the original white and red label Studio One issue.

21

THE WAILERS   circa: June 1966

Bunny Wailer, vocal; Peter Tosh, harmony vocal; Constantine "Vision" Walker, harmony vocal; Lloyd Knibbs, drums; Lloyd Brevett, bass; Lyn Taitt, guitar; Jackie Mittoo, piano; Count Ossie, percussion; Sydney Bucknor, engineer; recorded Studio One; four track; Clement Dodd, production. Overdubs c. 1975: unknown percussion (-1). Overdubs c. 1991: unknown drums (-2); unknown percussion (-2).

WIRL 1423-1	Sunday Morning	Coxsone 57, Island (UK) WI 3001, Coxsone lp, Heartbeat CD HB 251
WIRL 1423-2	"	Coxsone 57
WIRL 1438-1	He Who Feels It Knows It	Coxsone 56, Island (UK) WI 3001, Coxsone lp, Heartbeat CD HB 112, Heartbeat CD HB 319
	" (-1)	Calla lp 2 CAS-1240
WIRL 1499-1	Let Him Go	Coxsone 64, Island (UK) WI 3009, ND lp, Studio One lp
	" (-1)	Calla lp 2 CAS-1240
	" (-2)	Heartbeat CD HB 112, Heartbeat CD HB 319

Note: "He Who Feels It Knows It" was also known as "Who Feels It Knows It" and "Linger You Linger" which was the title handwritten on the vast majority of blank pre-release copies issued. The Coxsone lp is *The Best Of Bob Marley & The Wailers*. "Let Him Go" was included on the Studio One lp titled *Presenting Jamaica All Stars Vol. 1* and then later on the Studio One lp titled *Marley, Tosh, Livingston & Associates*. "Sunday Morning" is coupled with "He Who Feels It Knows It" on the original maroon and black Coxsone issue. "Let Him Go" was coupled with "Sinner Man" on the original red and black label Coxsone issue.

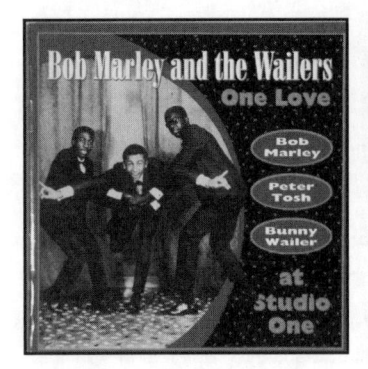

BOB ANDY   circa: June 1966

Bob Andy, vocal; Bunny Wailer, harmony vocal; Constantine "Vision" Walker, harmony vocal; Joe Isaacs, drums; Bryan "Bassie" Atkinson, bass; "Teacher," guitar; Jackie Mittoo, piano; Roland Alphonso, tenor sax; "Deadly" Headley Bennett, alto sax; Ron Wilson, trombone; Bobby Ellis, trumpet and arrangement; Sydney Bucknor, engineer; recorded Studio One; four track; Clement Dodd, production.

CSD 161	I've Got To Go Back Home	Coxsone, Heartbeat CD HB 201

Note: The original issue of "I've Got To Go Back Home" couples the song with "Lay It On" by the Melodians.

RITA & BUNNY   circa: June 1966

Bunny Wailer, vocal; Rita Marley, vocal; Lloyd Knibbs, drums; Lloyd Brevett, bass; Lyn Taitt, guitar; Jackie Mittoo, piano; Vin Gordon, trombone; "Dizzy" Johnny Moore, trumpet; Sydney Bucknor, engineer; recorded Studio One; four track; Clement Dodd, production.

CSD 192	Bless You	Studio One, Heartbeat CD HB 201

Note: Blank label pre-release copies of "Bless You"/ "Beard Man Ska" (Roland Alphonso) have been found with green or red plastic. This is probably a cover of an American song.

RITA MARLEY   circa: July 1966

Rita Marley, vocal; Bunny Wailer, harmony vocal; Peter Tosh, harmony vocal; Constantine "Vision" Walker, harmony vocal; Lloyd Knibbs, drums; Lloyd Brevett, bass; Jerome "Jah Jerry" Haines, guitar; Jackie Mittoo, piano or organ (-1); Roland Alphonso, tenor sax (-2); Sydney Bucknor, engineer; recorded Studio One; four track; Clement Dodd, production.

| CS Dodd-73-009 | Friends & Lovers (-2) | Studio One, Heartbeat CD HB 201 |
| CS Dodd-76-007 | I'm Sorry For You Baby (-1) | " |

Note: "Friends & Lovers" on the original black and silver Studio One label credits composition to Farrell and Burns. The composer of "I'm Sorry For You Baby" is unknown to the authors.

RITA MARLEY & THE SOULETTES WITH THE WAILERS   circa: July 1966

Rita Marley, vocal; Bob Marley, harmony vocal; Bunny Wailer, harmony vocal; Peter Tosh, harmony vocal; Constantine "Vision" Walker, harmony vocal; Marlene Gifford, harmony vocal; Lloyd Knibbs, drums; Lloyd Brevett, bass; Jerome "Jah Jerry" Haines, guitar; Jackie Mittoo, piano; Roland Alphonso, tenor sax; Lester Sterling, alto sax; Dennis "Ska" Campbell, baritone sax; "Dizzy" Johnny Moore, trumpet; Sydney Bucknor, engineer; recorded Studio One; four track; Clement Dodd, production.

                That Ain't Right   Heartbeat CD HB 201

Note: Composition of this tune is unknown by the authors. Although unissued in Jamaica, this song was a hit in Clement Dodd's sound systems.

THE WAILERS (-1)   PETER TOUCH & THE CHORUS (-2)   circa: July 1966

Bunny Wailer, vocal (-1) or harmony vocal (-2); Peter Tosh, vocal (-2) or harmony vocal (-1); Constantine "Vision" Walker, harmony vocal; Rita Marley, harmony vocal (-3); Lloyd Knibbs, drums; Lloyd Brevett, bass; Lyn Taitt, guitar; Jackie Mittoo, piano; Richard Ace, organ; Roland Alphonso, tenor sax; "Deadly" Headley Bennett, alto sax; Sydney Bucknor, engineer; recorded Studio One; four track; Clement Dodd, production.

WIRL CS 1533-1	Jerking Time (-1)	Coxsone 3, Heartbeat CD HB 191
WIRL CS 1534-1	Rock Sweet Rock (-1) (-3)	Coxsone 4, "
WIRL CD 1535-1	Don't Look Back (-2)	Coxsone 6, Heartbeat CD HB 150
	When The Well Runs Dry (-2)(-3)	Studio One lp, Heartbeat CD HB 150
	Little Boy Blue (-1)	unissued

Note: "Jerking Time" was later re-titled "Jerk In Time" for reissue. Studio One lp is *The Wailing Wailers*. Bunny Wailer remembers recording Curtis Mayfield's song "Little Boy Blue" at this session, but Clement Dodd has been unable to locate tape of this title. Both Bunny and Peter Tosh have claimed they wrote "Rock Sweet Rock." "Don't Look Back" was written by "Smokey" Bill Robinson and Ronald White and was a hit by the Temptations. "Jerking Time" was coupled with "Rock Sweet Rock" on the original white and red Coxsone issue. "Don't Look Back" was coupled with "Dancing Shoes" on the original white and red Coxsone issue.

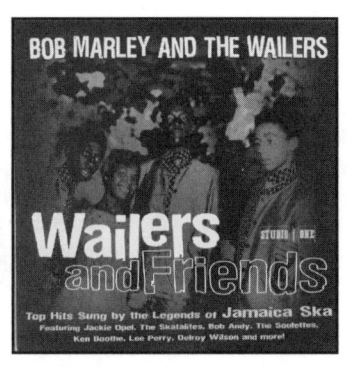

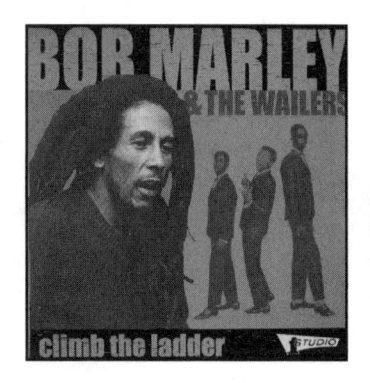

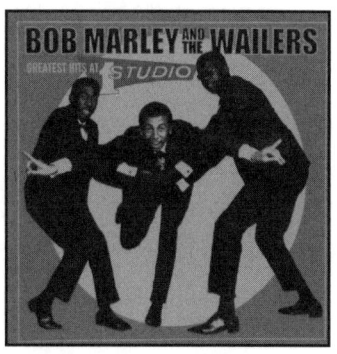

THE WAILERS   **PETER TOUCH & THE CHORUS**   circa: July 1966

Peter Tosh, vocal (-1) or harmony vocal (-2); Bunny Wailer, vocal (-2) or harmony vocal (-1); Constantine "Vision" Walker, harmony vocal; Rita Marley, harmony vocal; Marlene Gifford, harmony vocal (-3); Lloyd Knibbs, drums; Lloyd Brevett, bass; Lyn Taitt, guitar; Jackie Mittoo, piano; Roland Alphonso, tenor sax (-4); "Deadly" Headley Bennett, alto sax (-4); Sydney Bucknor, engineer; recorded Studio One; four track; Clement Dodd, production.

WIRL CS 1591-1	Making Love (-1) (-3) (-4)	Coxsone 7, Heartbeat CD HB 150
DIR CS 2002-B-1H	Lemon Tree (-1) (-2)	Coxsone, Heartbeat CD HB 251
	Sentimental Journey (-2) (-4)	unissued

   Note: "Lemon Tree" features a shared lead by Peter and Bunny. The song was first recorded by Peter, Paul, & Mary and was a minor hit when released in early 1962. Another popular version was cut in 1965 by Trini Lopez. Bunny remembers recording the big band jazz standard, "Sentimental Journey," at this session. "Making Love" was coupled with "Voo Doo Moon" by the Soul Brothers on the original black and white label Coxsone issue.

SOULETTES   circa: July 1966

Rita Marley, vocal; Bunny Wailer, harmony vocal; Peter Tosh, harmony vocal; Constantine "Vision" Walker, harmony vocal; Marlene Gifford, harmony vocal; Lloyd Knibbs, drums; Lloyd Brevett, bass; Lyn Taitt, guitar; Jackie Mittoo, piano; unknown percussion; Sydney Bucknor, engineer; recorded Studio One; four track; Clement Dodd, production.

CS-Dodd-75-006	A De Pon Dem	Studio One, Heartbeat CD HB 86

   Note: Title is as given on Heartbeat CD. The authors have only seen the Jamaican original on blank label pre-release and the original title may be "Deh Pon Dem." "Time To Cry" by Jackie Opel was coupled with "A De Pon Dem" on the original Studio One release.

JACKIE OPEL   circa: July 1966

Jackie Opel, vocal; Bunny Wailer, harmony vocal; Peter Tosh, harmony vocal; Constantine "Vision" Walker, harmony vocal; Lloyd Knibbs, drums; Lloyd Brevett, bass; Lyn Taitt, guitar; Jackie Mittoo, organ; Sydney Bucknor, engineer; recorded Studio One; four track; Clement Dodd, production.

CS Dodd 138	Time To Cry	Studio One, Studio One lp, Heartbeat CD HB 201

   Note: "Time To Cry" was coupled with "A De Pon Dem" by the Soulettes on the original Studio One release.

PETER TOSH AND THE CHORUS   **BOP & THE BELLTONES (-1)**   circa: August 1966

Peter Tosh, vocal; Bunny Wailer, harmony vocal; Constantine "Vision" Walker, harmony vocal; Rita Marley, harmony vocal (-1); unknown drums; Bryan "Bassie" Atkinson, bass; Lyn Taitt, guitar; unknown guitar; Bobby Aitken, guitar (-1); unknown piano (-1); Sydney Bucknor, engineer; recorded Studio One; four track; Clement Dodd, production. Overdubs c. 1988: unknown bongos (-2). Overdubs c. 1991: unknown drums (-3); unknown percussion (-3).

CC Dodd 64	Can't You See	Supreme, Heartbeat CD HB 150
	" (-2)	Studio One lp
	" (-3)	Heartbeat CD HB 112, Heartbeat CD HB 319
DIR CS 2005-A-1H	Treat Me Good (-1)	Studio One SO-3020, Heartbeat CD HB 150

   Note: "Treat Me Good" is mis-credited to Bop & the Belltones on both the white and green label Studio One original and later Coxsone label reissues. Studio One lp is *Marley, Tosh, Livingston & Associates*. "Can't You See" was coupled with "Time To Turn" by the Soulettes on the original Supreme label issue.

KEN BOOTHE   circa: Summer 1966

Ken Boothe, vocal; Peter Tosh, harmony vocal; Constantine "Vision" Walker, harmony vocal; Lloyd Knibbs, drums; Lloyd Brevett, bass; Jerome "Jah Jerry" Haines, guitar; Jackie Mittoo, piano; Roland Alphonso, tenor sax; Sydney Bucknor, engineer; recorded Studio One; four track; Clement Dodd, production.

| CD Dodd 88 | The Train Is Coming | Supreme, Heartbeat CD HB 201 |

Note: "The Train Is Coming" was coupled with Ken Boothe's "Feel It" on the original Supreme issue.

THE WAILERS   circa: August 1966

Bunny Wailer, vocal; Peter Tosh, harmony vocal; Constantine "Vision" Walker, harmony vocal; Lloyd Knibbs, drums; Lloyd Brevett, bass; Jerome "Jah Jerry" Haines, guitar; Jackie Mittoo, piano; Roland Alphonso, tenor sax; "Deadly" Headley Bennett, alto sax; Vin Gordon, trombone (-1); Sydney Bucknor, engineer; recorded Studio One; four track; Clement Dodd, production. Overdub c. 1970: Dennis Alcapone, DJ (-2).

WIRL CS 1748-1	What Am I Supposed To Do	Coxsone, Heartbeat CD HB 112, Heartbeat CD HB 319
CS Dodd 101	Dancing Shoes	Coxsone 5, Coxsone lp, Heartbeat CD HB 251
FCD 7448-A	"	Coxsone
	Dancing Version (-2)	Studio One lp
DIR CS 2005-B-1H	I Stand Predominant (-1)	Coxsone, Studio One (UK) SO 2024-B, Heartbeat CD HB 191

Note: Coxsone lp is *The Best Of Bob Marley & The Wailers*. Studio One lp is *Forever Version* by Dennis Alcapone. Both Jamaican and UK releases of "I Stand Predominant" share the same matrix number and both pair the song with "Come By Here" by Norma Fraser. "Dancing Shoes" was coupled with "Don't Look Back" on the original white and red Coxsone issue. "What Am I Supposed To Do" is coupled with "Do The Boogaloo" on the original Coxsone label issue.

THE WAILERS   circa: August 1966

Bunny Wailer, vocal (-1) or harmony vocal (-2); Peter Tosh, vocal (-2) or harmony vocal (-1); Constantine "Vision" Walker, harmony vocal; Lloyd Knibbs, drums; Lloyd Brevett, bass; Lyn Taitt, guitar; Jackie Mittoo, piano; Sydney Bucknor, engineer; recorded Studio One; four track; Clement Dodd, production. Overdubs c. 1991: unknown drums (-3); unknown guitar (-3); unknown percussion and sound effects (-3).

CS Dodd 122	I Need You (-1)	Studio One 7, Island (UK) WI 3042, Heartbeat CD HB 191
WIRL CS 2025-1	"	Studio One
	Dreamland (-1)	Heartbeat CD HB 251
	" (-1) (-3)	Studio One lp
	" (-1) (-3)	unissued
	Rolling Stone (-1)	Studio One lp
	" (-3)	Heartbeat CD HB 112. Heartbeat CD HB 319
	Blowing In The Wind (-2)	unissued

Note: CS Dodd 122/WIRL CS 2025-1 should not be confused with "I Need You" with Marley singing lead from August 1964. "I Need You" was re-titled as "I Need You So" on Heartbeat CD. "Rolling Stone" first appeared on a Studio One lp titled *Presenting Jamaica All Stars Vol. 1* and later reissued on Studio One lp *Marley, Tosh, Livingston & Associates*. Although Bunny Wailer clearly remembers "Blowing In The Wind," Clement Dodd doubts its existence and has been unable to find a tape of the title. Bob Dylan wrote both "Blowing In The Wind" and "Rolling Stone," but Bunny inserts some of his own lines. "I Need You," a "Smokey" Bill Robinson composition was originally titled "Baby, Baby I Need You" when performed by the Temptations on an August 1964 release. "Dreamland," long thought to be a classic Bunny Wailer composition and named as such by the authors in previous writings, was actually written by Al Johnson and was a 1962 American rhythm and blues release from Vee Jay records by a vocal group called El Tempos. "I Need You" was coupled with "Don't Want To See You Cry" by Ken Boothe on the original white and red label Studio One issue.

BOB MARLEY & THE WAILERS WITH THE SOUL BROTHERS
circa: November 1966

Bob Marley, vocal and guitar; Bunny Wailer, harmony vocal; Peter Tosh, harmony vocal; Lloyd Knibbs, drums; Lloyd Brevett, bass; Jackie Mittoo, piano; Sydney Bucknor, engineer; recorded Studio One; four track; Wailers production.

CS Dodd 127-1 RM01	Bend Down Low	Wail 'N Soul 'M, Island (UK) WI 3014, Coxsone lp, Tuff Gong (UK) CD TGCBX 1
CS Dodd 128-1 RM02	Freedom Time	Wail 'N Soul 'M, Island (UK) WI 3014, Heartbeat CD HB 112, JAD (FR) CD 537324-2, Heartbeat CD HB 319
WIRL BM 3408-2	"	Tuff Gong, Upsetter

Note: "Freedom Time" is also known as "Get Ready." Coxsone lp is *The Best Of Bob Marley & the Wailers*. Bob had returned to Jamaica from his sojourn in Delaware shortly before these titles were recorded. All three Wailers were unhappy with their previous relationship with Clement Dodd, but Bob wanted to give the relationship one more chance. Thus, they recorded their first self-produced single at Studio One and agreed to let Dodd distribute the disc. "Bend Down Low" was a major hit in Jamaica and the Wailers did well on the copies they personally sold, but their distribution deal with Dodd only resulted in more arguments over money. This was their last recording session at Studio One. This first Wail 'N Soul 'M release was initially marketed with a red and silver label. Early reissues were on a green and black Wail 'N Soul 'M label, and the coupling was later reissued on the Tuff Gong label.

THE CRACKERS & PRINCE BUSTER ALL STARS
circa: February 1967

Peter Tosh, vocal; unknown harmony vocal; Arkland "Drumbago" Parks, drums; unknown bass; Lyn Taitt, guitar; unknown piano; unknown tenor sax; Baba Brooks, trumpet; Carlton Lee, engineer; recorded West Indies Studio; four track; Prince Buster, production.

WIRL PB 7962-2	Simpleton	Olive Blossom

Note: Date of issue given on the label as 10/3/67, or March 10, 1967. When Bunny Wailer first heard this track in 1990, he was shocked that Peter would sing a lyric calling himself a simpleton. Peter often worked as a session guitarist during this period, and Bunny thinks he may have been hanging out at the studio when the Crackers attempted without success to voice their song for Prince Buster, who may have cajoled Peter into singing the lead.

BOB MARLEY AND THE WAILING WAILERS
circa: June 1967

Bob Marley, vocal; Bunny Wailer, harmony vocal; Peter Tosh, harmony vocal; Scotty, DJ vocal (-1); Hugh Malcolm, drums; Jackie Jackson, bass; Lyn Taitt, guitar; "Ranny," guitar; Winston Wright, piano; "Dizzy" Johnny Moore, trumpet; Vin Gordon, trombone; Carlton Lee, and Andy Capp, engineers; recorded West Indies Studio; four track; Wailers, production.

WIRL BM 3023-1	Nice Time	Wail N Soul M, Tuff Gong (US) 5003, Doctor Bird (UK) DB 1091, Tuff Gong (UK) CD TGCBX 1
DSR 8346 A	"	Tuff Gong
G-810-A	Nice Time Version	Giant (US) G810-A
	Nice Time Version	Rohit CD 7757, JAD (FR) CD
	Nice Time Version (-1)	unissued
WIRL BM 3084-1	Hypocrite	Wail N Soul M, Doctor Bird (UK) DB 1091, Tuff Gong (UK) CD TGCBX 1
DSR 8347 B	"	Tuff Gong
	Hypocrites	Rohit CD 7757, JAD (FR) CD
	Hypocrites Version	" , "
WIRL BM 3085-1	Mellow Mood	Wail N Soul M, Tuff Gong (US) 5006 A, Tuff Gong (UK) CD TGCBX 1
	Mellow Mood Version	Rohit CD 7757
WIRL BM 3086-1	Thank You Lord	Wail N Soul M, Tuff Gong (US) 5006 A, Tuff Gong (UK) CD TGCBX 1
	Thank You Lord Version	Rohit CD 7757

Note: Matrix designation of 3023-1 is surely a mistake at mastering and should have been 3083-1. Bunny Wailer leads on one verse of "Thank You Lord." All versions on Rohit CD are instrumental dubs and none features the voices of the Wailers. "Nice Time Version" on Giant (US) is quite different to that on the Rohit CD, and does feature the voices of the Wailers. "Nice Time"/ "Hypocrite" was released in July of 1967 and rose through the RJR Radio charts through August to rank in the top ten throughout September and October. Original releases of both "Nice Time"/ "Hypocrite" and "Mellow Mood"/ "Thank You Lord" were issued on the red, green and gold Wail N Soul M label with three interlocking hands designated as Bob, Peter, and Bunnie. Later pressings of "Hypocrite" were titled "Hypocrites". Pressings of "Hypocrites"/ "Nice Time" were either white label with red printing, black label with silver printing, or red label with black printing using the slightly altered imprint, Wail 'N Soul 'M. In "Hypocrite" Bob sings in patois "Dip for diplomatic, hip for hipocratic, dry for dryland tourist, top for Topper Norris. See the hypocrites dem a galong deh." A dryland tourist is one who claims to have traveled broadly but who has never left the island dryland of Jamaica. Topper Norris refers to upper class elites who run things and live on the surrounding hilltops looking down on Kingston. Also used in the lyric of "Hypocrite" is the patois term gravalicious, meaning greedy.

BOB MARLEY AND THE WAILING WAILERS circa: June 1967

Bob Marley, vocal; Bunny Wailer, harmony vocal; Peter Tosh, harmony vocal; Hugh Malcolm, drums; Jackie Jackson, bass; Lyn Taitt, guitar; Winston Wright, piano; "Ranny," guitar; Carlton Lee, engineer; recorded West Indies Studio; four track; Wailers, production.

| RM-45-628 A | Bus Dem Shut | Wail N Soul M, Tuff Gong (UK) CD TGCBX 1 |
| RM-45-628 B | Stir It Up | Wail N Soul M, Trojan (UK) 617, Tuff Gong (UK) CD TGCBX 1 |

Note: These titles were mastered in Miami and Bunny remembers that it took a long time to get the work back. "Stir It Up"/ "This Train" was finally released circa August 1968 and became another hit in the top ten of the RJR chart, ranking number 5 by the second week of October. Original issues of these titles were released using the red, gold, and green Wail N Soul M imprint. Later issues of "Stir It Up"/ "This Train" were red with black print or yellow with black lettering, and the label name is given as Wail 'N Soul M. "Bus Dem Shut" is patois for burst their shirts. This song was also known as "Payaka." Meaning dirty and unclean in the early part of the 1900s, by the 1950s the term payaka had acquired the additional meanings of greedy and covetous.

BOB MARLEY AND THE WAILING WAILERS circa: June 1967

Bunny Wailer, vocal (-1) and repeater (-1) or funda (-2); Bob Marley, harmony vocal (-1) and guitar; Peter Tosh, harmony vocal (-1) and guitar; Constantine "Vision" Walker, funda; Alvin "Seeco" Patterson, funda (-1) or repeater (-2); Carlton Lee, engineer; West Indies Studio; four track; Wailers, production.

WIRL BM 3273-1	Lyrical Satyrical I (-2)	Wail N Soul M, JAD (FR) CD 537324-2
WIRL BM 3274-1	This Train (-1)	Wail N Soul M, Trojan (UK) TR 617, JAD (FR) CD537324-2
WIRL BM 3274-2	"	Tuff Gong

Note: "Lyrical Satyrical I" is an acoustic instrumental track and was the original platter mate of "Bus Dem Shut" on a red, gold, and green Wail N Soul M label. In July Bunny went to prison following his conviction for possession of ganja and did not return to the group until September of 1968. "This Train" was originally recorded in January of 1927 by the Biddleville Quintette as "This Train Is Bound For Glory". The song was popularized in the 1950s by bluesman Big Bill Broonzy and it became a standard during the early sixties folk revival.

WAILERS circa: January 1968

Bob Marley, vocal and harmony vocal (-1) and guitar (-2); Peter Tosh, harmony vocal, piano (-3) or guitar (-4); Rita Marley, vocal (-5) and harmony vocal; unknown harmony vocal (-6); unknown percussion (-7); recorded in Danny Sims' rental house in Kingston; two track; Danny Sims, production.

	Fallin' In And Out Of Love (-3)	JAD CD 1001-2, JAD (FR) CD 537324-2
	Stranger On The Shore (-2) (-4) (-6)	" , "
	Splish For My Splash (-2) (-4) (-7)	" , "
	Wings Of A Dove (-4) (-5)	unissued
	Want Love True Love (-1) (-2) (-3) (-7)	"

Note: The three selections of JAD CD 1001-2 are only available on the CD-ROM portion of the disc. "Wings Of A Dove" is a traditional Jamaican song in the repertoire of most mento bands. Jimmy Norman wrote the other songs from this session with Joe Venneri and Al Pyfron except "Falling In And Out Of Love" which was written by Norman, Venneri, and M. Nash.

BOB MARLEY AND THE WAILING WAILERS
circa: **January 1968**

Peter Tosh, vocal; Bob Marley, vocal (-1) or harmony vocal (-2); Rita Marley, harmony vocal; Hugh Malcolm, drums; Jackie Jackson, bass; Lyn Taitt, guitar; Winston Wright, piano; Tommy McCook, tenor sax; "Dizzy" Johnny Moore, trumpet; Carlton Lee, engineer; recorded West Indies Studio; four track; Wailers, production.

WIRL BM 3672-1	Funeral (-2)	Wail N Soul M, JAD (FR) CD 537324-2
WIRL BM 3673-1	Pound Get A Blow (-1)	", Columbia CD C3K 65064, JAD (FR) CD 537324-2
	Hammer (-2)	Wail N Soul M (?)

Note: Although nobody has found a copy, Bunny Wailer remembers "Hammer" being released. Peter and Bob share lead on "Pound Get A Blow." "Funeral" also known as "Burial." The original label of "Funeral"/ "Pound Get A Blow" is the red, gold, and green variety. Bunny says that he and Peter wrote "Funeral" as a message to Clement Dodd, and that Peter wrote the other songs.

BOB MARLEY AND THE WAILING WAILERS   PETER TOSH & THE WAILERS (-2)   circa: **January 1968**

Peter Tosh, vocal and guitar; Bob Marley, harmony vocal; Rita Marley, harmony vocal; Hugh Malcolm, drums; Jackie Jackson, bass; "Ska" Campbell, baritone sax; Alvin "Seeco" Patterson, percussion; Carlton Lee, engineer; recorded West Indies Studio; four track; Wailers, production.

WIRL BM 3707-1	Stepping Razor	Wail N Soul M, Tuff Gong (US) 5009 A, JAD (FR) CD 537324-2
WIRL BM 3707-2	" (-2)	Intel Diplo

Note: "Stepping Razor" also known as "Walking Razor" or "Cutting Razor." Nobody has, as yet, found a labeled copy of the Wail N Soul M original; but Joe Higgs, who composed the song, verified the title.

BOB MARLEY AND THE WAILING WAILERS   SOULETTES (-2)   circa: **January 1968**

Bob Marley, vocal (-1) or harmony vocal (-2) and guitar; Peter Tosh, harmony vocal; Rita Marley, vocal (-2) or harmony vocal (-1); Hugh Malcolm, drums; Jackie Jackson, bass; Winston Wright, piano; Tommy McCook, tenor sax; "Dizzy" Johnny Moore, trumpet (-2); Alvin "Seeco" Patterson, percussion; Carlton Lee, engineer; recorded West Indies Studio; four track; Wailers, production.

WIRL BM 3708-1	I'm Hurting Inside (-1)	Wail N Soul M, JAD (FR) CD 537324-2
WIRL BM 3708-2	"	Wail N Soul M, Tuff Gong
WIRL BM 3709-1	Play Play Play (-2)	Wail N Soul M, JAD (FR) CD 537324-2
WIRL BM 3709-2	"	Wail N Soul M, Tuff Gong

Note: Joe Isaacs says he plays drums on this session. Details are given as Bunny Wailer remembers them. Titles are as given on later Tuff Gong reissues. The earliest pressings appear to have only been distributed on blank label pre-release. Bunny says Bob wrote "Play Play Play."

BOB MARLEY AND THE WAILING WAILERS   circa: **April 1968**

Peter Tosh, vocal and guitar; Bob Marley, vocal (-1) or harmony vocal (-2); Rita Marley, harmony vocal (-2); Hugh Malcolm, drums; Jackie Jackson, bass; Winston Wright, organ (-1) or piano (-2); "Ska" Campbell, baritone sax; Vin Gordon, trombone; Alvin "Seeco" Patterson, percussion; Carlton Lee, engineer; recorded West Indies Studio; four track; Wailers production.

WIRL Wailers 4229-1	Mus' Get A Beatin' (-1)	Wail N Soul M, JAD (FR) CD 537324-2
WIRL Wailers 4230-1	Fire Fire (-2)	", Columbia CD C3K 65064, JAD (FR) CD 537324-2
WIRL Wailers 4230-2	"	Wail N Soul M
WIRL Wailers 4230-3	"	"

Note: Peter and Bob share the lead on "Mus' Get A Beatin'." These titles have only been found on blank pre-release. The titles are as hand written on some copies. Bunny Wailer remembers 4229-1 as "Dem Ha' Fi Get A Beatin'." Titled "Dem A Fi Get A Beatin" on JAD CD. "Mus' Get A Beatin'" was coupled with WIRL Wailers 4230-1 "Fire Fire" on the original blank label Wail N Soul M pre-release. "Mus' Get A Beatin'" was later coupled with "The Lord Will Make A Way" on another blank label Wail N Soul M issue. "Fire Fire" was coupled with several different titles on later Wail N Soul M issues including "Don't Rock My Boat."

BOB MARLEY AND THE WAILING WAILERS   circa: April 1968

Bob Marley, vocal and guitar; Peter Tosh, harmony vocal; Rita Marley, harmony vocal; Hugh Malcolm, drums; Jackie Jackson, bass; unknown guitar; Winston Wright, organ; Roland Alphonso, tenor sax; unknown alto sax (-1); Alvin "Seeco" Patterson, percussion (-1); Carlton Lee, engineer; recorded West Indies Studio; four track; Wailers, production.

WIRL BM 4236-1	Chances Are	Wail N Soul M, Anansi/JAD (FR) Midem '97
		Sampler CD, JAD (FR) CD 474326 2
WIRL BM 4237-1	The Lord Will Make A Way	Wail N Soul M, JAD CD (FR) 474326 2
WIRL BM 4238-1	Don't Rock My Boat (-1)	Wail N Soul M, JAD (FR) 12" SP 2051,
		JAD (FR) CD 474326 2
WIRL BM 4238-2	"	Wail N Soul M

Note: These titles have only been found on blank pre-release. The titles are as Bunny Wailer remembers them. "Chances Are," written by Mortimo Planno, was coupled with "The Lord Will Make A Way" on the original blank label Wail N Soul M release. "Don't Rock My Boat" appeared on blank label pre release with several flip sides and it remains uncertain what the original reverse side was.

BOB MARLEY   circa: May 1968

Bob Marley, vocal; Peter Tosh, harmony vocal; Rita Marley, harmony vocal; Johnny Nash, harmony vocal; Al Pyfrom, harmony vocal; Dorothy Hughes, harmony vocal; Neville Willoughby, harmony vocal; Jimmy Norman, harmony vocal and piano; Damian Marley, harmony vocal (-1); Julian Marley, harmony vocal (-1); Steve Marley, harmony vocal (-1); Lynette Lewis, harmony vocal (-1); Bernard Purdie, drums; Chuck Rainey or Gordon Edwards, bass; Eric Gale, guitar; Richard Tee or Arthur Jenkins, piano; Roy Norman, keyboards; Arthur Jenkins, engineer; recorded at 43 Russell Heights; Nagra one track; overdub recordings and mix by Joe Venneri at his New York studio; Danny Sims, production.

	Falling In & Out Of Love	Anansi CD AN 0101-2, JAD CD 1001-2
	" (remix)	JAD CD 1001-2
	Splish For My Splash	Anansi CD AN 0101-2, JAD CD 1001-2
	" (remix)	JAD CD 1001-2
	What Goes Around Comes Around	JAD (FR) CD 474326 2
	" (version)	"
	" (album mix)	JAD 12" 5001-6, Anansi CD AN 0601-2,
		Anansi CD AN 0101-2, JAD CD 1001-2
	" (Alternative Mix)	JAD 12", Anansi CD AN 0601-2, Anansi CD AN 0101-2
	" (remix)	JAD CD 1001-2
	" (Roots Mix)	JAD 12" 5001-6, Anansi CD AN 0601-2
	" (Boom Remix)	JAD 12", JAD CD
	" (Yard Remix)	" , "
	" (Dancehall) (-1)	JAD 12" 5001-6, JAD CD
	" (Urban Reggae) (-1)	" , JAD CD
	" (Club Remix)	JAD 12", JAD CD
	" (Dub Remix)	" , "
	" (Original Mix)	" , "
	You Say I Have No Feelings	Anansi CD AN 0101-2
	Stranger On The Shore	JAD CD 1001-2

Mortimo Planno and Vincent "Tata" Ford, Kingston 2001. Photo by Roger Steffens.

Note: Virtually everything but Bob's lead and Peter and Rita's harmony vocals was overdubbed in NYC. The first listed "What Goes Around Comes Around" is the original track with no overdubs. "Falling In And Out of Love" and "Splish For My Splash" were written by Jimmy Norman and Joe Venneri. "What Goes Around Comes Around," "You Say I Have No Feelings," and "Stranger On The Shore" were written by Jimmy Norman, Joe Venneri, and A. Pyfrom.

BOB MARLEY   circa: May 1968

Bob Marley, vocal; Peter Tosh, harmony vocal; Rita Marley, harmony vocal; Johnny Nash, harmony vocal; Al Pyfron, harmony vocal; Dorothy Hughes, harmony vocal; Neville Willoughby, harmony vocal; Jimmy Norman, harmony vocal and piano; Bernard Purdie, drums; Chuck Rainey or Gordon Edwards, bass; Eric Gale, guitar; Richard Tee or Arthur Jenkins, piano; Roy Norman, keyboards; Errol Thompson, engineer; recorded at Randy's Studio; three track; overdub recording and mix by Joe Venerri at his New York studio; Danny Sims, production.

    Nice Time   Anansi CD AN 0101-2
    Soul Almighty   "
    Bend Down Low   "   , JAD CD 1001-2

Note: Virtually everything but Bob's lead and Peter and Rita's harmony vocals was overdubbed in NYC.

BOB MARLEY & THE WAILERS   circa: mid 1968

Bob Marley, vocal and guitar (-1); Peter Tosh, vocal and harmony vocal (-2) or harmony vocal (-1) and guitar; Rita Marley, harmony vocal; Hugh Malcolm, drums; Jackie Jackson, bass; Hux Brown, guitar (-1); Gladdy Anderson, piano; Winston Wright, organ (-1); Denzil Laing, percussion (-1); unknown engineer; unknown studio; four track; Danny Sims, production; Overdubs 1968: Bernard Purdie, drums (-3); Chuck Rainey, bass (-3); Eric Gale, guitar (-3); Richard Tee, keyboards (-3); Hugh Masekela, trumpet (-3); unknown saxophone (-3); unknown percussion (-3); Soul mixes produced in 2002 by Bruno Blum with Lou Anders, engineer.

	Rock To The Rock (-1) (-3)	Anansi/JAD (FR) Midem '97 Sampler CD, JAD (FR) Promo CD 4743232, JAD (FR) CD 474326 2
JN BB 001-A	" (-1) (Soul mix)	JAD BB 001, JAD (FR) CD 537324-2
JN BB 001-B	" (a cappella mix)	" , JAD (FR) lp 542 222-1
	Love (-2) (-3)	Anansi/JAD (FR) Midem '97 Sampler CD, JAD (FR) CD 474326 2
	" (-2) (Soul mix)	JAD (FR) CD 537324-2

Note: The a cappella mix on JAD BB 001 still has the basic instrumentation faintly audible in the mix. The Cayman Music Master Catalog lists Bob Marley as the composer of "Love," but the song was written by Peter Tosh. Neville Willoughby, in an interview with Roger Steffens published in *The Beat* volume 21 No. 3, recalls sitting with Peter as he strummed the guitar and composed the song late one night at Danny Sims' rental property in Russell Heights, Kingston.

BOB MARLEY & THE WAILERS   circa: mid 1968

Bob Marley, vocal; Peter Tosh, harmony vocal; Rita Marley, harmony vocal; Hugh Malcolm, drums; Jackie Jackson, bass; Hux Brown, guitar; Gladdy Anderson, piano (-1); Winston Wright, organ (-1); Denzil Laing, percussion (-1); unknown guitar (-2); unknown keyboard (-2); unknown tenor sax (-2); unknown trumpet (2); unknown engineer; unknown studio; four track; Danny Sims, production; unknown organ, synthesizer, and drum overdubs circa 1982 (-3); Clement Dodd, 1982 overdub and mixing engineer at Studio One; Dakota Macleod Backup Singers, harmony vocals (-4); Scott Zito, guitar (-4); Jim Ponzi, guitar (-4); Ray Naccari, keyboards (-4); unknown drum, bass, and percussion overdubs circa 1996 (-4); Joe Venneri, 1996 overdub and mixing engineer at Panther Studios, New Jersey; Soul mix produced in 2002 by Bruno Blum with engineer Lou Anders.

	Rocking Steady	Heartbeat CD HB 111/112, Heartbeat CD HB 319
	" (-1) (Soul mix)	JAD (FR) CD 537324-2
	" (-2)	JAD (FR) CD 474326 2
SO 0084 A	" (-3)	Studio One
	" (-4)	Anansi CD AN 0101-2, JAD CD 1001-2
SO 0084 B	Rocking Steady Pt. 2 (-3)	Studio One

Late '60s Wailers producer Joe Venneri, Marley's best friend, Allan "Skill" Cole, and JAD owner Danny Sims, Los Angeles 1999. Photo by Roger Steffens.

Note: Titled "Rock Steady" on Anansi and JAD CDs, this recording first appeared on Clement Dodd's Studio One label shortly after Bob's passing in 1981. Dodd also supplied Heartbeat with the original track without overdubs for issue in the mid-90s, but how he came by the recording is a mystery. The same recording was found on a reel of similar sounding material produced by Danny Sims in 1968. This identical voicing included horns, keyboard, and guitar additions to the basic rhythm probably also recorded in 1968. Bunny Wailer thought the tape and stampers were stolen from their shop on Beeston Street in May of that year. This suggests that the Wailers may have redone the song.

BOB MARLEY PLUS TWO   BOB, RITA & PETER (CANADA)   circa: May/June 1968

Bob Marley, vocal; Peter Tosh, harmony vocal, and guitar; Rita Marley, harmony vocal; Hugh Malcolm, drums; Jackie Jackson, bass; Hux Brown, guitar; unknown guitar; Gladdy Anderson, piano (-1); Winston Wright, organ (-1); unknown tenor sax (-2); unknown tenor sax (-2); "Ska" Campbell, baritone sax (-2); unknown violin (-3); unknown percussion; Carlton Lee, engineer; recorded West Indies Studio; eight track; Danny Sims, Johnny Nash, and Arthur Jenkins, production; Soul mixes produced in 2002 by Bruno Blum with engineer, Lou Anders.

	Bend Down Low (-1) (Soul mix)	JAD (FR) CD 537324-2
WIRL 4442	" (-1) (-3)	WIRL, JAD (Canada) J-211, JAD (FR) CD 474326 2
JN-BB-002 A	Nice Time (-2) (Soul mix)	JAD BB 002, JAD (FR) CD 537324-2
JN-BB-002 B	" (A cappella mix)	"
	" (-2) (-3)	JAD (FR) CD 474326 2

Note: The JAD (Canada) J-211 issue was also released in France.

BOB MARLEY PLUS TWO   BOB, RITA & PETER (CANADA)   circa: June 1968

Bob Marley, vocal; Peter Tosh, harmony vocal; Rita Marley, harmony vocal; Hugh Malcolm, drums; Jackie Jackson, bass; Hux Brown, guitar; Denzil Laing, percussion; Winston Wright, organ (-1); unknown guitar (-2); unknown keyboard synthesizer (-2); unknown tenor sax (-2); unknown baritone sax (-2); unknown percussion (-2); Carlton Lee, engineer; recorded West Indies Studio; eight track; Danny Sims, Johnny Nash, and Arthur Jenkins, production. Overdubs circa 1981 (-3); Overdubs circa 1996; Dakota Macleod Backup Singers, harmony vocals (-4); Scott Zito, guitar (-4); Ray Naccari, keyboards and programming (-4); Soul mix produced in 2002 by Bruno Blum with engineer, Lou Anders.

	Mellow Mood		Breakaway (UK) lp, JAD (FR) CD 474326 2
	"	(-1) (Soul mix)	JAD (FR) CD 537324-2
WIRL 4443	"	(-2)	WIRL, JAD (Canada) J-211
	"	(-3)	Cotillion lp SD 5228
	"	(-4)	Anansi CD AN 0101-2, JAD CD 1001-2

Note: JAD single was also released in France. Breakaway (UK) lp is titled *Jamaican Storm* and was also released in Germany on the Bellaphon label and in the United States on the Magnum label retitled *Bob Marley & The Wailers*. "Mellow Mood"/ "Treat Me Good" on the Hometown (US) label is a bootleg.

BOB MARLEY   circa: June 1968

Bob Marley, vocal and guitar; Peter Tosh, harmony vocal; Rita Marley, harmony vocal; Hugh Malcom, drums; Jackie Jackson, bass; Hux Brown, guitar (-1); Winston Wright, organ (-1); Denzil Laing, percussion (-1); Carlton Lee, engineer; recorded West Indies Studio; eight track; Danny Sims, Johnny Nash, and Arthur Jenkins, production. Overdubs circa 1996: Dakota Macleod Backup Singers, harmony vocals (-2); Scott Zito, guitar (-2); Jim Ponzi, guitar (-2); Ray Naccari, keyboards and programming (-2). "Chances Are" (Soul mix) produced in 2002 by Bruno Blum with engineer, Lou Anders.

There She Goes	Breakaway (UK) lp, JAD (FR) CD 474326 2
Put It On	" , "
" (-2)	Anansi CD AN 0101-2, JAD CD 1001-2
How Many Times	Breakaway (UK) lp, JAD (Fr) CD 474326 2
" (dub plate)	JAD CD B0003753-02
" (-2)	Anansi CD AN 0101-2
Chances Are	Breakaway (UK) lp, JAD (FR) CD 474326 2
" (-1) (Soul mix)	JAD (FR) CD 537324-2
Hammer	Breakaway (UK) lp , Tuff Gong (UK) CD TGCBX 1

Note: New York pressed singles of "Put It On" on the Eden label ER-05, "There She Goes"/ "Hammer" on the Flying Tiger label FT-04, and "How Many Times" on the Rock 'N Roll label RNR-07 have been identified by Danny Sims as bootlegs. The label numbering on these releases suggest there may have been additional pressings. Bunny Wailer says that Peter Tosh composed "Hammer."

BOB MARLEY AND THE WAILERS MORTIMO PLANNO June 8, 1968

Bob Marley, vocal (-1) or guitar (-2); Peter Tosh, harmony vocal and guitar (-1) or percussion (-2); Rita Marley, harmony vocal (-1); Constantine "Vision" Walker, harmony vocal (-1) (-2); Mortimo Planno, speech (-2); "Teego", repeater; Jeremiah, funda; Oswald Harvey, engineer; Barry Biggs, assistant engineer; recorded JBC Studio; four track; Mortimo Planno, production.

Dyna VR 238	Selassie Is The Chapel (-1)	blank, JAD CD 1001-2, JAD (FR) promo CD 4743232, JAD (FR) CD 474326 2, JAD (FR) 10"
Dyna VR 249	A Little Prayer (-2)	blank, JAD (FR) lp 542 222-1

Note: Titles and recording date were supplied by Mortimo Planno. Planno says only 26 copies were pressed and that Allan "Skill" Cole took 12 to Ethiopia. Cole confirms this figure for the initial pressing, but thinks a hundred more were subsequently pressed by Chin Randy's. This is mainly confirmed by Clive Chin who got the stamper from Mortimo Planno and thinks he pressed 150 to 200 copies. "Selassie Is The Chapel" on JAD CD 1001-2 is on the CD-ROM portion of the disc. "Selassie Is The Chapel" is based on the American hit "Crying In The Chapel," an Artie Glenn composition first popularized by country artist Rex Allen, and a hit in the 1950s by the Orioles and in the 1960s by Elvis Presley.

BOB MARLEY & THE WAILERS circa: September 1968

Bob Marley, vocal; unknown harmony vocals; unknown drums; unknown bass; unknown guitar; unknown keyboards; Carlton Lee, engineer; recorded West Indies Studio; four track; Danny Sims production.

Soul Rebel   Breakaway (UK) lp, Cotillion (US) lp 5228, JAD (FR) SPCD 2141, JAD (FR) CD 474326 2

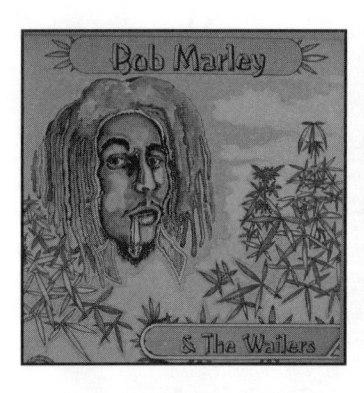

BOB MARLEY & THE WAILERS circa: late 1968

Bob Marley, vocal (-1) or harmony vocal (-2, -3, -4); Bunny Wailer, vocal (-2) or harmony vocal (-1, -3, -4); Peter Tosh, vocal (-3) or harmony vocal (-1, -2, -4) and melodica (-5); Rita Marley, vocal (-4) or harmony vocal (-1, -2, -3); unknown drums; unknown bass; unknown guitar; unknown keyboards; unknown xylophone (-6); unknown percussion; Carlton Lee, engineer; recorded West Indies Studio; eight track; Danny Sims, production. Overdubs circa 1996: Dakota Macleod Backup Singers, harmony vocals (-7); Scott Zito, guitar (-7); Jim Ponzi, guitar (-7); Ray Naccari, keyboards and programming (7). Overdubs circa 1997: unknown guitar (-8); unknown keyboards (-8); unknown drum program (-8); unknown percussion (-8).

Touch Me (-1)	Breakaway (UK) lp, JAD (FR) CD 474326 2
" (1988 remix)	Urban Teck lp 3002
" (7)	Anansi CD AN 0101-2
Treat You Right (-2)	Breakaway (UK) lp, JAD (FR) CD 474326 2
The World Is Changing (-3)	" , "

Lonely Girl (-4) (-5)		JAD (FR) lp 543 222-1
" (-8)		Jamaica (US) lp
Milkshake & Potato Chips (-1) (-5)		JAD (FR) lp 542 222-1
" (-8)		Jamaica (US) lp
It Hurts To Be Alone (-1) (-5) (-6)		JAD (FR) lp 542 222-1
" (-8)		Jamaica (US) lp
Soul Shake Down Party (-1)		"
Lonesome Feelings (-1)		JAD (FR) lp 542 222-1
" (1988 remix)		Urban Teck 3002
" (-7)		Anansi CD AN 0101-2
" (-8)		Jamaica (US) lp

Note: Jamaica (US) lp is *Bob, Bunny, Peter & Rita*. The vocal/harmony track of "Soul Shake Down Party" is identical to that used in May 1970 for the Beverley's recording of the title. It may be that Bob took it to Beverley's and overdubbed rhythm. It is also possible that Danny Sims got the vocal track from Beverley's at a later date. The title has been listed twice in this book to avoid confusion. New York-pressed singles of "Touch Me" on the Rock 'N Roll label RNR-07 and "The World Is Changing" re-titled as "You Can't Do That To Me" on the Eden label ER-05 have been identified as bootlegs by Danny Sims. "The World Is Changing" was also retitled as "You Can't Do That To Me" on Magnum (US) lp 601, a reissue of the Breakaway (UK) lp. "Treat You Right," "The World Is Changing," "Lonely Girl," and "Milk Shake & Potato Chips" were written by Jimmy Norman. "Gonna Get You" and "Stay With Me" were written by Jimmy Norman and Al Pyfrom. "Gonna Get You" was re-titled as "I'm Gonna Get You" on Anansi CD.

THE WAILERS   circa: January 1969

Bunny Wailer, vocal; Peter Tosh, harmony vocal and keyboards; Joe Sarky, harmony vocal; Ras Michael, percussion; Lloyd Brevett, bass; unknown guitar; Oswald Harvey, engineer; recorded JBC Studio; four track; Errol Thompson, mixing engineer; mixed at Randy's Studio 17; Wailers, production.

Dyna NL 524	Tread-O	Wail N Soul M, JAD (FR) CD 474326 2
Dyna NL 526	Tread-O Version	" , "

Note: Only blank pre-release copies have been found of the above coupling. Titles are supplied by Bunny Wailer.

PETER TOSH   circa: March 1969

Peter Tosh, vocal, harmony vocal (-1) and piano; unknown drums; unknown bass; unknown guitar; unknown organ; Errol Thompson, engineer; recorded Randy's Studio 17; four track; Randy's, production.

Dyna Randy 414-1	You Can't Fool Me Again	Randy's, Columbia CD C3K 65064
Randy's 414-B	Staright To Rag-Jah-Rabbit Head (-1)	Impact

Note: Randy's 414-B is a version of "You Can't Fool Me Again" released in 1998. The spelling is as given on the label. The title refers to this book's co-author Roger Steffens, whose reggae nick-name is "Ras RoJah." Randy's personnel combined that with "Roger Rabbit" and used a phonetic Cockney spelling for "straight." The Impact single was repressed on gold wax in 2002.

PRINCE BUSTER   circa: March 1969

Prince Buster, vocal; Bunny Wailer, harmony vocal; Peter Tosh, harmony vocal; unknown drums; unknown bass; unknown guitar; unknown organ; Carlton Lee, engineer; recorded West Indies Studio; four track; Prince Buster, production.

WIRL PB 4001-2	Don't Deceive Me	Olive Blossom
WIRL PB 4024-1	Don't You Know	"

Note: The few copies of this coupling that have been found have the titles written in pen with artist credit to Prince Buster, Bob Marley & The Wailers. Bob does not sing on either title. Bunny thinks there may have been a few additional titles recorded at this session.

HUGH ROY & PETER TOUCH   circa: summer 1969

Hugh Roy (U Roy), speech; Peter Tosh, speech; Carlton Barrett, drums; Aston "Family Man" Barrett, bass; Alva "Reggie" Lewis, guitar; Ranford "Ronnie Bop" Williams, guitar; Glen Adams, piano; Count Ossie, percussion (added at time of voicing); Errol Thompson, engineer; recorded Randy's Studio 17; four track; Lee Perry, production.

Upsetter 718-1	Earth's Rightful Ruler	Upsetter, Keith's (US) 200-B, Star (UK) PTLP 1023, Heartbeat CD HB 150

Note: Labeled copies of the Jamaican release have not been seen by the authors. U Roy says the proper title is "Earth's Rightful Ruler." Keith's (US) issue is titled "Righteous Ruler." Mis-titled on Star lp as "Nightfall Ruler." Heartbeat CD lists "Rightful Ruler." U Roy remembers this as his first recording. Instrumental session details given are for the basic rhythm track originally used for "Selassie" by the Reggae Boys, a vocal group anchored by Glen Adams and Alva Lewis. "Earth's Rightful Ruler" actually begins with Tosh speaking in Amharic over a rhythm called "Ethiopian National Anthem" by the Sons Of Negus Churchical Host originally issued on their Zion Disc label, but this rhythm is quickly spliced into "Selassie." These were lean times for the Wailers and Peter began to engage in a lot of session work as a guitarist or keyboard man. Eventually the Wailers again began the task of looking for an outside producer. In August both the Wailers and their friends The Wailing Souls auditioned material for producer Lloyd Daley (Lloyd the Matador). Lloyd loved both groups, but his wife vetoed the Wailers, convinced that they were too rough and ghetto tough to be trusted. She also found fault with the lyrical content of "Back Out," the song the Wailing Souls had auditioned. Their "Gold Digger" was instead chosen for the group's only Matador release.

BOB MARLEY AND THE WAILERS (?)   circa: late 1969 or early 1970

Bob Marley, vocal; Peter Tosh, harmony vocal and guitar; Bunny Wailer, harmony vocal; Rita Marley, harmony vocal; Cecile Campbell, harmony vocal; Hortense Lewis, harmony vocal; Carlton Barrett, drums; Aston "Family Man" Barrett, bass; Glen Adams, piano; Errol Thompson, engineer; recorded Randy's Studio 17; four track; Wailers, production.

BM 1006	Black Progress	Power, Anansi/JAD (FR) Midem '97 Sampler CD, JAD (FR) 12" SP 2051, JAD (FR) 10", JAD (FR) promo CD 4743232, JAD (FR) CD 474326 2
BM 1007	Version	Power, JAD (FR) 12" SP 2051, JAD (FR) CD 474326 2

Note: Only blank label pre release copies have been found of the above coupling. Most have the title hand written and are stamped, Power Label. "Black Progress" is a reworking of James Brown's "Say It Loud – I'm Black and I'm Proud," a chart hit in America during late 1968.

BOB MARLEY AND THE WAILERS   circa: late 1969 or early 1970

Bob Marley, vocal and guitar; Peter Tosh, harmony vocal and guitar, piano (-1), or organ (-2); Bunny Wailer, harmony vocal; Carlton Barrett, drums; Aston "Family Man" Barrett, bass; Errol Thompson, engineer; recorded Randy's Studio 17; four track; Wailers, production.

Dyna Wailers 833-1	Trouble On The Road Again (-1)	Wail N Soul M JAD (FR) CD 474326 2
AB 2648	Trouble Dub (-1)	Fam's, JAD (FR) CD 495250 2
Dyna Wailers 834	Comma Comma (-2)	Wail N Soul M, JAD (FR) CD 494250 2

Note: "Trouble Dub" is a remix of "Trouble On The Road Again" released in the early seventies. Only blank label pre-release copies of "Trouble On The Road Again"/ "Comma Comma" have been found, some stamped "Power Records." Titles are listed as remembered by Bunny Wailer.

WAILERS   circa: late 1969 or early 1970

Bob Marley, guitar; Peter Tosh, organ; Count Matchouki, DJ; Carlton Barrett, drums; Aston "Family Man" Barrett, bass; Errol Thompson, engineer; recorded Randy's Studio 17; four track; Randy's production.

AC-36	Stick Up	Randy's

Note: Issued on blank label with title "Stick Up'" credited to Wailers stamped on one side.

THE WAILERS   **circa: late 1969 or early 1970**

Bob Marley, vocal; Bunny Wailer, harmony vocal; Peter Tosh, harmony vocal and guitar; Rita Marley, harmony vocal; Hugh Malcolm, drums; Jackie Jackson, bass; Gladdy Anderson, piano; Errol Thompson, engineer; recorded Randy's Studio 17; four track; Randy's production.

Dyna Randy 1056-1   Sugar Sugar   Randy's, Anansi/JAD (FR) Midem '97 sampler CD,
                                            JAD (FR) CD SP 2051, JAD (FR) promo CD 4743232,
                                            JAD (FR) CD 474326 2

   Note: "Sugar Sugar" was originally a hit for American group the Archies. The Wailers rendition includes a verse from Bob's composition "You Pour Sugar On Me," a tune later covered by Judy Mowatt.

THE WAILERS (?)   **MAD DOGS**   **circa: early 1970**

Peter Tosh, vocal; Bob Marley, harmony vocal; Bunny Wailer, harmony vocal; Rita Marley, harmony vocal; probably Hugh Malcolm, drums; Jackie Jackson, bass; Hux Brown, guitar; unknown keyboards; Errol Thompson, engineer; recorded Randy's Studio 17; four track; Wailers, production.

Dyna RM 1478-1   Give Me A Ticket   Tempa B.P.N. 000200, Anansi/JAD (FR) Midem '97 Sampler CD,
                                            JAD (FR) CD 474326 2
Dyna RM 1480-1   Version   Tempa B.P.N. 000200, Tuff Gong (US) TG 5009-B,
                                            JAD (FR) CD 474326 2

   Note: The first recording of this Wayne Carson Thompson composition, originally titled "The Letter," was done by The Box Tops, who scored a number one chart hit in America circa August 1967. Labeled copies of the Tempa release credit music to the Mad Dogs and credit Bob Marley with arrangement. The label also lists Wail N Soul Rec., but does not feature title or artist credit. Some copies have "Give Me A Ticket" written in hand on the label. Bunny Wailer confirms this as the title.

WHALERS   **BOB MARLEY & THE WAILERS**   **circa: early 1970**

Bob Marley, vocal, guitar (-1); Peter Tosh, harmony vocal, guitar (-2); Bunny Wailer, harmony vocal; Rita Marley, harmony vocal; Hortense Lewis, harmony vocal (-3); Hugh Malcolm, drums; Jackie Jackson, bass; Hux Brown, guitar; Winston Wright, keyboards; Larry McDonald, bongos (-4); Buddy Davidson, engineer; recorded Federal Studio; four track; Ted Powder, production.

Dyna DS TP 1627-1   Adam And Eve   Tiger T-12, Trojan lp TRLS 221, JAD (FR) CD 474326 2
Dyna DS TP 1628-1   Wisdom (-4)   Tiger T-12, Trojan lp TRLS 221, JAD (FR) CD 474326 2
                       This Train (-1)   Tiger (?), Trojan lp TRLS 221, JAD (FR) CD 474326 2
                       Thank You Lord (-2) (-3) Tiger (?), Trojan lp TRLS 221, JAD (FR) CD 474326 2

   Note: "Wisdom" is also known as "Lips Of The Righteous," "Stiff Necked Fools," and "Fools Die." Although no one has as yet found a copy, Bunny Wailer is sure "This Train"/ "Thank You Lord" was released. The producer, whose name is given as Powder on the record label, actually used the Dutch spelling, Pouder. "This Train" is traditional. Composition of "Adam And Eve" is credited on the label to Llewlyn Graham, actually Leo Graham, who had previously recorded the song for the Tiger label with his vocal group, the Bleechers.

THE WAILERS   May 5, 1970

Bob Marley, vocal (-1) or harmony vocal (-2); Peter Tosh, vocal (-2) or harmony vocal (-1) and guitar; Bunny Wailer, harmony vocal; Mikey "Boo" Richards, drums; Jackie Jackson, bass; Hux Brown, guitar; Gladdy Anderson, piano; Winston Wright, organ; Carlton Lee, engineer; recorded Dynamic Sounds Studio; four track; Leslie Kong, production.

Dyna LK 1776-1	Soul Shake Down Party (-1)	Beverley's, Beverley's BLP 011, Trojan (UK) TR 7759, Trojan (UK) 12" TROT 9074, Tuff Gong (UK) CD TGCBX 1
Dyna LK 1777-1	Soul Shake Down Version (-1)	Beverley's, Trojan (UK) TR 7759, JAD (FR) CD 474326 2
Dyna LK 1780-1	Stop The Train (-2)	Beverley's SR 165, Beverley's BLP 011, JAD (FR) CD 474326 2

   Note: Rhythm tracks were recorded on April 29, 1970. Vocals were recorded on May 5, 1970. The vocal/harmony track for "Soul Shake Down Party" is identical to that also used by Danny Sims on Jamaica lp, *Bob, Bunny, Peter & Rita*. It may be that Bob took the vocal track to Beverley's and overdubbed rhythm. It is also possible that Danny Sims got the vocal track from Beverley's at a later date. The track is also listed on a late 1968 Sims session to avoid confusion.

THE WAILERS   May 19, 1970

Bob Marley, vocal; Peter Tosh, harmony vocal and guitar; Bunny Wailer, harmony vocal; Mikey "Boo" Richards, drums; Jackie Jackson, bass; Hux Brown, guitar; Gladdy Anderson, piano; Winston Wright, organ; Carlton Lee, engineer; recorded Dynamic Sounds Studio; four track; Leslie Kong, production.

	Cheer Up	Beverley's BLP 011, JAD (FR) CD 474326 2
	Cheer Up	unissued

THE WAILERS   circa: May 1970

Bob Marley, vocal (-1) or harmony vocal (-2); Peter Tosh, vocal (-2) or harmony vocal (-1) and guitar; Bunny Wailer, harmony vocal; Mikey "Boo" Richards, drums; Jackie Jackson, bass; Hux Brown, guitar; Alva "Reggie" Lewis, guitar (-3); Gladdy Anderson, piano; Winston Wright, organ; Carlton Lee, engineer; recorded Dynamic Sound Studio; four track; Leslie Kong, production.

Dyna LK 2264-1	Soon Come (-2)	Beverley's SR 133, Beverley's BLP 011, JAD (FR) CD 474326 2
Dyna LK 2265-1	Version (-2)	Beverley's SR 133, JAD (FR) CD 474326 2
FLK 3404	Caution (-1) (-3)	Beverley's SR 165, Beverley's BLP 011, Trojan (UK) 12" TROT 9074; Tuff Gong (UK) CD TGCBX 1
	Soul Captives (-1)	Beverley's BLP 011, JAD (FR) CD 474326 2
	Go Tell It On The Mountain (-2)	" , "
	Can't You See (-2)	" , "
	Back Out (-1)	" , Tuff Gong (UK) CD TGCBX 1
	Do It Twice (-1)	" , "
	Baby Baby Come Home (-1)	unissued
	Sophisticated Psychedelication (-1)	unissued

   Note: Leslie Kong passed away on April 9, 1971, the victim of heart failure. Other sources give the date of death as August 23, 1971. Paul Douglas says he played drums on some of these titles. "Go Tell It On The Mountain" is a traditional American song that was in Peter's repertoire when Bob and Bunny first met him. Jimmy Norman says he wrote "Soon Come" and that Peter just changed a few words.

BOB MARLEY & THE WAILERS   circa: summer 1970

Bunny Wailer, guitar; Peter Tosh, piano; Hugh Malcolm, drums; Lloyd Brevett, bass; Gladdy Anderson, piano; Ras Michael, percussion; Oswald Harvey, engineer; recorded JBC Studio; four track; Wailers, production.

Dyna NL 825-1	Rhythm	Wail 'N' Soul M, JAD (FR) CD 474326 2

Note: "Rhythm" is an instrumental track of an otherwise unknown Bunny Wailer song, "Homeward Bound," with voices barely audible in the mix. A blank label copy of "Rhythm"/ "Feel Alright" was found in a sleeve on which was written, "pre release date 24/12/69." Bunny insists that these songs were recorded just after the Beverley's sessions. Bunny does not recall if "Homeward Bound" was ever properly voiced.

BOB MARLEY & THE WAILERS   circa: summer 1970

Bob Marley, vocal and guitar; Bunny Wailer, harmony vocal and piano; Peter Tosh, harmony vocal and organ; Hugh Malcolm, drums; Lloyd Brevett, bass (-1); Errol Thompson, engineer; recorded Randy's Studio 17; four track; Wailers production; Overdubs circa 1971, Aston "Family Man" Barrett, bass (-2).

Dyna NL 823-1	Feel Alright (-1)	Wail 'N' Soul M, JAD (FR) CD 474326 2
AB 2649	Dub Feeling (-2)	Fam's, JAD (FR) CD 495250 2

Note: "Dub Feeling" is a remix of "Feel Alright" with a bass overdub.

PETER TOSH   circa: summer 1970

Peter Tosh, vocal; Carlton Barrett, drums; Aston "Family Man" Barrett, bass; Alva "Reggie" Lewis, guitar; Glen Adams, keyboards; Errol Thompson, engineer; recorded Randy's Studio 17; four track; Wailers, production.

FPT 7952-A	Oppressor Man	Trans Am
FPT 7952-B	Version	"

Note: This is Peter's second recording of the traditional "Sinner Man" which he first cut at Studio One.

PETER TOSH   circa: summer 1970

Peter Tosh, organ; unknown drums; unknown bass; unknown guitar; Errol Thompson, engineer; recorded Randy's Studio 17; four track; Randy's, production.

Selassie Serenade	Bullet (UK) 414
The Return Of Al Capone	Unity (UK) 525
Sun Valley	Unity (UK) 529
Romper Room	Escort (UK) 808 B
Crimson Pirate	Jackpot (UK) 706
Moon Dust	"
Green Duck	unknown

Note: Peter mentioned the "Green Duck" instrumental in an interview with this work's co-author, Roger Steffens, and his radio co-host, Hank Holmes.

PETER TOSH   circa: summer 1970

Peter Tosh, vocal; unknown drums; unknown bass; unknown guitar; unknown piano; unknown percussion; Errol Thompson, engineer; recorded Randy's Studio 17; four track; Randy's, production.

Little Green Apples	Impact

Note: This song was originally a hit for American soul artist O. C. Smith.

PETER TOSH & THE WAILERS   circa: summer 1970

Peter Tosh, keyboards; Bob Marley, guitar; Bunny Wailer, percussion; Carlton Barrett, drums; Aston "Family Man" Barrett, bass; Errol Thompson, engineer; recorded Randy's Studio 17; four track; Randy's, production.

        Field Marshall   Jah Guidance
        No Parshall   "

Note: The Jah Guidance disc was issued in 1995. "Field Marshall" and "Carly" were both nicknames for Carlton Barrett.

BOB & RITA   LESTER STERLING'S ALL STARS   circa: summer 1970

Bob Marley, vocal; Rita Marley, vocal; Bunny Wailer, harmony vocal; Peter Tosh, harmony vocal; Cecille Campbell, harmony vocal; Hortense Lewis, harmony vocal; Carlton Barrett, drums; Aston "Family Man" Barrett, bass; Alva "Reggie" Lewis, guitar; Glen Adams, piano; Lester Sterling, alto sax; "Deadly" Headly Bennett, tenor sax; Errol Thompson, engineer; recorded Randy's Studio 17; four track; Randy's, production.

Dyna WLRS 2117-1   Hold On To This Feeling Version   Tuff Gong, JAD (FR) 10", JAD (FR) CD 474326 2
Dyna WLRS 2148-1   Hold On To This Feeling   "   , JAD (FR) CD 474326 2

Note: Aston Barrett has stated that this recording was done at the same approximate time as "Black Progress," but this seems unlikely as the Junior Walker original did not reach the US charts until late February 1970.

SOULETTES   circa: summer 1970

Hortense Lewis, vocal; Rita Marley, harmony vocal; Cecille Campbell, harmony vocal; Carlton Barrett, drums; Aston "Family Man" Barrett, bass; Alva "Reggie" Lewis, guitar; Ranford "Ronnie Bop" Williams, guitar; Glen Adams, organ; Errol Thompson, engineer; recorded Randy's Studio 17; four track; Bob Marley/Lee Perry, production.

Dyna BM 3502-1   My Desire   Tuff Gong
Dyna B Marley 3515-1   Bring It Up   "
                           Bring It Up   Orchid ORCHCDB2

Note: Composition of both titles is credited on the Tuff Gong label to Bob Marley.

BOB MARLEY AND THE WAILERS   circa: August 1970

Bob Marley, vocal; Bunny Wailer, harmony vocal; Peter Tosh, harmony vocal; Dave Barker, harmony vocal; Carlton Barrett, drums; Aston "Family Man" Barrett, bass; Hux Brown, guitar; Alva "Reggie" Lewis, guitar; Glen Adams, piano; Carlton Lee, engineer; recorded Dynamic Sounds Studio; four track; Lee Perry, production.

Upsetter 574   My Cup (-1)   Upsetter, Upsetter (UK) US 340, Upsetter lp, JAD (FR) CD 823672 2
                         "   (extended)   Jamaican Gold CD JMC 200.277
Upsetter 573   Version Of Cup (-1)   Upsetter, Upsetter (UK) US 342, JAD (FR) CD 823672 2

Note: "My Cup" was re-titled as "I've Got To Cry" on Rohit CD 7757 and "Make Up" on Lagoon CD 1040. Upsetter lp is *Soul Rebels*.

BOB MARLEY AND THE WAILERS   circa: August 1970

Bob Marley, vocal; Bunny Wailer, harmony vocal; Peter Tosh, harmony vocal; Dave Barker, harmony vocal; Carlton Barrett, drums; Lloyd Parks, bass; Alva "Reggie" Lewis, guitar; Ranford "Ronnie Bop" Williams, guitar; Glen Adams, piano; Carlton Lee, engineer; recorded Dynamic Sounds Studio; four track; Lee Perry, production.

                         Try Me (-2)   Upsetter lp, JAD (FR) CD 823672 2
                           "   (extended)   Jamaican Gold CD JMC 200.277
                       Try Me Version (-2)   Lagoon CD 1040, JAD (FR) CD 823672 2

Note: "Try Me" was re-titled as "I've Got The Action" on Rohit CD 7757. Upsetter lp is *Soul Rebels*.

Lee "Scratch" Perry at his home in Kingston, 2003. Photo by Roger Steffens.

BOB MARLEY & THE WAILERS   DAVE BARKER (-1)   circa: September 1970

Bob Marley, vocal; Bunny Wailer, harmony vocal; Peter Tosh, harmony vocal; Dave Barker, vocal (-1); Carlton Barrett, drums; Jackie Jackson, bass; Alva "Reggie" Lewis, guitar; Ranford "Ronnie Bop" Williams, guitar; Glen Adams, organ; Tommy McCook, tenor sax; "Deadly" Headley Bennett, alto sax; Vin Gordon, trombone; unknown percussion (-1); Carlton Lee, engineer; recorded Dynamic Sounds Studio; four track; Lee Perry, production.

3921-1	Small Axe	Upsetter, Spinning Wheel, Upsetter (US), Upsetter (UK) US 357; Trojan lp TRLS 62, Tuff Gong (UK) CD TGCBX 1
	" (extended)	Jamaican Gold CD JMC 200.277
LP 3949-1	Axe Man	Upsetter, Spinning Wheel, Upsetter (US), Upsetter (UK) 372, JAD (FR) CD 823672 2
Us+358+A2	Small Axe V/2 (-1)	Spinning Wheel
	Battle Axe	Upsetter lp, Trojan (UK) TBL 167, JAD (FR) CD 823672 2

Note: "Axe Man" is a version cut of "Small Axe." "Battle Axe" is an alternate version cut of "Small Axe" which first appeared on the Upsetter lp also titled *Battle Axe*. "Small Axe" on Coxsone lp *The Best Of Bob Marley & The Wailers* is actually the take of "More Axe" originally issued on Upsetter single. "More Axe" is listed next in this text. The composer credit on copies of "Small Axe" reads L. Perry and B. Marley. According to Clancy Eccles and Niney the Observer, the song was originally penned by Lee Perry while he sat on the toilet in the back of Eccles' record shop. Perry is said to have emerged with the song written on toilet paper. The "big tree" referred to in the lyric works on two levels. Jamaicans routinely drop the letter H when pronouncing words. Thus Perry was also speaking of the "Big Three," the three dominant powers in Jamaican record manufacturing and production, Studio One, Treasure Isle, and Federal.

BOB MARLEY & THE WAILERS   circa: September 1970

Bob Marley, vocal; Bunny Wailer, harmony vocal; Peter Tosh, harmony vocal; Carlton Barrett, drums; Aston "Family Man" Barrett, bass; Alva "Reggie" Lewis, guitar; unknown guitar (-1); Glen Adams, organ; unknown percussion; Carlton Lee, engineer; recorded Dynamic Sounds Studio; four track; Lee Perry, production.

LP 3950-1	More Axe (-1)	Upsetter, Upsetter (US), Upsetter (UK) US 372, Coxsone lp, JAD (FR) CD 823672 2
	" (alternate long mix)	Orchid ORCHCDB2, JAD (FR) lp 542 222-1
	More More Axe	" , "

Note: "More Axe," a slow alternate recording of "Small Axe," was mis-titled as "Small Axe" on Coxsone lp *The Best Of Bob Marley & The Wailers*. "More More Axe" is not a version mix, but an alternate take of the song which is re-titled as "More Axe – alternate" on JAD (FR) CD. Composition credit on the original Upsetter pressing reads L. Perry and B. Marley.

BOB MARLEY & THE WAILERS   circa: September 1970

Bob Marley, vocal; Bunny Wailer, harmony vocal; Peter Tosh, harmony vocal; Dave Barker, vocal (-1); Carlton Barrett, drums; Aston "Family Man" Barrett, bass; Alva "Reggie" Lewis, guitar; Ranford "Ronnie Bop" Williams, guitar; Glen Adams, organ; Tommy McCook, tenor sax (-2); "Deadly" Headley Bennett, alto sax (-2); Carlton Lee, engineer; recorded Dynamic Sounds Studio; four track; Lee Perry, production.

KG 2269-1	Man To Man (-2)	Upsetter, JAD (FR) CD 823672 2
	" (alternate long mix)	JAD (FR) CD 537325-2
	" (dub plate mix)	unissued
KG 2270-1	Nicoteen (-2)	Upsetter, JAD (FR) CD 823672 2
	Mam To Man V/3 (-2)	Upsetter lp
LP 2246	Duppy Conqueror	Upsetter, Upsetter (UK) US 348, Shelter (US) P-7309 Clocktower (US) CT 505, Trojan lp TRLS 62, Tuff Gong (UK) CD TGCBX 1
Upsetter 2110-1	"	Upsetter
SRPO 6286-F-3	" (stereo mix)	Shelter (US) P-7309
	" (extended)	Jamaican Gold CD JMC 200.277
	" (vocal mix)	unissued
LP 3345	Zigzag	Upsetter, JAD (FR) CD 823672 2

Upsetter 2109-1	Zigzag	Upsetter
	" (alternate mix)	JAD (FR) CD 537325-2
Us+348+A	Conqueror Version 3 (-1)	Upsetter
	Duppy Conqueror V/4	Maroon lp, JAD (FR) CD 537325-2
	Duppy Conqueror V/5	Upsetter lp, JAD CD B0003300-02

Note: "Nicoteen" is a version of "Man To Man," as is "Mam To Man V/3" from the rare Jamaican issue of the lp *Good Bad & Upsetter*. "Zigzag" is a version of "Duppy Conqueror." "Duppy Conqueror V/4" is from the Maroon lp titled *Soul Revolution* on the label, but titled "Soul Revolution Part II" on the sleeve. "Duppy Conqueror V/5" is on Upsetter lp *Upsetter Revolution Rhythm*. Upsetter (UK) and Shelter (US) issues are wrongly titled as "Doppy Conqueror." The Shelter issue features mono and stereo mixes. Duppy is Jamaican patois for ghost or spirit. Composition credits for "Man To Man" and "Duppy Conqueror" both read B. Marley and L. Perry on the original Upsetter pressings. The initial lines of "Man To Man" were also used in a Perry composition from the early sixties called "The Unjust," originally recorded by Shenley Duffas and issued on Clement Dodd's Worldisc label. "Man To Man" was retitled as "Who The Cap Fit" when Bob recut the song in 1977. The alternate long mix of "Man To Man" features several lead vocal lines excised from the original single release on Upsetter.

LORD GLEN   circa: **September 1970**

Glen Adams, vocal and keyboard; Bob Marley, harmony vocal; Peter Tosh, harmony vocal, Bunny Wailer, harmony vocal; Carlton Barrett, drums, Aston "Family Man" Barrett, bass; Alva "Reggie" Lewis, guitar; Carlton Lee, engineer; recorded Dynamic Sound Studio; four track; Lee Perry, production.

FLP 3348	Never Had A Dream	Upsetter
FLP 3349	Version	"

Note: Glen Adams supplied the details of this session.

DAVE BARKER   circa: **September 1970**

Dave Barker, vocal; Bob Marley, harmony vocal; Bunny Wailer, harmony vocal; Peter Tosh, harmony vocal; Carlton Barrett, drums; Aston "Family Man" Barrett, bass; Alva "Reggie" Lewis, guitar; Ranford "Ronnie Bop" Williams, guitar; Glen Adams, organ; Carlton Lee, engineer; recorded Dynamic Sounds Studio; four track; Lee Perry, production.

Dyna Upsetter 2147-1	Don't Let The Sun Catch You Crying	Upsetter

Note: This song was originally a hit for English group, Gerry and the Pacemakers.

DAVE BARKER   circa: **September 1970**

Dave Barker, vocal; Bunny Wailer, harmony vocal; Carlton Barrett, drums; Aston "Family Man" Barrett, bass; Alva "Reggie" Lewis, guitar; Ranford "Ronnie Bop" Williams, guitar; Glen Adams, organ; Tommy McCook, tenor sax; unknown tenor sax; Uziah "Sticky" Thompson, percussion; Carlton Lee, engineer; recorded Dynamic Sounds Studio; four track; Lee Perry, production.

Dyna L Perry 3630	What A Confusion	Upsetter
Dyna L Perry 3632	Version	"

RAS DAWKINS & THE WAILERS   circa: **September 1970**

Carl Dawkins, vocal; Bob Marley, harmony vocal; Bunny Wailer, harmony vocal; Peter Tosh, harmony vocal; Carlton Barrett, drums; Aston "Family Man" Barrett, bass; Alva "Reggie" Lewis, guitar; Ranford "Ronnie Bop" Williams, guitar; Glen Adams, organ; Carlton Lee, engineer; recorded Dynamic Sounds Studio; four track; Lee Perry, production.

Dyna LP 4149-1	Picture On The Wall V/3	Upsetter, Upsetter (UK) US 368, Upsetter lp, Trojan (UK) TBL 167, Jamaican Gold CD JMC 200.229
Dyna LP 4156-1	Picture On The Wall V/4	Upsetter, Jamaican Gold CD JMC 200.229

Note: These titles, which seem to imply the existence of earlier Upsetter versions, actually refer to Freddy McKay's earlier hit recording of his song for Studio One and its original version mix. Upsetter/Trojan lp is titled *Battle Axe*.

CARL DAWKINS & THE WAILERS   circa: September 1970

Carl Dawkins, vocal; Bunny Wailer, harmony vocal; Peter Tosh, harmony vocal; Carlton Barrett, drums; Aston "Family Man" Barrett, bass; Alva "Reggie" Lewis, guitar; Ranford "Ronnie Bop" Williams, guitar; Glen Adams, organ; Val Bennett, sax (-2); Carlton Lee, engineer; recorded Dynamic Sounds Studio; four track; Lee Perry, production.

	True Love	Upsetter, Punch (UK) PH 39 (2)
	Cloud Nine (-2)	unissued
	Cloud Nine (-2)	"
	Cloud Nine (-2)	Upsetter lp, Heartbeat CD HB 101
	Cloud Nine (-2)	unissued

Note: "Cloud Nine" was originally a hit for Motown group, the Temptations. Upsetter lp is *Many Moods Of The Upsetters*.

BOB MARLEY & THE WAILERS   INTERNS   circa: October 1970

Bob Marley, vocal; Bunny Wailer, harmony vocal; Bunny Lee, speech (-1); Carlton Barrett, drums; Aston "Family Man" Barrett, bass; Alva "Reggie" Lewis, guitar; Ranford "Ronnie Bop" Williams, guitar; Glen Adams, organ; Carlton Lee, engineer; recorded Dynamic Sounds Studio; four track; Bunny Lee, production.

Dyna BL 1991-1	Mr. Chatterbox (-1)	Agro Sound, JAD (FR) CD 474326 2
	" (edited)	Jackpot (UK) JP 730, Trojan lp TRLS 182
	Chatterbox Version	Rohit CD 7757, JAD (FR) CD 474326 2

Note: A short conversation between Bunny Lee and Bob Marley precedes "Mr. Chatterbox" on original Agro Sound Jamaican release and JAD (FR) CD. This conversation has been edited out of Jackpot (UK) and Trojan reissues. Trojan lp wrongly credits The Inturns. Winston Grennan said that he played drums on this track. Details are as remembered by Bunny Wailer.

WAILERS/UPSETTERS   circa: November 1970

Carlton Barrett, drums; Aston "Family Man" Barrett, bass; Alva "Reggie" Lewis, guitar; Ranford "Ronnie Bop" Williams, guitar; Glen Adams, Keyboards; Uziah "Sticky" Thompson, percussion; recorded in rehearsal at Randy's Studio 17.

	Soul Rebel	unissued

WAILERS/UPSETTERS   circa: November 1970

Carlton Barrett, drums; Aston "Family Man" Barrett, bass; Alva "Reggie" Lewis, guitar; Ranford "Ronnie Bop" Williams, guitar; Peter Tosh, guitar (-1); Glen Adams, keyboards; Uziah "Sticky" Thompson, percussion; recorded in rehearsal at Randy's Studio 17.

	400 Years (-1)	unissued
	400 Years (-1)	"
	Corner Stone	"
	Corner Stone	"
	No Water	"
	No Water	"
	Reaction	"
	Reaction	"

Note: Vocals are not listed although they are occasionally barely audible in the mix. The tape also includes several false starts on all titles except "400 Years."

BOB MARLEY AND THE WAILERS   GLEN ADAMS (-1)   circa: November 1970

Bob Marley, vocal; Peter Tosh, harmony vocal; Bunny Wailer, harmony vocal; Carlton Barrett, drums; Lloyd Parks, bass; Alva "Reggie" Lewis, guitar; Ranford "Ronnie Bop" Williams, guitar; Glen Adams, keyboards; Uziah "Sticky" Thompson, percussion; Errol Thompson, engineer; recorded Randy's Studio 17; four track; Lee Perry, production.

Matrix	Title	Release
AB 2757	Soul Rebel	blank label, Upsetter lp, Trojan (UK) lp TBL 126, Tuff Gong (UK) CD TGCBX 1
Dyna CB 3039	"	Capo
	" (extended)	Jamaican Gold CD JMC 200.277
AB 2757	Version	blank label, JAD (FR) CD 823672 2
Dyna CB 3040	"	Capo
G-810-B	Rebel Version (-1)	Giant (US) 810-B, Capo, JAD (FR) CD 823672
	Soul Rebel V/4	Upsetter lp
	Soul Rebel	Lagoon CD 1040, JAD (FR) CD 537325-2
	Soul Rebels Version	"
Dyna Bob Morley 2208-1	Run For Cover	Tuff Gong T.G. 002, Escort (UK) ERT 842, JAD (FR) CD 823672 2
	It's Alright	Upsetter lp, Trojan (UK) lp TBL 126, JAD (FR) CD 823672 2
	" (extended)	Jamaican Gold CD JMC 200.277
	It's Alright (Version)	Upsetter lp, JAD (FR) CD 823672 2
	It's Alright	Lagoon CD 1040, JAD (FR) CD 537325-2
	It's Alright Version	"
	No Water	Upsetter lp, Trojan (UK) lp TBL 126, JAD (FR) CD 823672 2
	" (extended)	Jamaican Gold CD JMC 200.277
	No Water Version	JAD (FR) CD 823672 2

Note: "Soul Rebel V/4" and "It's Alright (Version)" are from Upsetter lp, *Good Bad & The Upsetter*. All other Upsetter lp tracks are from *Soul Rebels*. "No Water" re-titled "No Water Can Quench My Thirst" on Lagoon CD 1040. The matrix listing Dyna Bob Morley 2208-1 is not a misprint here, but rather in the matrix itself. Labeled copies of "Run For Cover" with full credits read "side 2 T.G. 002," but the title line reads "Side 1 Run For Cover." The AB matrixes stand for Aston Barrett. "Soul Rebel" incorrectly titled as "Soul Rebels" on Lagoon CD.

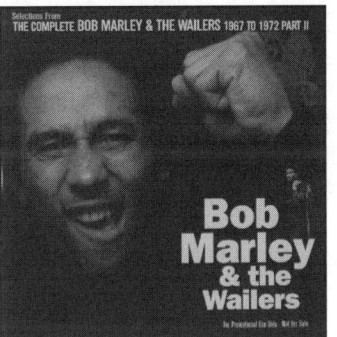

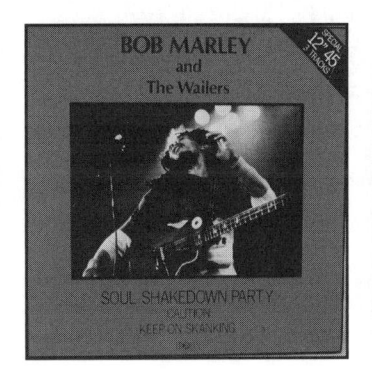

WAILERS   circa: November 1970

Peter Tosh, vocal and guitar; Bob Marley, harmony vocal; Bunny Wailer, harmony vocal; Carlton Barrett, drums; Lloyd Parks, bass; Alva "Reggie" Lewis, guitar; Ranford "Ronnie Bop" Williams, guitar; Glen Adams, keyboards; Uziah "Sticky" Thompson, percussion; Errol Thompson, engineer; recorded Randy's Studio 17; four track; Lee Perry, production.

Title	Release
400 Years	Upsetter lp, Trojan (UK) lp TBL 126, Heartbeat CD HB 150
" (extended)	Jamaican Gold CD JMC 200.277
400 Years version	Lagoon CD 1040
My Sympathy	Upsetter lp, Trojan (UK) lp TBL 126, JAD (FR) CD 823672 2

Note: "My Sympathy" is a version cut of "400 Years." Upsetter lp is titled *Soul Rebels*.

BOB MARLEY AND THE WAILERS
circa: November 1970

Bob Marley, vocal; Bunny Wailer, harmony vocal; Peter Tosh, harmony vocal; Carlton Barrett, drums; Lloyd Parks, bass; Alva "Reggie" Lewis, guitar; Ranford "Ronnie Bop" Williams, guitar; Glen Adams, keyboards; Uziah "Sticky" Thompson, percussion; Errol Thompson, engineer; recorded Randy's Studio 17; four track; Lee Perry, production.

	Reaction	Upsetter lp, Trojan (UK) lp TBL 126, JAD (FR) CD 823672 2
	" (extended)	Jamaican Gold CD JMC 200.277
	" (full length)	JAD (FR) CD 537325-2
	Reaction Version	JAD (FR) CD 823672 2

Note: Upsetter lp is titled *Soul Rebels*.

BOB MARLEY AND THE WAILERS
circa: December 1970

Bob Marley, vocal; Peter Tosh, harmony vocal and guitar; Bunny Wailer, harmony vocal; Lee Perry, vocal (-1); Carlton Barrett, drums; Lloyd Parks, bass (-2); Aston "Family Man" Barrett, bass (-3); Alva "Reggie" Lewis, guitar; Ranford "Ronnie Bop" Williams, guitar; Glen Adams, keyboards; Uziah "Sticky" Thompson, percussion; Errol Thompson, engineer; recorded Randy's Studio 17; four track; Lee Perry, production.

	Jah Is Mighty (-2)	Trojan (UK) lp 221, JAD (FR) CD 823672 2
Upsetter 003 B	Head Corner Stone	Upsetter (US) 003B, JAD (FR) lp 542 222-1
	Corner Stone (-2)	Upsetter lp, Trojan (UK) lp TBL 126, JAD (FR) CD 823672 2
	" (extended)	Jamaican Gold CD JMC 200.277
	Corner Stone Version	JAD (FR) CD 823672 2
	Rebel's Hop (-2)	Upsetter lp, Trojan (UK) lp TBL 126, JAD (FR) CD 823672 2
	" (extended)	Jamaican Gold CD JMC 200.277
	Rebel Hop Version	JAD (FR) CD 823672 2
	Soul Almighty (-3)	Upsetter lp, Trojan (UK) lp TBL 126, JAD (FR) CD 823672 2
	" (extended)	Jamaican Gold CD JMC 200.277
	Soul Almighty Version	JAD (FR) CD 823672 2
DRT 1-A-1	Shocks Of Mighty (-1) (-2)	blank (UK) 12", JAD (FR) CD 495250 2
DRT 1-B-1	Dub	blank (UK) 12", Jamaican Gold CD JMC 200.229

Note: All Upsetter lp titles are from *Soul Rebels*. "Soul Almighty" was re-titled "Hey Happy People" on Rohit CD 7757. Upsetter 003 B, "Head Corner Stone," is an alternate mix of "Jah Is Mighty."

WAILERS
circa: December 1970

Peter Tosh, vocal; Bob Marley, harmony vocal; Bunny Wailer, harmony vocal; Carlton Barrett, drums; Lloyd Parks, bass; Alva "Reggie" Lewis, guitar; Ranford "Ronnie Bop" Williams, guitar; Glen Adams, keyboards; Uziah "Sticky" Thompson, percussion; Errol Thompson, engineer; recorded Randy's Studio 17; four track; Lee Perry, production.

T+1023+B	No Sympathy	Upsetter (UK), Upsetter lp, Trojan (UK) lp TBL 126, Heartbeat CD HB 150
	" (full length)	JAD (FR) CD 537325-2
	No Sympathy Version	JAD (FR) CD 823672 2

Note: "No Sympathy" on Upsetter (UK) is a blank label pre-release.

BOB MARLEY AND THE WAILERS
circa: December 1970

Bob Marley, vocal; Bunny Wailer, harmony vocal; Peter Tosh, harmony vocal; Hugh Malcolm, drums; Aston "Family Man" Barrett, bass; Alva "Reggie" Lewis, guitar; Ranford "Ronnie Bop" Williams, guitar (-1); Glen Adams, organ; Uziah "Sticky" Thompson, percussion; Errol Thompson, engineer; recorded Randy's Studio 17; four track; Lee Perry, production.

Lee "Scratch" Perry in his home studio, in Kingston. LSD or Pounds, Shillings, Pence? 2003. Photo by Roger Steffens.

	Long Long Winter	JAD (FR) CD 823672 2
	" (extended)	Jamaican Gold CD JMC 200.277
	Long Long Winter Version	JAD (FR) CD 823672 2
	Put It On (-1)	Maroon lp, Upsetter lp, JAD (FR) CD 823672 2
	" (extended)	Jamaican Gold CD JMC 200.277
	Put It On (full length)	JAD (FR) CD 537325-2
	Put It On (version)	Upsetter lp, JAD (FR) CD 823672 2

Note: Maroon/Upsetter lp is titled *Soul Revolution* on the label, but the sleeve identifies the title as *Soul Revolution Part II*. Much confusion has been created by the fact that the instrumental dub version of this album, *Upsetter Revolution Rhythm*, was released in a very limited pressing, part of which was jacketed in plain sleeves and part of which was jacketed in *Soul Revolution Part II* sleeves. "Put It On (version)" is on *Upsetter Revolution Rhythm*. "Long Long Winter" is a cover of an Impressions song.

LITTLE ROY   BOB MARLEY & THE WAILERS   circa: January 1971

Earl "Little Roy" Lowe, vocal; Peter Tosh, guitar; Bunny Wailer, percussion; Carlton Barrett, drums; Aston "Family Man" Barrett, bass; glen Adams, keyboard; Errol Thompson, engineer; recorded Randy's Studio 17; four track; Lee Perry, production.

LP 3562-1	Don't Cross The Nation	Upsetter, Upsetter (US), Upsetter lp

Note: Although no Wailer actually sings on this track, it is included to avoid confusion. The Upsetter (US) pressing of this title credits Bob Marley & The Wailers. The green swirl Upsetter label Jamaican pressing does not include artist credits. "Don't Cross The Nation" is credited to "Mark & Luke" on Upsetter lp entitled *Battle Axe*.

BOB MARLEY AND THE WAILERS   circa: January 1971

Bob Marley, vocal (-1); Peter Tosh, harmony vocal (-1); Bunny Wailer, harmony vocal (-1); Carlton Barrett, drums; Aston "Family Man" Barrett, bass; Alva "Reggie" Lewis, guitar; Ranford "Ronnie Bop" Williams, guitar; Glen Adams, keyboard; Uziah "Sticky" Thompson, percussion; Errol Thompson, engineer; recorded Randy's Studio 17; four track; Lee Perry, production.

	Kaya (-1)	Anansi/JAD (FR) Midem '97 Sampler CD, JAD (FR) CD 823672 2
GPW+7	Kaya (-1)	Upsetter, Maroon lp, Upsetter lp, Upsetter (UK) US 356, Black Heart (US) 8043-B, JAD (FR) CD 823672 2
	" (extended)	Jamaican Gold CD JMC 200.277
GPW+8	Kaya Version (-1)	Upsetter, Upsetter (UK) US 356, JAD (FR) CD 823672 2
	Kaya (version)	Upsetter lp, JAD CD B0003300-02
	Kaya Skank	Upsetter lp

Note: Maroon/Upsetter lp is titled *Soul Revolution* on the record labels, but the sleeve identifies the title as *Soul Revolution Part II*. GPW+8 "Kaya Version" features two sections of scat vocals by Bob Marley. This track is identified as "Kaya (version 2)" on Jad CD. "Kaya (version)," an instrumental dub, is on Upsetter lp *Upsetter Revolution Rhythm*. "Kaya Skank" is a dub version mixed at King Tubby's and is included on the Upsetter lp *Upsetters 14 Dub Black Board Jungle*. Upsetter (UK) US 356 is titled "Kayah Now." "Kaya"/"Kaya Version" with the same matrix numbers has also been found on the Tuff Gong label. Both vocal takes of "Kaya" are sung over the same rhythm. "Turn Me Loose," a Bob Marley vocal recorded over the "Kaya" rhythm, was cut in January 1974 and is listed on that date.

BOB MARLEY AND THE WAILERS   circa: January 1971

Bob Marley, vocal; Peter Tosh, harmony vocal and guitar; Bunny Wailer, harmony vocal; Lee Perry, speech (-1); Carlton Barrett, drums; Aston "Family Man" Barrett, bass; Alva "Reggie" Lewis, guitar; Ranford "Ronnie Bop" Williams, guitar; Glen Adams, organ; Gladdy Anderson, piano; Uziah "Sticky" Thompson, percussion; Errol Thompson, engineer; recorded Randy's Studio 17; four track; Lee Perry, production.

8043-A	All In One	Black Heart (US) 8043-A, Upsetter (UK) US 357, JAD (FR) CD 8235672 2
3332-1	All In One (-1)	Upsetter, JAD (FR) CD 823672 2
3333-1	Part Two (-1)	" , "

Dyna LP 3561-1	Copasetic	Upsetter, Jamaican Gold CD JMC 200.229, JAD (FR) CD 537325-2

Note: "All In One" is a medley of Wailers hits including "Bend Down Low," "Nice Time," "One Love," "Simmer Down," "It Hurts to Be Alone," "Lonesome Feeling," "Love And Affection," "I'm Gonna Put It On," "Duppy Conqueror," and ending with another portion of "I'm Gonna Put It On." "All In One" on Black Heart and Upsetter (UK) is the uninterrupted track, but edits out Marley's final return to "I'm Gonna Put It On." "All In One" and "Part Two" on Upsetter (JA) is an alternate longer mix including the return to "I'm Gonna Put It On" and cut into two parts with spoken introductions by Lee Perry. "Copasetic" is a version cut of "All In One" and appeared in Jamaica as the flip side of "Don't Cross The Nation" by Little Roy.

PETER TOSH & THE WAILERS — circa: January 1971

Peter Tosh, vocal; Bob Marley, harmony vocal; Bunny Wailer, harmony vocal; Carlton Barrett, drums; Aston "Family Man" Barrett, bass; Alva "Reggie" Lewis, guitar; Glen Adams, keyboards; Gladdy Anderson, piano; Uziah "Sticky" Thompson, percussion; Errol Thompson, engineer; recorded Randy's Studio 17; four track; Lee Perry, production.

	Brand New Secondhand	Trojan lp 221, Heartbeat CD HB 150
LP 5972-1	Secondhand	Justice League, "
Upsetter, 002 A	"	Upsetter (US) 002A
GPW+46+B	Secondhand Part Two	Justice League, JAD (FR) CD 823672 2
LP 4157-1	Downpresser	Upsetter, Punch (UK) PH 77, Heartbeat CD HB 150,
LP 4159-1	Downpresser Version	Upsetter, JAD (FR) CD 823672 2

Note: "Brand New Secondhand" is an alternate vocal take of "Secondhand." Adding to the confusion, the Upsetter (US) pressing of "Secondhand" is titled "Brand New Secondhand" as is Peter's 1974 recut of the song. "Downpresser" is Peter's third recording of the traditional "Sinner Man" which he first cut at Studio One in 1966.

BOB MARLEY AND THE WAILERS — circa: January 1971

Bob Marley, vocal; Bunny Wailer, harmony vocal; Peter Tosh, harmony vocal and organ; Glen Adams, organ; Carlton "Santa" Davis, drums; George "Fully" Fullwood, bass; Tony Chin, guitar; Cleon Douglas, guitar; Errol Thompson, engineer; recorded Randy's Studio 17; four track; Lee Perry, production.

Dyna SEP LP 3014-1	Who Is Mister Brown	Upsetter, Upsetter (UK) US, Tuff Gong (UK) CD TGCBX 1
	" (extended)	Jamaican Gold CD JMC 200.277
GPW+6	"	Upsetter
Dyna SEP LP 3015-1	Dracular (Dracula on UK)	Upsetter, Upsetter (UK) US 354, JAD (FR) CD 495250 2
	Dracula	Upsetter lp

Note: Some Upsetter labels read "Mister Brown" or "Whose Mr. Brown." "Dracula" and "Dracular" are versions. Vocals for "Who Is Mister Brown" were recorded over the original rejected riddim for "Duppy Conqueror."

BOB MARLEY AND THE WAILERS   UPSETTERS (-1) — circa: January 1971

Bob Marley, vocal; Bunny Wailer, harmony vocal; Peter Tosh, harmony vocal; Lee Perry, vocal (-1); Carlton Barrett, drums; Aston "Family Man" Barrett, bass; Alva "Reggie" Lewis, guitar; Ranford "Ronnie Bop" Williams, guitar; Glen Adams, keyboard; "Deadly" Headley Bennett, tenor sax (-2); Errol Thompson, engineer; recorded Randy's Studio 17; four track; Lee Perry, production.

FLP 7695	In The Iwah (-1)	Upsetter
	" (alternate mix)	Black Art LP, Trojan (UK) lp TRLS 70
FLP 7659	Version	Upsetter
	Fussing & Fighting	Maroon lp, Upsetter lp, JAD (FR) CD 823672 2
	" (extended)	Jamaican Gold CD JMC 200.277
	Fussing & Fighting (version)	Upsetter lp, JAD (FR) CD 823672 28042-B
8042-B	Stand Alone (-2)	Blackheart (US) 8042-B, Maroon lp, Upsetter lp, JAD (FR) CD 823672 2

Stand Alone (extended)	Jamaican Gold CD JMC 200.277
Stand Alone (version)	Upsetter lp, JAD (FR) CD 823672 2

Note: Black Art/Trojan lp is titled *Double Seven*. "In The Iwah" is mis-titled as "In the Iaah" on the Trojan lp. All issues of "Iwah" are credited to the Upsetters. Maroon/Upsetter lp is *Soul Revolution/Soul Revolution Part II*. Instrumental dub versions of "Fussing & Fighting" and "Stand Alone" are on Upsetter lp *Upsetter Revolution Rhythm*. Composition of "Stand Alone" is credited to Lee Perry on the Blackheart (US) pressing of the title, but Bunny says Bob wrote the song.

WAILERS   circa: February 1971

Bunny Wailer, vocal; Bob Marley, harmony vocal; Peter Tosh, harmony vocal and piano (-1); Carlton Barrett, drums; Aston "Family Man" Barrett, bass; Alva "Reggie" Lewis, guitar; Ranford "Ronnie Bop" Williams, guitar; Glen Adams, keyboards; Winston Wright, organ (-2); Errol Thompson, engineer; recorded Randy's Studio 17; four track; Lee Perry, production.

Riding High (-1)	Maroon lp, Upsetter lp, JAD (FR) CD 823672 2
" (extended)	Jamaican Gold CD JMC 200.277
Riding High (version)	Upsetter lp, JAD (FR) CD 823672 2
Brainwashing (-2)	Maroon lp, Upsetter lp, JAD (FR) CD 823672 2
" (extended)	Jamaican Gold CD JMC 200.277
Brainwashing (version)	Upsetter lp, JAD (FR) CD 823672 2

Note: Maroon/Upsetter lp is titled *Soul Revolution* on the label but *Soul Revolution Part Two* on the sleeve. Instrumental dub versions of "Riding High" and "Brainwashing" are on Upsetter lp *Upsetter Revolution Rhythm*.

WAILERS   circa: February 1971

Peter Tosh, melodica; Carlton Barrett, drums; Aston "Family Man" Barrett, bass; Alva "Reggie" Lewis, guitar; Ranford "Ronnie Bop" Williams, guitar; Glen Adams, keyboards; Errol Thompson, engineer; recorded Randy's Studio 17; four track; Lee Perry, production.

Memphis	Maroon lp, Upsetter lp, JAD (FR) CD 823672 2
" (extended)	Jamaican Gold CD JMC 200.277
Memphis (version)	Upsetter lp, JAD (FR) CD 823672 2

Note: Maroon/Upsetter lp is titled *Soul Revolution* on the record label, but titled *Soul Revolution Part II* on the sleeve. The instrumental dub version of "Memphis" is on Upsetter lp *Upsetter Revolution Rhythm*.

BOB MARLEY AND THE WAILERS   BIG YOUTH (-1)   WONG CHU (-2)   circa: February 1971
BOB MARLEY (-4)   BOB & UPSETTERS BAND (-4)

Bob Marley, vocal; Bunny Wailer, harmony vocal; Peter Tosh, harmony vocal; Big Youth, DJ (-1); Wong Chu, DJ (-2); Carlton Barrett, drums; Aston "Family Man" Barrett, bass; Alva "Reggie" Lewis, guitar; Ranford "Ronnie Bop" Williams, guitar (-3); Glen Adams, keyboard; Errol Thompson, engineer; recorded Randy's Studio 17; four track; Lee Perry, production. Overdubs circa 1995: unknown drums, bass, guitar, synthesizer, and percussion (-4).

LP 6933-A	Keep On Moving (-3)	Justice League, Upsetter (UK) US 392, Maroon lp, Upsetter lp, JAD (FR) CD 823672 2
	" (extended)	Jamaican Gold CD JMC 200.277
Lee Perry 931 B	" (-2) (-3)	Upsetter 12", JAD (FR) CD 495250 2
A	" (-3) (-4)	Upsetter
B	Keep On Moving Version (-4)	Upsetter
	Keep On Moving Version (-3)	Upsetter lp, JAD (FR) CD 823672 2
	Mooving Skank	Upsetter lp
	Keep On Moving (-3)	Lagoon CD 1044, JAD ((FR) CD 537325-2
	Keep On Moving Version (-3)	"
DSR LP 6568-1	Mooving Version (-1) (-3)	Justice League

LP 6951-1		African Herbsman	Justice League, Upsetter (UK) US 392, Blackheart (US) 8042-A, Maroon lp, Upsetter lp, JAD (FR) CD 823672 2
	"	(extended)	Jamaican Gold CD JMC 200.277
		African Herbsman Version	Upsetter lp, JAD (FR) CD 823672 2

Note: Maroon/Upsetter lp is titled *Soul Revolution* on the record label, but titled *Soul Revolution Part II* on the record sleeve. The instrumental dub versions of "Keep On Moving" and "African Herbsman" are on the Upsetter lp *Upsetter Revolution Rhythm*. "Mooving Skank," a mix done at King Tubby's studio, is on Upsetter lp *Upsetters 14 Dub Black Board Jungle*. "Keep On Moving" with matrix Lee Perry 931 B is a 1977 12" remix with DJ Wong Chu. "African Herbsman" is correctly credited to Richie Havens on the Blackheart (US) pressing.

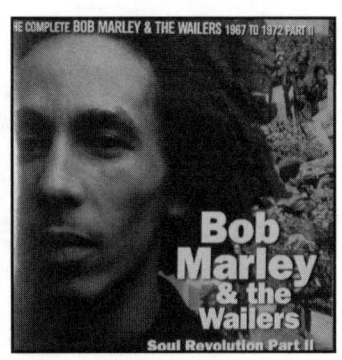

WAILERS ISTAN (-1) U ROY (-2) circa: February 1971

Bunny Wailer, vocal; Bob Marley, harmony vocal; Peter Tosh, harmony vocal and guitar; Istan, DJ (-1); U Roy, DJ (-2); Carlton Barrett, drums; Aston "Family Man" Barrett, bass; Karl Pitterson, bass (-3); Alva "Reggie Lewis, guitar; Ranford "Ronnie Bop" Williams, guitar; Glen Adams, keyboards; Tyrone Downie, keyboards (-3); H. Butler, keyboards (-3); Tommy McCook, tenor sax (-3); Richard "Dirty Harry" Hall, tenor sax (-3); "Jackey," alto sax (-3); Errol Thompson, engineer; recorded Randy's Studio 17; four track; King Tubby and Lee Perry, remix at King Tubby's studio (-4); Lee Perry, original production; Bunny Wailer, production of Solomonic issues; 1975 overdubs (-3); 1975 recordings and remix, Karl Pitterson (-3); recorded at Aquarius Studio in Kingston; twenty four track; Peter Weston, production of PW1 matrix title with U Roy.

LP 3770-1	Dreamland	Upsetter, Upsetter (UK) US 371, JAD (FR) CD 495250 2
Bunny Wailer 2649 A	" (1972 remix)	Solomonic, Solomonic lp, Mango MLPS 9629
	" (-3) (1975 remix)	Solomonic lp, Island ILPS 9415
BW 2733-B	Vision Land (-1)	Solomonic
	Dreamland Version	Upsetter, Upsetter (UK) US 371, JAD (FR) CD 495250 2
	Dreamland (version)	Upsetter lp
	Dreamland Skank (-4)	Upsetter lp
PW 1	Dreamland Version (-2)	Soul Beat pre
Bunny Wailer 2650 B	Dub'd Version	Solomonic
	Dream Land (Dubd'sco) (-3)	Solomonic lp

Note: "Dreamland (version)" is on Upsetter lp, *Africa's Blood*. "Dreamland Skank" was mixed at King Tubby's studio and is on Upsetter lp *Upsetters 14 Dub Black Board Jungle*. Some copies of the original Upsetter label single are wrongly labeled and couple "Dreamland" with an Upsetters instrumental titled "Good Luck." "Vision Land" on Solomonic is a 1972 remix of the original Upsetter track with the addition of DJ, Istan. Solomonic/Mango lp is *Bunny Wailer Sings The Wailers*. Solomonic/Island lp is *Blackheart Man*. "Dream Land (Dubd'sco)" is on Solomonic lp *Dubd'sco Vol. 1*. Bunny first cut "Dreamland" for Studio One in 1966. The song was first recorded as "My Dream Island" by El Tempos circa 1962 on the U.S. Vee Jay label.

BOB MARLEY & THE WAILERS circa: March 1971

Bob Marley, vocal and guitar; Bunny Wailer, harmony vocal and bass; Peter Tosh, harmony vocal and xylophone; Rita Marley, harmony vocal; Hortense Lewis, harmony vocal; Hugh Malcolm, drums; Carlton Lee and Andy Capp, engineers; recorded West Indies Studio; four track; Wailers/Lee Perry, production.

Dyna Bob Marley 3176-1	Send Me That Love	Upsetter, Tuff Gong, JAD (FR) CD 495250 2

Reasoning with The Upsetter at his home in Kingston, 2003. Photo by Roger Steffens.

BOB MARLEY & THE WAILERS   circa: March 1971

Bob Marley, vocal; Bunny Wailer, harmony vocal; Peter Tosh, harmony vocal; Rita Marley, harmony vocal (-1); Hortense Lewis, harmony vocal (-1); Carlton Barrett, drums; Aston "Family Man" Barrett, bass; Alva "Reggie" Lewis, guitar; Glen Adams, organ; Gladdy Anderson, piano; Uziah "Sticky" Thompson, percussion; Errol Thompson, engineer; recorded Randy's Studio 17; four track; Wailers/Lee Perry, production.

Dyna Bob Marley 3177-1	Love Light	Upsetter, Tuff Gong, JAD (FR) CD 495250 2
	Love Light (-1)	Lagoon CD 1044, JAD (FR) CD 823672 2
	" (extended)	Jamaican Gold CD JMC 200.277
	Love Light Version	Lagoon CD 1044, JAD (FR) CD 495250 2

Note: "Love Life" on Lagoon CD is a mis-titled alternate take of "Love Light." "Love Light" as issued on Upsetter and Tuff Gong singles is also mis-titled as "Love Life" on Jamaican Gold CD.

BOB MARLEY & THE WAILERS   **JOHNNY LOVER (-2)**   circa: March 1971

Bob Marley, vocal; Bunny Wailer, harmony vocal, repeater (-1); Peter Tosh, harmony vocal and melodica; Johnny Lover, DJ (-2); Carlton Barrett, drums; Aston "Family Man" Barrett, bass; Alva "Reggie" Lewis, guitar; Ranford "Ronnie Bop" Williams, guitar; Tyrone Downie, organ; Uziah "Sticky" Thompson, percussion; Errol Thompson, engineer; recorded Randy's Studio 17; four track; Wailers/Lee Perry, production.

Dyna Bob Morley 2209-1	Sun Is Shining	Tuff Gong T.G. 001, Escort (UK) ERT 842, Maroon lp,
		Upsetter lp, Tuff Gong (UK) CD TGCBX 1
	" (extended)	Jamaican Gold CD JMC 200.277
Dyna Bob Marley 3359-1	Sun Is Shining V/2 (-1) (-2)	Tuff Gong, JAD (FR) CD537325-2
Dyna Bob Marley 3360-1	Sun Is Shining V/3 (-1)	" , "
	Sun Is Shining Version	Upsetter lp, JAD (FR) CD 823672 2

Note: "Sun Is Shining" was re-titled "To The Rescue" on Escort 842. Maroon/Upsetter lp is titled *Soul Revolution* on the record label, but is titled *Soul Revolution Part II* on the record sleeve. The instrumental dub version of "Sun Is Shining" is on Upsetter lp *Upsetter Revolution Rhythm*. The matrix, Dyna Bob Morley 2209-1 is not a misprint here, but rather a misprint in the original mastering. The label of "Sun Is Shining" reads "side 1 T.G. 001," but also reads "Side 2 Sun Is Shining" on the title line. Drummer "Santa" Davis remembers recording a take of "Sun Is Shining" featuring "Fully" Fullwood on bass and Cleon Douglas on guitar. He says this recording was issued. It seems unlikely that a commercial release exists, and the recording was probably used for a sound system "special." George "Fully" Fullwood remembers playing bass on this session. This is confirmed by his Soul Syndicate band mate, guitarist Tony Chin. The details listed are as Bunny Wailer remembers the session.

BOB MARLEY & THE WAILERS   **JOHNNY LOVER (-2)**   circa: March 1971

Bob Marley, vocal; Bunny Wailer, harmony vocal (-1); Peter Tosh, harmony vocal (-1); Johnny Lover, DJ (-2); Carlton Barrett, drums; Aston "Family Man" Barrett, bass; Alva "Reggie" Lewis, guitar; Ranford "Ronnie Bop" Williams, guitar; Glen Adams, organ; Errol Thompson, engineer; recorded Randy's Studio 17; four track; Wailers/Lee Perry, production.

	Don't Rock My Boat	Maroon lp, Upsetter lp, Tuff Gong (UK) CD TGCBX 1
	" (extended)	Jamaican Gold CD JMC 200.277
	Don't Rock My Boat (version)	Upsetter lp, JAD (FR) CD 823672 2
	Don't Rock My Boat	Supreme (UK) 216, JAD (FR) CD 537325-2
Dyna Bob Marley 3358-1	I Like It Like This (-1) (-2)	Tuff Gong, Bullet (UK) BU 464, JAD (FR) CD 537325-2
Dyna Bob Marley 3516-1	Rock My Boat (-1)	Tuff Gong, JAD (FR) CD 823672 2

Note: Maroon/Upsetter lp is titled *Soul Revolution* on the record label, but titled *Soul Revolution Part II* on the record sleeve. The instrumental dub version of "Don't Rock My Boat" is on Upsetter lp *Upsetter Revolution Rhythm*. Dyna Bob Marley 3358-1 is titled "I Like It Like This" on Tuff Gong labels with the artist credit Bob Marley & the Wailers, but titled "Like It Like This" on labels crediting Johnny Lover, and re-titled as "Soultown" on Bullet (UK) BU 464. "Don't Rock My Boat" on Supreme is retitled as "Don't Rock My Boat (alt. 3)" on JAD (FR) CD.

BOB MARLEY & THE WAILERS   circa: March 1971

Bob Marley, vocal; Bunny Wailer, harmony vocal; Peter Tosh, harmony vocal and guitar; Rita Marley, harmony vocal; Hugh Malcolm, drums; Jackie Jackson, bass; Gladdy Anderson, piano; Alvin "Seeco" Patterson, percussion; Carlton Lee and Andy Capp, engineers; West Indies Studio; four track; Wailers, production.

Dyna Bob Marley 3361-1	Let The Sun Shine On Me	Tuff Gong, Bullet (UK) BU 464, Anansi/JAD (FR)
		Midem '97 Sampler CD, JAD (FR) CD 495250 2

Note: Title is as given on the UK release. Although labeled copies from Jamaica have been found, none has been reported with title credits. Titled "Pour Down The Sunshine" on JAD CD. Bob Marley left Jamaica during the spring of 1971 and spent a short amount of time in New York City before proceeding on to Stockholm, Sweden, where he spent about two months. He returned to Jamaica probably in late June or early July. John "Rabbit" Bundrick says Bob arrived in Sweden in early May. Both Bob and "Rabbit" were there to work on the soundtrack of *North Scene*, a movie starring Johnny Nash.

PETER TOSH   BUNNY FLIP   JOE GIBBS & NOW/LOVE GENERATION   circa: April 1971

Peter Tosh, vocal and guitar, piano and organ; Cecille Campbell, harmony vocal; Hortense Lewis, harmony vocal; Winston Scotland (Bunny Flip), DJ (-1); Johnny Lover, DJ (-2); Carlton Barrett, drums; Aston "Family Man" Barrett, bass; unknown tenor sax (-3); unknown trombone (-3); unknown trumpet (-4); Joe Gibbs, engineer; recorded Joe Gibbs Studio; four track; Joe Gibbs, production.

	Maga Dog (take 1)	unissued
FJG 7581	Maga Dog (take 2)	Pressure Beat, Heartbeat CD HB 73
FJG 7582	Bull Dog	"
FJG 7785-A	Boney Dog (-3) (-4)	Pressure Beat, Pressure Beat (UK) 5510
FJG 7785-B	Skanky Dog (-1)	" , "
FJG 6688-A	Maingy Dog (-2) (-3)	Jogibs
FJG 6688-B	Hot Dog (-2) (-3)	"

Note: "Skanky Dog," credited to Bunny Flip on Jamaican issue, is credited to Winston Scotland on UK issue. Joe Gibbs has stated that Rita Marley and Judy Mowatt sang harmony. Bunny Wailer remembers the details as listed above. "Maga Dog" was also recorded at Studio One in 1964 and this early release credits Bob Marley with composition. In Jamaican patois, a maga dog is a very skinny and rough looking beast.

THE 3RD & 4TH GENERATION   circa: April 1971

Peter Tosh, vocal and harmony vocal; unknown harmony vocal; Carlton Barrett, drums; Aston "Family Man" Barrett, bass; Alva "Reggie" Lewis, guitar; Glen Adams, keyboards; Joe Gibbs, engineer; Joe Gibbs Studio; four track; Joe Gibbs, production.

FJG 7582	Rudie's Medley	Jogib, Punch (UK) PH 91
FJG 7584	Rude Boy Version	" , "

Note: Medley includes Desmond Dekker's compositions "007 Shanty Town" and "Rude Boy Train" and concludes with Tosh's "The Toughest." Although many have suspected Dekker's presence on this track, Bunny Wailer confirms that Peter sings the entire lead, imitating Dekker's classic style in the beginning of the performance. "Rudie's Medley" and "Bull Dog," a track from the previous session, unaccountably share the same matrix number.

PETER TOUSH/TOSH MR. X & SWEETIE WINSTON WRIGHT & LARRY McDONALD   circa: May 1971

Peter Tosh, vocal, piano, and organ; Cecille Campbell, harmony vocal; Hortense Lewis, harmony vocal; "Mr. X & Sweetie," vocals (-1); Arkland "Drumbago" Parks, drums; Aston "Family Man" Barrett, bass; Alva "Reggie" Lewis, guitar; Winston Wright, piano (-2); Larry McDonald, percussion (-2); Joe Gibbs, engineer; Joe Gibbs Studio; four track; Joe Gibbs, production.

FJG 7705-A	Them A, Fi Get A Beaten	Pressure Beat, Pressure Beat (UK) PB-5509
FJG 7784	"	"
FJG 7705-B	Get A Beaten	" , Pressure Beat (UK) PB-5509

6251-A	White Liver Mabel (-2)	Jogibs (US) 7970 A
6251-B	Reuben (-1) (-2)	"

Note: Joe Gibbs has stated that harmony vocals on this session were performed by Rita Marley and Judy Mowatt. Bunny Wailer remembers the details as listed above. Some copies read "Them Have To Get A Beating" with the version side re-titled as "You Can't Get Away" and credited to the Love Generations. "White Liver Mabel" and "Reuben" are version tracks of "Them A, Fi Get A Beaten."

BOB MARLEY   circa: May 1971

Bob Marley, vocal and guitar; recorded informally by John "Rabbit" Bundrick in Stockholm, Sweden.

Guava Jelly	Tuff Gong (UK) CD TGCBX 1
This Train	"
Cornerstone	"
Comma Comma	"
Dewdrops	"
Stir It Up	"
Cry To Me	Anansi/Jad (FR) Midem '97 sampler CD, Jad (FR) CD 495250-2
I'm Hurting Inside	Tuff Gong (UK) CD TGCBX 1

Note: Titles are given in the order originally recorded. It is unclear why "Cry To Me" was not included on the Tuff Gong (UK) CD issue.

PETER TOSH   circa: June 1971

Peter Tosh, vocal and organ; unknown bass; unknown drums; unknown percussion; probably Errol Thompson, engineer; Randy's Studio; four track; Joe Gibbs, production.

JG 1687-1	Black Dignity (?)	Jogibs pre-release, Columbia CD C3K 65064

Note: Although labeled, neither title nor artist credit is printed on the Jogibs pre-release. "Black Dignity," our best guess at a title, was used on Columbia CD issue. The artist credit may be to Peter Touch. Some of the lyrics are in the Amharic language.

PETER TOUCH   WINSTON WRIGHT   DESTROYERS   circa: June 1971

Peter Tosh, vocal (-1); Winston "Pipe" Matthews, harmony vocal (-1); Lloyd "Bread" McDonald, harmony vocal (-1); Constantine "Vision" Walker, harmony vocal (-1); Joe Gibbs, speech (-1); Carlton "Santa" Davis, drums; George "Fully" Fullwood, bass; Earl "Chinna" Smith, guitar; unknown piano; Winston Wright, organ (-2); unknown tenor sax; unknown trombone; "Dizzy" Johnny Moore, trumpet; Joe Gibbs, engineer, production, and studio; four track.

FJG 3552-A	Here Comes The Judge (-1)	Shock, Columbia CD C3K 65064
FJG 3552-B	Rebeloution (-2)	"
Dyna JG 3599-1	Ah-So	Shock
Dyna JG 3600-1	If Ah-So	"

Note: "Ah-So," credited to The Destroyers, is an instrumental cut of the Abyssinians "Satta Massa Ganna" and is the basic rhythm track over which "Here Comes The Judge" and "Rebeloution" were performed. "Ah So" may have been recorded elsewhere (probably Randy's with Errol Thompson) and only voiced at Gibbs'. The courtroom drama of "Here Comes The Judge" recalls rock steady era courtroom hits by Prince Buster, Derrick Morgan and Lee Perry.

PIPE & THE PIPERS   circa: June 1971

Winston "Pipe" Matthews, vocal; Lloyd "Bread" McDonald, harmony vocal; George "Buddy" Haye, harmony vocal; Norman "Fats" Davis, harmony vocal; Carlton Barrett, drums; Aston "Family Man" Barrett, bass; Bob Marley, guitar; Alva "Reggie" Lewis, guitar; Tyrone Downie, organ; Errol Thompson, engineer; recorded Randy's Studio 17; four track; Wailers, production.

DSR BM 4412-1	Harbour Shark	Tuff Gong

DSR BM 4413-1   Shark   Tuff Gong
                     Turn Me Loose   unissued

Note: These titles are included because Bob Marley both played on and produced the tracks. These vocalists were also known as the Wailing Souls. Session details supplied by "Pipe" and "Bread."

BOB MARLEY & THE WAILERS   PIPE & THE PIPERS (-2)   circa: July 1971

Bob Marley, vocal (-1) and guitar; Bunny Wailer, harmony vocal (-1) and bass; Peter Tosh, harmony vocal (-1) and piano (-1) or organ (-2); Winston "Pipe" Matthews, vocal (-2) or harmony vocal (-1); Lloyd "Bread" McDonald, harmony vocal; George "Buddy Haye, harmony vocal (-2); Norman "Fats" Davis, harmony vocal (-2); Carlton Barrett, drums; Wally Williams, guitar; Alvin "Seeco" Patterson, percussion; Carlton Lee and Andy Capp, engineers; recorded West Indies Studio; four track; Wailers production.

No matrix, GH 001 A	Trench Town Rock (-1)	Tuff Gong, G & C (US) 5000-A
	" (remix)	Tuff Gong (UK) CD TGCBX 1
DSR BM 4410-1	" (short mix)	Tuff Gong, Green Door (UK) GD 4005, Trojan lp TRLS 62
DSR BM 4411-1	Grooving KNG.12 (-1)	Tuff Gong, G & C (US) 5000-A, Green Door (UK) GD 4005, JAD (FR) CD 495250 2
FBM 7730-A	Back Biter (-2)	Tuff Gong, Tuff Gong (US) 5008-A
FBM 7762-B	Back Biter Version (-2)	" , "

Note: "Trench Town Rock" with no matrix on Tuff Gong, G & C (US) 5000, and Tuff Gong (UK) CD TGCBX-1 is the original long version, from which the final verse was excised when DSR BM 4410-1 was mixed and mastered for release. "Grooving KGN.12" was titled "Grooving Kingston" on G & C (US) 5000. Allan "Skill" Cole says G & C stands for Gary Hall and Allan Cole. Cole says of Hall, "Bob used to give him some tapes to release in America and dem place deh." It was Hall who actually pressed and released singles on the Tuff Gong (US) and G & C imprints. Cole has referred to these pressings as bootlegs, maintaining that Hall never paid any royalties to the Wailers. "Back Biter" credits R. Marley as the composer on the original label. Winston "Pipe" Matthews and Lloyd "Bread" McDonald both say that "Pipe" wrote the song which was recorded at this session. Bunny Wailer remembers the tune as having been recorded in the same session as "Redder Than Red" listed below. Pipe & The Pipers were also known as Wailing Souls.

U ROY & BOB MARLEY   BOB MARLEY & HUGH ROY   circa: July 1971

Bob Marley, vocal and guitar; Bunny Wailer, harmony vocal and bass; Peter Tosh, harmony vocal, piano, and melodica; U Roy, DJ; Carlton Barrett, drums; Wally Williams, guitar; Alvin "Seeco" Patterson, percussion; Carlton Lee and Andy Capp, engineers; recorded West Indies Studio; four track; Wailers, production.

DSR AC BM 4811-1	Kingston 12 Shuffle	Tuff Gong, Tuff Gong (US) 5002-A, JAD (FR) CD 537225-2
5002-A-1	Kingston 12 Shuffle Version	Tuff Gong (US) 5002-A, JAD (FR) CD 485250 2

Note: This recording, which uses the same rhythm track as "Trench Town Rock," is listed separately because the Wailers re-voiced the tune and added melodica when U Roy voiced the DJ part. Most copies of Tuff Gong (US) 5002-A feature "Kingston 12 Shuffle"/ "Ammunition," but a few actually couple "Kingston 12 Shuffle Version" and "Ammunition." To complicate matters further, both US issues of "Kingston 12 Shuffle" and its version use the same matrix number. Copies that feature "Kingston 12 Shuffle" have the final "1" of the matrix struck boldly over a faint "2."

BOB MARLEY & THE WAILERS   circa: July 1971

Bob Marley, vocal and guitar; Bunny Wailer, harmony vocal and bass; Peter Tosh, harmony vocal and organ; Carlton Barrett, drums; Wally Williams, guitar; Tommy McCook, tenor sax; "Deadly" Headly Bennett, alto sax; Alvin "Seeco" Patterson, percussion; Carlton Lee and Andy Capp, engineers; recorded West Indies Studio; four track; Wailers, production.

Screw Face	Tuff Gong (UK) CD TGCBX 1
Screw Faces	Lagoon CD 1044, JAD (FR) CD 495250 2
Screw Faces Version	" , "

The Wailers in Kingston, circa 1971. © Franco Agresta, courtesy of www.distantdrums.org.

Note: Screwface is a term used for an angry facial expression designed to keep others at a distance. Duppy is Jamaican patois for ghost or spirit.

BOB MARLEY & THE WAILERS   circa: July 1971

Bob Marley, vocal and guitar; Bunny Wailer, harmony vocal and bass; Peter Tosh, harmony vocal and organ; Winston "Pipe" Matthews, harmony vocal; Lloyd "Bread" McDonald, harmony vocal; Carlton Barrett, drums; Wally Williams, guitar; Tyrone Downie, organ (-1); Alvin "Seeco" Patterson, percussion; Carlton Lee and Andy Capp, engineers; recorded West Indies Studio; four track; Wailers, production.

DSR TG 4946-11	Redder Than Red (-1)	Tuff Gong, Green Door (UK) GD 4025,
		Anansi/JAD (FR) Midem '97 Sampler CD,
		JAD (FR) CD 495250 2
DSR TG 4914-1	Red (-1)	Tuff Gong, JAD (FR) CD 495250 2
	" (-1)	JAD (FR) CD 537325-2

Note: "Red" is a version cut of "Redder Than Red." A blank label of DSR TG 4946-11 exists with the title "Red Red Red" written in Bob's own hand according to identification by Allan "Skill" Cole.

BOB MARLEY & THE WAILERS   circa: July 1971

Bob Marley, vocal and guitar; Bunny Wailer, harmony vocal and bass; Peter Tosh, harmony vocal; Carlton Barrett, drums; Wally Williams, guitar (-1); Winston Wright, organ; Tommy McCook, tenor sax (-2); Vin Gordon, trombone
(-2); Alvin "Seeco" Patterson, percussion; Errol Thompson, engineer; recorded Randy's Studio 17; four track;
Wailers, production.

TG 5003 A	Concrete Jungle (-2)	Tuff Gong (US) 5003-A, JAD (FR) CD 537325-2
TG 5003 A 1	"	"
DSR BM 4812-1	Ammunition	Tuff Gong, Tuff Gong (US) 5002-B
	Concrete Jungle (-2)	Lagoon CD 1044, JAD (FR) CD 495250 2
	Concrete Jungle Version	" , "
	Guava Jelly (-1)	unissued
TG 5005-B	Guava Jelly (-1)	Tuff Gong (US) 5005-B, Tuff Gong (UK) CD TGCBX 1
FBM 7732-A	Guava Jelly (-1)	Tuff Gong, Green Door (UK) GD 4025,
		Anansi/JAD (FR) Midem'97 Sampler CD,
		JAD (FR) CD 495250 2
FBM 7732-B	Guava	Tuff Gong, JAD (FR) CD 495250 2

Note: "Ammunition" is a version cut of "Concrete Jungle." "Concrete Jungle Version" was re-titled as "Jungle Dub" on JAD (FR) CD. "Guava" is a version cut of "Guava Jelly."

PETER TOSH   circa: July 1971

Peter Tosh, vocal and guitar, melodica, and keyboards; Bunny Wailer, harmony vocal; Carlton Barrett, drums; Aston "Family Man" Barrett, bass; Errol Thompson, engineer; recorded Randy's Studio 17; four track; Peter Tosh, production.

FPT 7916-A	Leave My Business (-1)	Jogibs, Columbia CD C3K 65064
FPT 7916-B	Business Man Version (-1)	"

Note: Although issued on a label owned by Joe Gibbs, the FPT matrix prefix indicates a Tosh production. This is a rewrite of the old blues standard "Ain't Nobody's Business" first popularized by Bessie Smith.

- Plate 1 -

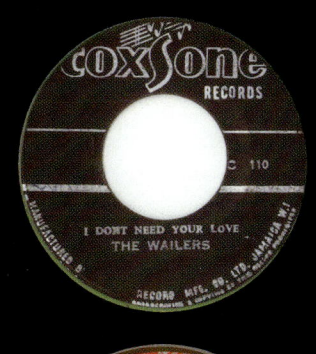

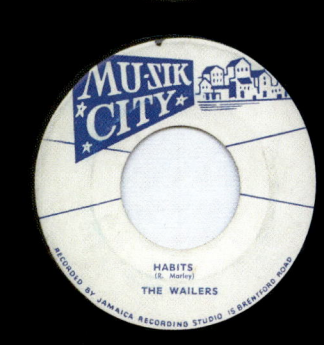

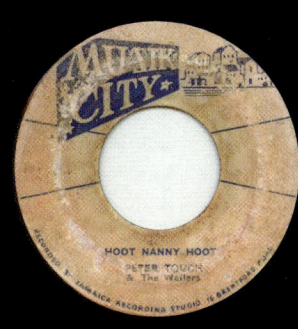

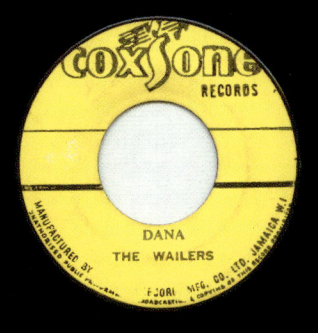

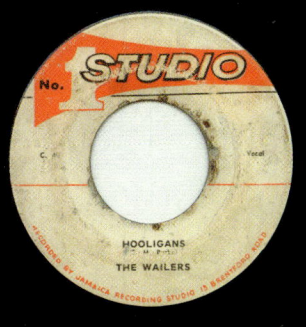

- Plate 2 -

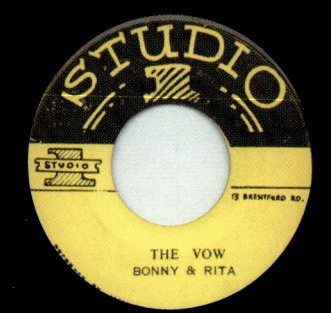

- Plate 3 -

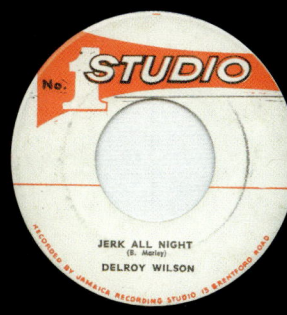

- Plate 4 -

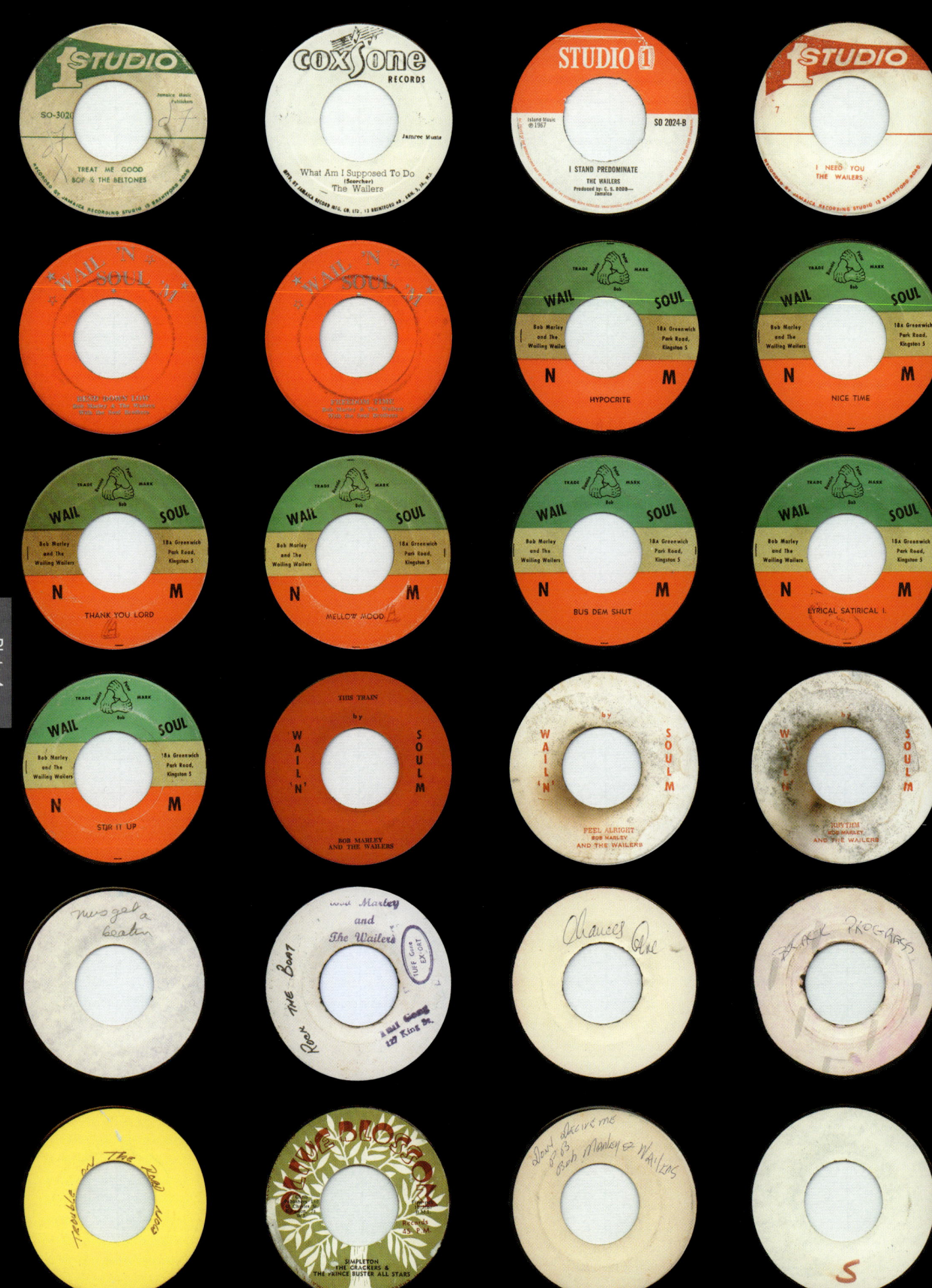

- Plate 5 -

- Plate 6 -

- Plate 7 -

- Plate 8 -

- Plate 9 -

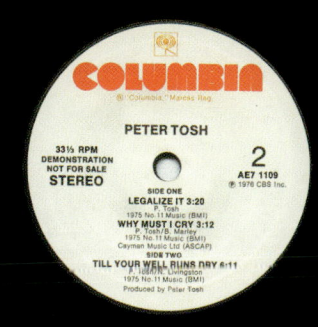

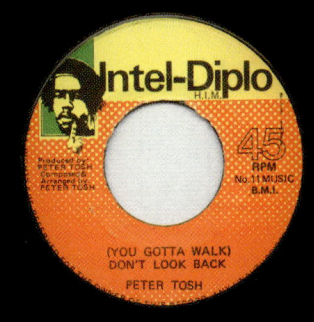

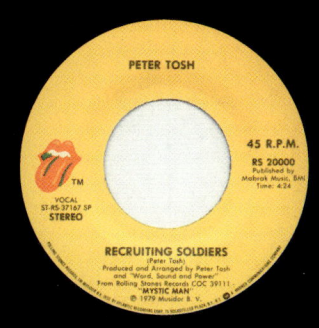

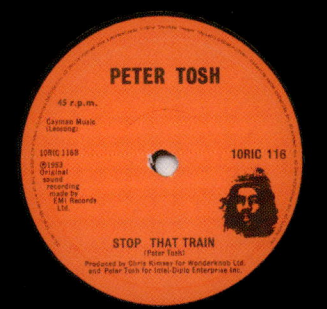

- Plate 10 -

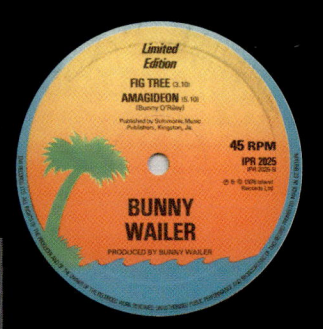

- Plate 11 -

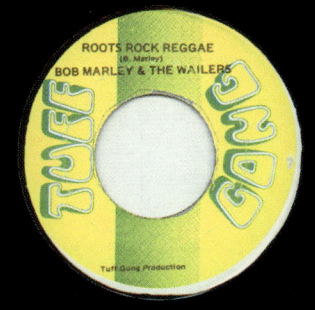

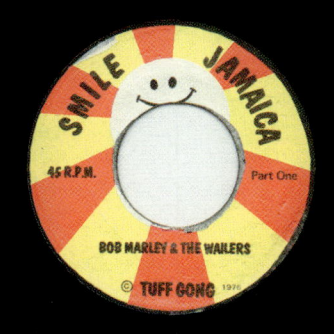

- Plate 12 -

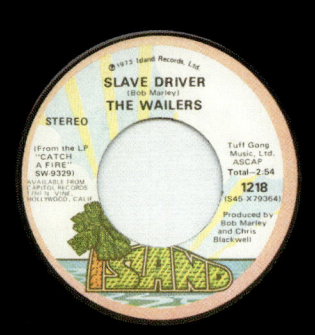

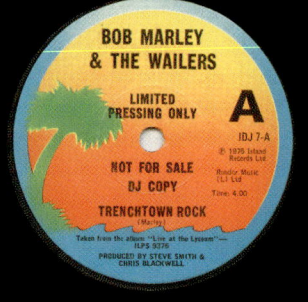

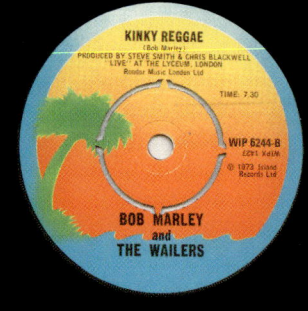

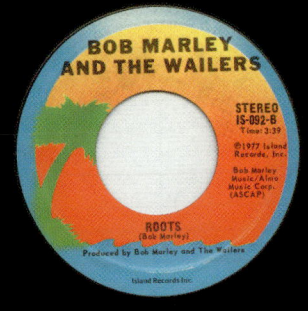

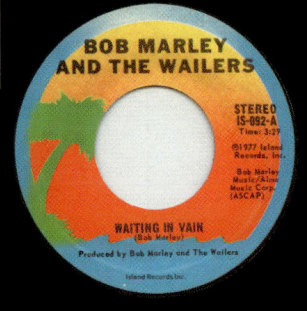

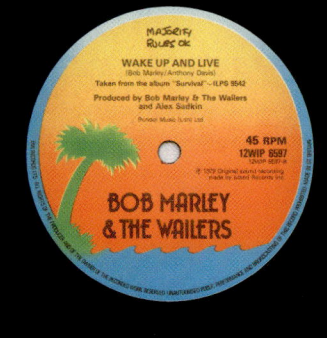

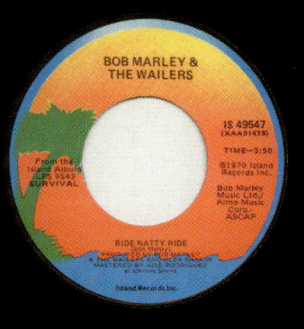

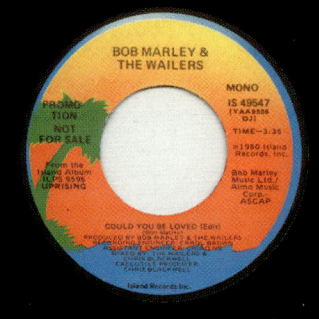

PETER TOSH
circa: July 1971

Peter Tosh, vocal and guitar; Bunny Wailer, harmony vocal and percussion; Carlton Barrett, drums; Aston "Family Man" Barrett, bass; Winston Wright, organ; Errol Thompson, engineer; recorded Randy's Studio 17; four track; Joe Gibbs, production.

DSR JG 6562-1	Arise Blackman	Joe Gibbs, Columbia CD C3K 65064
DSR JG 6563-1	Version	"

Note: This song shares the melody and lyrical ideas of "Awake Rasta," a 1970 Lee Perry production by an unknown vocal group.

BOB MARLEY & THE WAILERS   THE WAILERS GROUP
circa: August 1971

Bob Marley, vocal and guitar; Bunny Wailer, harmony vocal; Peter Tosh, harmony vocal and guitar; Carlton Barrett, drums; Aston "Family Man" Barrett, bass; Tyrone Downie, organ; Tommy McCook, tenor sax (-1); "Deadly" Headley Bennett, alto sax (-1); Alvin "Seeco" Patterson, percussion; Errol Thompson, engineer; recorded Randy's Studio 17; four track; Wailers, production.

DSR TG 4915-1	Screw Face (-1)	Tuff Gong, Tuff Gong (US) TG 5004-B, Punch (UK) PH 101, Anansi/JAD (FR) Midem '97 Sampler CD, JAD (FR) CD 495250 2
DSR TG 4916-1	Face Man (-1)	Tuff Gong, Punch (UK) PH 101, JAD (FR) CD 495250 2
FRM 8107-A	Satisfy My Soul Jah Jah (-1)	Tuff Gong, JAD (FR) CD 495250 2
FRM 8107-B	Version (-1)	", JAD (FR) lp 542 222-1
	Satisfy My Soul Jah Jah Version	Rohit CD RRTG 7757, JAD (FR) CD 495250 2
DSR RM 7163	Satisfy My Soul Babe	Tuff Gong, JAD (FR) lp 542 222-1
	Satisfy My Soul	Lagoon CD 1044, JAD (FR) CD 495250 2
	" (extended mix)	Jamaican Gold CD JMC 200.277
	Satisfy My Soul Version	Lagoon CD 1044, JAD (FR) CD 495250 2

Note: "Face Man" is a version cut of "Screwface." Tuff Gong 7" issues of "Satisfy My Soul Jah Jah" and "Satisfy My Soul Babe" both feature FRM 8107-B as the reverse. "Satisfy My Soul" on Lagoon CD and Jamaican Gold CD is an alternate take of "Satisfy My Soul Babe." FRM 8107-A is titled "Satisfy My Soul Jah Jah Dub" on JAD (FR) lp. On Rohit CD "Satisfy My Soul Jah Jah" and its version are incorrectly titled "Power & More Power." The title "Satisfy My Soul Jah Jah Version" is as given on JAD (FR) CD. Some copies of FRM 8107-A have FBM 7762-A, "Choke," as the reverse. Details of "Choke" are in the next section.

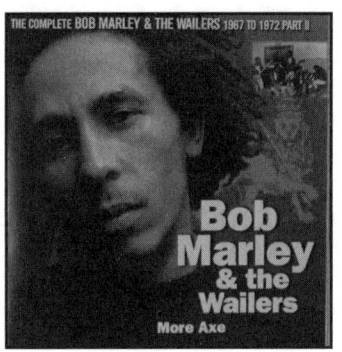

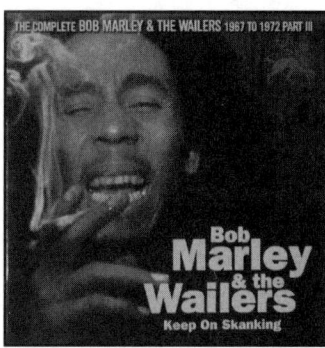

BOB MARLEY & THE WAILERS   TOMMY McCOOK   BIG YOUTH (-3)
circa: August 1971

Bob Marley, vocal and guitar; Bunny Wailer, harmony vocal; Peter Tosh, harmony vocal and melodica (-1) or piano (-2); Rita Marley, harmony vocal (-1); Cecille Campbell, harmony vocal (-1); Hortense Lewis, harmony vocal (-1); Big Youth, DJ (-3); Carlton Barrett, drums; Aston "Family Man" Barrett, bass; Alva "Reggie" Lewis, guitar; Tyrone Downie, organ; Tommy McCook, tenor sax (-2); Vin Gordon, trombone (-2); Uziah "Sticky" Thompson, percussion; Errol Thompson, engineer; recorded Randy's Studio 17; four track; Wailers, production.

DSR TG 4917-1	Lively Up Yourself (-2)	Tuff Gong, Tuff Gong (US) TG 5005-A, Green Door (UK) GD 4002, Trojan lp TRLS 62, JAD (FR) CD 495250 2
DSR TG 4918-1	Live (-2)	Tuff Gong, Green Door (UK) GD 4002, JAD (FR) CD 495250 2
FBM 7730-B	Craven Choke Puppy (-2)	Tuff Gong, Tuff Gong (US) TG 5007-A, Tuff Gong (UK) CD TGCBX 1
FBM 7762-A	Choke (-2)	Tuff Gong, Tuff Gong (US) TG 5007-B, JAD (FR) CD 495250 2
DSR RM 7103-1	Craven Version (-2) (-3)	Tuff Gong
FBM 7731-A	Lick Samba (-1)	Tuff Gong, Tuff Gong (US) 5004-A, Bullet (UK) BU 493, Tuff Gong (UK) CD TGCBX-1
FBM 7731-B	Samba (-1)	Tuff Gong, Bullet (UK) BU 493, JAD (FR) CD 495250 2

Note: "Live" is a version cut of "Lively Up Yourself" credited to Tommy McCook. "Choke" is a version cut of "Craven Choke Puppy." "Samba" is a version cut of "Lick Samba." A Jamaican proverb states "Craven a go choke puppy," meaning that gluttony will hurt you. The word craven probably derives from craving. Lick samba literally means "Lick some back," Jamaican slang for making love.

PETER TOUCH & PAT   circa: August 1971

Peter Tosh, melodica; Pat Satchmo, vocal; unknown drums, bass, guitar, and keyboards; unknown engineer and recording studio; Tony Robinson, production.

DSR TS 4785-1	We Can Make It Uptight	High School

Note: This title is the version side of "We Can Make It" by Pat Satchmo.

PETER TOSH & THE WAILERS   circa: August 1971

Peter Tosh, vocal, speech (-1) and clavinet; Bob Marley, harmony vocal and guitar; Bunny Wailer, harmony vocal; Errol Thompson, speech (-1); Carlton Barrett, drums; Aston "Family Man" Barrett, bass; Tyrone Downie, organ; Gladdy Anderson, piano; Errol Thompson, engineer; recorded Randy's Studio 17; four track; Wailers, production.

DSR PT 7736-1	Once Bitten	Tuff Gong, Columbia CD C3K 65064
DSR PT 7737-1	Version	"
PPTD 2135-A	Dog Teeth (-1)	Intel Diplo, Columbia CD C3K 65064

Note: These recordings use a remake of the "Maga Dog" rhythm.

PETER TOSH & THE WAILERS   circa: August 1971

Peter Tosh, vocal and organ; Bunny Wailer, harmony vocal; Carlton Barrett, drums; Aston "Family Man" Barrett, bass; Lloyd "Gits" Willis, guitar; Tyrone Downie, organ; Errol Thompson, engineer; recorded Randy's Studio 17; four track; Wailers, production.

DSR PT 7740-1	Lion	Tuff Gong, Columbia CD C3K 65064
DSR PT 7741-1	Version	"
FPT 7898-A	Here Comes The Sun	Tuff Gong, Columbia CD C3K 65064
FPT 7898-B	Version	"

Note: "Here Comes The Sun" was written by George Harrison of the Beatles.

BOB MARLEY & THE WAILERS   circa: September 1971

Bob Marley, vocal and guitar; Bunny Wailer, harmony vocal; Peter Tosh, harmony vocal and guitar; Carlton Barrett, drums; Aston "Family Man" Barrett, bass; Tyrone Downie, keyboards; Alvin "Seeco" Patterson, percussion; Sylvan Morris, engineer; recorded Harry J Studio; eight track; Wailers, production. 1992 overdubs with Rita Marley, Marcia Griffiths, and Judy Mowatt, harmony vocals (-1).

	Why Should I	unissued
	" (-1)	Tuff Gong (UK) CD TGCBX 1

ORIGINAL WAILERS   circa: October 1971

Bob Marley, vocal; Bunny Wailer, harmony vocal; Peter Tosh, harmony vocal; Rita Marley, harmony vocal; additional details of this session are unknown. Overdubs circa 1984 include Sly Dunbar and Carlton "Santa" Davis, drums; Robbie Shakespeare and Derrick Barnett, bass; Constantine "Vision" Walker, guitar; Robbie Lyn and Keith Sterling, keyboards; "Dizzy" Johnny Moore and Bobby Ellis, trumpets; Barrington Bailey, trombone; Bunny Wailer, Harry T Powell and Hugh "Sticky" Thompson, percussion; David Hamilton, Steven Stanley and Solgie Hamilton, engineers; Tuff Gong and Channel One studios; originally a four track, then transferred to twenty four track; Wailers, production.

	I'm Still Waiting	unissued
	" (demo mix)	"
	" ('85 mix)	"
	" (12 Tribes mix)	"
	" (alternate mix)	Universal CD B0002093-02
	" ('93 mix)	RAS lp 3501
	Hammer	unissued
	" (demo mix)	"
	" ('85 mix)	"
	" (12 Tribes mix)	"
	" ('93 mix)	RAS lp 3501
	How Many Times	unissued
	" (demo mix)	"
	" ('85 mix)	"
	" (12 Tribes mix)	"
	" ('93 mix)	RAS lp 3501
	It Hurts To Be Alone	unissued
	" (demo mix)	"
	" ('85 mix)	"
	" (12 Tribes mix)	"
	" ('93 mix)	RAS lp 3501
	Music Lesson	unissued
	" (demo mix)	"
TG12 001-A	" ('85 mix)	Tuff Gong 12" TG12 001
	" (12 Tribes mix)	unissued
	" (alternate mix)	Universal CD B0002093-02
	" ('93 mix)	RAS lp 3501
	Music Gonna Teach Version	Universal CD B0002093-02

    Note: "Music Lesson"/ "Nice Time" on Tuff Gong 12", released by Bunny Wailer in 1990, was bootlegged by Rita Marley on her own Tuff Gong imprint. "Music Lesson" is correctly listed on the label of Tuff Gong 12" TG12 001 but the title is given on the picture sleeve as "Musical Lesson." The original Tuff Gong 12" credits Bob Marley, N. O. Livingston, and Peter Macintosh with composition of "Music Lesson." The songs detailed above were extensively overdubbed and remixed in 1989 and were intended for inclusion on an album tentatively called *Together Again*. This album was not released for legal reasons, but was subsequently remixed in 1993 and finally released under the title *The Never Ending Wailers*. "Music Lesson" is re-titled as "Music Gonna Teach" on Universal CD. Bob again left Jamaica for Stockholm, Sweden in November 1971. He stayed in Sweden until January 27, 1972 when he traveled to London, England where he reunited with Johnny Nash and John "Rabbit" Bundrick.

BOB MARLEY & THE WAILERS   circa: February 1972

Bob Marley, vocal (-1) or harmony vocal (-2); Peter Tosh, vocal (-2) or harmony vocal (-1); Bunny Wailer, harmony vocal; unknown drums; unknown bass; "Geeshie," guitar; Carl Levy, keyboards; unknown horns, unknown engineer; CBS Studios, London; eight track; Danny Sims, production.

Stir It Up (-1)	unissued
Concrete Jungle (-1)	"
Midnight Ravers (-1)	"

Slave Driver (-1) unissued
400 Years (-2) "

BOB MARLEY   circa: April 4, 1972

Bob Marley, vocal and guitar; Johnny Nash, harmony vocal; Doris Troy, harmony vocal; Richard Bailey, drums; Trevor, bass; Gordon Hunt, guitar; John "Rabbit" Bundrick, keyboards; Anthony "Rebop" Kwaku Baah, percussion; Sons Of The Jungle, horns (-1); recorded CBS Studio in London, England; Jim Czak and John Post, remix engineers; originally remixed at Nolan Recording, New York; eight track; Johnny Nash, production; Danny Sims, executive production. 1996 overdubs: Dakota MacLeod Backup Singers (-2); Scott Zito, guitar (-2); Jim Ponzi, guitar (-2); Ray Naccari, keyboards and programming (-2); recorded at Panther Studios in Jackson, New Jersey.

	I'm Hurting Inside (-1)	Cotillion (US) lp 5228
	" (remix)	JAD (FR) CD 495250 2
	" (Alternate Mix)	Tuff Gong (UK) CD TGCBX 1
	" (remix)	JAD (US) CD 1003
	Dance Do The Reggae (-1)	Cotillion (US) lp 5228
	" (remix)	JAD (FR) CD 495250 2
	" (remix)	unissued
	" (remix)	JAD (US) CD 1003
	Oh Lord I Got To Get There (-1)	CBS (UK) 8114, JAD (FR) lp 542 222-1
	" (remix)	JAD (FR) CD 495250 2
	" (remix)	Jamaica (US) lp
	" (remix)	unissued
	Reggae On Broadway (-1)	CBS (UK) 8114, JAD (FR) lp 542 222-1
	" (remix)	Cotillion (US) lp 5228
	" (remix)	JAD (FR) CD 495250 2
	" (remix)	JAD (US) CD 1003
	Gonna Get You	Cotillion (US) lp 5228, JAD (FR) CD 495250 2
	" (-2)	Anansi (US) CD AN 0101-2
	" (Alt. version)	JAD (US) CD 1003
	" (radio single)	JAD (FR) SPCD 2292
	Stay With Me	Cotillion (US) lp 5228
	" (-2)	Anansi (US) CD AN 0101-2
	" (alternate mix)	JAD (FR) CD 495250 2

Note: Original mixes were done on April 30, 1971. According to John "Rabbit" Bundrick, Bob returned to Jamaica immediately following the mixing session. CBS (UK) 8114 was released on May 26, 1972. All four tracks were remixed by Ingmar King at Island Studios, London in 1990 for possible inclusion on Tuff Gong CD TGCBX 1. "Gonna Get You" and "Stay With Me" were composed by Jimmy Norman and Al Pyfrom. Jamaica (US) lp is *Bob, Bunny, Peter & Rita*.

HEAT, AIR & WATER (-1)   WAILERS (-2)   TUFF GONG ALL STARS   circa: 1972

Bunny Wailer, vocal and harmony vocal (-2); Peter Tosh, guitar and piano (-1) or organ (-2) and melodica (-2); Rita Marley, harmony vocal (-1); Judy Mowatt, harmony vocal (-1); Marcia Griffiths, harmony vocal (-1); Sangie Davis, harmony vocal (-2); Carlton Barrett, drums; Aston "Family Man" Barrett, bass (-1); Robbie Shakespeare, bass (-2); Tyrone Downie, organ (-1) or piano (-2); Tommy McCook, flute (-1); Vin Gordon, trombone (-1); Bobby Ellis, trumpet (-1); Carlton Lee, engineer; recorded Dynamic Studio; eight track; Bunny Wailer, production; 1981 remix by Bunny Wailer and Sylvan Morris at Harry J Studio.

DSR NL 7759-1	Searching For Love (-1)	Solomonic
	" (long remix)	Nighthawk lp 306
DSR NL 7760-1	Must Skank (-1)	Solomonic
RRS 2093	Life Line (-2)	Solomonic
NHR-1001-B	" (remix)	Nighthawk 12" 1001, Nighthawk lp 301
NHR-1001-B	Life Line Version (-2)	"

Note: "Searching For Love" was re-titled "Search For Love" when coupled with "Bide Up" on a later release credited to Bunny Wailer. The original issue of "Searching For Love" paired with "Must Skank," a dub version, is credited to Heat, Air & Water while the version side is credited to Tuff Gong All Stars. "Must Skank" was also released on Solomonic backed with "Got To Leave This Place" by A. Hudson on Tuff Gong, the only known pairing of these two labels on one disc. Composition of "Searching For Love" is credited to Neville Livingston (Bunny Wailer) while the composition of "Search For Love" is credited to Bunny's wife, Jean Watt, who also gets writing credit for "Life Line." The Solomonic issue of "Life Line" shows "Version" on the flip side, but this is not a version cut of "Life Line." Rather some copies play "Choke," a previously issued version cut of "Craven Choke Puppy," and some copies play "Grooving KGN 12," a previously issued version cut of "Trench Town Rock." Nighthawk issues are credited to Bunny Wailer.

BUNNY WAILER   circa: 1972

Bunny Wailer, vocal and jaw harp, harmony vocal (-2) and guitar (-2); Peter Tosh, harmony vocal, guitar and harmonica; Joe Higgs, harmony vocal (-1); Carlton Barrett, drums; Robbie Shakespeare, bass (-1); Karl Pitterson, bass (-2); Tyrone Downie, keyboards; Tommy McCook, flute (-2); Uziah "Sticky" Thompson, percussion; Larry McDonald, bongos (-2); Errol Thompson, engineer; recorded Randy's Studio 17; four track; Bunny Wailer, production; 1975 Overdubs: Bunny Wailer, harmony vocal and guitar (-2); Karl Pitterson, bass (-2); Tommy McCook, flute (-2); Larry McDonald, bongos (-2); engineered by Karl Pitterson at Aquarius Studio; twenty four track; Bunny Wailer, production.

FNL 7652-A	Bide up (-1)	Solomonic
	" (-2)	Solomonic lp, Island ILPS 9415

Note: Jean Watt is credited with composition of "Bide Up."

BONY & BIG YOUTH   BIG YOUTH   circa: 1972

Big Youth, dj vocal; Bunny Wailer, vocal (-1) and jaw harp; Peter Tosh, guitar and harmonica; Carlton Barrett, drums; Robbie Shakespeare, bass; Tyrone Downie, keyboards; Uziah "Sticky" Thompson, percussion; Errol Thompson, engineer; recorded Randy's Studio 17; four track; Bunny Wailer, production; 1981 remix by Bunny Wailer and Sylvan Morris at Harry J Studio.

BL 5075 A	Bide (-1)	Solomonic, Solomonic CD
	" (-1) (remix)	Nighthawk 12" NH1001, Nighthawk lp 306
BL 5076 B	Black On Black	Solomonic, Solomonic CD

Note: Bunny Wailer vocals on "Bide Up" and "Bide" are different. Bunny re-voiced with Big Youth. In the wax of "Black On Black" after the matrix number is the title, "Related To Life." Composition of both songs is credited to Jean Watt and M. Buchanan (Big Youth). Solomonic CD is titled *World Piece*.

WAILERS   circa: 1972

Bunny Wailer, vocal and harmony vocal; Rita Marley, harmony vocal; Judy Mowatt, harmony vocal; Peter Tosh, guitars and keyboard; Carlton Barrett, drums; Aston "Family Man" Barrett, bass; Bobby Ellis, trumpet and piano; Richard "Dirty Harry" Hall, tenor sax; Errol Thompson, recording engineer; Dennis Thompson, mixing engineer; recorded and mixed Randy's Studio 17; Bunny Wailer, production; 1981 remix by Bunny Wailer and Sylvan Morris at Harry J Studio.

BW 3668-2	Arabs Oil Weapon	Solomonic
NHR-1001-A	" (remix)	Nighthawk 12" NH 1001, Nighthawk lp 301
BW 3676	Dub'd Version	Solomonic

Note: Although the Arab oil crisis was over a year away, Bunny insists that he recorded this title well before that event. Titled as "Arab Oil Weapon," the Nighthawk remix is an extended version. Composition of "Arabs Oil Weapon" is credited to Jean Watt.

THE WAILERS   circa: 1972

Bunny Wailer, vocal and harmony vocal; Peter Tosh, harmony vocal, guitars and keyboards; Carlton Barrett, drums; Robbie Shakespeare, bass; Tommy McCook, tenor sax; Errol Thompson, engineer; recorded Randy's Studio 17; four track; Bunny Wailer, production; 1981 remix by Bunny Wailer and Sylvan Morris at Harry J Studio.

NL 1684	Pass It On	Solomonic
	" (remix)	Nighthawk lp 306

No. 11 Music 1683   Trod On   Solomonic

Note: "Trod On" is a version of "Pass It On." Composition of "Pass It On" is credited to Jean Watt. The 1981 remix by Bunny Wailer & Sylvan Morris was done at Harry J Studio in Kingston, Jamaica. Bunny is sure that he recorded "Pass It On" before the Wailers began work on the *Catch A Fire* album, but the track was apparently not released until 1975 and shares the distinct label style of another later issue, "Battering Down Sentence." Both labels credit publishing to No. 11 Music and production to Tuff Gong. Both labels also share a block style rendering of "Solomonic" not found on other issues. Bunny says that the chorus of this song is traditional. In late August 1972 the Wailers traveled to England for their first live shows in the UK. Included in this tour was an August 27 appearance at the Telegraph in Brixton, England. It was on this trip that the Wailers first met Chris Blackwell, owner of Island Records, who financed production of the *Catch A Fire* album sessions, details of which follow. Riddims were recorded on two consecutive days in early October. The Wailers then rehearsed their vocals for a week or two before recording all the vocals in one day. Because of the complexity of this work, it is impractical to list it in one block, so it has been broken into seven sections comprising all the Wailers' October 1972 recordings.

THE WAILERS   circa: October 1972

Bob Marley, vocal and guitar; Peter Tosh, harmony vocal and guitar; Bunny Wailer, harmony vocal and percussion; Carlton Barrett, drums; Robbie Shakespeare, bass; Wayne Perkins, guitar (-1); Tyrone Downie, organ; John "Rabbit" Bundrick, keyboards (-1); Alvin "Seeco" Patterson, percussion; Carlton Lee, engineer; recorded Dynamic Sounds Studio; eight track; Stu Barrett and Tony Platt, mixing engineers; mixed at Island Studios (UK); Wailers, production. Overdubs 2000, recorded Island Studios (UK): Rakim, DJ and vocal (-2); Renae Neusville, harmony vocal (-2); Damian Marley, drum program (-2); Earl "Chinna" Smith, guitar (-2); 2001 "original" mix: Errol Brown, engineer (-3); mixed at Universal Studios, East.

DSR-RM –8601-A   Concrete Jungle (-1)   Tuff Gong, Island (UK) WIP 6164A, Island (US) 1215
                                                                                   Tuff Gong lp 101, Island lp SW 9329
                         Concrete Jungle (-3)   Tuff Gong/Island CD 314 548 935-2
                         Concrete Jungle   unissued
                             "   (-2) (demo)   "
                             "   (-2)   Tuff Gong/Island CD 314 546 404-2

Note: Wayne Perkins' guitar and "Rabbit" Bundrick's keyboards were overdubbed at Island Studios. The Errol Brown "original" mix is listed as an alternate take because it contains alternate vocals and no overdubs. The original issue of Tuff Gong lp 101 featured a red, black and white label with a drawing of a dreadlocks striking a gong.

THE WAILERS   circa: October 1972

Bob Marley, vocal; Bunny Wailer, harmony vocal; Peter Tosh, harmony vocal and guitar; Carlton Barrett, drums; Aston "Family Man" Barrett, bass; Earl "Wya" Lindo, piano; Winston Wright, organ; Carlton Lee, engineer; recorded Dynamic Sounds Studio; eight track; Wailers, production; 2001 mix by Errol Brown (-1) at Universal Studios, East.

                         High Tide Or Low Tide   Tuff Gong (UK) CD TGCBX 1
                               "   (-1)   Tuff Gong/Island CD 314 546 404-2

THE WAILERS   circa: October 1972

Bob Marley, vocal and guitar; Peter Tosh, harmony vocal and guitar; Bunny Wailer, harmony vocal and percussion; Carlton Barrett, drums; Aston "Family Man" Barrett, bass; Earl "Wya" Lindo, piano and keyboards; Winston Wright, keyboards; Alvin "Seeco" Patterson, percussion; Carlton Lee, engineer; recorded Dynamic Sounds Studio; eight track; Stu Barrett and Tony Platt, mixing engineers; mixed at Island Studios (UK); Wailers, production. Overdubs 1999: Ghetto Youths Crew, vocals and DJ vocal (-1); Damian Marley, drum program (-1/-2); Julian Marley, keyboards (-1, -2); R. Lyfook, keyboards (-1); Erykah Badu, vocal (-2); unknown harmony vocals (-2); Damian Marley, drum program (-2); Stephen Marley, keyboards (-2). 2001 mix by Errol Brown (-3) at Universal Studios, East.

X79364   Slave Driver   Island (US) 1218, Island (UK), Tuff Gong lp 101,
                                                                                       Island lp SW 9329
                          "   (-3)   Tuff Gong/Island CD 314 546 404-2
                       Kinky Reggae   Tuff Gong lp 101, Island lp SW 9329
                       Kinky Reggae (-3)   Tuff Gong/Island CD 314 546 404-2

	Kinky Reggae	unissued
	" (-1) (demo)	"
	" (-1)	Tuff Gong/Island CD 314 546 404-2
X79370	No More Trouble	Island (US) 1215, Tuff Gong lp 101, Island lp SW 9329
	" (-3)	Tuff Gong/Island CD 314 546 404-2
	No More Trouble	unissued
	" (-2) (demo)	"
	" (-2)	Tuff Gong/Island CD 314 546 404-2
	No More Trouble	"

Note: The Errol Brown mix of "Kinky Reggae" is listed as an alternate take because it features an alternate vocal line throughout. The Brown mix of "No More Trouble" runs an additional 75 seconds and features previously edited verses. "Kinky Reggae" contains the line "She had brown sugar all over her bugga wugga." The short stalk of sugar cane left in the ground after harvest is brown and worthless. The cane cutters wear a cheap canvas shoe known as bugga wuggas and these shoes get covered with the dark sugar residues abundant on the remaining stalks.

THE WAILERS   circa: October 1972

Peter Tosh, vocal and guitar and keyboards; Bob Marley, harmony vocal; Bunny Wailer, harmony vocal and percussion; Carlton Barrett, drums; Aston "Family Man" Barrett, bass; Earl "Wya" Lindo, keyboards; Winston Wright, organ (-1); John "Rabbit" Bundrick, organ (-2); Alvin "Seeco" Patterson, percussion; Carlton Lee, engineer; recorded Dynamic Sounds Studio; eight track; Stu Barrett and Tony Platt, mixing engineers; mixed at Island Studios (UK); Wailers, production. 2001 mix by Errol Brown (-3) at Universal Studios, East.

	400 Years	Tuff Gong/Island CD 314 546 404-2
	Stop That Train	"
	400 Years	Tuff Gong lp 101, Island lp SW 9329
	" (-3)	Tuff Gong/Island CD 314 546 404-2
	Stop That Train (-2)	Tuff Gong lp 101, Island lp SW 9329
	" (-1) (-3)	Tuff Gong/Island CD 314 546 404-2
S-45-79499-F-3	Stop That Train (Instrumental)	Island (US) 1211, Blue Mountain (UK) BM 1021

THE WAILERS   circa: October 1972

Bob Marley, vocal and guitar; Peter Tosh, harmony vocal and guitar; Bunny Wailer, harmony vocal, bass, and percussion; Rita Marley, harmony vocal; Marcia Griffiths, harmony vocal; Carlton Barrett, drums; Wayne Perkins, guitar (-1); Earl "Wya" Lindo, piano; Winston Wright, organ; Alvin "Seeco" Patterson, percussion; Carlton Lee, engineer; recorded Dynamic Sounds Studio; eight track; Stu Barrett and Tony Platt, mixing engineers; mixed at Island Studios (UK); Wailers, production. 2001 mix by Errol Brown (-2) at Universal Studios, East.

FM 7500-A	Rock It Babe (-1)	Tuff Gong, Island (US) 1211, Blue Mountain (UK) BM 1021, Tuff Gong lp 101, Island lp SW 9329
	" (-2)	Tuff Gong/Island CD 314 546 404-2
DSR RM 7685-1	Rock It Version	Tuff Gong

Note: "Rock It Babe" was re-titled as "Rock It Baby" on Island (US) 1211, and re-titled as "Baby We've Got A Date" on Blue Mountain (UK) BM 1021 and on Tuff Gong/Island album issues. Wayne Perkins' guitar was overdubbed at Island Studios. Lloyd "Bread" McDonald of Pipe & The Pipers has stated that this song was recorded over the "Back Biter" riddim from July 1971. They are indeed similar, but distinctly different as well. Perhaps this was an alternate recording of the "Back Biter" riddim, but not the one used for the original Tuff Gong single issue of that song.

Bob's companion shot this picture in England in early 1973 for *Catch A Fire*. From left: Earl "Wya" Lindo, Aston "Family Man" Barrett, Bob Marley, Peter Tosh, Carly Barrett, Bunny Wailer. Photo by Esther Anderson.

THE WAILERS circa: October 1972

Bob Marley, vocal and guitar; Peter Tosh, harmony vocal and guitar; Bunny Wailer, harmony vocal, bass, and percussion; Carlton Barrett, drums; Earl "Wya" Lindo, piano; Bernard "Touter" Harvey, keyboards; John "Rabbit" Bundrick, keyboards (-1); Alvin "Seeco" Patterson, percussion; Carlton Lee, engineer; recorded Dynamic Sounds Studio; eight track; Stu Barrett and Tony Platt, mixing engineers; Wailers, production; Bill Laswell, 1997 remix. 2001 mix by Errol Brown (-2) at Universal Studios, East.

DSR RM 7682-1	Midnight Ravers (-1)	Tuff Gong, Tuff Gong (US) 5014, Tuff Gong lp 101, Island lp SW 9329
	" (-2)	Tuff Gong/Island CD 314 546 404-2
	" ('97 remix) (-1)	Island CD 314 524 419-2
DSR RM 7684-1	Ravers Version (-1)	Tuff Gong, Tuff Gong (US) 5014

Note: "Rabbit" Bundrick's keyboards were overdubbed at Island Studios.

THE WAILERS circa: October 1972

Bob Marley, vocal; Peter Tosh, harmony vocal; Bunny Wailer, harmony vocal; Sparrow Martin, drums; Ian Lewis (-1) or Robbie Shakespeare, bass (-2); Roger Lewis, guitar; "Cat" Coore, guitar; Wayne Perkins, guitar (-3); Earl "Wya" Lindo, piano; Tyrone Downie, organ (-2); Alvin "Seeco" Patterson, percussion; Carlton Lee, engineer; recorded Dynamic Sounds Studio; eight track; Stu Barrett and Tony Platt, mixing engineers; mixed at Island Studios (UK); Wailers, production. 2001 mix by Errol Brown (-4) at Universal Studios, East.

Stir It Up (-2) (-3)	Tuff Gong lp 101, Island lp SW 9329
" (-2) (-4)	Tuff Gong/Island CD 314 546 404-2
All Day All Night (-1)	"
Walk The Proud Land (-1)	unissued

Note: Details supplied by "Cat" Coore, Roger Lewis and Ian Lewis. Wayne Perkins' guitar was overdubbed at Island Studios (UK). Robbie Shakespeare says he played on "Stir It Up."

PETER TOSH & THE WAILERS circa: late 1972

Peter Tosh, vocal, guitar, organ, and clavinet; Bunny Wailer, harmony vocal, repeater (-1); "Tin Leg", drums; Aston "Family Man" Barrett, bass; Noel "Scully" Simms, percussion; Errol Brown, engineer; Duke Reid Studio; eight track; Peter Tosh, production.

PT 2259 A	Can't Blame The Youth	Intel Diplo, Columbia CD C3K 65064
TSL PT 1155	"	"
PT 2262 B	Version	"
PT 1156 TSL	"	"
PT 2260 A	No Mercy (-1)	Intel Diplo, Columbia CD C3K 65064
PT 2261 B	Version (-1)	"

BOB MARLEY — EARL LINDO — PETER TOSH

JOE HIGGS — ASTON "FAMILY MAN" BARRETT — CARLTON BARRETT

THE WAILERS

island records
available from capitol records

Burnin' publicity picture, with Joe Higgs briefly replacing Bunny Wailer, late 1973

PETER TOSH & THE WAILERS   circa: early 1973

Peter Tosh, vocal, harmony vocal, guitar and keyboards; Bunny Wailer, harmony vocal; Carlton Barrett, drums; Aston "Family Man" Barrett, bass; Noel "Scully" Simms, percussion; Uziah "Sticky" Thompson, percussion; Errol Brown, engineer; recorded Duke Reid Studio; eight track; Peter Tosh, production.

PT 4615 A	The Mark Of The Beast	Intel Diplo, Columbia CD C3K 65064
TIS PT 777	Version	"

WAILERS   circa: April 1973

Bob Marley, vocal (-1) or harmony vocal (-2, -3) and guitar; Bunny Wailer, vocal (-2) or harmony vocal (-1, -3) and percussion; Peter Tosh, vocal (-3) or harmony vocal (-1, -2) and guitar; Carlton Barrett, drums; Aston "Family Man" Barrett, bass; Earl "Wya" Lindo, keyboards; Alvin "Seeco" Patterson, percussion; Sylvan Morris, engineer; recorded Harry J Studio; eight track; mixed by Tony Platt, Phil Brown and Frank Owen at Island Studio in London; Wailers, production.

Small Axe (-1)	unissued
Oppressed Song (-2)	"
" (remix)	Tuff Gong/Island CD 314 548 894-2
Reincarnated Soul (-2)	unissued
" (remix)	Tuff Gong/Island CD 314 548 894-2
One Foundation (-3)	unissued
No Sympathy (-3)	Columbia CD C3K 65064
Get Up Stand Up (-1)	Tuff Gong/Island CD B0003359-2

Note: These recordings were made as "demos" for Island Records. "Get Up Stand Up" features a shared lead with Peter Tosh. "Oppressed Song" and "Reincarnated Soul" were both originally mixed on May 14, 1973 and then remixed in mid-June. "One Foundation" and "No Sympathy" were both mixed between May and July of 1973.

WAILERS   circa: April 1973

Bunny Wailer, vocal and harmony vocal and percussion; Peter Tosh, harmony vocal and guitar; Bob Marley, harmony vocal; Carlton Barrett, drums; Aston "Family Man" Barrett, bass; Earl "Wya" Lindo, keyboards; Alvin "Seeco" Patterson, percussion; Sylvan Morris, engineer; recorded Harry J Studio; eight track; Wailers, production.

WIPV 1263-IU	Reincarnated Soul	Island (UK) WIP 6164
	Hallelujah Time	Tuff Gong LP 102, Island ILPS 9256
IDJ2-B	Pass It On	Island (UK) IDJ2-B, Tuff Gong LP 102, Island ILPS 9256

Note: Composition of all three titles is credited to Bunny's wife, Jean Watt.

WAILERS   circa: April 1973

Peter Tosh, vocal and guitar and keyboards; Bunny Wailer, harmony vocal and percussion; Bob Marley, harmony vocal; Carlton Barrett, drums; Aston "Family Man" Barrett, bass; Earl "Wya" Lindo, keyboards; Alvin "Seeco" Patterson, percussion; Sylvan Morris, engineer; recorded Harry J Studio; eight track; Wailers, production.

One Foundation	Tuff Gong lp 102, Island ILPS 9256
No Sympathy	Island lp ILPS 9391

Note: A recording of Tosh's "Can't Blame The Youth" may have been cut at this session.

WAILERS   circa: April 1973

Bob Marley, vocal and harmony vocal (-1) and guitar; Peter Tosh, harmony vocal and guitar; Bunny Wailer, harmony vocal and percussion; Carlton Barrett, drums; Aston "Family Man" Barrett, bass; Earl "Wya" Lindo, keyboards; Alvin "Seeco" Patterson, percussion; Sylvan Morris, engineer; recorded Harry J Studio; eight track; Wailers, production; Bill Laswell, 1997 remix. 1992 overdubs: Rita Marley, harmony vocal (-2); Judy Mowatt, harmony vocal (-2); Marcia Griffiths, harmony vocal (-2); unknown horns (-2); unknown keyboards (-2); unknown percussion (-2). Overdubs 1999: The Roots featuring Black Thought, vocals and DJ vocals (-3); Ahmir "Roots" Thompson, drums (-3); Damian Marley, drum program (-3); D. Copper, bass and keyboards (-3); Stephen Marley, keyboards (-3); Julian Marley, keyboards (-3); Scott "Roots" Starch, keyboards (-3).

	Get Up Stand Up	Tuff Gong lp 102, Island ILPS 9256
IS 005-A	I Shot The Sheriff	Island (US) IS 005, Island (UK) IDJ2-A,
		Tuff Gong LP 102, Island ILPS 9256
SCRM #12 #2205-A	Curfew (Burnin' And Lootin') (-1)	Tuff Gong, Tuff Gong lp 102, Island ILPS 9256
	" (1997 remix)	Island CD 314 524 419-2
	Burnin' And Lootin'	unissued
	" (-3) (demo)	unissued
	" (-3)	Tuff Gong/Island CD 314 546 414-2
IS 005-B	Put It On	Island (US) IS 005, Tuff Gong lp 102, Island ILPS 9256
	Small Axe	Tuff Gong lp 102, Island ILPS 9256
	" (remix)	Island lp MSTDA 1
IDJ2-B	Duppy Conqueror	Island (UK) IDJ2-B, Tuff Gong lp 102, Island ILPS 9256
	Iron Lion Zion (original mix)	unissued
MML 3143-A	" (-2)	Tuff Gong, Tuff Gong (UK) CD TGCBX-1
12 TGX2-A	" (12" mix)	Tuff Gong 12"
MML 3143-B	" (12" edit)	Tuff Gong

Note: Peter sings lead on one verse of "Get Up Stand Up." "Curfew" was re-titled "Burnin' and Lootin'" on all album issues. The alternate vocal take of this title was issued as "Burnin' And Lootin'" on Tuff Gong/Island CD 314 546 414-2.

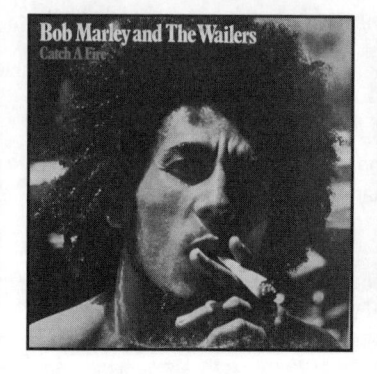

WAILERS   circa: early 1973

Bob Marley, vocal and percussion; Bunny Wailer, harmony vocal and percussion; Peter Tosh, harmony vocal and percussion; Carlton Barrett, drums; Aston "Family Man" Barrett, bass; Earl "Wya" Lindo, keyboards; Sylvan Morris, engineer; recorded Harry J Studio; eight track; Wailers, production. Overdubs 1999: Busta Rhymes and Flipmore Squad, vocals and DJ vocals (-1); Damian Marley, drum program (-1); R. Lyfook, keyboards (-1).

RM #2266	Chant (Rasta Man Chant)	Tuff Gong, Tuff Gong lp 102, Island ILPS 9256
		Tuff Gong 12"
	" (-1) (demo)	unissued
	" (-1)	Tuff Gong/Island CD 314 546 404-2

Note: Some labels of "Chant" read, "Chant I." "Chant" was re-titled "Rasta Man Chant" on all lp issues. This session was the last featuring all three Wailers together in the studio. In late April the Wailers embarked on an extensive UK tour beginning April 27 at the Coleman Club in Nottingham and ending May 29 at the Coach House in Southampton. Scheduled between these dates were twenty-six additional shows including the following well-recorded appearances.

BOB MARLEY & THE WAILERS   May 1, 1973

Bob Marley, vocal and guitar (-1) or percussion (-2); Bunny Wailer, harmony vocal and percussion; Peter Tosh, harmony vocal and guitar (-1) or percussion (-2); Carlton Barrett, drums; Aston "Family Man" Barrett, bass; Earl "Wya" Lindo, keyboards; unknown engineer; recorded at the Langham, London; probably four track; John Walters, production.

        Rasta Man Chant (-2)   unissued
        Concrete Jungle (-1)   "
        Slave Driver (-1)   "

Note: These titles were recorded for John Peel's Top Gear program on National Radio 1. They were first broadcast on May 15, 1973.

BOB MARLEY & THE WAILERS   May 1, 1973

Bob Marley, vocal and guitar; Bunny Wailer, vocal and percussion; Peter Tosh, vocal and guitar; Carlton Barrett, drums; Aston "Family Man" Barrett, bass; Earl "Wya" Lindo, keyboards; unknown engineer; recorded at BBC Broadcasting House, London; probably four track; BBC, production.

        Concrete Jungle   unissued
        Stir It Up   "

Note: Rhythm tracks were recorded in the studio. Then, while being filmed, the Wailers sang over the recorded riddims and pretended to play their instruments. The film was broadcast on BBC's The Old Grey Whistle Test.

BOB MARLEY & THE WAILERS   May 24, 1973

Bob Marley, vocal (-1) or harmony vocal (-2) and guitar, percussion (-1); Peter Tosh, vocal (-2) or harmony vocal (-1) and guitar, percussion (-3); Bunny Wailer, harmony vocal and percussion; Carlton Barrett, drums; Aston "Family Man" Barrett, bass; Earl "Wya" Lindo, keyboards; unknown engineer; recorded live at the Paris Theatre, London; probably eight track; BBC, production.

        Rasta Man Chant (-1) (-3)   BBC Transcription Services lp CN 1813/S
        Slave Driver (-1)   "
        Stop The Train (-2)   "
        No More Trouble (-1)   "
        400 Years (-2)   "
        Midnight Raver (-1)   "
        Stir It Up (-1)   "
        Concrete Jungle (-1)   "
        Get Up, Stand Up (-1) (-2)   "
        Kinky Reggae (-1)   "

Note: This concert was broadcast on BBC Radio 1's "In Concert" program. Chris Blackwell's remark that the Wailers would play "freak clubs" on the upcoming American portion of their tour, convinced Bunny that he should return to Jamaica and let the others go without him. In early July the Wailers, with Joe Higgs filling in for Bunny, came to the United States and toured through early August. Their first job was a weeklong appearance in Boston at Paul's Mall and the last was at the Matrix Club in San Francisco. Below are listed a few of their best-recorded shows.

BOB MARLEY & THE WAILERS   July 11, 1973

Bob Marley, vocal (-1) or harmony vocal (-2) and guitar; Peter Tosh, vocal (-2) or harmony vocal (-1) and guitar; Joe Higgs, harmony vocal and percussion; Carlton Barrett, drums; Aston "Family Man" Barrett, bass; Earl "Wya" Lindo, keyboards; recorded live at Paul's Mall, Boston.

        Lively Up Yourself (-1)   unissued
        400 Years (-2)   "
        Stir It Up (-1)   "
        Slave Driver (-1)   "

Stop That Train (-2)	unissued
Kinky Reggae (-1)	"
Concrete Jungle (-1)	"
Get Up Stand Up (-1) (-2)	"

BOB MARLEY & THE WAILERS　　　　　　　　　　　　　　　　　　　　　　　　circa: late July 1973

Bob Marley, vocal (-1) or harmony vocal (-2) and guitar; Peter Tosh, vocal (-2) or harmony vocal (-1) and guitar; Joe Higgs, harmony vocal and percussion; Carlton Barrett, drums; Aston "Family Man" Barrett, bass; Earl "Wya" Lindo, keyboards; three sets recorded live at Max's Kansas City, New York.

I'm Gonna Put It On (-1)	unissued
Slave Driver (-1)	"
Curfew (Burnin' And Lootin') (-1)	"
Stop That Train (-2)	"
Kinky Reggae (-1)	"
Stir It Up (-1)	"
Bend Down Low (-1)	unissued
Lively Up Yourself (-1)	"
Slave Driver (-1)	"
Stop That Train (-2)	"
Stir It Up (-1)	"
Kinky Reggae (-1)	"
Get Up Stand Up (-1)	"
Rude Boy (-1)	"
Bend Down Low (-1)	unissued
Lively Up Yourself (-1)	"
Slave Driver (-1)	"
400 Years (-2)	"
Stir It Up (-1)	"
Kinky Reggae (-1)	"
Don't Rock My Boat (-1)	"
Get Up Stand Up (-1)	"
I'm Gonna Put It On (-1)	"

BOB MARLEY & THE WAILERS　　　　　　　　　　　　　　　　　　　　　　　　circa: late July 1973

Bob Marley, vocal and guitar; Peter Tosh, vocal and guitar; Carlton Barrett, drums; Aston "Family Man" Barrett, bass; Earl "Wya" Lindo, keyboards; eight track; recorded at A&R Studios in New York City; Wailers, production.

Get Up, Stand Up	Tuff Gong/Island CD B0003359-2

Note: This recording uses the basic rhythm track of the title included on the original *Burnin'* album, but is so extensively re-voiced and overdubbed that it deserves separate listing. The Wailers resumed touring in October with a scheduled seventeen dates opening for Sly & The Family Stone. The tour fell apart for the Wailers after the fourth show and they were stranded in Las Vegas for a time before traveling to California for the following well-recorded dates.

BOB MARLEY & THE WAILERS　　　　　　　　　　　　　　　　　　　　　　　　October 19, 1973

Bob Marley, vocal (-1) or harmony vocal (-2) and guitar, percussion (-3); Peter Tosh, vocal (-2) or harmony vocal (-1) and guitar, percussion (-3); Joe Higgs, harmony vocal and percussion; Carlton Barrett, drums; Aston "Family Man" Barrett, bass; Earl "Wya" Lindo, keyboards; recorded live at the Matrix San Francisco.

Rasta Man Chant (-1) (-3)	unissued
Duppy Conqueror (-1)	"
Slave Driver (-1)	"
Curfew (Burnin' And Lootin') (-1)	"

Stop That Train (-2)   unissued
unknown titles   "

BOB MARLEY & THE WAILERScirca: late October 1973

Bob Marley, vocal (-1) or harmony vocal (-2) and guitar, percussion (-3); Peter Tosh, vocal (-2) or harmony vocal (-1) and guitar, percussion (-3); Joe Higgs, harmony vocal and percussion; Carlton Barrett, drums; Aston "Family Man" Barrett, bass; Earl "Wya" Lindo, keyboards; recorded Record Plant in Sausalito, CA; eight track; Wailers, production.

Rasta Man Chant (-1) (-3)Tuff Gong lp 422-848 243-1
Bend Down Low (-1)Tuff Gong/Island CD 314 548 906-2
Slave Driver (-1)Tuff Gong lp 422-848 243-1
You Can't Blame The Youth (-2)"
Stop That Train (-2)Tuff Gong/Island CD 314 548 906-2
Burnin' & Lootin' (-1)Tuff Gong lp 422-848 243-1
Kinky Reggae (-1)"
Get Up Stand Up (-1) (-2)"
Lively Up Yourself (-1)Tuff Gong/Island CD 314 548 906-2
Walk The Proud Land (-1)Tuff Gong lp 422-848 243-1

BOB MARLEY & THE WAILERSOctober 30, 1973

Bob Marley, vocal (-1) or harmony vocal (-2) and guitar, percussion (-3); Peter Tosh, vocal (-2) or harmony vocal (-1) and guitar, percussion (-3); Joe Higgs, harmony vocal and percussion; Carlton Barrett, drums; Aston "Family Man" Barrett, bass; Earl "Wya" Lindo, keyboards; recorded live at the Matrix, San Francisco.

Rasta Man Chant (-1) (-3)unissued
Duppy Conqueror (-1)"
Lively Up Yourself (-1)"
Can't Blame the Youth (-2)"
No More Trouble (-1)"
Kinky Reggae (-1)"
Get Up Stand Up (-1) (-2)"
Jam"
Bend Down Low (-1)"
I'm Gonna Put It On (-1)"
Curfew (Burnin' And Lootin') (-1)"
Stop That Train (-2)"
Small Axe (-1)"
Stir It Up (-1)"

BOB MARLEY & THE WAILERScirca: early November 1973

Bob Marley, vocal (-1) or harmony vocal (-2) and guitar, percussion (-3); Peter Tosh, vocal (-2) or harmony vocal (-1) and guitar, percussion (-3); Joe Higgs, harmony vocal and percussion; Carlton Barrett, drums; Aston "Family Man" Barrett, bass; Earl "Wya" Lindo, keyboards; unknown engineer; recorded at the Capitol Record Tower in Los Angeles; sixteen track; Lee Jaffe, production.

Can't Blame The Youth (-1)unissued
Rasta Man Chant (-1) (-3)"
Rasta Man Chant (-1) (-3)"
Duppy Conqueror (-1)"
Duppy Conqueror (-1)"
Slave Driver (-1)"
Curfew (Burnin' And Lootin') (-1)"
Midnight Ravers (-1)"
Midnight Ravers (-1)"
Midnight Ravers (-1)"

I'm Gonna Put It On (-1)	unissued
Stop That Train (-2)	"
Kinky Reggae (-1)	"
Stir It Up (-1)	"
No More Trouble (-1)	"
Get Up Stand Up (-1) (-2)	"
Rasta Man Chant (-1) (-3)	"
Duppy Conqueror (-1)	"
Midnight Ravers (-1)	"
Midnight Ravers (-1)	"
Midnight Ravers (-1)	"
I'm Gonna Put It On (-1)	"
Stop That Train (-2)	"
Kinky Reggae (-1)	"
Stir It Up (-1)	"
No More Trouble (-1)	"
Can't Blame The Youth (-2)	"
Rasta Man Chant (-1) (-3)	"
Rasta Man Chant (-1) (-3)	"
Rasta Man Chant (-1) (-3)	"

Note: This complete session was filmed in color. Shortly afterwards Joe Higgs returned to Jamaica. The rest of the band went to England to play a benefit.

BOB MARLEY & THE WAILERS   circa: early November 1973

Bob Marley, vocal (-1) or harmony vocal (-2) and guitar; Peter Tosh, vocal (-2) or harmony vocal (-1) and guitar; Carlton Barrett, drums; Aston "Family Man" Barrett, bass; Earl "Wya" Lindo, keyboards; recorded live at Ethiopian Famine Relief Benefit at the Edmonton Sundown Club in London, England.

Slave Driver (-1)	unissued
Stop That Train (-2)	"
Get Up Stand Up (-1) (-2)	"

Note: In November, the Wailers returned to the UK, but had to cancel the first five dates due to Peter being ill. The tour ultimately began on November 22 at the Locarno in Blackpool and ended in Northampton on the 30th when Peter's bronchitis returned. A few of the better-recorded dates from this tour are listed below.

BOB MARLEY & THE WAILERS   November 23, 1973

Bob Marley, vocal (-1) or harmony vocal (-2) and guitar, percussion (-3); Peter Tosh, vocal (-2) or harmony vocal (-1) and guitar, percussion (-3); Carlton Barrett, drums; Aston "Family Man" Barrett, bass; Earl "Wya" Lindo, keyboards; recorded live at Leeds Polytechnic, England.

Duppy Conqueror (-1)	Tuff Gong/Island CD B0003359-2
Slave Driver (-1)	"
Curfew (Burnin' And Lootin')	"
Can't Blame The Youth (-2)	"
Stop That Train (-2)	"
Midnight Ravers (-1)	"
No More Trouble (-1)	"
Kinky Reggae (-1)	"
Get Up, Stand Up (-1) (-2)	"
Stir It Up (-1)	"
I'm Gonna Put It On (-1)	"
Lively Up Yourself (-1)	"

Note: A few days after this concert the Wailers returned to Jamaica, where Peter announced his decision to leave the group. Bunny had reached the same decision while waiting for the group's return.

BOB MARLEY & THE WAILERS   November 26, 1973

Bob Marley, vocal (-1) or harmony vocal (-2) and guitar; Peter Tosh, vocal (-2) or harmony vocal (-1) and guitar; Carlton Barrett, drums; Aston "Family Man" Barrett, bass; Earl "Way" Lindo, keyboards; unknown engineer; recorded at BBC Studio, Kensington House; probably four track; produced for the BBC by John Walters and Pete Dauncey.

        Kinky Reggae (-1)   unissued
        Can't Blame The Youth (-2)   "
        Get Up, Stand Up (-1) (-2)   "

PETER TOUCH & MUDIE'S ALL STARS   circa: late 1973

Peter Tosh, melodica; unknown drums, bass, guitar, keyboards, and percussion; unknown engineer and studio; Harry A Mudie, production.

FHM 10128-B   Wellbread   Moodisc

Note: "Wellbread" is the version side of "It May Sound Silly" by I Roy. Recently, "Wellbread" was re-issued on Moodisc wrongly titled as "It May Sound Silly" with a version side that does not feature Tosh.

PETER TOSH & THE WAILERS   PETER TOSH   circa: late 1973

Peter Tosh, vocal, guitar, and keyboards; Bunny Wailer, harmony vocal and percussion; Carlton Barrett, drums; Aston "Family Man" Barrett, bass; Al Anderson, guitar; Tyron Downie, keyboards; Robbie Shakespeare, bass (-1); Lee Jaffe, harmonica (-1); Tommy McCook, tenor sax (-2); David Madden, trumpet (-2); Errol Brown, engineer; recorded at Duke Reid's Treasure Isle Studio; eight track; Peter Tosh, production.

PT-002-4385	What You Gonna Do (-1)	Intel Diplo, Intel Diplo lp, Columbia lp PC 34253
PT 002 A	"	Intel Diplo
PT-003-4387	Version (-1)	"
PT 002 B	"	"
DSR-TC-9808-A	Burial (-2)	Intel Diplo, Intel Diplo lp, Columbia lp PC 34253
001 A PT	"	Intel Diplo
Intel A	"	"
DSR-TC 9809-B	Version (-2)	Intel Diplo, Tuff Gong
P. Tosh 4225 B	"	Intel Diplo
Intel B	Version (-2)	"

Note: Matrix Intel B is an alternate mix appearing only as the flip side of matrix Intel A. The Tuff Gong coupling of "Burial"/ "Version" is an oddity coupling the 1967 recording of the song (WIRL BM 3672-1) originally titled "Funeral," with the 1974 version cut, DSR-TC 9809-B. Composition credit for "Burial" on Intel Diplo lp and Columbia lp is listed Tosh/Livingston.

BOB MARLEY   circa: December 1973

Bob Marley, spoken word; interviewed by Neville Willoughby in Bull Bay, Jamaica.

        Bob Marley Interview   V & N S lp 21, JAD (FR) SPCD2002
        "   (excerpts)   Tuff Gong lp

Note: V & N S lp is titled *The Bob Marley Interviews*. The Tuff Gong lp is titled *Bob Marley Interviews*.

Peter Tosh. Photo by Kate Simon.

UPSETTERS   BOB MARLEY & THE WAILERS   circa: January 1974

Bob Marley, vocal; Lee Perry, speech (-1) or percussion (-2); Bunny Wailer, harmony vocal (-2); Peter Tosh, harmony vocal (-2); Carlton Barrett, drums; Aston "Family Man" Barrett, bass; Alva "Reggie" Lewis, guitar; Ranford "Ronnie Bop" Williams, guitar; Earl "Chinna" Smith, guitar (-2); Glen Adams, keyboards; Winston Wright, organ (-1); Uziah "Sticky" Thompson, percussion (-2); Carlton Lee, engineer; West Indies Studio; four track; Lee Perry, production.

	Turn Me Loose (-2)	Trojan (UK) lp 221
	Keep On Skanking (-1)	Trojan (UK) lp 183, Heartbeat (US) CD HB 37
Lyn 13670-1	" (long mix)	Trojan (UK) 12" 9074

Note: When first issued on Trojan lp 183, "Keep On Skanking" was credited to the Upsetters. Heartbeat CD and Trojan (UK) 12" issues credit Bob Marley & The Wailers. Trojan 12" long mix is not just versioned out, but features a longer edit and much more of Marley's vocal. Actually, the riddim track for this tune was recorded circa 1971 for Leo Graham's "Black Candle." The riddim track used for "Turn Me Loose" is the Wailers' own 1971 "Kaya" riddim. The Bunny Wailer and Peter Tosh harmony was recorded in 1971. The date is confirmed by journalist/photographer Chris Lane, who was in the studio at the time and took photographs of Marley and Perry at work.

PETER TOSH   circa: early 1974

Peter Tosh, vocal, harmony vocal, guitar and keyboards; Bunny Wailer, harmony vocal and percussion; Carlton Barrett, drums; Aston "Family Man" Barrett, bass; Al Anderson, guitar; Tyrone Downie, keyboards; Errol Brown, engineer; recorded at Duke Reid's Treasure Isle Studio; eight track; Peter Tosh, production.

ZSM162494-1A	Why Must I Cry	Intel Diplo lp, Columbia AE 71109, Columbia lp PC 34253
ZSM162495-1B	Till Your Well Runs Dry	Intel Diplo lp, Columbia AE 71109, Columbia lp PC 34253

Note: Matrix numbers given are from Columbia AE 71109, a three-track promotional ep. The third track on the ep is "Legalize It" which shares the ZSM162494-1A matrix with "Why Must I Cry," a Tosh/Marley composition. "Till Your Well Runs Dry" is a Tosh/Livingston composition.

77

PETER TOSH
circa: early 1974

Peter Tosh, vocal, harmony vocal, guitar and keyboards; Bunny Wailer, harmony vocal and percussion; Carlton "Santa" Davis, drums; Robbie Shakespeare, bass; Al Anderson, guitar; Tyrone Downie, keyboards; Errol Brown, engineer; recorded at Duke Reid's Treasure Isle Studio; eight track; Peter Tosh, production.

CP 5001-A	Ketchy Shubby	Intel Diplo, Intel Diplo lp, Columbia lp PC 34253
115-A	"	Intel Diplo
DSR 3628-A	"	"
PT 5003	Iration	"
PT 212 B	"	"
DSR 3629-B	"	"

Note: "Iration" is a version of "Ketchy Shubby." In Rasta patois, "Iration" means creation. Another recording of this song with different lyrics is "Ketchy Huby" by the Mighty Revelation on the Wag label from Kingston, and this version of the song may predate Tosh's. Although recorded in 1974, "Ketchy Shubby" was not released as a single in Jamaica until June 22, 1976. The title refers to a children's game.

PETER TOSH
circa: early 1974

Peter Tosh, vocal and guitar; Rita Marley, harmony vocal (-1); Judy Mowatt, harmony vocal (-1); Carlton "Santa" Davis, drums; Robbie Shakespeare, bass; Donald Kinsey, guitar; Tyrone Downie, keyboards; Errol Thompson, engineer; recorded at Randy's Studio 17; eight track; Peter Tosh, production.

	No Sympathy	Intel Diplo lp, Columbia lp PC 34253
PT-5084	Brand New Second Hand (-1)	Intel Diplo, Intel Diplo lp, Columbia lp PC 34253
PT-5085	Version (-1)	Intel Diplo

BOB MARLEY & THE WAILERS
circa: early 1974

Bob Marley, vocal and guitar; Carlton Barrett, drums; Aston "Family Man" Barrett, bass; Al Anderson, guitar; Bernard "Touter" Harvey, keyboards; Alvin "Seeco" Patterson, percussion; recorded in rehearsal, Kingston.

	Revolution	unissued

BOB MARLEY & THE WAILERS
circa: early 1974

Bob Marley, vocal and guitar; Rita Marley, harmony vocal; Judy Mowatt, harmony vocal; Marcia Griffiths, harmony vocal; I Roy, DJ (-1); Carlton Barrett, drums; Aston "Family Man" Barrett, bass; Al Anderson, guitar; Bernard "Touter" Harvey, keyboards; Lee Jaffe, harmonica; Tommy McCook, tenor sax (-2); Glen DaCosta, tenor sax (-2); David Madden, trumpet (-2); Alvin "Seeco" Patterson, percussion; Sylvan Morris, engineer; recorded Harry J Studio; sixteen track; Phil Ault, overdub engineer; overdubbed at Island Studios (UK); Sydney Bucknor, mixing engineer; mixed at Basing Street Studios (UK); Wailers, production; Paul "Groucho" Smykle, 1986 remix engineer; Bill Laswell, 1997 remix engineer. Overdubs 1999: Krayzie Bone, dj vocal (-3); Stephen Marley, drum program and keyboards (-3); W. Cole, drum program and keyboards (-3); D. Copper, bass (-3).

AB 4709-A	Road Block (Rebel Music)	Tuff Gong, Tuff Gong lp, Island lp 90037-1
TG 1468	" (alternate mix)	Tuff Gong
TG 1649	" (long alternate mix)	Tuff Gong
	" (1986 remix)	Island lp 90520-1
	" (1997 remix)	Island CD 314 524 419-2
	Road Block	unissued
	Rebel Music (-3) (demo)	"
	" (-3)	Tuff Gong/Island CD 314 546 404-2
AB 4710-B	Rebel Music	Tuff Gong
TG 1469	" (short alternate mix)	Tuff Gong
DSR BM 9602-B	" (long alternate mix)	Tuff Gong
	" (alternate mix)	unissued
	Talkin' Blues (-2)	Tuff Gong lp 422 848 243-1

Micron 6088	Talking Blues (-2)	Tuff Gong, Tuff Gong lp, Island lp 90037-1
4861-B	"	Black Art
Micron 1675	Talking Blues (Version) (-1)	Tuff Gong
	Talking Blues (Version) (-1)	unissued

Note: "Rebel Music" is the version of "Road Block." Titles are given as found on the original singles. On the album *Road Block* was re-titled as "Rebel Music (3 O'clock Road Block)," the title used on all subsequent reissues and remixes. A state of emergency was declared in Jamaica on April 1. In addition, the government established the infamous Gun Court. At this point in Bob's career he began assigning composer credits on many of his best songs to friends, in an attempt to avoid old contractual obligations which he felt robbed him of his proper royalties. All the songs done in this manner required royalties to be paid to an account in the Cayman Islands, which only Bob and manager Don Taylor had access to. "Road Block" was credited to A. Barrett and H. Peart. "Talkin' Blues" was credited to Carlton Barrett and Cogil Leghorn on the original Tuff Gong single. The later name is credited as Legon Cogill on the Island lp. "Talking Blues" is rendered as "Talkin' Blues" on the Island lp. Rita Marley, Judy Mowatt and Marcia Griffiths are collectively known as the I Three. Bob had rehearsed these songs and others from Island lp 90037-1 ("Natty Dread") with Bunny Wailer and Peter Tosh singing harmony, but decided to use the I Three at the last minute. British-based artist Delroy Washington says he sang harmony on some tracks from the *Natty Dread* lp. "Talking Blues" on Black Art single was issued on an odd black and white label with no production credits. The label design is the same as the typical production on Lee Perry's Black Art label, but is not in the normal red, gold, and green, and looks like a bad copy. Although issued in Jamaica, this disc may be a bootleg.

BOB MARLEY & THE WAILERS   circa: early 1974

Bob Marley, vocal and guitar; Rita Marley, harmony vocal (-1); Judy Mowatt, harmony vocal (-1); Marcia Griffiths, harmony vocal (-1); Carlton Barrett, drums; Aston "Family Man" Barrett, bass; Al Anderson, guitar; Bernard "Touter" Harvey, keyboards; Alvin "Seeco" Patterson, percussion; Tommy McCook, flute (-2); Sylvan Morris, engineer; recorded Harry J Studio; sixteen track; Phil Ault, overdub engineer; overdubbed at Island Studios (UK); Sydney Bucknor, mixing engineer; mixed at Basing Street Studios (UK); Wailers, production; Bill Laswell, 1997 remix engineer.

AB 4704	Belly Full (-1)	Tuff Gong, Tuff Gong lp, Island lp 90037-1
AB 4772	"	Tuff Gong
Tuff Gong AB 4944/2	"	"
	" (1997 remix)	Island CD 314 524 419-2
AB 4696-B	Version	Tuff Gong
AB 4773-B	"	"
Tuff Gong AB 4945/B	"	"
A 4861	Bend Down Low (-1)	Black Art, Tuff Gong lp, Island lp 90037-1
	Bend Down Low (-1) (-2)	Tuff Gong lp 422 848 243-1
	Bend Down Low Version (-2)	unissued
	Am-A-Do	"
	Am-A-Do (-1)	Tuff Gong lp 422 848 243-1

Note: "Belly Full" was re-titled on the album and remix as "Them Belly Full (But We Hungry)." Legon Cogill and Carlton Barrett are assigned composer credit on "Belly Full." The Black Art single of "Bend Down Low"/ "Talking Blues" is an odd-looking issue and, although issued in Jamaica, may be a bootleg.

BOB MARLEY & THE WAILERS   circa: early 1974

Bob Marley, vocal and guitar; Rita Marley, harmony vocal; Judy Mowatt, harmony vocal; Marcia Griffiths, harmony vocal; Carlton Barrett, drums; Aston "Family Man" Barrett, bass; Al Anderson, guitar; Bernard "Touter" Harvey, keyboards and harmony vocal (-1); Tommy McCook, tenor sax; Glen DaCosta, tenor sax; David Madden, trumpet; Vin Gordon, trombone; Alvin "Seeco" Patterson, percussion; Sylvan Morris, engineer; recorded Harry J Studio; sixteen track; Phil Ault, overdub engineer; overdubbed at Island Studios (UK); Sydney Bucknor, mixing engineer; mixed at Basing Street Studios (UK); Wailers, production. 1984 remix by Eric Thorngren.

	Lively Up Yourself	Tuff Gong lp, Island lp 90037-1
	" (1984 remix)	Tuff Gong/Island CD 314 586 741-2
	So Jah Seh (-1)	Tuff Gong lp, Island (UK) WIP 1612, Island lp 90037-1
FCT 45-A	Knotty Dread (Natty Dread)	Tuff Gong, Tuff Gong lp, Island (UK) WIP 1612, Island lp 90037-1
FCT 45-B	Version	Tuff Gong

Revolution		unissued
Revolution		"
Revolution		Tuff Gong lp, Island lp 90037-1

Note: "Knotty Dread" was re-titled as "Natty Dread" on album. Composer credit for "So Jah Seh" is assigned to Willy San Francisco, a pseudonym of Alvin "Seeco" Patterson. The original Tuff Gong single of "Knotty Dread" lists Bob Marley as the composer, but on the *Natty Dread* album the composer credit is assigned to Allan Cole and Aston Barrett. According to Aston Barrett, Chris Blackwell objected to some lyrics of the militant "Revolution," which was re-voiced to eliminate those passages.

THE WAILERS   FAMILY MAN & REBEL ARMS   circa: early 1974

Carlton Barrett, drums; Aston "Family Man" Barrett, bass; Eric "Rickanbaca" Frater, guitar; Tyrone Downie, piano; Earl "Wya" Lindo, organ, clavinet and synthesizer; Errol Thompson, engineer; recorded Randy's Studio 17; four track; Aston "Family Man" Barrett, production.

FM RRS 3890	Eastern Memphis	Cobra, Heartbeat CD HB 157
FM RRS 3891-B	Version Rebel Am I	Cobra, Heartbeat CD HB 159

Note: This track is included because of the artist credit on the original label, and the information "Distributed By Tuff Gong – 127 King Street" on the same label.

FAMILY MAN & KNOTTY ROOTS   WAILERS BAND   circa: early 1974

Aston "Family Man" Barrett, guitar and repeater; Carlton Barrett, drums; Robbie Shakespeare, bass; Tyrone Downie, piano; "Dirty" Harry Hall, clarinet; Herman Marquis, clarinet; Bob Marley, repeater; Peter Tosh, repeater; Bunny Wailer, funda; Errol Thompson, engineer; recorded Randy's Studio 17; four track; Aston "Family Man" Barrett, production.

AB 5009-A	Distant Drums	Fam's, Heartbeat CD HB 157
AB 5010-B	Version	Fam's, Heartbeat CD HB 159

Note: This track utilizes the same riddim originally released on Family Man's Defenders label as "Love Thy Neighbor" by Vivian Jackson & The Defenders. Bob, Bunny, and Peter are not present on that recording. AB 5010-B is re-titled as "Distant Dub" on Heartbeat CD.

BOB MARLEY & THE WAILERS   circa: early 1974

Bob Marley, vocal and guitar; unknown female harmony vocals; Carlton Barrett, drums; Aston "Family Man" Barrett, bass; Al Anderson, guitar; Earl "Wya" Lindo, keyboards; recorded Island Studios, London; Wailers and Chris Blackwell, production. Eric Thorngren, 1984 remix engineer; Bill Laswell, 1997 remix engineer.

	No Woman No Cry	Tuff Gong lp, Island lp 90037-1
	" (1984 remix)	Island (UK) 12 IS 210, Island lp 90169-1
	" (1997 remix)	Island CD 314 524 419-2

Note: Bob and the Wailers band returned to Jamaica shortly after this session. The absence of the I Three harmony group from this session was revealed in an interview with Aston Barrett. Credit for the composition of "No Woman No Cry" was assigned to Vincent "Tata" Ford who is said to have actually written much of the lyric.

WAILERS   circa: 1974

Bunny Wailer, vocal, harmony vocal and percussion; Peter Tosh, harmony vocal and guitar; Carlton Barrett, drums; Aston "Family Man" Barrett, bass (-1) or keyboards (-2); Robbie Shakespeare, bass (-2); Tyrone Downie, keyboards (-1); Winston Wright, keyboards (-2); Tommy McCook, tenor sax and flute (-2); Richard "Dirty Harry" Hall, tenor sax (-2); Glen DaCosta, alto sax (-1); Herman Marquis, alto sax (-2); Bobby Ellis, trumpet (-2); Sylvan Morris, engineer; recorded Harry J Studio; eight track; 1975 Overdubs (-2); 1975 remix by Karl Pitterson at Aquarius Studio; twenty four track; Bunny Wailer, production.

TC-2729-A	Battering Down Sentence (-1)	Solomonic
Talent A	"	Solomonic
	Fighting Against Convictions (-2)	Solomonic lp, Island lp ILPS 9415
TC-2729-B	Version (-1)	Solomonic
Talent B	"	Solomonic
	Battering Down (Dubd'sco) (-2)	Solomonic lp SP 007-34

Note: Matrix Talent A plays a few seconds longer than matrix TC-2729-A. "Battering Down Sentence" was re-titled as "Fighting Against Convictions" when overdubbed and remixed for inclusion on Solomonic lp, *Blackheart Man*. This song was written by Bunny during his fourteen-month incarceration for possession of ganja which began in July of 1967 and ended in September of 1968.

PETER TOSH   circa: early 1975

Peter Tosh, vocal, guitar, and keyboards (-1); Rita Marley, harmony vocal (-1); Judy Mowatt, harmony vocal (-1); Carlton Barrett, drums; Aston "Family Man" Barrett, bass; Al Anderson, guitar; Tyrone Downie, keyboards; Errol Brown, engineer; recorded Duke Reid's Studio; eight track; Peter Tosh, production.

	Igziabeher (Let Jah Be Praised)	Intel Diplo lp, Columbia lp PC 34253
PT-177-A	Legalize It (-1)	Intel Diplo,
	" (lp mix)	Intel Diplo lp, Columbia ep AE 71109,
		Columbia lp PC 34253
DSR 2770-A	" (alternate mix)	Intel Diplo
DSR 3687-A	" (alternate mix)	"
PT-177-B	Version (-1)	Intel Diplo
DSR 2770-B	" (early fade)	" , Columbia CD C3K 65064
DSR 3688-B	" (early fade)	"

Note: PT-177-A coupled with PT-177-B appeared on the older style Intel Diplo label with Intel on the top of the label and Diplo on the bottom. This early issue is dated 1975 and has been seen with a variety of colors including red and black, yellow and black, light blue and black, orange and red, white and blue, and white and green. It is not known which is the original issue. DSR matrices appeared on the later Intel Diplo label with yellow top, orange bottom with mid label yellow dots, and Peter's picture on green background in the upper left hand side of the label. This issue is undated. The PT prefix matrices are extremely well mastered and loud. The DSR prefix matrixes are dull in comparison. All versions seem to derive from the same mix, but the DSR matrices fade several seconds earlier than PT-177-B.

BOB MARLEY (-1)   BOB MARLEY & THE WAILERS (-2)   circa: summer 1975

Bob Marley, vocal and guitar; unknown female harmony vocals (-1); unknown male harmony vocals (-2); Carlton Barrett, drums; Aston "Family Man" Barrett, bass; Julian "Junior" Marvin, guitar; Tyrone Downie, keyboards; Earl "Wya" Lindo, keyboards; Glen DaCosta, tenor sax; Dave Madden, trumpet; Vin Gordon, trombone; Lee Perry, percussion; Alvin "Seeco" Patterson, percussion; Lee Perry, engineer; recorded at Black Ark Studio; Lee Perry, production.

101-A	Rainbow Country (-1)	Disco (US) 12" 101
DK 451-A	" (vocal)	Daddy Cool (UK) 12" DK 12 101, JAD (FR) CD 537325-2
	"	Lagoon CD LG2-1044

101-B	Rainbow Country Rhythm Track	Disco (US) 12" 101,
DK 451-A	" (Dub)	Daddy Cool (UK) 12" DK 12 101, JAD (FR) CD 537325-2
	" (Version)	Lagoon CD LG2-1044
102-A	Natural Mystic (-2)	Disco (US) 12" 102, JAD (FR) CD 537325-2
102-B	Natural Mystic Rhythm Track	" , "

Note: The Disco (US) 12" of "Natural Mystic" credits Lee Perry with composition. Bob recorded the song again in 1977 for the Island label, and all Island issues credit Bob Marley with composition. The mix of "Rainbow Country" and its dub used on Lagoon CD are nearly a minute and a half shorter than the mixes used on the Daddy Cool (UK) 12" and JAD CD.

WAILERS June 1975

Bob Marley, vocal (-1), harmony vocal (-2 or -3), and guitar; Peter Tosh, vocal (-2), harmony vocal (-1 or -2) and guitar; Bunny Wailer, vocal (-3) or harmony vocal (-1 or -2) and percussion; Rita Marley, harmony vocal; Marcia Griffiths, harmony vocal; Judy Mowatt, harmony vocal; Carlton Barrett, drums; Aston "Family Man" Barrett, bass; Al Anderson, guitar; Tyrone Downie, keyboards; Alvin "Seeco" Patterson, percussion; Lee Jaffe, harmonica (-4); recorded live at Carib Theatre in Kingston, Jamaica.

Curfew (Burnin' And Lootin') (-1)	unissued
Slave Driver (-1)	"
Can't Blame The Youth (-2)	"
Arab's Oil Weapon (-3)	"
Get Up Stand Up (-1, -2)	"
Road Block (-1, -4)	"

Note: This appearance was on a show headlined by American soul artist Marvin Gaye.

BOB MARLEY & THE WAILERS July 17, 1975

Bob Marley, vocal and guitar; Rita Marley, harmony vocal; Judy Mowatt, harmony vocal; Carlton Barrett, drums; Aston "Family Man" Barrett, bass; Al Anderson, guitar; Tyrone Downie, keyboards; Alvin "Seeco" Patterson, percussion; Lee Jaffe, harmonica (-1); Dave Harper, engineer; recorded live at the Lyceum, London; Chris Blackwell, Danny Holloway and Steve Smith, production.

I Shot The Sheriff	Tuff Gong lp 422-848 243-1
Road Block (-1)	unissued
Unknown titles	"

Note: This show was remembered by Wailers band members as consisting of a virtually identical song list to that of the next show, presented the next night at the same venue.

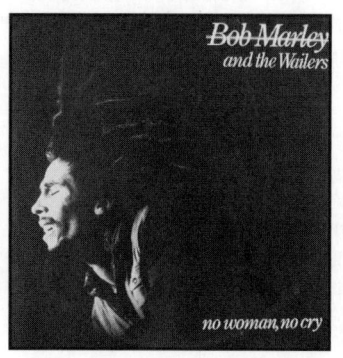

BOB MARLEY & THE WAILERS   July 18, 1975

Bob Marley, vocal and guitar; Rita Marley, harmony vocal; Judy Mowatt, harmony vocal; Carlton Barrett, drums; Aston "Family Man" Barrett, bass; Al Anderson, guitar; Tyrone Downie, keyboards; Alvin "Seeco" Patterson, percussion; Lee Jaffe, harmonica (-1); Dave Harper, engineer; recorded at the Lyceum, London; Chris Blackwell, Danny Holloway and Steve Smith, production.

1DJ7-A	Trench Town Rock	Island (UK) promo 1DJ7, Island ILPS 9376
	Slave Driver	unissued
	Burnin' & Lootin'	Island ILPS 9376
	Concrete Jungle	unissued
IS-037-B	Kinky Reggae	Tuff Gong, Island (UK) WIP 6244, Island ILPS 9376
	Midnight Ravers	unissued
	Lively Up Yourself	Island ILPS 9376
TS-7830-A	No Woman, No Cry	Tuff Gong, Island (UK) WIP 6244, Island ILPS 9376
	" (1984 remix)	Island lp 90169-1
	Road Block (-1)	unissued
	Belly Full	Island ILPS 9376
	Knotty Dread	unissued
1DJ7-B	I Shot The Sheriff	Island (UK) promo 1DJ7, Island ILPS 9376
	Nice Time	unissued
	Talking Blues (-1)	"
	Bend Down Low	"
	So Jah Seh	"
	Get Up, Stand Up	Island ILPS 9376

BUNNY WAILER   SOLOMONIC REGGAE STAR PETER TOSH (-3)   circa: Summer 1975

Bunny Wailer, vocal, harmony vocal, repeater (-1), funda (-2); Peter Tosh, guitar and melodica; Carlton Barrett, drums; Aston "Family Man" Barrett, bass and guitar (-2); Earl "Chinna" Smith, guitar; "Fratter," guitar; Tyrone Downie, keyboards; H. Butler, keyboards; Tommy McCook, flute (-2); Bobby Ellis, trumpet; Herman Marquis, alto sax; Richard "Dirty Harry" Hall, tenor sax; Willie Pep, bongos; Karl Pitterson, engineer; recorded Aquarius Studio; twenty-four track; Bunny Wailer, production.

BW 2733-A	Rasta Man (-1)	Solomonic, Solomonic lp, Island ILPS 9415
	Rasta Man (Dubd'sco) (-1)	Solomonic lp AP 007-34
I-2 Bunny 1-A2	Amagideon (Armagedon) (-2)	Island (UK) 12" Bunny 1, Solomonic lp, Island ILPS 9415
	Amagideon (Armagedon) (-2)	Island (UK) 12" IPR 2025
	Armagedon (Dubd'sco) (-2)	Solomonic lp
DSR 7177-A	Anti-Apartheid (-2) (-3)	Solomonic
DSR 7178-B	Solidarity (-2) (-3)	"

Note: "Amagideon (Armagedon)" on Island (UK) 12" IPR 2025 is a dub version different from the title found on Island (UK) 12" Bunny 1 or on Solomonic/Island lps. "Anti-Apartheid" and "Solidarity" are both version tracks of "Amagideon" credited to Solomonic Reggae Star Peter Tosh. Jean Watt is credited with the composition of "Rasta Man" on Solomonic single, but Solomonic and Island albums credit Bunny O'Reilly (Bunny Wailer).

BUNNY WAILER   circa: Summer 1975

Bunny Wailer, vocal, harmony vocal, guitar and percussion; Carlton Barrett, drums; Aston "Family Man" Barrett, bass; Peter Tosh, guitar; Earl "Chinna" Smith, guitar; M. Murray, guitar; Tyrone Downie, keyboards; Harold Butler, keyboards; Richard "Dirty Harry" Hall, tenor sax; Herman Marquis, alto sax; Bobby Ellis, trumpet; Karl Pitterson, engineer; recorded Aquarius Studio; twenty-four track; Bunny Wailer, production.

The Oppressed Song	Solomonic lp, Island ILPS 9415

BUNNY WAILER   circa: Summer 1975

Bunny Wailer, vocal, harmony vocal and percussion; Carlton Barrett, drums; Robbie Shakespeare, bass; Aston "Family Man" Barrett,

Alvin "Seeco" Patterson on tour in Europe, 1977. Photo by Kate Simon.

guitar; Tyrone Downie, keyboards; Tommy McCook, tenor sax and flute; Karl Pitterson, engineer; recorded Aquarius Studio; twenty-four track; Bunny Wailer, production.

| I-2 Bunny 1-B2 | Blackheart Man | Island (UK) 12" Bunny 1, Solomonic lp, Island ILPS 9415 |

BUNNY WAILER   circa: Summer 1975

Bunny Wailer, vocal and harmony vocal; Peter Tosh, guitar; Carlton Barrett, drums; Robbie Shakespeare, bass; Earl "Chinna" Smith, guitar; Bernard "Touter" Harvey, keyboards; H. Butler, keyboards; Tommy McCook, tenor sax; Richard "Dirty Harry" Hall, tenor sax; Bobby Ellis, trumpet; M. West, horn; Karl Pitterson, engineer; recorded Aquarius Studio; twenty-four track; Bunny Wailer, production.

Fig Tree	Solomonic lp, Island ILPS 9415
Fig Tree	Island (UK) 12" IPR 2025
Fig Tree (Dubd'sco)	Solomonic lp

Note: "Fig Tree" on Island (UK) 12" is a dub version different from that found on the Solomonic lp.

BUNNY WAILER   circa: Summer 1975

Bunny Wailer, vocal, harmony vocal, bass, timbales, and bongos; Peter Tosh, guitar; Carlton Barrett, drums; Aston "Family Man" Barrett, guitar and keyboards; Tyrone Downie, keyboards; H. Butler, keyboards; Tommy McCook, tenor sax; Richard "Dirty Harry" Hall, tenor sax; Karl Pitterson, engineer; recorded Aquarius Studio; twenty-four track; Bunny Wailer, production.

| Reincarnated Souls | Solomonic lp, Island ILPS 9415 |

BUNNY WAILER   circa: Summer 1975

Bunny Wailer, vocal, harmony vocal, guitar, repeater, funda, and percussion; Carlton Barrett, funda; Robbie Shakespeare, bass; Karl Pitterson, guitar; Tyrone Downie, keyboards and melodica; Neville Garrick, percussion; Karl Pitterson, engineer; recorded Aquarius Studio; twenty-four track; Bunny Wailer, production.

| IPR 2003-B | This Train | Island (UK) 12" IPR-2003, Solomonic lp, Island ILPS 9415 |

BOB MARLEY & THE WAILERS   August 10, 1975

Bob Marley, vocal and guitar; Rita Marley, harmony vocal; Judy Mowatt, harmony vocal; Carlton Barrett, drums; Aston "Family Man" Barrett, bass; Al Anderson, guitar; Tyrone Downie, keyboards; Alvin "Seeco" Patterson, percussion; recorded live for the Manhattan Transfer television program.

| Kinky Reggae | unissued |
| Get Up Stand Up | " |

BOB MARLEY & THE WAILERS   August 29, 1975

Bob Marley, vocal and guitar; Rita Marley, harmony vocal; Judy Mowatt, harmony vocal; Carlton Barrett, drums; Aston "Family Man" Barrett, bass; Al Anderson, guitar; Tyrone Downie, keyboards; Alvin "Seeco" Patterson, percussion; recorded live at the National Arena in Kingston, Jamaica.

Trench Town Rock	unissued
Talking Blues	"
Belly Full	"
Road Block	"
Natty Dread	"

BOB MARLEY & THE WAILERS   August/September 1975

Bob Marley, vocal and guitar; Rita Marley, harmony vocal; Marcia Griffiths, harmony vocal; Judy Mowatt, harmony vocal; Carlton Barrett, drums; Aston "Family Man" Barrett, bass; Earl "Chinna" Smith, guitar; Donald Kinsey, guitar; Tyrone Downie, keyboards, harmony vocal (-1); Bernard "Touter" Harvey, keyboards; Alvin "Seeco" Patterson, percussion; Tommy McCook, tenor sax (-2); Sylvan Morris, recording engineer; recorded Harry J Studio; sixteen track; Alex Sadkin, mixing engineer; mixed Criteria Studio, Miami by Aston "Family Man" Barrett and Chris Blackwell; Wailers, production. Overdubs 1999: Steven Tyler, vocal (-3); Joe Perry, guitar (-3); Eric Adams, drums (-3); Guru, DJ vocal (-4); Damian Marley, drum program (-4); M. Morgan, drum program (-4); D. Cole, drum program (-4); F. Lyfook, bass synth (-4).

	Positive Vibration (-1)	Tuff Gong lp, Island ILPS 9383
DSR 2376-A	Roots Rock Reggae (-1) (-2)	Tuff Gong, Island (US) IS-060, Tuff Gong lp, Island ILPS 9383
	" (alt. mix)	Tuff Gong/Island CD 440 063 446-2
	Roots Rock Dub	"
	Roots Rock Reggae	unissued
	" (-3) (demo)	"
	" (-3)	Tuff Gong/Island CD 314 546 404-2
WIPX 1536-1U	Johnny Was	Island (UK) WIP 6296, Tuff Gong lp, Island ILPS 9383
	" (alternate mix)	Tuff Gong/Island CD 440 063 446-2
	Johnny Was	unissued
	" (-4) (demo)	"
	" (-4)	Tuff Gong/Island CD 314 546 404-2
WIPX 1537-1U	Cry To Me	Island (UK) WIP 6296, Island (US) IS-060, Tuff Gong lp, Island ILPS 9383
	Want More	Tuff Gong lp, Island ILPS 9383
	" (alternate mix)	Tuff Gong/Island CD 440 063 446-2
IS 072 A	Who The Cap Fit	Island (US) IS-072, Tuff Gong lp, Island ILPS 9383
	" (alternate mix)	unissued
IS 072 B	Version (Who The Cap Fit)	Island (US) IS-072
	Night Shift	Tuff Gong lp, Island ILPS 9383

Note: "Johnny Was" is said to be about Trevor Wilson, Delroy Wilson's younger brother, who penned the reggae classic "Johnny Too Bad," a song originally recorded by the Slickers and later rewritten and recorded by Bunny Wailer. Rita Marley is credited with the composition of "Johnny Was." "Who The Cap Fit" is the same song Bob previously recorded in 1971 as "Man To Man." The original Upsetter issue of "Man To Man" credits composition to B. Marley and L. Perry. "Who The Cap Fit" credits composition to A. Barrett and C. Barrett. Vincent "Tata" Ford is credited with writing "Positive Vibration" and "Roots Rock Reggae." Composition of "Want More" is credited to Aston Barrett.

BOB MARLEY & THE WAILERS   late August/early September 1975

Bob Marley, vocal and guitar; Rita Marley, harmony vocal; Marcia Griffiths, harmony vocal; Judy Mowatt, harmony vocal; Carlton Barrett, drums; Aston "Family Man" Barrett, bass; Al Anderson, guitar; Tyrone Downie, keyboards; Lee Perry, percussion; Sylvan Morris, engineer; recorded and mixed at Harry J Studio; sixteen track; Bob Marley and Lee Perry, production.

BM 2381	Jah Live	Tuff Gong, Island (UK) WIP 6265, Island lp MSTDA 1, Tuff Gong (UK) CD TGCBX 1
DSR 5301	" (1982 remix)	Tuff Gong
BM 2382	Concrete	Tuff Gong, Island (UK) WIP 6265, Tuff Gong/Island CD 440 063 446-2
RMI-3-83-B	" (alt. mix)	Tuff Gong

Note: The alternate mix of "Concrete" omits the trademark Marley scream from the beginning. According to Aston "Family Man" Barrett, this scream was Bob's imitation of Martha Velez clearing her throat prior to singing. The original 7" release came in a picture sleeve with a drawing of Bob on one side and a drawing of Haile Selassie on the other. Selassie was reported to have passed away on August 27, 1975, and "Jah Live" was cut within days of the event. Composition is credited to Lee Perry and Bob Marley.

BOB MARLEY & THE WAILERS   September 1975

Bob Marley, vocal and guitar; Rita Marley, harmony vocal; Marcia Griffiths, harmony vocal; Judy Mowatt, harmony vocal; Carlton Barrett, drums; Aston "Family Man" Barrett, bass; Earl "Chinna" Smith, guitar; Donald Kinsey, guitar; Tyrone Downie, keyboards; Bernard "Touter" Harvey, keyboards; Ian Winter, keyboards; Tommy McCook, tenor sax; Glen DaCosta, alto sax; David Madden, trumpet; Vin Gordon, trombone; Alvin "Seeco" Patterson, percussion; Errol Thompson, recording engineer; recorded Joe Gibbs Studio; sixteen track; Alex Sadkin, mixing engineer; mixed Criteria Studio, Miami by Aston "Family Man" Barrett and Chris Blackwell; Wailers, production.

DSR 2377 B	War (-1)	Tuff Gong, Tuff Gong lp, Island ILPS 9383
	" (alternate mix)	Tuff Gong/Island CD 440 063 446-2
	" (long mix)	unissued

Note: The lyrics of "War" were drawn primarily from a speech given to the United Nations by Haile Selassie on October 4, 1963. Composition of this track is credited to Bob Marley on the Tuff Gong single but is assigned to Alan [Allan] Cole and Carlton Barrett on the Island lp. The long mix contains an additional 35 seconds of the Selassie speech sung by Bob.

WAILERS   FAMILY MAN & REBEL ARMS   circa: September 1975

Aston "Family Man" Barrett, bass, drum machine, and synthesizer; Ian Winter, piano and vocal; Aston "Family Man" Barrett, engineer; recorded at the Tuff Gong rehearsal studio in the rear of 56 Hope Road; Aston "Family Man" Barrett, production.

FM 2007	Work	Tuff Gong, Heartbeat CD HB 157
FM 2009 (A)	Guided Missile	" , "

Note: "Guided Missile" is a version track of "Work." Although these tracks do not feature Bob, Peter, or Bunny, they are included because the original release credited the Wailers and was distributed on the Wailers' label. Heartbeat CD credits Family Man & Rebel Arms.

BOB MARLEY & THE WAILERS   circa: September 1975

Bob Marley, vocal and guitar; Rita Marley, harmony vocal; Marcia Griffiths, harmony vocal; Judy Mowatt, harmony vocal; Carlton Barrett, drums; Aston "Family Man" Barrett, bass; Earl "Chinna" Smith, guitar; Al Anderson, guitar; Tyrone Downie, keyboards; Bernard "Touter" Harvey, keyboards; Alvin "Seeco" Patterson, percussion; Sylvan Morris, recording engineer; recorded Harry J Studio; sixteen track; Errol Brown and Aston "Family Man" Barrett, mixing engineers; mixed Tuff Gong Studio circa 1981; Wailers, production.

TG 457-A	I Know	Tuff Gong 12", Tuff Gong lp, Island (US) lp 90085-1
TG 77056	"	"
DSR 3161-A	"	"
DSR 2918-A	Version	"
DSR 3162-B	"	"

Note: "I Know" was first released in 1981 shortly after Bob's passing.

BOB MARLEY & THE WAILERS circa: September 1975

Bob Marley, vocal, harmony vocal, and guitar; Carlton Barrett, drums; Aston "Family Man" Barrett, bass; Earl "Chinna" Smith, guitar; Al Anderson, guitar; Tyrone Downie, keyboards; Bernard "Touter" Harvey, keyboards; Alvin "Seeco" Patterson, percussion; Sylvan Morris, engineer; recorded Harry J Studio; sixteen track; Wailers, production.

BM 2816	Rat Race	Tuff Gong pre-release
BM 2817	Part II	"

Note: BM 2816 evidently appeared only as a blank label 7" pre-release. BM 2817 is also the version side of most copies of BM 2812-A listed next. This take is very different, both lyrically and musically to the better known BM 2812-A, and it has a loose earlier feel. Bob sings, "Some are lawful, some are bastard, some are jacket." Jacket is a term used for a child in the family not actually sired by the patriarch. He then sings, "Some are gorgon, some are hooligan, some are guinea gog." Guinea gog means a criminal big shot. Bob then sings, "Some are chicken, some a' scratch, some are bun, some a' batch." Bun means cheat or an unwanted child, and batch refers to cutting a batch of different vocals using the same rhythm track. The first part of the line needs no direct explanation, but it contains an indirect reference to producer Lee Perry, whose early nickname was "Chicken Scratch."

BOB MARLEY & THE WAILERS circa: September 1975

Bob Marley, vocal and guitar; Rita Marley, harmony vocal; Marcia Griffiths, harmony vocal; Judy Mowatt, harmony vocal; Carlton Barrett, drums; Aston "Family Man" Barrett, bass; Earl "Chinna" Smith, guitar; Al Anderson, guitar; Tyrone Downie, keyboards; Bernard "Touter" Harvey, keyboards; Tommy McCook, tenor sax (-1); Glen DaCosta, alto sax (-1); David Madden, trumpet (-1); Vin Gordon, trombone (-1); Alvin "Seeco" Patterson, percussion; Sylvan Morris, recording engineer; recorded Harry J Studio; sixteen track; Alex Sadkin, mixing engineer; mixed Criteria Studio, Miami by Aston "Family Man" Barrett and Chris Blackwell; Wailers, production.

BM-2812-A	Rat Race (-1)	Tuff Gong, Tuff Gong lp, Island ILPS 9383
BM 2837 B	Part II (-1)	"
	Crazy Baldhead	Tuff Gong lp, Island ILPS 9383
	" (alternate mix)	Tuff Gong/Island CD 440 063 446-2
	" (no harmony)	unissued
	Crazy Baldhead Version	"

Note: The version side of the labeled Tuff Gong 7" release of BM-2812-A "Rat Race" is most commonly BM 2817, previously listed. Some copies have an alternate version mix BM 2837 B which features horns. Both BM-2812-A and the earlier voicing BM 2816 are structured on the same drum, bass and guitar riddim, but everything else is different. Rita Marley is credited with the composition of "Rat Race." Rita shares credit with Vincent "Tata" Ford for writing "Crazy Baldhead."

BOB MARLEY & THE WAILERS circa: September 1975

Bob Marley, vocal and guitar; Rita Marley, harmony vocal; Marcia Griffiths, harmony vocal; Judy Mowatt, harmony vocal; Carlton Barrett, drums; Aston "Family Man" Barrett, bass; Earl "Chinna" Smith, guitar; Donald Kinsey, guitar; Tyrone Downie, keyboards; Bernard "Touter" Harvey, keyboards; Tommy McCook, flute; Alvin "Seeco" Patterson, percussion; Sylvan Morris, engineer; Karl Pitterson, engineer; recorded Harry J Studio; sixteen track; Lee Hulko, mixing engineer; mixed by Aston "Family Man" Barrett, Chris Blackwell and Karl Pitterson; mixed at Sterling Sound (US); Wailers, production.

	Roots	unissued
IS 092 B-1	Roots	Island (US) IS-092, Island lp 90520-1
	" (alternate mix)	unissued
	Roots Version	unknown issue

Note: The authors have heard a tape of "Roots Version" taken from a single, but can supply no details.

BOB MARLEY & THE WAILERS   circa: September 1975

Bob Marley, vocal and guitar; Rita Marley, harmony vocal; Marcia Griffiths, harmony vocal; Judy Mowatt, harmony vocal; Carlton Barrett, drums; Aston "Family Man" Barrett, bass; Earl "Chinna" Smith, guitar; Donald Kinsey, guitar; Tyrone Downie, keyboards; Bernard "Touter" Harvey, keyboards; Alvin "Seeco" Patterson, percussion; Sylvan Morris, engineer; Karl Pitterson, engineer; recorded Harry J Studio; sixteen track; mixed at Island Studio.

The Heathen	unissued
One Love/People Get Ready	"

Note: These tracks were mixed at Island Studio in early 1977, but Bob subsequently recorded alternate vocal tracks on these riddims. The alternate vocal takes were recorded in early 1977 and were included in the 1977 "Exodus" album. These alternates are listed in early 1977.

BOB MARLEY & THE WAILERS   circa: September 1975

Bob Marley, vocal (-1) or harmony vocal (-2,-3) and guitar; Bunny Wailer, vocal (-2) or harmony vocal (-1,-3) and percussion; Peter Tosh, vocal (-3) or harmony vocal (-1,-2) and guitar; Carlton Barrett, drums; Aston "Family Man" Barrett, bass; Earl "Chinna" Smith, guitar; Donald Kinsey, guitar; Earl "Wya" Lindo, keyboards; Tyrone Downie, keyboards; Alvin "Seeco" Patterson, percussion; live at National Stadium in Kingston, Jamaica.

Trench Town Rock (-1)	unissued
Blackheart Man (-2)	"
Mark Of The Beast (-3)	"
unknown titles	"

Note: The Jackson Five were the headliners on this show.

BOB MARLEY & THE WAILERS   circa: October 4, 1975

Bob Marley, vocal (-1) or harmony vocal (-2, -3) and guitar; Bunny Wailer, vocal (-2) or harmony vocal (-1, -3) and percussion; Peter Tosh, vocal (-3) or harmony vocal (-1, -2) and guitar; Rita Marley, harmony vocal (-4); Marcia Griffiths, harmony vocal (-4); Judy Mowatt, harmony vocal (-4); Carlton Barrett, drums; Aston "Family Man" Barrett, bass; Earl "Chinna" Smith, guitar; Donald Kinsey, guitar; Tyrone Downie, keyboards; Bernard "Touter" Harvey, keyboards; unknown tenor sax (-5); unknown trumpet (-5); Vin Gordon, trombone (-5); Alvin "Seeco" Patterson, percussion; live at National Stadium, Kingston.

Rasta Man Chant (-1)	unissued
Nice Time (-1) (-5)	"
Simmer Down (-1) (-4) (-5)	"
One Love (-1) (-4)	"
Dreamland (-2) (-4)	"
Battering Down Sentence (-2) (-5)	"
Mark Of The Beast (-3)	"
Can't Blame The Youth (-3)	"
Legalize It (-3) (-4)	"
So Jah Seh (-1) (-4) (-5)	"
No Woman No Cry (-1) (-4)	"
Jah Live (-1) (-4)	"

Bob Marley, vocal; Stevie Wonder, vocal and keyboards; unknown drums; unknown bass; unknown guitar; unknown keyboards; unknown male and female harmony singers.

I Shot The Sheriff (-1) (-4)	unissued

Note: This show headlined by Stevie Wonder is remembered as the Wailers' final reunion. In the following months Bob would begin relentless rehearsals in preparation for an April/May tour of North America.

BOB MARLEY & THE WAILERS   May 26, 1976

Bob Marley, vocal and guitar; Rita Marley, harmony vocal; Marcia Griffiths, harmony vocal; Judy Mowatt, harmony vocal; Carlton Barrett, drums; Aston "Family Man" Barrett, bass; Earl "Chinna" Smith, guitar; Donald Kinsey, guitar; Earl "Wya" Lindo, keyboards; Tyrone Downie, keyboards; Alvin "Seeco" Patterson, percussion; Wally Heider, recording engineer; recorded live at the Roxy Theatre, Los Angeles; sixteen track; Ingmar King, remix engineer; Wailers, production.

	Trench Town Rock	Tuff Gong/Island CD 440 063 446-2
	Curfew (Burnin' And Lootin')	"
	Them Belly Full	"
	Rebel Music	"
	I Shot The Sheriff	"
	Want More	"
	No Woman No Cry	Tuff Gong (UK) CD TGCBX 1
	Lively Up Yourself	Tuff Gong/Island CD 440 063 446-2
	Roots Rock Reggae	"
	Rat Race	"
	Positive Vibration	Tuff Gong/Island CD B0000516-02
	Medley: Get Up Stand Up	"
	No More Trouble	"
	War	"

Note: Several selections from this show, including "No Woman No Cry" and "Want More" were remixed by Ingmar King in 1991 for possible inclusion on Tuff Gong TGCBX 1. "No Woman No Cry" is also on both Tuff Gong/Island CDs, and CD B0000516-02 includes all titles.

BOB MARLEY & THE WAILERS   circa: October 1976

Bob Marley, vocal and guitar; Rita Marley, harmony vocal; Marcia Griffiths, harmony vocal; Judy Mowatt, harmony vocal; Carlton Barrett, drums; Aston "Family Man" Barrett, bass, guitar, and organ; Tyrone Downie, keyboards; Alvin "Seeco" Patterson, percussion; Lee Perry, engineer; recorded Black Ark Studio; Bob Marley and Lee Perry, production.

Smile 1976 B	Smile Jamaica Part One	Tuff Gong
BFM 1977 A	"	Tuff Gong
DSR 5300	" (1981 remix)	Tuff Gong
BFM 1977 B	Smile Jamaica Part Two	Tuff Gong

BOB MARLEY & THE WAILERS   circa: October 1976

Bob Marley, vocal and guitar; Rita Marley, harmony vocal; Marcia Griffiths, harmony vocal; Judy Mowatt, harmony vocal; Neville Garrick, harmony vocal; Antonio "Gilly" Gilbert, harmony vocal; Carlton Barrett, drums; Aston "Family Man" Barrett, bass, guitar and organ; Tyrone Downie, keyboards; David Madden, trumpet; Glen DaCosta, tenor sax; Vin Gordon, trombone; Alvin "Seeco" Patterson, percussion; Sylvan Morris, engineer; recorded Harry J Studio; sixteen track; Bob Marley and Lee Perry, production.

Smile 1976 A	Smile Jamaica Part One	Tuff Gong, Island (UK) WIP 6640, Island (UK) 12",
		Tuff Gong (UK) CD TGCBX 1
BM 3400 A	"	Tuff Gong
BM 3436 A	"	Tuff Gong
BM 3400 B	Smile Jamaica Part Two	Tuff Gong, Tuff Gong/Island CD 440 063 446-2
BM 3436 B	"	Tuff Gong

PETER TOSH   circa: 1976

Peter Tosh, vocal and guitar; unknown drums; unknown bass; unknown guitar; unknown keyboards; recorded in rehearsal in Kingston, Jamaica.

	What You Gonna Do	unissued
	Igziabeher	"

No Sympathy	unissued
Ketchy Shubby	"
Legalize It	"
Brand New Secondhand	"
Why Must I Cry	"

Note: This rehearsal session is said to include members of Eric Clapton's 1976 touring band. Peter played several dates at the Beacon Theatre in New York City in mid-October.

PETER TOSH   **November 26, 1976**

Peter Tosh, vocal and guitar; Sly Dunbar, drums; Robbie Shakespeare, bass; Al Anderson, guitar; Donald Kinsey, guitar; Earl "Wya" Lindo, keyboards; Errol "Tarzan" Nelson, keyboards; recorded live at the Sanders Theatre in Cambridge, Massachusetts.

Instrumental Intro	Columbia/Legacy CD CK 85478
Igziabeher	"
400 Years	"
No Sympathy	"
Burial	"
Mark Of The Beast	"
Babylon Queendom	"
Why Must I Cry	"
Whatcha Gonna Do	"
Steppin' Razor	"
Ketchy Shubby	"

PETER TOSH   **circa: late 1976**

Peter Tosh, vocal, harmony vocals, guitar, and keyboards; Sly Dunbar, drums; Robbie Shakespeare, bass; Al Anderson, guitar; Earl "Wya" Lindo, keyboards; Karl Pitterson, engineer; recorded Randy's Studio 17; sixteen track; Peter Tosh, production.

	400 Years	unissued
DSR 9122-A	Jah Man	Intel Diplo pre-release
DSR 9123-B	Hammer	"
	Mark Of The Beast	unissued

Note: "Jah Man" was apparently only issued on blank pre-release coupled with "Hammer," which also saw release on an Intel Diplo label issue paired with "Can't Blame The Youth." The title is as Peter's manager Herbie Miller remembers it, and as written on the only copy known to the authors. "Hammer" was called "Hammer Dem Dung" on a poster for the Jamaican single release of the title.

PETER TOSH
circa: late 1976

Peter Tosh, vocal, harmony vocal, guitar, and keyboards; Bunny Wailer, harmony vocal; Sly Dunbar, drums; Robbie Shakespeare, bass; Al Anderson, guitar; Earl "Wya" Lindo, keyboards; Karl Pitterson, engineer; recorded Randy's Studio 17; sixteen track; Peter Tosh, production.

DSR 5679-A	Vampire	Intel Diplo	
DSR 7167-A	"	"	
DSR 5680-B	Dracula	"	, Columbia CD C3K 65064
DSR 7169-B	"	"	
PT-3011	Babylon Queendom (mix 1)	Intel Diplo	
DSR 3118-A	" (mix 2)	"	
PT-3127	" (mix 3)	"	
DSR 3632-A	" (mix 4)	"	
	" (rough mix)	unissued	
PT-3310	Iration (mix 1)	Intel Diplo	
DSR 3119-B	" (mix 2)	"	
PT-3128	" (mix 3)	"	
DSR 3633-B	" (mix 4)	"	
DS 20370-B	Can't Blame The Youth	Intel Diplo	
9123 B	"	"	

Note: "Dracula" is the version track of "Vampire," and should not be confused with "Dracula," a version of "Who Is Mr. Brown" recorded in January 1971. "Iration" is the version track of "Babylon Queendom," not to be confused with the like-titled "Iration," a version cut of "Ketchy Shubby." The different mixes of "Babylon Queendom" are not noted on the labels.

BOB MARLEY & THE WAILERS
December 5, 1976

Bob Marley, vocal; Rita Marley, harmony vocal; Judy Mowatt, harmony vocal; Carlton Barrett, drums; Earl "Chinna" Smith, guitar; Tyrone Downie, bass and keyboards; Earl "Wya" Lindo, keyboards; Glen DaCosta, tenor sax; David Madden, trumpet; Alvin "Seeco" Patterson, percussion; recorded live at National Stadium, Kingston at the Smile Jamaica Concert.

	War	BBC Film
	No More Trouble	unissued
	Get Up Stand Up	"
	Crazy Baldhead	"
	Positive Vibration	"
	Smile Jamaica	"
	Rat Race	"
	Trench Town Rock	"
	Keep On Moving	"
	Want More	"
	Belly Full	"
	Jah Live	"
	Rasta Man Chant	"
	Road Block	"
	So Jah Seh	"

Note: Bob appeared on this show despite a well-publicized attempt on his life two days before. After his appearance, Bob left Jamaica and showed up a few weeks later in London, England, where he began rehearsals and recording at Island Studio.

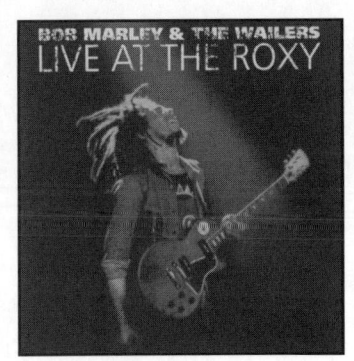

PETER TOSH
circa: early 1977

Peter Tosh, vocal, harmony vocal, guitar, keyboards (-1), and percussion; Bunny Wailer, harmony vocal; Sly Dunbar, drums; Robbie Shakespeare, bass; Al Anderson, guitar (-2); Karl Pitterson, guitar (-3); Earl "Wya" Lindo, keyboards; Noel "Scully" Simms, percussion; Karl Pitterson, engineer; recorded Randy's Studio 17; sixteen track; overdubs at Aquarius, Joe Gibbs, and Dynamic Studios; mixed at Criteria, Miami, by Karl Pitterson, Alex Sadkin, and Jack Nuber; Peter Tosh, production.

	Get Up Stand Up (-2)	Intel Diplo lp
XSS162931-2A	Get Up Stand Up (mono) (-2)	Columbia 12" ASF 310, Intel Diplo lp, Columbia, lp 34670
XSS162932-2A	" (stereo) (-2)	Columbia 12" ASF 310, Intel Diplo lp, Columbia lp 34670
	Stepping Razor (-2)	Intel Diplo lp, Columbia lp 34670
	Downpressor Man (-1) (-3)	" , "
	Apartheid (-1) (-3)	" , "

Note: The original voicing of "Get Up Stand Up" included the line "Don't be no nigger now." Herbie Miller, Tosh's manager, reports that CBS demanded that the phrase be deleted and Peter re-voiced that part of the vocal. The first voicing did appear on early copies of the Jamaican release of the "Equal Rights" album with matrix numbers reading DSR 9413 A and DSR 9414 B.

PETER TOSH
circa: early 1977

Peter Tosh, vocal, harmony vocal, and guitar; Bunny Wailer, harmony vocal; Sly Dunbar, drums; Robbie Shakespeare, bass; Harold Butler, clavinet; Karl Pitterson, engineer; recorded Randy's Studio 17; sixteen track; mixed Criteria, Miami by Karl Pitterson, Alex Sadkin, and Jack Nuber; Peter Tosh, production.

	Equal Rights	Intel Diplo lp, Columbia lp 34670

PETER TOSH
circa: early 1977

Peter Tosh, vocal, harmony vocal, guitar, and clavinet; Bunny Wailer, harmony vocal; Carlton Barrett, drums; Robbie Shakespeare, bass; Al Anderson, guitar (-1); Tyrone Downie, keyboards; Richard "Dirty Harry" Hall, tenor sax; Bobby Ellis, trumpet; Karl Pitterson, engineer; recorded Randy's Studio 17; sixteen track; mixed Criteria, Miami by Karl Pitterson, Alex Sadkin, and Jack Nuber; Peter Tosh, production.

	I Am That I Am	Intel Diplo lp, Columbia lp 34670
	Jah Guide (-1)	" , "
DSR 4222-A	African	Intel Diplo, Intel Diplo lp, Columbia lp 34670
DSR 4223-B	African Version	"

BOB MARLEY & THE WAILERS circa: early 1977

Bob Marley, vocal and guitar; Carlton Barrett, drums; Aston "Family Man" Barrett, bass; Julian "Junior" Marvin, guitar; Tyrone Downie, keyboards; Alvin "Seeco" Patterson, percussion; rehearsal in London, England.

            Jamming   unissued

BOB MARLEY & THE WAILERS January/February 1977

Bob Marley, vocal and guitar; Rita Marley, harmony vocal; Marcia Griffiths, harmony vocal; Judy Mowatt, harmony vocal; Carlton Barrett, drums; Aston "Family Man" Barrett, bass; Julian "Junior" Marvin, guitar; Tyrone Downie, keyboards and harmony vocal (-1); Alvin "Seeco" Patterson, percussion; David Madden, trumpet (-1); Glen DaCosta, alto sax (-1); Vin Gordon, trombone (-1); Karl Pitterson, engineer; recorded at Island Studios in London, England; twenty four track; Lee Hulko, mixing engineer; mixed by Aston "Family Man" Barrett, Chris Blackwell and Karl Pitterson; mixed at Sterling Sound (US); Wailers, production. 1984 remix of "Exodus" by Eric Thorngren; 1984 remix of "Waiting In Vain" by Julian Mendelsohn; 1997 remix by Bill Laswell.

	Exodus (-1)	unissued
	Exodus (-1)	"
	" (alternate mix)	"
TS 3880-A	Exodus (-1)	Tuff Gong, Island (UK) WIP 6390, Island (UK) 12"
		IPR 2000-A, Island (US) IS-0898,
		Tuff Gong lp, Island DLPS 9498
	" (1984 remix)	Island (UK) 12 IS 236, Island lp 90169-1
	" (1997 remix)	Island CD 314 524 419-2
TS 3880-B	Exodus Instrumental	Tuff Gong, Island (UK) WIP 6390, Island (UK) 12",
		IPR 2000-B, Island (US) IS-0898
	Waiting In Vain	unissued
	Waiting In Vain	"
	Waiting In Vain	Tuff Gong/Island CD 314 586 408-2
	" (alt. mix)	unissued
	" (alt. mix)	"
	" (alt. mix)	"

   Note: Unissued alternate takes from this session and the January/February sessions that follow are alternate lead vocals over a single riddim track. Marcia Griffiths has said that Bob and Rita were frequently at odds during the course of these sessions and that Rita often found an ally in Judy Mowatt. Marcia has said that the two sometimes boycotted the sessions to protest Bob's behavior with a current love interest. Thus, Marcia says that she often voiced all of the I Three backing vocals by herself. We have listed the session credits as given on the albums.

BOB MARLEY & THE WAILERS January/February 1977

Bob Marley, vocal, harmony vocal (-1); Rita Marley, harmony vocal (-2); Marcia Griffiths, harmony vocal (-2); Judy Mowatt, harmony vocal (-2); Carlton Barrett, drums; Aston "Family Man" Barrett, bass; Julian "Junior" Marvin, guitar; Tyrone Downie, keyboards and harmony vocal (-1); Alvin "Seeco" Patterson, percussion; Karl Pitterson, engineer; recorded at Island Studios in London, England; twenty-four track; Lee

Hulko, mixing engineer; mixed by Aston "Family Man" Barrett, Chris Blackwell, and Karl Pitterson; mixed at Sterling Sound (US); Wailers, production. 1997 remix by Bill Laswell.

IS 092 A-2	Waiting In Vain (-1)	Island (US) IS-092, Island (UK) WIP 640, Tuff Gong lp, Island DLPS 9498
12 IS 180-A	" (1984 remix)	Island (UK) 12 IS 180, Island lp 90169-1
	" (Advert Mix)	Tuff Gong CD TGCBX 1
	" (1997 remix)	Island CD 314 524 419-2
DSR 2642-B	Waiting In Vain Dub	Tuff Gong
	She's Gone (-2)	unissued
	She's Gone (-2)	Tuff Gong lp, Island ILPS 9517
	Crisis (-2)	unissued
	Crisis (-2)	Tuff Gong lp, Island ILPS 9517
	Crisis Version (-2) (vocal mix)	unissued
IS 099 B-5	Crisis Version	Island (US) IS-099

BOB MARLEY & THE WAILERS   January/February 1977

Bob Marley, vocal, guitar, and harmony vocal; Carlton Barrett, drums; Aston "Family Man" Barrett, bass; Julian "Junior" Marvin, guitar; Tyrone Downie, keyboards; Alvin "Seeco" Patterson, percussion; Karl Pitterson, engineer; recorded at Island Studio in London, England; twenty four track; Lee Hulko, mixing engineer; mixed by Aston "Family Man" Barrett, Chris Blackwell, and Karl Pitterson at Sterling Sound (US); Wailers production.

	Time Will Tell	Tuff Gong lp, Island ILPS 9517
	" (1982 remix)	Island MSTDA 1

BOB MARLEY & THE WAILERS   January/February 1977

Bob Marley, vocal and guitar; Rita Marley, harmony vocal; Marcia Griffiths, harmony vocal; Judy Mowatt, harmony vocal; Carlton Barrett, drums; Aston "Family Man" Barrett, bass; Julian "Junior" Marvin, guitar; Tyrone Downie, keyboards; Alvin "Seeco" Patterson, percussion; David Madden, trumpet; Glen DaCosta, alto sax; Vin Gordon, trombone; Karl Pitterson, engineer; recorded at Island Studios in London, England; twenty four track; Lee Hulko, mixing engineer; mixed by Aston "Family Man" Barrett, Chris Blackwell and Karl Pitterson; mixed at Sterling Sound (US); Wailers production.

	Satisfy My Soul	unissued
	Satisfy My Soul	Island (UK) WIP 6440, Tuff Gong lp, Island ILPS 9517
	" (alternate mix)	unissued
	" (alternate mix)	"
	Misty Morning	"
	Misty Morning	Tuff Gong lp, Island lp RSS1-A, Island ILPS 9517
	Natural Mystic	unissued
	Natural Mystic	Tuff Gong lp, Island DLPS 9498
	" (full horns mix)	unissued
	" (no horns mix)	"
WIP 6774 A-2U	" (1982 remix)	Island (UK) WIP 6774, Island MSTDA 1
	Guiltiness	Tuff Gong lp, Island DLPS 9498
	Guiltiness	unissued
	" (alternate mix)	"

Note: The 1975 recording of "Natural Mystic" credits Lee Perry with composition. All Island issues credit Bob Marley with writing the song.

BOB MARLEY & THE WAILERS   January/February 1977

Bob Marley, vocal and guitar; Rita Marley, harmony vocal; Marcia Griffiths, harmony vocal; Judy Mowatt, harmony vocal; Carlton Barrett, drums; Aston "Family Man" Barrett, bass; Julian "Junior" Marvin, guitar; Tyrone Downie, keyboards; Alvin "Seeco" Patterson, percussion;

David Madden, trumpet (-1); Glen DaCosta, alto sax (-1); Vin Gordon, trombone (-1); Karl Pitterson, engineer; recorded at Island Studio, London England; twenty-four track; Lee Hulko, mixing engineer; mixed by Aston "Family Man" Barrett, Chris Blackwell, and Karl Pitterson; mixed at Sterling Sound (US); Wailers, production; Bill Laswell, 1997 remix engineer. Overdubs 1999: Stephen Marley, synth (-1); W. Cole, drums and synth (-1); D. Cooper, bass (-1); Lauryn Hill, vocal and DJ vocal (-1); R. Lyfook, synth (-1); Ziggy Marley, organ (-1); Errol Brown, engineer (-1); MC Lyte, DJ vocal (-2); Earl "Chinna" Smith, guitar (-2); D. Cooper, bass (-2).

	Running Away (-1)	unissued
	Running Away (-1)	"
	Running Away (-1)	Tuff Gong lp, Island ILPS 9517
	Running Away Dub (-1)	unissued
	Turn Your Lights Down Low	Tuff Gong lp, Island DLPS 9498
	Turn Your Lights Down Low	unissued
	" (-1) (demo)	"
	" (-1)	Tuff Gong/Island CD 314 546 404-2
	Is This Love	unissued
	Is This Love	"
IS 099 A-5	Is This Love	Island (US) 1S-099, Tuff Gong lp, Island lp RSS1-A, Island ILPS 9517
	" (-1) (Horns Mix)	Tuff Gong CD TGCBX 1
	" (-1) (alt. Horns Mix)	unissued
	" (1997 remix)	Island CD 314 524 419-2
	Jamming	unissued
	" (alternate mix)	"
	Jamming	"
	" (-2) (demo)	"
	" (-2)	Tuff Gong/Island CD 314 546 404-2
	Jamming	Tuff Gong lp, Island (UK) WIP 6410-AA, Island DLPS 9498
12WIP 6410-A	" (long version)	Island (UK) 12 WIP 6410, Tuff Gong (UK) CD TGCBX 1
12 IS 210-A	" (1984 remix)	Island (UK) 12 IS 210, Island lp 90169-1

BOB MARLEY & THE WAILERS   circa: early 1977

Bob Marley, vocal and guitar; Rita Marley, harmony vocal; Marcia Griffiths, harmony vocal; Judy Mowatt, harmony vocal; Carlton Barrett, drums; Aston "Family Man" Barrett, bass; Julian "Junior" Marvin, guitar; Tyrone Downie, keyboards; Alvin "Seeco" Patterson, percussion; original rhythm tracks and scratch vocal recorded circa: September 1975 at Harry J Studio in Kingston, Jamaica; engineered by Sylvan Morris; subsequent overdub vocals recorded at Island Studio in London, England; Lee Hulko, mixing engineer; mixed by Aston "Family Man" Barrett, Chris Blackwell, and Karl Pitterson at Sterling Sound (US); Wailers, production. Bill Laswell, 1997 remix engineer.

	The Heathen	Tuff Gong lp, Island DLPS 9498
	" (1997 remix)	Island CD 314 524 419-2
12 ISX 169-B	One Love/People Get Ready	Island (UK) 12 ISX 169, Tuff Gong lp, Island DLPS 9498, Tuff Gong (UK) CD TGCBX 1
12 ISX 169-A	" (Dub Version)	Island (UK) 12 ISX 169
	" (Dub Version)	unissued
12 IS 169-A	" (extended version)	Island (UK) 12 IS 169
	" (1997 remix)	Island CD 314 524 419-2

Note: The early scratch vocal versions of these songs are listed in September 1975.

BOB MARLEY & THE WAILERS   circa: early 1977

Bob Marley, vocal and guitar; Rita Marley, harmony vocal; Marcia Griffiths, harmony vocal; Judy Mowatt, harmony vocal; Carlton Barrett, drums; Aston "Family Man" Barrett, bass; Julian "Junior" Marvin, guitar; Tyrone Downie, keyboards; Bernard "Touter" Harvey, keyboards; Alvin "Seeco" Patterson, percussion; Karl Pitterson, engineer; recorded Island Studio in London, England; twenty four track; Lee Hulko, mixing engineer; mixed by Aston "Family Man" Barrett, Chris Blackwell, and Karl Pitterson; mixed at Sterling Sound (US); Wailers, production.

	Three Little Birds	Tuff Gong lp, Island DLPS 9498
	" (alternate mix)	Tuff Gong (UK) CD TGCBX 1
12 IS 236-A	" (1984 remix)	Island (UK) 12 IS 236
12 IS 236-A	Three Little Birds Dub	"

BOB MARLEY & THE WAILERS   circa: early 1977

Bob Marley, vocal and guitar; Rita Marley, harmony vocal; Marcia Griffiths, harmony vocal; Judy Mowatt, harmony vocal; Carlton Barrett, drums; Aston "Family Man" Barrett, bass; Julian "Junior" Murvin, guitar; Tyrone Downie, keyboards; Earl "Wya" Lindo, keyboards; Alvin "Seeco" Patterson, percussion; Karl Pitterson, engineer; recorded at Island Studio in London, England; twenty-four track; Lee Hulko, mixing engineer; mixed by Aston "Family Man" Barrett, Chris Blackwell, and Karl Pitterson at Sterling Sound (US); Wailers, production.

Easy Skanking	unissued
Easy Skanking	Tuff Gong lp, Island ILPS 9517
Easy Skanking Version	unissued
Kaya	"
Kaya	Tuff Gong lp, Island lp RSS1-A, Island ILPS 9517
Sun Is Shining	unissued
Sun Is Shining	Tuff Gong lp, Island ILPS 9517
Sun Is Shining Version	unissued
So Much Things To Say	Tuff Gong lp, Island DLPS 9498
" (alt. mix)	unissued
" (alt. mix)	"

BUNNY WAILER   circa: early 1977

Bunny Wailer, vocal, harmony vocal and percussion; Peter Tosh, harmony vocal and guitar; Marcia Griffiths, harmony vocal (-1); Leroy "Horsemouth" Wallace or Mikey "Boo" Richards, drums; Robbie Shakespeare, bass; Earl "Chinna" Smith, guitar; Earl "Wya" Lindo, keyboards; Bernard "Touter" Harvey, keyboards; Keith Sterling, keyboards; Tommy McCook, tenor sax (-2); Richard "Dirty Harry" Hall, tenor sax (-2); Herman Marquis, alto sax (-2); Bobby Ellis, trumpet (-2); Sylvan Morris, engineer; recorded Harry J Studio; sixteen track; Bunny Wailer, production.

	Moses Children (-2)	Solomonic lp, Island ILPS 9512
IPR 2003-A	Get Up Stand Up (-2)	Island (UK) 12" IPR 2003, Solomonic lp, Island ILPS 9512
	Scheme Of Things (-2)	Solomonic lp, Island ILPS 9512
	Quit Trying (-2)	Solomonic lp, Island ILPS 9512
IS 062-A	Follow Fashion Monkey (-1)(-2)	Solomonic, Island (UK) IS-062, Solomonic lp, Island ILPS 9512
IS 062-B	Follow Fashion Monkey Inst.	Solomonic, Island (UK) IS-062
	Wanted Children	Solomonic lp, Island ILPS 9512
	Who Feels It (-2)	" , "
	Johnny Too Bad (-2)	" , "

Note: Both Jamaican and UK 7" releases of "Follow Fashion Monkey" share the same matrix numbers. "Get Up Stand Up" was written by Bob Marley and Peter Tosh. "Johnny Too Bad" was written by Trevor Wilson and originally performed by the Slickers. Bunny has added a few of his own verses to complete the story of Trevor Wilson.

BOB MARLEY & THE WAILERS   May 11, 1977

Bob Marley, vocal and guitar; Rita Marley, harmony vocal; Marcia Griffiths, harmony vocal; Judy Mowatt, harmony vocal; Carlton Barrett, drums; Aston "Family Man" Barrett, bass; Julian "Junior" Murvin, guitar and harmony vocal; Tyrone Downie, keyboards and harmony vocal; Alvin "Seeco" Patterson, percussion; recorded live in Brussels, Belgium.

Road Block	unissued
Concrete Jungle	"
Curfew (Burnin' And Lootin')	"

Bunny Wailer and Big Youth, Kingston, mid '70s. Photo by Kate Simon.

I Shot The Sheriff	unissued
Belly Full	"
War	"
No More Trouble	"
No Woman no Cry	"
Lively Up Yourself	"
Positive Vibration	"
Get Up Stand Up	"
Exodus	"

Note: Following this show, the Wailers played several dates in Germany and Holland performing the basic show with the addition of songs like "Natural Mystic," "The Heathen," and "Jamming" on some shows. They returned to Jamaica toward the end of the month.

BOB MARLEY & THE WAILERS   May 31, 1977

Bob Marley, vocal; Rita Marley, harmony vocal; Marcia Griffiths, harmony vocal; Judy Mowatt, harmony vocal; Carlton Barrett, drums; Aston "Family Man" Barrett, bass; Julian "Junior" Marvin, guitar and harmony vocals; Tyrone Downie, keyboards and harmony vocals; Alvin "Seeco" Patterson, percussion; recorded live in London at a rehearsal.

Exodus	unissued
I Shot The Sheriff	"
No Woman No Cry	"
No More Trouble	"
Positive Vibration	"
Natty Dread	"
Jamming	"
Guiltiness	"
Natural Mystic	"
Lively Up Yourself	"
Crazy Baldhead	"
Running Away	"

BUNNY WAILER   circa: mid 1977

Bunny Wailer, vocal, harmony vocal, and percussion; Peter Tosh, harmony vocal and guitar; Leroy "Horsemouth" Wallace, drums; Robbie Shakespeare, bass; Earl "Chinna" Smith, guitar; Earl "Wya" Lindo, keyboards; Tommy McCook, tenor sax; Bobby Ellis, trumpet; Ronald "Nambo" Robinson, trombone; Sylvan Morris, engineer; recorded Harry J Studio; sixteen track; Bunny Wailer, production.

DSR 7448-A	Bright Soul	Solomonic, Solomonic lp
DSR 710-A	"	Solomonic 12" 010
DSR 7449-B	Falling Angel	Solomonic
DSR 711-B	"	Solomonic 12" 010

Note: "Falling Angel" is a version of "Bright Soul." Solomonic lp is *Struggle*.

MARCIA GRIFFITHS   circa: 1977

Marcia Griffiths, vocal; Bunny Wailer, percussion; Leroy "Horsemouth" Wallace, drums; Robbie Shakespeare, bass; Earl "Chinna" Smith, guitar; Earl "Wya" Lindo, keyboards; Tommy McCook, tenor sax; Bobby Ellis, trumpet; Ronald "Nambo" Robinson, trombone; Sylvan Morris, engineer; recorded Harry J Studio; sixteen track; Bunny Wailer, production.

DSR 6852-A	Tribulation	Solomonic 12"
DSR 6853-B	Version	"

Note: This is included because Bunny Wailer composed, produced, and played on the track.

BUNNY WAILER　　　　　　　　　　　　　　　　　　　　　　　　　　　　circa: summer 1977

Bunny Wailer, vocal, harmony vocal, and percussion; Peter Tosh, vocal and guitar; Leroy "Horsemouth" Wallace, drums; Robbie Shakespeare, bass; Earl "Chinna" Smith, guitar; Earl "Wya" Lindo, keyboards; Tommy McCook, tenor sax; Bobby Ellis, trumpet; Ronald "Nambo" Robinson, trombone; Sylvan Morris, engineer; recorded Harry J Studio; sixteen track; Bunny Wailer, production.

DSR 5693-A	Love Fire	Solomonic 12" B.W. 0078, Island (UK) 12" IPR 2015-A, Solomonic lp
DSR 5694-B	Love's Version	Solomonic 12" B.W. 0078, Island (UK) 12" IPR 2015-B
	Love Fire (Dubd'sco)	Solomonic lp

　　Note: "Love Fire" is on Solomonic lp, *In I Father's House*. "Love Fire (Dubd'sco)" is on Solomonic lp, *Dubd'sco Vol. 1*.

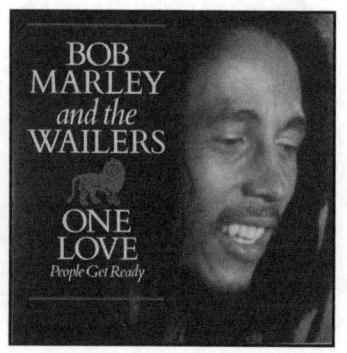

BOB MARLEY AND THE WAILERS　　　　　　　　　　　　　　　　　　　　　　circa: June 1977

Bob Marley, vocal and guitar; Rita Marley, harmony vocal; Marcia Griffiths, harmony vocal; Judy Mowatt, harmony vocal; Carlton Barrett, drums; Aston "Family Man" Barrett, bass; Julian "Junior" Marvin, guitar; Tyrone Downie, keyboards; Alvin "Seeco" Patterson, percussion; recorded live at the Rainbow Theatre, London.

Curfew (Burnin' And Lootin')	unissued
Concrete Jungle	"
I Shot The Sheriff	"
Belly Full	"
Rebel Music	"
War	"
No More Trouble	"
No Woman No Cry	"
Positive Vibration	"
Get Up Stand Up	"
Exodus	"

BOB MARLEY AND THE WAILERS　　　　　　　　　　　　　　　　　　　　　　circa: June 1977

Bob Marley, vocal and guitar; Rita Marley, harmony vocal; Marcia Griffiths, harmony vocal; Judy Mowatt, harmony vocal; Carlton Barrett, drums; Aston "Family Man" Barrett, bass; Julian "Junior" Marvin, guitar; Tyrone Downie, keyboards; Alvin "Seeco" Patterson, percussion; recorded live at the Rainbow Theatre, London; Scott Millaney, production.

Trench Town Rock	CBS Sony Video 002m 48
Belly Full	"
I Shot The Sheriff	"
Rebel Music	"

Lively Up Yourself	CBS Sony Video 002M 48	
Crazy Baldhead/Running Away	Tuff Gong/Island CD 314 546 404-2	
War/No More Trouble	"	
The Heathen	"	
No Woman No Cry	CBS Sony Video 002m 48	
Jamming	Tuff Gong/Island CD 314 546 404-2	
Get Up Stand Up	CBS Sony Video 002m 48	
Exodus	Tuff Gong/Island CD 314 546 404-2	

BOB MARLEY   circa: July/August 1977

Bob Marley, vocal and guitar; Candy McKenzie, harmony vocal; Yvonne McKenzie, harmony vocal (-1); Aurelia "Aura" Lewis, harmony vocal (-2); Ansel Cridland, harmony vocal (-2); Danny Clarke, harmony vocal (-2); Winston Watson, harmony vocal (-2); Angus Gaye, drums; Richie, bass; Cat Coore, guitar; Ibo Cooper, keyboards; Phil Ramacon, keyboards; "Deadly" Headly Bennett, alto sax (-2); Cedric "Im" Brooks, tenor sax (-2); Michael "Reuben" Campbell and "Drummie" Zeb, and Lee Perry, engineers; recorded at Island Studios, London and Black Ark Studio; mixed at Island Studios, Criteria Studio, Miami, and Black Ark Studio; twenty-four track; Lee Perry, production.

12 ISX 169-B	Keep on Moving (-1)	Island (UK) 121SX 169, Island (UKJ) 12IS 169
	" (London Version)	Tuff Gong (UK) CD TGCBX 1
	" (original mix)	Tuff Gong/Island CD 314 546 404-2
	Keep On Moving (Dub) (orig. mix)	"
	Keep On Moving Version	unissued
	Keep On Moving Version 2	"
	Punky Reggae Party (-2)	unissued
Lee Perry 2060-A	Punky Reggae Party Pt. 1 (-2)	Tuff Gong 12", Island (UK) WIP 6410, Island (UK) 12WIP 6410, Tuff Gong/Island CD 314 546 404-2
DSR 2886-A	"	Tuff Gong 12"
Lee Perry 2060-B	Punky Reggae Version Pt. 2 (-2)	Tuff Gong 12", Island (UK) WIP 6410, Island (UK) 12WIP 6410, Tuff Gong/Island CD 314 546 404-2
DSR 2887-B	"	Tuff Gong 12"
LP 4050-A	Punky Reggae Part of Park 1 (-2)	Black Art 12"
LP 4050-B	Punky Party Part 2 (-2)	"
	Punky Reggae Party (-2)	Island (Holland) lp BV 25272-A

Note: Three distinct vocal takes exist of "Punky Reggae Party." The oddly titled "Punky Reggae Part Of Park 1"/ "Punky Party Part 2" on Black Art 12" is a unique Lee Perry mix, probably done at the Black Ark Studio, utilizing the same basic track as that used on Tuff Gong/Island. Original mixes of "Keep On Moving," "Keep On Moving (Dub)," and the unissued voicing of "Punky Reggae Party" were done in London at Island Studios by Lee Perry.

Bob Marley, live in Europe, 1977. Photo by Kate Simon.

PETER TOSH
circa: late 1977

Peter Tosh, vocal and guitar; recorded live in Eugene, Oregon on radio station KZEL.

Pick Myself Up	JAD CD-1012
Guitar Solo	"
Guitar Solo #2	unissued
Can't You See	JAD CD-1012
Fire Fire	"
Don't Want To Get Busted	"
Legalize It	"

PETER TOSH
circa: late 1977

Peter Tosh, vocal and guitar; recorded live in Chicago, Illinois on radio station WXFM.

Stop That Train	JAD CD-1012
Get Up Stand Up	Legacy Columbia CD C3K 65064
Fools Die	JAD CD-1012
Jah Guide	"
I Am That I Am	"
Can't You See Instrumental	"
WXFM Radio ID	unissued

BOB MARLEY & THE WAILERS
circa: late 1977

Bob Marley, vocal and guitar; Carlton Barrett, drums; Aston "Family Man" Barrett, bass; Julian "Junior" Marvin, guitar; Tyrone Downie, keyboards; Earl "Wya" Lindo, keyboards; Alvin "Seeco" Patterson, percussion; rehearsals at Tuff Gong Studio.

Rasta Man Chant	unissued
Curfew (Burnin' And Lootin')	"
Curfew (Burnin' And Lootin')	"
Time Will Tell	"
Time Will Tell	"
Lively Up Instrumental	"
Who The Cap Fit	"
Easy Skanking	"
Want More	"
Jamming	"
Crisis	"
Running Away	"
Crazy Baldhead	"
Positive Vibration	"
Soul Rebel	"
Waiting In Vain	"

Note: In early December, the Wailers began an American tour using the same basic song list that they used at the Rainbow Theatre concerts previously listed.

PETER TOSH
April 22, 1978

Peter Tosh, vocal and guitar; Junior Moore, harmony vocal; Carlton Smith, harmony vocal; Winston Morgan, harmony vocal; Sly Dunbar, drums; Robbie Shakespeare, bass; Mikey "Mao" Chung, guitar; Al Anderson, guitar; Robbie Lyn, keyboards; Keith Sterling, keyboards; Uziah "Sticky" Thompson, percussion; recorded live before midnight at National Stadium in Kingston, Jamaica at the One Love Peace Concert.

Carly Barrett, Tyrone Downie, Family Man, Bob, and Junior Marvin soundcheck in Europe, 1977. Photo by Kate Simon.

	Igziabeher	JAD CD 1009
	400 Years	"
	Stepping Razor	"
	Intro Rap	"
	Burial/Speech	"
	Speech	"
	Equal Rights	"
	Speech	"
	Legalize It/Get Up Stand Up	"

Note: The harmony singers are collectively known as the Tamlins.

BOB MARLEY & THE WAILERS   April 23, 1978

Bob Marley, vocal and guitar; Rita Marley, harmony vocal; Marcia Griffiths, harmony vocal; Judy Mowatt, harmony vocal; Carlton Barrett, drums; Aston "Family Man" Barrett, bass; Earl "Chinna" Smith, guitar; Julian "Junior" Marvin, guitar; Tyrone Downie, keyboards; Earl "Wya" Lindo, keyboards; Glen DaCosta, tenor sax (-1); "Deadly" Headly Bennett, alto sax (-1); David Madden, trumpet (-1); Vin Gordon, trombone (-1); Alvin "Seeco" Patterson, percussion; recorded live after midnight at the National Stadium in Kingston, Jamaica at the One Love Peace Concert.

	Conquering Lion	unissued
	Natural Mystic (-1)	"
	Trench Town Rock	Continental Video
	Natty Dread (-1)	"
	Positive Vibration	unissued
	War (-1)	Continental Video
	Jamming	"
	One Love	unissued
	Jah Live	Continental Video

Note: The Continental Video is titled *Heartland Reggae*.

BOB MARLEY & THE WAILERS   circa: mid 1978

Bob Marley, vocal and guitar; unknown female harmony vocals (-1); Carlton Barrett, drums; Aston "Family Man" Barrett, bass; Julian "Junior" Marvin, guitar; Tyrone Downie, keyboards; Earl "Wya" Lindo, keyboards; Lee Perry, percussion; Alvin "Seeco" Patterson, percussion; Lee Perry, engineer; recorded Black Ark Studio; Lee Perry, production. 2001 remix by Peter Hoff (-2); 2001 remix by Peter Black (-3); 2001 remix by Fresca Boys (-4); overdubs 2001: Davide Aldrighetti, keyboards (-4); Diego Polimeno, guitars (-4).

	Who Colt The Game	Orchid CD ORCHCD82, Trojan CD 06076-80261-2
	" (alt. mix)	unissued
	" (alt. mix)	"
	Who Colt The Dub	Orchid CD ORCHCD82
	I Know A Place (-1)	"
	" (alt. mix)	unissued
12 TGX 10 B2	" (alt. mix)	Tuff Gong (US) 12 TGX 10/588 844-1
12 TGX 10 A1	" (-2)	"
12 TGX 10 B2	" (-3)	"
12 TGX 10 A1	" (-4)	"
	I Know A Dub	Orchid CD ORCHCD82

BUNNY WAILER
circa: mid 1978

Bunny Wailer, vocal, harmony vocal, and percussion; Leroy "Horsemouth" Wallace, drums; Robbie Shakespeare, bass; Earl "Chinna" Smith, guitar; Earl "Wya" Lindo, keyboards; Tommy McCook, tenor sax; Bobby Ellis, trumpet; Ronald "Nambo" Robinson, trombone; Sylvan Morris, engineer; recorded Harry J Studio; sixteen track; Bunny Wailer, production.

Bunny Wailer 204-A	Roots, Radics, Rockers & Reggae	Solomonic 12" 0079, Island (UK) 12" IPR 2025
Bunny Wailer 204-B	Peace Talk	" , Shanachie CD 45014
	Roots Radics (Dubd'sco)	Solomonic lp

Note: Titled "Peace Talks" on Shanachie, "Peace Talk" is a version of "Roots, Radics, Rockers & Reggae."

BUNNY WAILER
circa: mid 1978

Bunny Wailer, vocal, harmony vocal, and percussion; Leroy "Horsemouth" Wallace, drums; Robbie Shakespeare, bass; Earl "Chinna" Smith, guitar; Gladdy Anderson, piano; Earl "Wya" Lindo, keyboards; Sylvan Morris, engineer; recorded Harry J Studio; sixteen track; Bunny Wailer, production.

	The Old Dragon	Solomonic lp 012

BUNNY WAILER
circa: mid 1978

Bunny Wailer, vocal, harmony vocals, and percussion; Leroy "Horsemouth" Wallace or Eric "Fish" Clarke, drums; Robbie Shakespeare or Errol "Flabba" Holt, bass; Earl "Chinna" Smith, guitar; Douglas "Dougie" Bryan or Ernest Ranglin, guitar; Earl "Wya" Lindo, keyboards; Keith Sterling, keyboards; Bobby Kalphat, keyboards; Gladdy Anderson, piano; Tommy McCook, tenor sax; "Deadly" Headly Bennett, alto sax; Bobby Ellis, trumpet; Ronald "Nambo" Robinson, trombone; Uziah "Sticky" Thompson, percussion; Sylvan Morris, engineer; recorded Harry J Studio; sixteen track; Bunny Wailer, production.

	Got To Move	Solomonic lp 012
	Let The Children Dance	"
	Struggle	"
DSR 9374-A	Power Struggle	Solomonic BW 0078, Solomonic lp 012
DSR 9375-B	Version	"
DSR 8120-A	Free Jah Children	Solomonic BW 0078, Solomonic lp 012
DSR 8121-B	Dub Wise	"

Note: Issues sharing the release number BW 0078 are printed over a common label stock.

BUNNY WAILER
circa: mid 1978

Bunny Wailer, vocal, harmony vocal, and percussion; Leroy "Horsemouth" Wallace, drums; Errol "Flabba" Holt, bass; Douglas "Dougie" Bryan, guitar; Keith Sterling, keyboards; Bobby Kalphat, keyboards; Dean Fraser, alto sax; Sylvan Morris, engineer; recorded Harry J Studio; sixteen track; Bunny Wailer, production.

Bob Marley at the One Love Peace Concert at the National Stadium in Kingston, April 22, 1978. Photo by Kate Simon.

DSR 8703-A   Let Him Go   Solomonic BW 0078, Solomonic lp
DSR 8704-B   Version   "

Note: Issues sharing the release number BW 0078 are printed over a common label stock. "Let Him Go" is on Solomonic lp, *In I Father's House*.

PETER TOSH   circa: mid 1978

Peter Tosh, vocal, guitar, and keyboards; Sly Dunbar, drums; Robbie Shakespeare, bass; Mikey "Mao" Chung, guitar; Donald Kinsey, guitar; Robbie Lyn, keyboards; Lee Jaffe, harmonica; Larry McDonald, percussion; Noel "Scully" Simms, percussion; Errol Thompson, engineer; recorded at Joe Gibbs Studio; sixteen track; Peter Tosh, production.

        Lesson In My Life   Capitol EMI CD 72435 39181 25

PETER TOSH   circa: mid 1978

Peter Tosh, vocal, guitar, and autoharp; Gwen Guthrie, harmony vocal; Yvonne Lewis, harmony vocal; Brenda White, harmony vocal; Geoffrey Chung, engineer; recorded Dynamic Sounds Studio; sixteen track; Karl Pitterson, remix engineer; remixed at Bearsville Studio (US); Peter Tosh, production.

        Creation   Intel Diplo lp, Rolling Stone lp COC 39109

PETER TOSH   circa: mid 1978

Peter Tosh, vocal and guitar; Junior Moore, harmony vocal; Carlton Smith, harmony vocal; Winston Morgan, harmony vocal; Sly Dunbar, drums; Robbie Shakespeare, bass; Mikey "Mao" Chung, guitar; Donald Kinsey, guitar; Robbie Lyn, keyboards; Larry McDonald, percussion; Noel "Scully" Simms, percussion; Geoffrey Chung, engineer; recorded Dynamic Sounds Studio; sixteen track; Karl Pitterson, remix engineer; remixed at Bearsville Studio (US); Peter Tosh, production.

        Pick Myself Up   Intel Diplo lp, Rolling Stones lp COC 39109

PETER TOSH   circa: mid 1978

Peter Tosh, vocal and guitar; Sly Dunbar, drums; Robbie Shakespeare, bass; Mikey "Mao" Chung, guitar; Donald Kinsey, guitar; Keith Richards, guitar (-1); Robbie Lyn, keyboards; unknown flute (-2); unknown horns (-2); Larry McDonald, percussion; Noel "Scully" Simms, percussion; Geoffrey Chung, engineer; recorded Dynamic Sounds Studio; sixteen track; Karl Pitterson, remix engineer; remixed at Bearsville Studio (US); Peter Tosh, production.

        Stand Firm (-1)   Intel Diplo lp, Rolling Stones lp COC 39109
        Moses – The Prophets (-2)   "   ,   "

PETER TOSH
circa: mid 1978

Peter Tosh, vocal, harmony vocal, guitar, and keyboards; Mick Jagger, vocal (-1); Gwen Guthrie, harmony vocal; Yvonne Lewis, harmony vocal; Brenda White, harmony vocal; Sly Dunbar, drums; Robbie Shakespeare, bass; Mikey "Mao" Chung, guitar; Donald Kinsey, guitar; Keith Richards, guitar (-2); Robbie Lyn, keyboards; Larry McDonald, percussion; Noel "Scully" Simms, percussion; unknown horns (-3); Luther Francois, soprano sax (-4); Geoffrey Chung, engineer; recorded Dynamic Sounds Studio; Errol Thompson, engineer; recorded at Joe Gibbs Studio; Karl Pitterson, remix engineer; remixed at Bearsville Studio (US); Peter Tosh, production.

2859-A	(You Gotta Walk) Don't Look Back (-1, -3, -4)	Intel Diplo, Intel Diplo lp, Rolling Stones (US) RS 19308, Rolling Stones lp COC 39109
DK 7500-A	" (long mix)	Rolling Stones (UK) 12" DK 7500
DK 7500-B	Don't Space Out	"
	I'm The Toughest (-4)	Intel Diplo lp, Rolling Stones lp COC 39109
12 RSR 103-A	" (long mix)	Rolling Stones (UK) 12 RS 103
12 RSR 103-B	Toughest Version	"
2859-B	Soon Come (-3)	Intel Diplo, Intel Diplo lp, Rolling Stones lp COC 39109
	" (long mix)	Rolling Stones (UK) 12"
	Bush Doctor (-2)	Intel Diplo lp, Rolling Stones lp COC 39109
	" (long mix)	Rolling Stones (UK) 12"
	Dem Ha Fe Get A Beaten (-3)	Intel Diplo lp, Rolling Stones lp COC 39109
	Tough Rock Soft Stones	Capitol EMI CD 72435 39181 25

Note: "Don't Space Out" is re-titled "(You Gotta Walk) Don't Look Back (Version)" on Capitol EMI CD. Rolling Stones 7" RS 19308 features mono and stereo mixes of "Don't Look Back" back to back. "Tough Rock Soft Stones" is an instrumental. "Don't Look Back" was written by Smokey Robinson and Ronald White. The original 1966 release of "The Toughest" credits Jackie Mittoo and Clement Dodd with writing the song. "I'm The Toughest" is credited to Peter Tosh.

BOB MARLEY & THE WAILERS
June 13, 1978

Bob Marley, vocal and guitar; Rita Marley, harmony vocal; Marcia Griffiths, harmony vocal; Judy Mowatt, harmony vocal; Carlton Barrett, drums; Aston "Family Man" Barrett, bass; Julian "Junior" Marvin, guitar; Al Anderson, guitar; Tyrone Downie, keyboards; Earl "Wya" Lindo, keyboards; Alvin "Seeco" Patterson, percussion; Jack Nuber, engineer; recorded live at Jaap Edenhal in Amsterdam, Holland; sixteen track; Bob Marley and the Wailers, production.

SMX 53812	Rat Race	Island (UK) 12" IX 13009, Island lp ISLD 11

BOB MARLEY & THE WAILERS
June 25, 1978

Bob Marley, vocal and guitar; Rita Marley, harmony vocal; Marcia Griffiths, harmony vocal; Judy Mowatt, harmony vocal; Carlton Barrett, drums; Aston "Family Man" Barrett, bass; Julian "Junior" Marvin, guitar; Al Anderson, guitar; Tyrone Downie, keyboards; Earl "Wya" Lindo, keyboards; Alvin "Seeco" Patterson, percussion; Jack Nuber, engineer; recorded live at the Paris Pavillion in Paris, France; sixteen track; Bob Marley & The Wailers, production.

	Punky Reggae Party	Island lp ISLD 11
SMX 53672	Exodus	Island (UK) 12" IX 13006, Island lp ISLD 11
	Kinky Reggae	Island lp ISLD 11
	Rebel Music	"
	Is This Love	"

BOB MARLEY & THE WAILERS
June 26, 1978

Bob Marley, vocal and guitar; Rita Marley, harmony vocal; Marcia Griffiths, harmony vocal; Judy Mowatt, harmony vocal; Carlton Barrett, drums; Aston "Family Man" Barrett, bass; Julian "Junior" Marvin, guitar; Al Anderson, guitar; Tyrone Downie, keyboards; Earl "Wya" Lindo, keyboards; Alvin "Seeco" Patterson, percussion; Jack Nuber, engineer; recorded live in Paris, Copenhagen, London and Amsterdam; sixteen track; Bob Marley and the Wailers, production.

"RAT RACE"

Bob Marley & The Wailers

	Positive Vibration	Island lp ISLD 11
	Concrete Jungle	"
	Lively Up Yourself	"
SMX 53671	War	Island (UK) 12" IX 13006, Island lp ISLD 11
SMX 53671	No More Trouble	" , "
	Heathen	Island lp ISLD 11
12WIP 6244-B	Jamming	Island 12WIP 6244, Island lp ISLD 11

BOB MARLEY & THE WAILERS   July 18, 1978

Bob Marley, vocal and guitar; Rita Marley, harmony vocal; Marcia Griffiths, harmony vocal; Judy Mowatt, harmony vocal; Carlton Barrett, drums; Aston "Family Man" Barrett, bass; Julian "Junior" Marvin, guitar; Al Anderson, guitar; Tyrone Downie, keyboards; Earl "Wya" Lindo, keyboards; Alvin "Seeco" Patterson, percussion; Jack Nuber, engineer; recorded live at the Lyceum in London, England.

SMX 53811	Stir It Up	Island (UK) 12" IX 13009, Island lp ISLD 11

Note: This recording and those listed from June 13 through June 26 were high points of a hectic tour that began on May 4 in Tampa, Florida and ended August 5 in Miami, Florida.

BOB MARLEY & THE WAILERS   July 21, 1978

Bob Marley, vocal and guitar; Peter Tosh, vocal (-1); Rita Marley, harmony vocal; Marcia Griffiths, harmony vocal; Judy Mowatt, harmony vocal; Carlton Barrett, drums; Aston "Family Man" Barrett, bass; Julian "Junior" Marvin, guitar; Al Anderson, guitar; Tyrone Downie, keyboards; Earl "Wya" Lindo, keyboards; Alvin "Seeco" Patterson, percussion; recorded live at the Burbank Starlight Bowl in Los Angeles, California;

Positive Vibration	unissued
Belly Full	"
Road Block	"
The Heathen	"
Crisis	"
War	"
No More Trouble	"
Running Away	"
Crazy Baldhead	"
I Shot The Sheriff	"
No Woman No Cry	"
Jamming	"
Is This Love	"
Easy Skanking	"
Get Up Stand Up (-1)	"
Exodus	"

Note: Peter surprised Bob with an impromptu appearance on this show. It was their last stage appearance together.

PETER TOSH   circa: December 1978

Peter Tosh, vocal and guitar; Mick Jagger, vocal (-1); Sly Dunbar, drums; Robbie Shakespeare, bass; Mikey "Mao" Chung, guitar; Donald Kinsey, guitar; Robbie Lyn, keyboards; recorded live for Saturday Night Live television program.

Don't Look Back (-1)	unissued
Bush Doctor	"

Carly Barrett at his drum kit, Europe 1977. Photo by Kate Simon.

PETER TOSH
circa: late 1978

Peter Tosh, vocal, guitar, and keyboards; Junior Moore, harmony vocal; Carlton Smith, harmony vocal; Winston Morgan, harmony vocal; Sly Dunbar, drums and percussion; Robbie Shakespeare, bass; Mikey "Mao" Chung, guitar, keyboards and percussion; Robbie Lyn, keyboards; Keith Sterling, piano (-1); Ed Walsh, synthesizer (-2); Uziah "Sticky" Thompson, percussion; Sammy Figueroa, congas (-3); Noel "Scully" Simms, repeater (-4); George Young, alto sax and flute (-5); Louis Marini, tenor sax and flute (-5); Howard J. Johnson, baritone sax (-5); Barry Rogers, trombone (-5); Mike Lawrence, trumpet; Geoffrey Chung, engineer; recorded Dynamic Sound Studio; twenty-four track; mixed at Sound Mixer (US); Peter Tosh, production.

	Mystic Man (-1) (-3) (-5)	Intel Diplo lp, Rolling Stones lp CUN 39110
	" (long version)	EMI CD 72435 37696 28
ST-RS-37167-1	Recruiting Soldiers (-2) (-5)	Rolling Stones (US) RS 20000, Intel Diplo lp, Rolling Stones lp CUN 39110
	Recruiting Soldiers (Version)	EMI CD 72435 37696 28
	Jah Seh No (-2)	Intel Diplo lp, Rolling Stones lp CUN 39110
	Fight On (-4)	" , "
	Fight On (Instrumental)	EMI CD72435 37696 28
12 RSP 104B	The Day The Dollar Die (-5)	Rolling Stones 12 YRSR 104, Rolling Stones (UK) RSR 104 B, Intel Diplo lp, Rolling Stones lp CUN 39110

PETER TOSH
circa: late 1978

Peter Tosh, vocal, guitar, and keyboards; Gwen Guthrie, harmony vocal; Yvonne Lewis, harmony vocal; Brenda White, harmony vocal; Sly Dunbar, drums and percussion; Robbie Shakespeare, bass; Mikey "Mao" Chung, guitar, keyboards, and percussion; Robbie Lyn, keyboards; Ed Walsh, synthesizer; Uziah "Sticky" Thompson, percussion; Sammy Figueroa, congas; George Young, alto sax and flute; Lou Marini, tenor sax and flute; Howard J. Johnson, baritone sax; Barry Rogers, trombone; Mike Lawrence, trumpet; Geoffrey Chung, engineer; recorded Dynamic Sounds Studio; twenty-four track; mixed at Sound Mixers, New York; Peter Tosh, production.

DSR 9548-B	Buk-In-Hamm Palace	Intel Diplo, Rolling Stones (US) RS 2000, Rolling Stones (UK) RSR 104 A, Intel Diplo lp, Rolling Stones lp CUN 39110
12 RSR 104A	"	Rolling Stones 12 YRSR 104
DSR 9547-A	Buk-In-Hamm Version	Intel Diplo
12 RSP 104B	Dubbing In Buk-In-Hamm	Rolling Stones 12 YRSR 104

PETER TOSH
circa: late 1978

Peter Tosh, vocal, guitar, and keyboards; Gwen Guthrie, harmony vocal; Yvonne Lewis, harmony vocal; Brenda White, harmony vocal; Sly Dunbar, drums; Robbie Shakespeare, bass; Mikey "Mao" Chung, guitar, keyboards, and percussion; Ed Elizalde, guitar (-1); Robbie Lyn, keyboards; Uziah "Sticky" Thompson, percussion; Geoffrey Chung, engineer; recorded Dynamic Sounds Studio; twenty-four track; mixed at Sound Mixers (US); Peter Tosh, production.

	Can't You See (-1)	Intel Diplo lp, Rolling Stones lp CUN 39110
	Crystal Ball	" , "
	Rumours Of War	" , "

Bob Marley, vocal and guitar; Rita Marley, harmony vocal; Marcia Griffiths, harmony vocal; Judy Mowatt, harmony vocal; Carlton Barrett, drums; Aston "Family Man" Barrett, bass; Julian "Junior" Marvin, guitar and harmony vocal; Tyrone Downie, keyboards and harmony vocal; Earl "Wya" Lindo, keyboards; Alvin "Seeco" Patterson, percussion; Errol Brown, engineer; recorded Dynamic Sounds Studio; sixteen track; Bob Marley and the Wailers, production.

	Rastaman Live Up	Island lp 90085-1
12IS 180-A	Blackman Redemption	Island 12IS 180, Island lp 90085-1

Note: Bob may not have liked these recordings, as he re-cut both songs later in the year with harmony by the Meditations and released these later recordings as singles in Jamaica.

BUNNY WAILER   circa: early 1979

Bunny Wailer, vocal, harmony vocal, bongos, and harp; Leroy "Horsemouth" Wallace, drums; Robbie Shakespeare, bass; Earl "Chinna" Smith, guitar; Douglas "Dougie" Bryan, guitar; Earl "Wya" Lindo, keyboards; Keith Sterling, keyboards; Tommy McCook, tenor sax or flute (-1); Richard "Dirty Harry" Hall, tenor sax; Herman Marquis, alto sax; Bobby Ellis, trumpet; Ronald "Nambo" Robinson, trombone; Vin "Trammie" Gordon, trombone; Errol Thompson, recording engineer; recorded Joe Gibbs Studio; sixteen track; Sylvan Morris, mixing engineer; mixed at Harry J Studio; Bunny Wailer, production.

DSR 6519-A	Rockers	Solomonic 12" SP 008-34, Island lp ILPS 9587
	" (alternate mix)	Solomonic lp
DSR 6517-B	Theme From Rockers	Solomonic 12" SP 008-34

Note: This composition was the theme song for the movie *Rockers*.

BUNNY WAILER   circa: early 1979

Bunny Wailer, vocal, harmony vocal, and percussion; Leroy "Horsemouth" Wallace, drums; Robbie Shakespeare, bass; Earl "Chinna" Smith, guitar; Douglas "Dougie" Bryan, guitar; Earl "Wya" Lindo, keyboards; Keith Sterling, keyboards; Tommy McCook, tenor sax or flute (-1); Richard "Dirty Harry" Hall, tenor sax; Herman Marquis, alto sax; Bobby Ellis, trumpet; Ronald "Nambo" Robinson, trombone; Vin "Trammie" Gordon, trombone; Errol Thompson, recording engineer; recorded Joe Gibbs Studio; sixteen track; Sylvan Morris, mixing engineer; mixed at Harry J Studio; Bunny Wailer, production.

DSR 8928-A	Rock In Time (-1)	Solomonic BW 0078, Solomonic lp
DSR 8928-B	Rock	"
	Wirly Girly	Solomonic lp
	Worly Girly	Solomonic lp

Note: All Solomonic lp tracks are from *In I Father's House*, except "Worly Girly" from *Dubd'sco Vol. 2*. Issues sharing the release number BW 0078 are printed over a common label stock. "Rock" is a version track of "Rock In Time."

BOB MARLEY & THE WAILERS   circa: early 1979

Bob Marley, vocal and guitar; Carlton Barrett, drums; Aston "Family Man" Barrett, bass; Julian "Junior" Marvin, guitar; Tyrone Downie, keyboards; Earl "Wya" Lindo, keyboards; Alvin "Seeco" Patterson, percussion; recorded live in rehearsal at Tuff Gong Studio in Kingston, Jamaica.

	So Much Trouble	unissued
	Babylon System	"
	Survival	"
	Survival	"
	Ride Natty Ride	"

BOB MARLEY & THE WAILERS
circa: early 1979

Bob Marley, vocal and guitar; Rita Marley, harmony vocal (-1); Judy Mowatt, harmony vocal (-1); Marcia Griffiths, harmony vocal (-1); Carlton Barrett, drums; Aston "Family Man" Barrett, bass; Julian "Junior" Marvin, guitar; Tyrone Downie, keyboards and harmony vocal; Earl "Way" Lindo, keyboards; Alvin "Seeco" Patterson, percussion; unknown trumpet (-2); unknown tenor sax (-2); unknown trombone (-2); recorded in rehearsal at Tuff Gong Studio in Kingston, Jamaica.

	Could You Be Loved	unissued
	Could You Be Loved	"
	Survival	"
	Zimbabwe (-2)	"
	Ride Natty Ride (-1) (-2)	"

Note: Although appearing on the same tape, it is possible that the two takes of "Could You Be Loved" were taped over earlier material, as this seems an early date for its inclusion in a rehearsal.

BOB MARLEY & THE WAILERS
circa: early 1979

Bob Marley, vocal and guitar; Rita Marley, harmony vocal; Marcia Griffiths, harmony vocal; Judy Mowatt, harmony vocal; Carlton "Santa" Davis, drums; Aston "Family Man" Barrett, bass; Julian "Junior" Marvin, guitar and harmony vocal; Tyrone Downie, keyboards and harmony vocal; Earl "Wya" Lindo, keyboards and harmony vocal; Dean Fraser, alto sax; Alvin "Seeco" Patterson, percussion; Alex Sadkin, engineer; recorded Tuff Gong Studio; Bob Marley, production.

12WIP 6597-A	Africa Unite	Island (UK) 12WIP 6597, Tuff Gong lp, Island ILPS 9542

BOB MARLEY & THE WAILERS
circa: early 1979

Bob Marley, vocal and guitar; Rita Marley, harmony vocal (-1); Marcia Griffiths, harmony vocal (-1); Judy Mowatt, harmony vocal (-1); Carlton Barrett, drums; Aston "Family Man" Barrett, bass; Julian "Junior" Marvin, guitar and harmony vocal (-1); Al Anderson, guitar; Tyrone Downie, keyboards and harmony vocal (-1); Earl "Wya" Lindo, keyboards and harmony vocal (-1); Alvin "Seeco" Patterson, percussion; Dean Fraser, tenor sax (-2); "Deadly" Headly Bennett, alto sax (-2); Ronald "Nambo" Robinson, trombone (-2); Melba Liston, trombone (-2); Luther Francois, trombone (-2); Junior "Chico" Chin, trumpet (-2); Jackie Willacy, trumpet (-2); Micky Hanson, trumpet (-2); Alex Sadkin, engineer; recorded Tuff Gong Studio; Bob Marley, production. Overdubs 1999: Chuck D, vocal and DJ vocal (-3); Damian Marley, drums (-3), Stephen Marley, bass and keyboards (-3); Julian Marley, keyboards (-3).

	One Drop	unissued
DSR 9358-A	One Drop (-1) (-2)	Tuff Gong, Island (UK) WIP 6610, Island (UK) 12WIP 6610, Tuff Gong lp, Island ILPS 9542
	" (long mix)	unissued
DSR 9359-B	One Dub (-1) (-2)	Tuff Gong, Tuff Gong CDE TGCBX 1
12WIP 6597-A	Zimbabwe (-1)	Island (UK) 12 WIP 6597, Island (UK) WIP 6597, Tuff Gong lp, Island ILPS 9542
	Zimbabwe Version	unissued
	Zimbabwe Version (bass)	"
	Survival (-1) (-2)	Island (UK) WIP 6597, Tuff Gong lp, Island ILPS 9542
	Survival (-1)	unissued
	" (-3) (demo)	"
	" (-3)	Tuff Gong/Island CD 314 546 404-2

BOB MARLEY & THE WAILERS   circa: early 1979

Bob Marley, vocal, guitar, and percussion; Rita Marley, harmony vocal; Marcia Griffiths, harmony vocal; Judy Mowatt, harmony vocal; Carlton Barrett, drums and percussion; Aston "Family Man" Barrett, bass and percussion; Julian "Junior" Marvin, guitar; Tyrone Downie, keyboards and percussion; Earl "Wya" Lindo, keyboards and percussion; Alvin "Seeco" Patterson, percussion; Alex Sadkin, engineer; recorded Tuff Gong Studio; Bob Marley, production.

	Babylon System	Tuff Gong lp, Island ILPS 9542
	Babylon System	unissued
	Babylon System Dub	"

BOB MARLEY & THE WAILERS   circa: early 1979

Bob Marley, vocal, and guitar; Rita Marley, harmony vocal (-1); Marcia Griffiths, harmony vocal (-1); Judy Mowatt, harmony vocal (-1); Carlton Barrett, drums; Aston "Family Man" Barrett, bass; Julian "Junior" Marvin, guitar; Tyrone Downie, keyboards and harmony vocal; Earl "Wya" Lindo, keyboards; Lee Jaffe, harmonica; Dean Fraser, tenor sax; "Deadly" Headly Bennett, alto sax; Ronald "Nambo" Robinson, trombone; Alex Sadkin, engineer; recorded Tuff Gong Studio; Bob Marley, production.

	Ride Natty Ride	unissued
145 9843-A	Ride Natty Ride (-1)	Tuff Gong, Tuff Gong lp, Island (US) IS 49547, Island ILPS 9542
12WIP 6610-B	" (12" mix) (-1)	Island (UK) 12WIP 6610, Island ILPS 9542

BOB MARLEY & THE WAILERS   circa: early 1979

Bob Marley, vocal and guitar; Rita Marley, harmony vocal (-1); Marcia Griffiths, harmony vocal (-1); Judy Mowatt, harmony vocal (-1); Carlton Barrett, drums except (-3); Carlton "Santa" Davis, drums (-3); Aston "Family Man" Barrett, bass; Julian "Junior" Marvin, guitar; Al Anderson, guitar; Tyrone Downie, keyboards; Earl "Wya" Lindo, keyboards; Alvin "Seeco" Patterson, percussion; Dean Fraser, tenor sax (-2); "Deadly" Headly Bennett, alto sax (-2); Ronald "Nambo" Robinson, trombone (-2); Melba Liston, trombone (-2); Luther François, trombone (-2); Junior "Chico" Chin, trumpet (-2); Jackie Willacy, trumpet (-2); Micky Hanson, trumpet (-2); Alex Sadkin, engineer; recorded Tuff Gong Studio; Bob Marley, production; Bill Laswell, 1997 remix engineer.

DSR 8619-A	Ambush (-1) (-2)	Tuff Gong, Tuff Gong lp, Island ILPS 9542
	Ambush	unissued
DSR 8620-B	Ambush In Dub	Tuff Gong
12IS 169-B	So Much Trouble In World (-1)	Island (UK) 12IS 169, Island (UK) WIP 65103, Tuff Gong lp, Island ILPS 9542
	" (1977 remix)	Island CD 314 524 419-2
	So Much Trouble Dub	unissued
	Instrumental	Island (UK) WIP 65103
	Top Rankin'	unissued
	Top Rankin'	"
	Top Rankin' (-1) (-2)	Tuff Gong lp, Island ILPS 9542
	Top Rankin' Dub	unissued

BOB MARLEY & THE WAILERS   circa: early 1979

Bob Marley, vocal and guitar; Rita Marley, harmony vocal; Marcia Griffiths, harmony vocal; Judy Mowatt, harmony vocal; Mikey "Boo" Richards, drums; Val Douglas, bass; Aston "Family Man" Barrett, guitar; Tyrone Downie, keyboards and harmony vocal; Earl "Wya" Lindo, keyboards and harmony vocal; Dean Fraser, tenor and alto saxes; Junior "Chico" Chin, trumpet; Alvin "Seeco" Patterson, percussion; Alex Sadkin, engineer; recorded Tuff Gong Studio; Bob Marley, production.

XAA9165S	Wake Up And Live (stereo)	Island (US) IS 49080, Island (UK) 12WIP 6597, Tuff Gong lp, Island ILPS 9542
XAA9165	" (mono)	Island (US) IS 49080
	Wake Up And Live Version	Island (US)

PETER TOSH   March 8, 1979

Peter Tosh, vocal and guitar; Junior Moore, harmony vocal; Carlton Smith, harmony vocal; Winston Morgan, harmony vocal; Sly Dunbar, drums; Robbie Shakespeare, bass; Mikey "Mao" Chung, guitar; Donald Kinsey, guitar; Robbie Lyn, keyboards; Uziah "Sticky" Thompson, percussion; recorded live at the Bottom Line in New York City; broadcast live on WNEW radio.

Stepping Razor	unissued
Pick Myself Up	"
Burial	"
Soon Come	"
I'm The Toughest	"
Bush Doctor	"
Get Up Stand Up	"
Babylon Queendom	"

Note: A well-recorded and representative show from Peter's American tour which began in late January in California and concluded in mid March on the East Coast. He resumed touring with the same group in July with several European dates. Bob toured Japan and Australia in April.

BOB MARLEY & THE WAILERS   circa: mid 1979

Bob Marley, vocal and guitar; Rita Marley, harmony vocal; Marcia Griffiths, harmony vocal; Judy Mowatt, harmony vocal; Carlton Barrett, drums; Aston "Family Man" Barrett, bass; Julian "Junior" Marvin, guitar and harmony vocal; Tyrone Downie, keyboards and harmony vocal; Earl "Wya" Lindo, keyboards; Alvin "Seeco" Patterson, percussion; Errol Brown, engineer; recorded Tuff Gong Studio; twenty-four track; Bob Marley and the Wailers, production.

DSR 1288-A	Mix Up, Mix Up	Tuff Gong, Island lp 90085-1

BOB MARLEY & THE WAILERS   circa: mid 1979

Bob Marley, vocal and guitar; Ansel Cridland, harmony vocal; Danny Clark, harmony vocal; Winston Watson, harmony vocal; Carlton Barrett, drums; Aston "Family Man" Barrett, bass; Julian "Junior" Marvin, guitar; Al Anderson, guitar; Tyrone Downie, keyboards; Earl "Wya" Lindo, keyboards; Alvin "Seeco" Patterson, percussion; Errol Brown, engineer; recorded Tuff Gong Studio; twenty-four track; Bob Marley and Lee Perry, production.

6051-A	Blackman Redemption	Tuff Gong
6052-B	Version	"
FRM 6923-A	Rastaman Live Up	Tuff Gong
FRM 6924-B	Don't Give Up	"

Note: "Don't Give Up" is a version mix of "Rastaman Live Up." The harmony singers are collectively known as The Meditations. Bob had recorded versions of both tunes with harmony by the I Three early in 1979.

BUNNY WAILER circa: mid 1979

Bunny Wailer, vocal, harmony vocal, and percussion; Leroy "Horsemouth" Wallace, drums; Robbie Shakespeare, bass; Earl "Chinna" Smith, guitar; Douglas "Dougie" Bryan, guitar; Earl "Wya" Lindo, keyboards; Keith Sterling, keyboards; Tommy McCook, tenor sax; Bobby Ellis, trumpet; Errol Thompson, recording engineer; recorded Joe Gibbs Studio; sixteen track; Sylvan Morris, mixing engineer; mixed at Harry J Studio; Bunny Wailer, production.

DSR 0241-A	Gamblings	Solomonic BW 0078
DSR 0079-B	Version	"

Note: Issues sharing the release number BW 0078 are printed over a common label stock.

BOB MARLEY & THE WAILERS July 7, 1979

Bob Marley, vocal and guitar; Rita Marley, harmony vocal; Marcia Griffiths, harmony vocal; Judy Mowatt, harmony vocal; Carlton Barrett, drums; Aston "Family Man" Barrett, bass; Julian "Junior" Marvin, guitar; Tyrone Downie, keyboards; Earl "Wya" Lindo, keyboards; Alvin "Seeco" Patterson, percussion; recorded live at Reggae Sunsplash in Montego Bay, Jamaica.

Road Block	Columbia Video (Japan) 148C68-9038
War	unissued
No More Trouble	"
Running Away	"
Crazy Baldhead	"
Who The Cap Fit	"
The Heathen	"
Belly Full	"
Hypocrites	Columbia Video (Japan) 148C68-9038
Blackman Redemption	unissued
Rastaman Live Up	Columbia Video (Japan) 148C68-9038
No Woman No Cry	"
Lively Up Yourself	"
Jamming	unissued
Get Up Stand Up	Columbia Video (Japan) 148C68-9038
Natural Mystic	unissued
Ambush In The Night	"
Exodus	Columbia Video (Japan) 148C68-9038

BOB MARLEY & THE WAILERS circa: July 21, 1979

Bob Marley, vocal and guitar; Rita Marley, harmony vocal; Marcia Griffiths, harmony vocal; Judy Mowatt, harmony vocal; Carlton Barrett, drums; Aston "Family Man" Barrett, bass; Julian "Junior" Marvin, guitar; Tyrone Downie, keyboards; Earl "Wya" Lindo, keyboards; Alvin "Seeco" Patterson, percussion; recorded live at the Amandla Festival Of Unity held at Harvard University Stadium in Boston, Massachusetts.

Positive Vibration	unissued
Slave Driver	"
Belly Full	"
Running Away	"
Crazy Baldhead	"
The Heathen	"
War	"
No More Trouble	"
Lively Up Yourself	"
No Woman No Cry	"
Jamming	"
Get Up, Stand Up	"
Exodus	"
Zimbabwe	"
Wake Up And Live	"

Bob Marley's only Sunsplash appearance, July 7, 1979 in Montego Bay, with Rita Marley, Judy Mowatt, and Marcia Griffiths: the I Three. Photo by Leroy Pierson.

Note: A film of this exceptional show with excellent sound has for years been rumored to be ready for commercial release.

BOB MARLEY & THE WAILERS   circa: October 25, 1979

Bob Marley, vocal and guitar; Rita Marley, harmony vocal; Marcia Griffiths, harmony vocal; Judy Mowatt, harmony vocal; Carlton Barrett, drums; Aston "Family Man" Barrett, bass; Julian "Junior" Marvin, guitar; Tyrone Downie, keyboards; Earl "Wya" Lindo, keyboards; Alvin "Seeco" Patterson, percussion; recorded live at the Apollo Theatre, New York City.

Natural Mystic	unissued
Belly Full	"
I Shot The Sheriff	"
Concrete Jungle	"
Ambush In The Night	"
Ride Natty Ride	"
Running Away	"
Crazy Baldhead	"
Wake Up And Live	"
One Drop	"
No Woman No Cry	"
Jamming	"
So Much Trouble	"
Zimbabwe	"
Africa Unite	"
War	"
No More Trouble	"

Note: This was the first of seven shows the Wailers performed at the Apollo Theatre from October 25 to the 28th. These shows at the legendary Harlem venue were of particular importance to Bob, who had long dreamed of penetrating the US soul market.

BOB MARLEY & THE WAILERS   November 25, 1979

Bob Marley, vocal and guitar; Rita Marley, harmony vocal; Judy Mowatt, harmony vocal; Carlton Barrett, drums; Aston "Family Man" Barrett, bass; Julian "Junior" Marvin, guitar and harmony vocal; Al Anderson, guitar; Tyrone Downie, keyboards and harmony vocal; Earl "Wya" Lindo, keyboards; Glen DaCosta, tenor sax; David Madden, trumpet; Alvin "Seeco" Patterson, percussion; Devon Evans, percussion; recorded live at the Santa Barbara County Bowl.

Positive Vibration	Trojan DVD 06076-88364-9
Wake Up And Live	"
I Shot The Sheriff	Thorn EMI Video TVF 2909
Ambush In The Night	"
Concrete Jungle	Trojan DVD 06076-88364-9
Running Away	Thorn EMI Video TVF 2909
Crazy Baldhead	"
Them Belly Full	Trojan DVD 06076-88364-9
Heathen	Thorn EMI Video TVF 2909
Ride Natty Ride	Trojan DVD 06076-88365-9
Africa Unite	Thorn EMI Video TVF 2909
One Drop	Trojan DVD 06076-88364-9
Exodus	Thorn EMI Video TVF 2909
So Much Things To Say	Trojan DVD 06076-88364-9
Zimbabwe	Thorn EMI Video TVF 2909
Jamming	"
Is This Love	Trojan DVD 06076-88364-9
Kinky Reggae	Thorn EMI Video TVF 2909
Stir It Up	"
Get Up Stand Up	"

Hank Holmes, Judy Mowatt, and Rita Marley, San Diego Sports Arena, November 1979. Photo by Roger Steffens.

        Medley: War   Trojan DVD 06076-88364-9
             No More Trouble   "

Note: Thorn EMI Video TVF 2909 was released in 1981. Trojan DVD 06076-88364-9 was released in 2004 and includes all titles above.

PETER TOSH   circa: late 1979

Peter Tosh, vocal; Junior Moore, harmony vocal; Carlton Smith, harmony vocal; Winston Morgan, harmony vocal; Sly Dunbar, drums; Robbie Shakespeare, bass; Mikey "Mao" Chung, guitar; Donald Kinsey, guitar; Keith Lyn, keyboards; Uziah "Sticky" Thompson, percussion; recorded live in Munich, Germany.

        Get Up Stand Up   Columbia (Japan) video 148C68-9038
        Legalize It   "
        Buk-In-Hamm Palace   "
        Pick Myself Up   "

BOB MARLEY   circa: late 1979/early 1980

Bob Marley, vocal and guitar (-1) or keyboard (-2); unknown bass (-3); unknown guitar (-4); unknown keyboards (-5); unknown bongos (-6); drum machine (-3); private composing tapes produced by Bob Marley.

        Jailbreaker (-1)   unissued
        Place Of Peace (-1)   "
        Record A New Song (-1)   "
        We And Dem (-1)   "
        Vexation (-1)   "
        Jump Them Outta Babylon (-1)   "
        Pray For Me (-1) (-3) (-4)   "
        Can't Take Your Slogans No More
            (-1) (-4) (-5) (-6)   "
        Right On (-2)   "

BOB MARLEY   circa: late 1979/early 1980

Bob Marley, vocal and guitar; unknown harmony vocal; unknown harmony vocal; drum machine; unknown bass; unknown guitar; unknown keyboard; unknown percussion; private composing tapes produced by Bob Marley.

        Pomps And Pride   unissued
        Show Your Dreads On   "
        Rumors   "
        Zion Train (fragment)   "
        Can't Take Your Slogans No More "
        Can't Take Your Slogans No More "

Note: "Show Your Dreads On" is also known as "The Russians Are Coming."

BOB MARLEY & THE WAILERS   circa: late 1979/early 1980

Bob Marley, vocal and guitar; Carlton Barrett, drums; Aston "Family Man" Barrett, bass; Julian "Junior" Marvin, guitar; Al Anderson, guitar; Tyrone Downie, keyboards; Earl "Wya" Lindo, keyboards; Alvin "Seeco" Patterson, percussion; recorded live at rehearsals in Kingston, Jamaica.

        Pimper's Paradise   unissued
        Work   "
        Could You Be Loved   "
        Forever Loving Jah   "

	Redemption Song	unissued
	Redemption Song	"
	Redemption Song	"

BOB MARLEY & THE WAILERS   circa: late 1979/early 1980

Bob Marley, vocal and guitar; Carlton Barrett, drums; Aston "Family Man" Barrett, bass; Julian "Junior" Marvin, guitar; Tyrone Downie, keyboards; Earl "Wya" Lindo, keyboards; Alvin "Seeco" Patterson; recorded and filmed at Tuff Gong Studio in Kingston, Jamaica during rehearsals.

	Concrete Jungle	unissued
	Forever Loving Jah	"
	Zion Train	"
	So Much Trouble	"
	Bad Card	"

BOB MARLEY & THE WAILERS   circa: late 1979/early 1980

Bob Marley, guitar; Carlton Barrett, drums; Aston "Family Man" Barrett, bass; Julian "Junior" Marvin, guitar; Tyrone Downie, keyboards; Earl "Wya" Lindo, keyboards; Alvin "Seeco" Patterson, percussion; Errol Brown, engineer; recorded Tuff Gong Studio; sixteen track; Bob Marley and the Wailers, production.

	Uprising Theme	unissued

BOB MARLEY & THE WAILERS   circa: late 1979/early 1980

Bob Marley, vocal and guitar; Joe Higgs, harmony vocal; Rita Marley, harmony vocal; Marcia Griffiths, harmony vocal; Judy Mowatt, harmony vocal; Carlton "Santa" Davis, drums; Aston "Family Man" Barrett, bass; Julian "Junior" Marvin, guitar and harmony vocal; Al Anderson, guitar; Tyrone Downie, keyboards and harmony vocal; Earl "Wya" Lindo, keyboards and harmony vocal; Alvin "Seeco" Patterson, percussion; Errol Brown, engineer; recorded Tuff Gong Studio; sixteen track; Bob Marley and the Wailers, production.

	Coming In From The Cold		unissued
DSR128-A	Coming In From The Cold		Tuff Gong, Tuff Gong lp, Island ILPS 9596
	"	(alternate mix)	unissued
12 IS 210-B	"	('84 remix)	Island 12 IS 210, Tuff Gong (UK) CD TGCBX 1
	Version		unissued

Note: The Island 12" issue is incorrectly titled "Coming From The Cold."

BOB MARLEY & THE WAILERS   circa: late 1979/early 1980

Bob Marley, vocal and guitar; Rita Marley, harmony vocal (-1); Marcia Griffiths, harmony vocal (-1); Judy Mowatt, harmony vocal (-1); Carlton Barrett, drums; Aston "Family Man" Barrett, bass, guitar and piano; Julian "Junior" Marvin, guitar; Al Anderson, guitar; Tyrone Downie, keyboards and harmony vocal (-1); Earl "Wya" Lindo, keyboards and harmony vocal (-1); Alvin "Seeco" Patterson, percussion; Errol Brown, engineer; recorded Tuff Gong Studio; sixteen track; Bob Marley and the Wailers, production.

	Jungle Fever		unissued
	Could You Be Loved		"
	Could You Be Loved (-1)		Island ISP 210, Tuff Gong lp, Island ILPS 9596
12 IS 210-A	"	(12" mix)	Island 12 IS 210, Tuff Gong (UK) CD TGCBX 1
IS 49547	"	(edit/mono)	Island (US) IS 49547
	"	(edit/stereo)	"
	"	(alt. mix)	unissued

BOB MARLEY & THE WAILERS circa: late 1979/early 1980

Bob Marley, vocal and guitar; Rita Marley, harmony vocal (-1); Marcia Griffiths, harmony vocal (-1); Judy Mowatt, harmony vocal (-1); Carlton Barrett, drums; Aston "Family Man" Barrett, bass; Julian "Junior" Marvin, guitar; Al Anderson, guitar; Tyrone Downie, keyboards; Earl "Wya" Lindo, keyboards; Alvin "Seeco" Patterson, percussion; Errol Brown, engineer; recorded Tuff Gong Studio; sixteen track; Bob Marley and the Wailers, production.

	Real Situation	unissued
	Real Situation (-1)	Tuff Gong lp, Island ILPS 9596
	Bad Card	unissued
Bad Card A	" (-1)	Tuff Gong, Tuff Gong lp, Island ILPS 9596
Bad Card B	Rub-A-Dub-Style	"
	Zion Train (-1)	Tuff Gong lp, Island ILPS 9596
TF 086-B	Zion Express	Tuff Gong 12"

Note: "Zion Express" is a remix of "Zion Train" with deleted harmony vocals. "Rub-A-Dub-Style" is a version of "Bad Card."

BOB MARLEY & THE WAILERS circa: late 1979/early 1980

Bob Marley, vocal and guitar; Rita Marley, harmony vocal; Marcia Griffiths, harmony vocal; Judy Mowatt, harmony vocal; Carlton Barrett, drums; Aston "Family Man" Barrett, bass, piano, and guitar; Julian "Junior" Marvin, guitar and harmony vocal; Al Anderson, guitar; Tyrone Downie, keyboards and harmony vocal; Earl "Wya" Lindo, keyboards; Alvin "Seeco" Patterson, percussion; Errol Brown, engineer; recorded Tuff Gong Studio; sixteen track; Bob Marley and the Wailers, production.

	We And Them	Tuff Gong lp, Island ILPS 9596
	" (no harmony mix)	unissued
	Work (-1)	Tuff Gong lp, Island ILPS 9596
	Pimper's Paradise	" , "
	" (alternate mix)	unissued
	Forever Loving Jah	"
	Forever Loving Jah (-1)	Tuff Gong lp, Island ILPS 9596
	Forever Loving Jah Version	unissued

BOB MARLEY & THE WAILERS circa: late 1979/early 1980

Bob Marley, vocal and guitar; Rita Marley, harmony vocal (-1); Marcia Griffiths, harmony vocal (-1); Judy Mowatt, harmony vocal (-1); Carlton Barrett, drums; Aston "Family Man" Barrett, bass; Julian "Junior" Marvin, guitar; Al Anderson, guitar; Tyrone Downie, keyboards; Earl "Wya" Lindo, keyboards; Glen DaCosta, tenor sax; David Madden, trumpet; Ronald "Nambo" Robinson, trombone; Alvin "Seeco" Patterson, percussion; Errol Brown, engineer; recorded Tuff Gong Studio; sixteen track; Bob Marley and the Wailers, production.

	Give Thanks & Praises	unissued
	Give Thanks & Praises (-1)	Tuff Gong lp, Island lp 90085-1

BOB MARLEY & THE WAILERS circa: early 1980

Bob Marley, vocal and guitar; Carlton Barrett, drums; Aston "Family Man" Barrett, bass; Julian "Junior" Marvin, guitar; Al Anderson, guitar; Tyrone Downie, keyboards; Earl "Wya" Lindo, keyboards; Alvin "Seeco" Patterson, percussion; Errol Brown, engineer; recorded Tuff Gong Studio; Bob Marley and the Wailers, production.

TG 086-A	Redemption Song (-1)	Tuff Gong 12", Island (UK) WIP 6653, Island 12WIP 6653

BOB MARLEY & THE WAILERS   circa: early 1980

Bob Marley, vocal and guitar; unknown vocal and guitar (-1); Errol Brown, engineer; recorded Tuff Gong Studio; twenty-four track; Bob Marley, production.

WIP 6653-A	Redemption Song	Island (UK) WIP 6653, Island 12 WIP 6653,
		Tuff Gong lp, Island ILPS 9596
	Redemption Song	Island video
	Redemption Song (-1)	Island video

BUNNY WAILER   circa: early 1980

Bunny Wailer, vocal, harmony vocal, and percussion; Leroy "Horsemouth" Wallace, drums; Robbie Shakespeare, bass; Earl "Chinna" Smith, guitar; Douglas "Dougie" Bryan, guitar; Earl "Wya" Lindo, keyboards; Keith Sterling, keyboards; Tommy McCook, tenor sax (-1); Bobby Ellis, trumpet (-1); Ronald "Nambo" Robinson, trombone (-1); Sylvan Morris, engineer; recorded Harry J Studio; sixteen track; Bunny Wailer, production.

DSR 0245-A	Togawar Game (-1)	Solomonic, Shanachie CD 45014
DSR 0246-B	Crucial	" , "
DSR 1754-A	" (12" mix)	Solomonic 12"
DSR 1755-B	Version	"
DSR 1140-A	Cease Fire	Solomonic
DSR 1141-B	Version	"
DSR 1012-A	Innocent Blood	Solomonic, Shanachie CD 45014
DSR 1013-B	Version	"

BOB MARLEY   circa: mid 1980

Bob Marley, vocal; recorded over original riddims. Bob Marley, production.

Kilamanjaro Specials:
    Bad Play (Bad Card)   unissued
    Get Up Stand Up   "
    Redemption Song   "
    No Sound Boy No Cry   "

Note: These titles were recorded as sound system specials exclusively for the use of Kilamanjaro.

BOB MARLEY & THE WAILERS   April 28, 1980

Bob Marley, vocal and guitar; Rita Marley, harmony vocal (-1); Marcia Griffiths, harmony vocal (-1); Judy Mowatt, harmony vocal (-1); Carlton Barrett, drums; Aston "Family Man" Barrett, bass; Julian "Junior" Marvin, guitar; Al Anderson, guitar; Tyrone Downie, keyboards; Earl "Wya" Lindo, keyboards; Alvin "Seeco" Patterson, percussion; Devon Evans, percussion; recorded live at Rufaro Stadium in Salisbury, Zimbabwe.

    Natural Mystic   unissued
    Positive Vibration (-1)   "
    Roots Rock Reggae (-1)   "
    Lively Up Yourself (-1)   "
    Zimbabwe (-1)   "
    Running Away (-1)   "
    Crazy Baldhead (-1)   "
    Get Up, Stand Up (-1)   "
    Exodus (-1)   "

Note: This show was so important to Bob that he and the Wailers played for free and paid their own expenses.

BUNNY WAILER circa: mid 1980

Bunny Wailer, vocal and harmony vocals; Sly Dunbar, drums; Robbie Shakespeare, bass; Earl "Chinna" Smith, guitar; Keith Sterling, keyboards; Winston Wright, keyboards; Dean Fraser, tenor sax; "Deadly" Headly Bennett, alto sax; Ronald "Nambo" Robinson, trombone; Uziah "Sticky" Thompson, percussion; David Hamilton, engineer; recorded at Harry J Studio; sixteen track; Bunny Wailer, production.

	Mellow Mood	Solomonic lp, Mango MLPS 9629
	Mellow Mood – Dub	Solomonic lp
	Hypocrite	Solomonic lp, Mango MLPS 9629
	Hypocrite – Dub	Solomonic lp
	I Stand Predominate	Solomonic lp, Mango MLPS 9629
	I Stand Predominate – Dub	Solomonic lp
12WIP 6685-B	Walk The Proud Land	Island (UK) 12WIP 6685, Solomonic lp, Mango MLPS 9629
	Walk The Proud Land – Dub	Solomonic lp

Note: Dub titles are from the lp *Dubd'sco Vol. 2*. All other titles are from the *Bunny Wailer Sings The Wailers* album.

BUNNY WAILER circa: mid 1980

Bunny Wailer, vocal and harmony vocals; Sly Dunbar, drums; Robbie Shakespeare, bass; Earl "Chinna" Smith, guitar; Keith Sterling, keyboards; Winston Wright, keyboards; Dean Fraser, tenor sax (-1) and alto sax (-2); Uziah "Sticky" Thompson, percussion; David Hamilton, engineer; recorded at Harry J Studio; sixteen track; Bunny Wailer, production.

12WIP 6685-A	Dancing Shoes (-1) (-2)	Island (UK) 12WIP 6685, Solomonic lp, Mango MLPS 9629
	Dancing Shoe – Dub	Solomonic lp
	Rule This Land (-2)	Solomonic lp, Mango MLPS 9629
	Rule This Land – Dub	Solomonic lp
	I'm The Toughest (-2)	Solomonic lp, Mango MLPS 9629
	Toughest – Dub	Solomonic lp

Note: Dub titles are from the lp, *Dubd'sco Vol. 2*. Other titles are from the *Bunny Wailer Sings The Wailers* album.

BUNNY WAILER circa: mid 1980

Bunny Wailer, vocal and harmony vocals; Sly Dunbar, drums; Robbie Shakespeare, bass; Earl "Chinna" Smith, guitar; Keith Sterling, keyboards; Winston Wright, keyboards; Uziah "Sticky" Thompson, percussion; David Hamilton, engineer; recorded at Harry J Studio; sixteen track; Bunny Wailer, production.

Keep On Moving	Solomonic lp, Mango MLPS 9629
Keep On Moving – Dub	Solomonic lp
Burial	Solomonic lp, Mango MLPS 9629
Burial – Dub	Solomonic lp
Soul Rebel	Solomonic lp
I Shot The Sheriff	"
Slave Driver	"
Cry To Me	Shanachie lp 43043

Note: "Soul Rebel," "I Shot The Sheriff," and "Slave Driver" are from the *Tribute* lp. "Cry To Me" is from the Shanachie lp, *Rootsman Skanking*. Dub titles are from the lp *Dubd'sco Vol. 2*. All other titles are from the *Bunny Wailer Sings The Wailers* lp. That album also contained "Dreamland," but this cut is a 1970 recording.

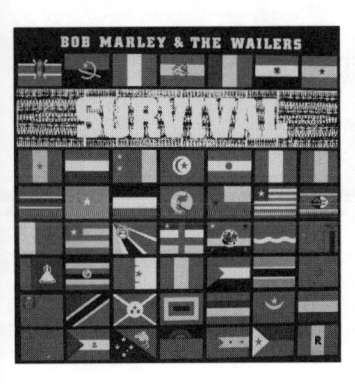

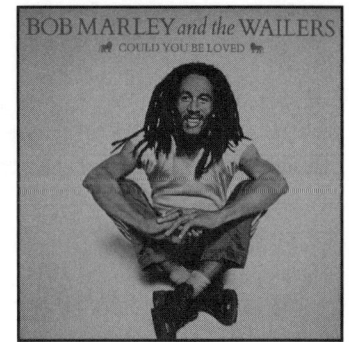

BOB MARLEY
circa: mid 1980

Bob Marley, vocal; Charib Ellis, drums; Carl Crowder, bass; Burt Bailer, guitar; Timmy Thompson, keyboards; Dimp Liptrott, tenor sax; Ron Lewis Smith, trumpet; Charles Williams, trombone; King Sporty, percussion; Sylvan Morris, engineer; recorded Criteria Studio, Miami; sixteen track; mixed Harry J Studio; King Sporty, production.

BOB 1-A   Buffalo Soldier   BOB (UK) 1

Note: This was released as a blank label single with stamped title, packaged with a picture sleeve 7" of "Three Little Birds." The reverse side is also BOB 1-A. Composition is credited to Bob Marley and N. G. Williams (King Sporty).

BOB MARLEY & THE WAILERS
circa: mid 1980

Bob Marley, vocal and guitar; Rita Marley, harmony vocal; Marcia Griffiths, harmony vocal; Judy Mowatt, harmony vocal; Carlton Barrett, drums; Aston "Family Man" Barrett, bass; Al Anderson, guitar; Tyrone Downie, keyboards and harmony vocal; Glen DaCosta, tenor sax; David Madden, trumpet; Ronald "Nambo" Robinson, trombone; Alvin "Seeco" Patterson, percussion; Errol Brown, engineer; recorded Tuff Gong Studio; twenty-four track; Wailers, production.

RM 2-3-83-A   Buffalo Soldier   Rita Marley Music, Island Tuff Gong (US) 7-99882,
                                                                     Island Tuff Gong (US) 12" 0-99883,
                                                                     Tuff Gong lp, Island lp 90085-1
                               "   (1984 remix)   Island (UK) lp BMW 1
RM 2-3-83-B   Buffalo Dub   Rita Marley Music, Island Tuff Gong (US) 12" 0-99883
                            Buffalo Soldier   Island (US) lp 90169-1
                            Buffalo Soldier Version   unissued

Note: "Buffalo Dub" is re-titled as "Buffalo Soldier Instrumental" on Island Tuff Gong (US) 12".

BOB MARLEY & THE WAILERS
circa: mid 1980

Bob Marley, vocal and guitar; Carlton Barrett, drums; Aston "Family Man" Barrett, bass; Julian "Junior" Marvin, guitar; Tyrone Downie, keyboards; Earl "Wya" Lindo, keyboards; Alvin "Seeco" Patterson, percussion; Errol Brown, engineer; recorded Tuff Gong Studio; twenty-four track; Wailers, production.

                                Trench Town   unissued
                                Chant Down Babylon   "
                                Jump Nyabinghi   "

BOB MARLEY & THE WAILERS   circa: mid 1980

Bob Marley, vocal and guitar; Rita Marley, harmony vocal; Marcia Griffiths, harmony vocal; Judy Mowatt, harmony vocal; Carlton "Santa" Davis, drums; Aston "Family Man" Barrett, bass; Julian "Junior" Marvin, guitar; Tyrone Downie, keyboards; Earl "Wya" Lindo, keyboards; Alvin "Seeco" Patterson, percussion; Errol Brown, engineer; recorded Tuff Gong Studio; twenty-four track; Wailers, production.

                        Chant Down Babylon   Tuff Gong lp, Island lp 90085

BOB MARLEY & THE WAILERS   circa: mid 1980

Bob Marley, vocal and guitar; Rita Marley, harmony vocal; Marcia Griffiths, harmony vocal; Judy Mowatt, harmony vocal; Carlton Barrett, drums; Aston "Family Man" Barrett, bass; Julian "Junior" Marvin, guitar and harmony vocal; Tyrone Downie, keyboards and harmony vocal; Earl "Wya" Lindo, keyboards; Glen DaCosta, tenor sax (-1); David Madden, trumpet (-1); Ronald "Nambo" Robinson, trombone (-1); Alvin "Seeco" Patterson, percussion; Devon Evans, percussion; Bunny Wailer, repeater (-2); Errol Brown, engineer; recorded Tuff Gong Studio; sixteen track; Wailers, production.

	Jump Nyabinghi (-1)	Tuff Gong lp, Island lp 90085-1
	Version	unissued
TG 12-11-83-A	Trench Town (-1) (-2)	56 Hope Road 12", Tuff Gong lp, Island lp 90085-1
	" (alternate mix)	unissued
TF 12-11-83-B	Dub In Trench Town	56 Hope Road 12"
	Stiff Necked Fools	Tuff Gong lp, Island lp 90085-1
	" (alternate mix)	unissued
	Stiff Necked Dub	"

BOB MARLEY & THE WAILERS   circa: mid 1980

Bob Marley, vocal and guitar; Carlton Barrett, drums; Aston "Family Man" Barrett, bass; Julian "Junior" Marvin, guitar; Tyrone Downie, keyboards; Earl "Wya" Lindo, keyboards; Alvin "Seeco" Patterson, percussion; Errol Brown, engineer; rehearsal or demo recording at Tuff Gong Studio; twenty-four track; Wailers, production.

	Babylon Feel This One	unissued
	Babylon Feel This One	"
	She Used To Call Me Da Da	"

PETER TOSH   July 3, 1980

Peter Tosh, vocal; Junior Moore, harmony vocal; Carlton Smith, harmony vocal; Winston Morgan, harmony vocal; Sly Dunbar, drums; Robbie Shakespeare, bass; Mikey "Mao" Chung, guitar; Robbie Lyn, keyboards; Uziah "Sticky" Thompson, percussion; recorded live at Reggae Sunsplash held at the Ranny Williams Center in Kingston, Jamaica.

	400 Years	unissued
	Stepping Razor	"
	African	"
	I'm The Toughest	"
	Bush Doctor	"
	Speech	"
	Don't Look Back	"
	Get Up Stand Up	"
	Recruiting Soldiers	"
	Hammer	"
	Babylon Queendom	"
	Buk-In-Hamm Palace	"

    Note: Peter was booked to perform on July 2, but did not appear until 12:20 a.m. on the morning of Thursday, July 3. The harmony vocalists, collectively known as the Tamlins, also performed on this show.

Bob Marley live in Europe, 1977. Photo by Kate Simon.

CHRIS HINZE
circa: summer 1980

Peter Tosh, vocal and guitar; Junior Moore, harmony vocal; Carlton Smith, harmony vocal; Winston Morgan, harmony vocal; Sly Dunbar, drums; Robbie Shakespeare, bass; Mikey "Mao" Chung, guitar, keyboards, and percussion; Hiram L. Bullock, guitar; Chris Hinze, flute; Uziah "Sticky" Thompson, percussion; Mervin Williams, engineer; recorded Aquarius Studio; twenty-four track; Chris Hinze, production.

	Silver And Gold	Keytone (Holland) lp KYT 719
	Puss And Dog	"

Note: Peter and the band also perform backup for Hinze on an additional nine instrumental tracks. "Puss And Dog" is an answer to Bob Marley's "Rat Race." It is said that the musicians balked at recording an attack on Marley until Peter agreed to tone down or omit certain lyrics.

BOB MARLEY & THE WAILERS
September 23, 1980

Bob Marley, vocal and guitar; Rita Marley, harmony vocal; Judy Mowatt, harmony vocal; Carlton Barrett, drums; Aston "Family Man" Barrett, bass; Julian "Junior" Marvin, guitar and harmony vocal; Al Anderson, guitar; Tyrone Downie, keyboards and harmony vocal; Earl "Wya" Lindo, keyboards; Glen DaCosta, tenor sax; David Madden, trumpet; Alvin "Seeco" Patterson, percussion; recorded live at the Stanley Theatre, Pittsburgh.

	Natural Mystic	unissued
	Positive Vibration	"
	Curfew (Burnin' And Lootin')	"
	Belly Full	"
	The Heathen	Tuff Gong (Japan) lp
	Running Away	unissued
	Crazy Baldhead	"
	War	Tuff Gong (Japan) lp
	No More Trouble	unissued
	Zimbabwe	Tuff Gong (Japan) lp
	Zion Train	"
	No Woman No Cry	"
	Jamming	"
	Exodus	"
	Redemption Song	Tuff Gong, Tuff Gong (UK) CD TGCBX 1, Tuff Gong (Japan) lp
	Coming In From The Cold	Tuff Gong (Japan) lp
	Could You Be Loved	"
	Is This Love	"
	Medley: Work	"
	Get Up Stand Up	"

Note: These were Bob Marley's last recordings.

BUNNY WAILER
circa: 1980

Bunny Wailer, vocal, harmony vocal, and percussion; Anthony "Style" Scott, drums; Errol "Flabba" Holt, bass; Eric "Bingy Bunny" Lamont, guitar; Dwight Pinkney, guitar; Wycliffe "Steely" Johnson, keyboards; Uziah "Sticky" Thompson, percussion; David Hamilton, engineer; Lancelot "Maxie" McKenzie, assistant engineer; recorded Dynamic Sounds Studio; sixteen track; Bunny Wailer, production.

	Crazy Baldhead	Solomonic lp
	Time Will Tell	"
	War	"
SM 016A	Redemption Song	Solomonic (UK), Solomonic lp
	No Woman No Cry	Solomonic lp
	Belly Full	Shanachie (US) lp 43072

Note: Above tracks are from the *Tribute* lp.

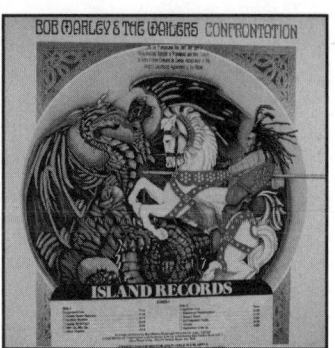

PETER TOSH   January 19, 1981

Peter Tosh, vocal, harmony vocal, guitar, and keyboards; Junior Moore, harmony vocal; Carlton Smith, harmony vocal; Winston Morgan, harmony vocal; Sly Dunbar, drums; Robbie Shakespeare, bass; Mikey "Mao" Chung, guitar; Darryl Thompson, guitar; Robbie Lyn, keyboards; Keith Sterling, keyboards; Uziah "Sticky" Thompson, percussion; Geoffrey Chung, engineer; recorded Dynamic Sounds Studio; twenty-four track; mixed at A&R Studios (US); Peter Tosh, production.

        That's What They Will Do   unissued
        That's What They Will Do   Intel Diplo lp, EMI lp SO-17055

PETER TOSH   January 20, 1981

Peter Tosh, vocal, harmony vocal, and guitar; Junior Moore, harmony vocal (-1); Carlton Smith, harmony vocal (-1); Winston Morgan, harmony vocal (-1); Sly Dunbar, drums; Robbie Shakespeare, bass; Darryl Thompson, guitar; Mikey "Mao" Chung, guitar; Uziah "Sticky" Thompson, percussion; Noel "Scully" Simms, percussion; Geoffrey Chung, engineer; recorded Dynamic Sounds Studio; twenty-four track; Peter Tosh, production.

        Feel No Way (-1)   Intel Diplo lp, EMI lp RDC 2005
        Feel No Way Dub Mix One   unissued
        Too Much Rats   "
        Wicker Man   "
        Jah Guide Me   "

PETER TOSH   January 20, 1981

Peter Tosh, vocal and guitar; Gwen Guthrie, harmony vocal; Pam Hall, harmony vocal; Yvonne Lewis, harmony vocal; Nadine Sutherland, harmony vocal; Sly Dunbar, drums; Aston "Family Man" Barrett, bass; Mikey "Mao" Chung, guitar; Darryl Thompson, guitar; Robbie Lyn, keyboards; Keith Sterling, keyboards; Uziah "Sticky" Thompson, percussion; Geoffrey Chung, engineer; recorded Dynamic Sounds Studio; twenty-four track; mixed at A&R Studios (US); Peter Tosh, production.

        The Poor Man Feel It   Intel Diplo lp, EMI lp SO-17055

PETER TOSH   January 21, 1981

Peter Tosh, vocal, harmony vocal, guitar, and keyboards; Junior Moore, harmony vocal; Carlton Smith, harmony vocal; Winston Morgan, harmony vocal; Sly Dunbar, drums; Robbie Shakespeare, bass; Mikey "Mao" Chung, guitar; Darryl Thompson, guitar; Robbie Lyn, keyboards; Keith Sterling, keyboards; Uziah "Sticky" Thompson, percussion; Geoffrey Chung, engineer; recorded Dynamic Sounds Studio; twenty-four track; mixed at A&R Studios (US); Peter Tosh, production.

	Cold Blood	unissued
12 RSR 107B	Cold Blood	Rolling Stones 12 RSR 107, Intel Diplo lp, EMI lp SO-17055
	Wanted Dread & Alive	Intel Diplo lp, EMI lp SO-17055

PETER TOSH
January 28, 1981

Peter Tosh, vocal and guitar (-1) or percussion (-2); Junior Moore, harmony vocal; Carlton Smith, harmony vocal; Winston Morgan, harmony vocal; Sly Dunbar, drums; Robbie Shakespeare, bass; Mikey "Mao" Chung, guitar; Darryl Thompson, guitar; Robbie Lyn, keyboards; Keith Sterling, keyboards; Dean Fraser, alto sax (-3); David Madden, trumpet (-3); Arnold Brakenridge, trumpet (-3); Ronald "Nambo" Robinson, trombone (-3); "Pee Wee", flute (-3); Uziah "Sticky" Thompson, percussion; Scully Simms, percussion; Geoffrey Chung, engineer; recorded Dynamic Sounds Studio; twenty-four track; mixed at A&R Studios (US); Peter Tosh, production.

A 8094-S45-500613	Reggae Mylitis (-1) (-3)	EMI (US) A-8094, Intel Diplo lp, EMI lp SO-17055
	Rastafari Is (-2)	Intel Diplo lp, EMI lp SO-17055
DSR 5932-A	Peace Treaty (-1) (12" mix)	Intel Diplo 12", Peter Tosh (UK) 10" 10RIC 115
DSR 5934-A	"	Intel Diplo, EMI (US) X 501091, Intel Diplo lp, EMI lp RDC 2005

Note: The 12" mix of "Peace Treaty" is listed first because the matrix reveals it to have been mastered earlier than the 7" pressing.

PETER TOSH
January 29, 1981

Peter Tosh, vocal and keyboards; Robbie Lyn, piano; "Pee Wee," flute; Geoffrey Chung, engineer; recorded Dynamic Sounds Studio; twenty-four track; mixed at A&R Studios (US); Peter Tosh, production.

                Fools Die   Intel Diplo lp, EMI lp SO-17055

Note: The original recording studio track sheet from Dynamic Sounds lists this track as "Lips Of The Righteous." Bob sang lead on the Wailers' 1970 cut of this song titled "Wisdom."

PETER TOSH
February 2, 1981

Peter Tosh, vocal, harmony vocal, guitar, and keyboards; Junior Moore, harmony vocal; Carlton Smith, harmony vocal; Winston Morgan, harmony vocal; Sly Dunbar, drums; Robbie Shakespeare, bass; Mikey "Mao" Chung, guitar; Darryl Thompson, guitar; Robbie Lyn, keyboards; Keith Sterling, keyboards; Uziah "Sticky" Thompson, percussion; Geoffrey Chung, engineer; recorded Dynamic Sounds Studio; twenty-four track; mixed at A&R Studios (US); Peter Tosh, production.

A 8094-Ss45-500611	Coming In Hot	EMI (US) A-8094, Intel Diplo lp, EMI lp SO 17055
DSR 1396-A	Rock With Me	Intel Diplo, EMI (UK) lp
	" (alternate long mix)	EMI CD72435 37693 21
DSR 1632-B	Version	Intel Diplo

Note: The original recording studio track sheet from Dynamic Sounds lists "Coming In Hot" as "Red Hot."

PETER TOSH WITH GWEN GUTHRIE
circa: early 1981

Peter Tosh, vocal; Gwen Guthrie, vocal; Pam Hall, harmony vocal; Yvonne Lewis, harmony vocal; Nadine Sutherland, harmony vocal; Sly Dunbar, drums; Robbie Shakespeare, bass; Mikey "Mao" Chung, guitar; Darryl Thompson, guitar; Robbie Lyn, keyboards; Keith Sterling, keyboards; Lou Marini, tenor sax; Barry Roger, trombone; Lew Soloff, alto sax; Jim Faddis, trumpet; Uziah "Sticky" Thompson, percussion; Geoffrey Chung, engineer; recorded Dynamic Sounds Studio; twenty-four track; Billy Jackson, mixing engineer; mixed at A&R Studios (US); Peter Tosh, production.

S45-500612-A-25	Nothing But Love	Rolling Stones (US) 8043, Intel Diplo lp, EMI lp SO-17055
12 RSR 107A	"	Rolling Stones (UK) 12" RSR 107

Note: "Nothing But Love" was written by Fred Harris and Ella Mitchell.

PETER TOSH circa: early 1981

Peter Tosh, vocal and guitar; Junior Moore, harmony vocal; Carlton Smith, harmony vocal; Winston Morgan, harmony vocal; Sly Dunbar, drums; Robbie Shakespeare, bass; Mikey "Mao" Chung, guitar; Darryl Thompson, guitar; Robbie Lyn, keyboards; Keith Sterling, keyboards; Dean Fraser, tenor sax; David Madden, trumpet; Arnold Brakenridge, trumpet; Ronald "Nambo" Robinson, trombone; Uziah "Sticky" Thompson, percussion; Geoffrey Chung, engineer; recorded Dynamic Sound Studio; twenty-four track; mixed at A&R Studios (US); Peter Tosh, production.

DSR 2958-A	Bumbo Klaat	Intel Diplo, Rolling Stones (US) 8083, Rolling Stones (UK) RSR 107, EMI (UK) lp
Sterling	Version	Intel Diplo

Note: The title "Bumbo Klaat" is as given on Intel Diplo single. On Rolling Stones labels, the title is given as "Oh Bumbo Klaat." Although listed on disc one of Columbia CD C3K 65064, the cut of "Bumbo Klaat" included is not this recording, but rather a live performance of the song.

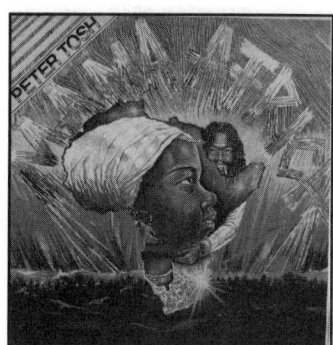

BUNNY WAILER circa: 1981

Bunny Wailer, vocal and harmony vocal; Anthony "Style" Scott or Sly Dunbar, drums; Errol "Flabba" Holt, or Robbie Shakespeare, bass; Eric "Bingy Bunny" Lamont, guitar; Dwight Pinkney, guitar; Wycliffe "Steely" Johnson, keyboards; Keith Sterling, keyboards; Dean Fraser, tenor sax and alto sax; "Deadly" Headly Bennett, alto sax; Ronald "Nambo" Robinson, trombone; Uziah "Sticky" Thompson, percussion; David Hamilton, engineer; Lancelot "Maxie" McKenzie, assistant engineer; recorded Channel One Studio and Harry J Studio; sixteen track; Bunny Wailer, production.

DSR 2207-A	Riding	Solomonic, Solomonic 12", Solomonic lp 008,
RT 83 A	"	Solomonic (UK) RT 83
DSR 2208-B	Version	Solomonic, Solomonic 12"
DSR 3050-A	Galong So	Solomonic, Solomonic 12", Solomonic (US) 12"
DSR 3051-B	Version	"
BW-981-NY	Rock And Groove	Solomonic (US) 12", Solomonic lp
SM 018B	Another Dance	Solomonic (UK), Solomonic lp
	Dance Rock	Solomonic lp
	Ballroom Floor	Solomonic, Solomonic lp
	Baldheaded Woman	Shanachie DC 45014

Note: "Riding" is on Solomonic lp *Hook Line & Sinker*. Other Solomonic lp titles are from the lp *Rock And Groove*.

BUNNY WAILER   circa: 1981

Bunny Wailer, vocal and harmony vocals; Anthony "Style" Scott or Sly Dunbar, drums; Errol "Flabba" Holt or Robbie Shakespeare, bass; Eric "Bingy Bunny" Lamont, guitar; Dwight Pinkney, guitar; Wycliffe "Steely" Johnson, keyboards; Keith Sterling, keyboards; Uziah "Sticky" Thompson, percussion; David Hamilton, engineer; Lancelot "Maxie" McKenzie, assistant engineer; recorded Channel One Studio and Harry J Studio; sixteen track; Bunny Wailer, production.

DSR 1704-A	Unity	Solomonic, Solomonic 12", Shanachie CD 45014
DSR 1705-B	Version	" , "
SM 007-A	Rise & Shine	Solomonic (US) 12", Solomonic lp,
RT 83 B	"	Solomonic (UK) RT 83
SM 007-B	Solomonic Dub	"
DSR 2034-A	Cool Runnings	Solomonic, Solomonic 12", Solomonic lp
DSR 2035-B	Version	" , "
	Roots Man Skanking	Solomonic lp
	Jammins	"

Note: Solomonic lp titles are from the lp *Rock And Groove*.

PETER TOSH   circa: Summer 1981

Peter Tosh, vocal, and guitar; Constantine "Dream" Walker, harmony vocal and percussion; Winston Morgan, harmony vocal and percussion; Steve Golding, harmony vocal and guitar; Carlton "Santa" Davis, drums; George "Fully" Fullwood, bass; Donald Kinsey, guitar; Robbie Lyn, keyboards; Keith Sterling, keyboards; recorded live at unknown location.

Bumbo Klaat	Columbia CD C3K 65064

Note: Peter toured Europe in June and then played dates in America ending on August 1. He then returned to Jamaica for a few weeks before returning to America for another five weeks of touring.

PETER TOSH   August 7, 1981

Peter Tosh, vocal, harmony vocal, and guitar; Junior Moore, harmony vocal (-1); Carlton Smith, harmony vocal (-1); Winston Morgan, harmony vocal (-1); Sly Dunbar, drums; Robbie Shakespeare, bass; Darryl Thompson, guitar; Mikey "Mao" Chung, guitar; Uziah "Sticky" Thompson, percussion; Noel "Scully" Simms, percussion; Geoffrey Chung, engineer; recorded Dynamic Sounds Studio; twenty-four track; Peter Tosh, production.

	Maga Dog	Intel Diplo lp, EMI lp RDC 2005
10-RIC-116-B	Stop That Train	Peter Tosh (UK) 10" 10RIC 116, Intel Diplo lp, EMI lp RDC 2005
	Not Gonna Give It Up (-1)	unissued
	Not Gonna Give It Up (-1)	"

PETER TOSH   circa: early 1982

Peter Tosh, vocal and guitar; Donald Kinsey, guitar; Tyrone Downie, keyboards; Lee Jaffe, harmonica; unknown engineer; unknown studio; Peter Tosh, production.

Rock This Music	unissued
Dub	"

Note: These tracks were recorded as demos.

PETER TOSH June 1982

Peter Tosh, vocal, harmony vocal, and guitar; Junior Moore, harmony vocal (-1); Carlton Smith, harmony vocal (-1); Winston Morgan, harmony vocal (-1); Carlton "Santa" Davis, drums; Lebert "Gibby" Morrison, bass; Steve Golding, guitar; Donald Kinsey, guitar and harmony vocal; Keith Sterling, keyboards; Robbie Lyn, keyboards; Dean Fraser, tenor or alto sax (-2); Uziah "Sticky" Thompson, percussion; Noel "Scully" Simms, percussion; Lancelot "Maxie" McKenzie, engineer; recorded Dynamic Sounds Studio; twenty-four track; Peter Tosh, production.

	Reggae Mylitis	unissued
	Come Together	"
	Glass House	"
DSR 5933-B	Glass House (-2) (12" mix)	Intel Diplo 12", EMI (US) 12" 7807
DSR 5935-B	" (7" mix)	Intel Diplo, Intel Diplo lp, EMI lp RDC 2005
	Me No Go A Jail Fe Gang Jah	unissued
RIC-177-AA-A	Not Gonna Give It Up (-1) (-2)	Peter Tosh (UK) 10" 10RIC 117, Intel Diplo lp, EMI lp RDC 2005

Note: 12" mix of "Glass House" is listed first because the matrix numbers reveal it to have been mastered earlier than the 7" pressing.

PETER TOSH circa: mid 1982

Peter Tosh, vocal, harmony vocal and guitar; Junior Moore, harmony vocal (-1); Carlton Smith, harmony vocal (-1); Winston Morgan, harmony vocal (-1); Betty Wright, harmony vocal; Dorrett Myers, harmony vocal; Pam Hall, harmony vocal; Audrey Hall, harmony vocal; Raymond Hall, harmony vocal; Carlton "Santa" Davis, drums; Lebert "Gibby" Morrison, bass; Steve Golding, guitar; Donald Kinsey, guitar and harmony vocal; Keith Sterling, keyboards; Robbie Lyn, keyboards; Dean Fraser, tenor sax and alto sax; David Madden, trumpet; Arnold Brackenridge, trumpet; Junior "Chico" Chin, trumpet; Frank, trumpet; Ronald "Nambo" Robinson, trombone; Uziah "Sticky" Thompson, percussion; Noel "Scully" Simms, percussion; Lancelot "Maxie" McKenzie, engineer; recorded Dynamic Sounds Studio; twenty-four track; Peter Tosh and Chris Kimsey, production.

RIC 117-A-1	Mama Africa	Peter Tosh (UK) 10" 10RIC 117, Intel Diplo lp, EMI lp RDC 2005
	" (short edit)	Peter Tosh (UK) RIC 117
	Mama Africa Dub (girls)	unissued
SPRO-29913-R2	Johnny B Good (short mix)	EMI (US) 12" 501090, EMI (US) X501090A, Intel Diplo lp, EMI lp RDC 2005
SPRO-1-9912-P-2	" (long mix)	EMI (US) 12" 501090, EMI (US) 12" 7807, Peter Tosh (UK) 10" 10RIC 115
	" (Dub mix max)	unissued
	" (Dub mix drums)	"
	Where You Gonna Run	Intel Diplo lp, EMI lp RDC 2005
10-RIC-116-A	" (long version)	Peter Tosh (UK) 10" 10RIC 116

PETER TOSH November 5, 1982

Peter Tosh, vocal and percussion (-1); Constantine "Vision" Walker, harmony vocal and percussion; Winston Morgan, harmony vocal and percussion; Carlton "Santa" Davis, drums; George "Fully" Fullwood, bass; Steve Golding, guitar; Donald Kinsey, guitar; Keith Sterling, keyboards; recorded live at the Roxy in Los Angeles, California.

	Stepping Razor	unissued
	African	"
	Coming In Hot	"
	Not Gonna Give It Up	"
	Don't Look Back	"
	Rastafari Is (-1)	Columbia CD C3K 65064
	Medley: I'm The Toughest	unissued
	Bush Doctor	"
	Johnny B. Good	"

                Get Up Stand Up   unissued
            Medley: Babylon Queendom   "
                    Legalize It   "

PETER TOSH   circa: November 1982

Peter Tosh, vocal; Constantine "Vision" Walker, harmony vocal and percussion; Winston Morgan, harmony vocal and percussion; Carlton "Santa" Davis, drums; George "Fully" Fullwood, bass; Steve Golding, guitar; Donald Kinsey, guitar; Keith Sterling, keyboards; recorded live at the Country Club in Reseda, California.

                Glass House (spoken)   Columbia CD C3K 65064

PETER TOSH   circa: November 1982

Peter Tosh, vocal; Constantine "Vision" Walker, harmony vocal and percussion; Winston Morgan, harmony vocal and percussion; Carlton "Santa" Davis, drums; George "Fully" Fullwood, bass; Steve Golding, guitar; Donald Kinsey, guitar; Keith Sterling, keyboards; recorded live in Calgary, Alberta, Canada.

                Glass House   Columbia CD C3K 65064
                Don't Look Back   unissued
                Mystic Man   Columbia CD C3K 65064

PETER TOSH   circa: 1982

Peter Tosh, vocal and percussion (-1); Constantine "Vision" Walker, harmony vocal and percussion; Winston Morgan, harmony vocal and percussion; Carlton "Santa" Davis, drums; George "Fully" Fullwood, bass; Steve Golding, guitar; Donald Kinsey, guitar; Keith Sterling, keyboards; recorded live in Detroit, Michigan.

                Johnny B Good   Columbia CD C3K 65064
                Rock With Me   "
                Rastafari Is (-1)   unissued

PETER TOSH   circa: November 1982

Peter Tosh, vocal; Constantine "Vision" Walker, harmony vocal and percussion; Winston Morgan, harmony vocal and percussion; Carlton "Santa" Davis, drums; George "Fully" Fullwood, bass; Steve Golding, guitar; Donald Kinsey, guitar; Keith Sterling, keyboards; recorded live in Boulder, Colorado.

                Coming In Hot   Columbia CD C3K 650564
                Get Up Stand Up   "
                Not Gonna Give It Up   "

BUNNY WAILER
circa: November 1982

Bunny Wailer, vocal and harmony vocal; Anthony "Style" Scott, drums; Errol "Flabba" Holt, bass; Eric "Bingy Bunny" Lamont, guitar; Dwight Pinkney, guitar; Wycliffe "Steely" Johnson, keyboards; Dean Fraser, tenor sax (-1); "Deadly" Headly Bennett, alto sax (-1); Ronald "Nambo" Robinson, trombone (-1); Uziah "Sticky" Thompson, percussion; David Hamilton, engineer; Lancelot "Maxie" McKenzie, assistant engineer; recorded Dynamic Sounds Studio; sixteen track; Bunny Wailer, production.

Collie Man A-5016	Collie Man (-1)	Solomonic, Solomonic (UK) 12", Shanachie lp 43043
Collie Man Version	Version	" , "
DSR 6592-A	Trouble Is On The Road Again	Solomonic, Solomonic (UK) 12", Shanachie CD 45014
DSR 6593-B	Version	" , "
DSR 3428-A	Back To School	Solomonic, Solomonic 12", Solomonic lp 008
DSR 3429-B	Version	" , "
	Hook Line & Sinker (-1)	Solomonic lp 008
SM7 021B	Soul Rocking Party (-1)	Solomonic (UK), Solomonic (UK) 12" SM 12-021, Solomonic lp 008
	Swop Shop (-1)	Solomonic lp 008
	" (alternate mix)	unissued
	" (alternate mix)	"
	Simmer Down (-1)	Solomonic lp 008

BUNNY WAILER
circa: November 1982

Bunny Wailer, vocal and harmony vocal; Anthony "Style" Scott, drums; Errol "Flabba" Holt, bass; Eric "Bingy Bunny" Lamont, guitar; Dwight Pinkney, guitar; Wycliffe "Steely" Johnson, keyboards; Dean Fraser, tenor sax; "Deadly" Headly Bennett, alto sax; Ronald "Nambo" Robinson, trombone; Uziah "Sticky" Thompson, percussion; David Hamilton, engineer; Lancelot "Maxie" McKenzie, assistant engineer; recorded Harry J Studio; sixteen track; Bunny Wailer, production.

The Monkey Speaks	Solomonic lp 008

Note: This song was originally recorded for Imperial Records in 1957 by New Orleans rhythm and blues giant Dave Bartholomew.

PETER TOSH
November 27, 1982

Peter Tosh, vocal and guitar; Constantine "Vision" Walker, harmony vocal and percussion; Winston Morgan, harmony vocal and percussion; Carlton "Santa" Davis, drums; George "Fully" Fullwood, bass; Steve Golding, guitar; Donald Kinsey, guitar; Keith Sterling, keyboards; recorded live at the World Music Festival in Kingston, Jamaica.

You Can't Blame The Youth	unissued
Them A, Fi Get A Beaten	"
Babylon Queendom	"
Stepping Razor	JAD CD-1014
Speech	"
African	"
Coming In Hot	"
Not Gonna Give It Up	"
Don't Look Back	"
Rastafari Is (-1)	"
I'm The Toughest	"
Legalize It	"
Get Up Stand Up	"

Note: Although booked to appear on the 26th, Peter did not take the stage until dawn of the 27th.

PETER TOSH
December 26, 1982

Peter Tosh, vocal and guitar or percussion (-1); Junior Moore, harmony vocal; Carlton Smith, harmony vocal; Winston Morgan, harmony vocal and percussion; Carlton "Santa" Davis, drums; George "Fully" Fullwood, bass; Steve Golding, guitar; Donald Kinsey, guitar; Keith Sterling, keyboards; recorded live at the Youth Consciousness Festival in Kingston, Jamaica.

Creation	unissued
Pick Myself Up	"
African	"
Coming In Hot	"
Not Gonna Give It Up	"
Medley: Can't Blame The Youth	"
Them A, Fi Get A Beaten	"
Rastafari Is (-1)	"
I'm The Toughest	"
Bush Doctor	"
Johnny B Good	"
Speech	"
Medley: Ketchy Shubby	"
Brand New Secondhand	"
Babylon Queendom	"
Legalize It	"

Note: Also see the following Bunny Wailer listing for additional performances by Tosh on this program.

BUNNY WAILER
December 27, 1982

Bunny Wailer, vocal; Gem, harmony vocal; Anna, harmony vocal; Vern, harmony vocal; Carl Ayton, drums; Lebert "Gibby" Morrison, bass; Winston "Bo Peep" Bowen, guitar; Douglas "Dougie" Bryan, guitar; Franklyn "Bubbler" Waul, keyboards; Errol "Tarzan" Nelson, keyboards; Dean Fraser, tenor or alto sax; Junior "Chico" Chin, trumpet; Ronald "Nambo" Robinson, trombone; Uziah "Sticky" Thompson, percussion; Harry T. Powell, percussion; Dennis Thompson and David Hamilton, engineers; recorded live at the Youth Consciousness Festival in Kingston, Jamaica.

Rastaman	unissued
Blackheart Man	Solomonic lp
Armagedon	"
Dreamland	unissued
Battering Down Sentence	"
Let Him Go	"
Love Fire	"
The Old Dragon	"
Struggle	"

Bunny Wailer, vocal; Gem, harmony vocal; Anna, harmony vocal; Vern, harmony vocal; Anthony "Style" Scott, drums; Errol "Flabba" Holt, bass; Eric "Bingy Bunny" Lamont, guitar; Dwight Pinkney, guitar; Wycliffe "Steely" Johnson, keyboards; Dean Fraser, tenor or alto sax; Junior "Chico" Chin, trumpet; Ronald "Nambo" Robinson, trombone; Uziah "Sticky" Thompson, percussion; Dennis Thompson and David Hamilton, engineers; recorded live at the Youth Consciousness Festival in Kingston, Jamaica.

Speech	unissued
Dance Rock	Solomonic lp
Rock And Groove	"
Rootsman Skanking	unissued
Galong So	"
Jamming	"
Cool Runnings	"

Bunny Wailer, vocal; Peter Tosh, harmony vocal and occasional lead (-1); Jimmy Cliff, harmony vocal and occasional lead (-1); Marcia Griffiths, harmony vocal (-2); Judy Mowatt, harmony vocal (-2); Gem, harmony vocal; Anna, harmony vocal; Vern, harmony vocal; Sly Dunbar, drums; Robbie Shakespeare, bass; Winston "Bo Peep" Bowen, guitar; Douglas "Dougie" Bryan, guitar; Franklyn "Bubbler" Waul, keyboards; Errol "Tarzan" Nelson, keyboards; Dean Fraser, tenor or alto sax; Junior "Chico" Chin, trumpet; Ronald "Nambo" Robinson, trombone; Uziah "Sticky" Thompson, percussion; Harry T. Powell, percussion; Dennis Thompson and David Hamilton, engineers; recorded live at the Youth Consciousness Festival in Kingston, Jamaica.

Crucial	Solomonic lp
Rudie	unissued
I'm The Toughest	Solomonic lp
Ballroom Floor	"
Soul Rocking Party	unissued
Back To School	"
Get Up Stand Up (-1)	"
Soul Rebel (-1)	"
Run For Cover (-1)	"
Hypocrite (-1)	"
No Woman No Cry (-1) (-2)	"
Keep On Moving (-1) (-2)	"

Note: Solomonic lp is titled *Bunny Wailer Live!* The show began on the 26th with Bunny going on at 4:49 a.m. on the morning of the 27th.

BUNNY WAILER   circa: 1983

Bunny Wailer, vocal and harmony vocal; Anthony "Style" Scott, drums; Errol "Flabba" Holt, bass; Eric "Bingy Bunny" Lamont, guitar; Dwight Pinkney, guitar; Wycliffe "Steely" Johnson, keyboards; Dean Fraser, tenor sax; "Deadly" Headly Bennett, alto sax; Uziah "Sticky" Thompson, percussion; David Hamilton, engineer; Harry J Studio; sixteen track; Bunny Wailer, production.

DSR 6386-A	The Conqueror	Solomonic, Solomonic (UK) 12", Shanachie (US) lp 43013
DSR 6387-B	Version	" , "
SM 018A	Boderation	Solomonic (UK), Solomonic 12", Solomonic (UK) 12",
		Shanachie (US) CD 45014
	Badder Ridim	Solomonic 12", Solomonic (UK) 12"

BUNNY WAILER   MARCIA GRIFFITHS   circa: 1983

Bunny Wailer, vocal and harmony vocal; Marcia Griffiths, vocal (-1); Anthony "Style" Scott, drums; Errol "Flabba" Holt, bass; Eric "Bingy Bunny" Lamont, guitar; Dwight Pinkney, guitar; Wycliffe "Steely" Johnson, keyboards; Uziah "Sticky" Thompson, percussion; David Hamilton, engineer; Dynamic Sounds Studio; sixteen track; Bunny Wailer, production.

Elec Boog A	Electric Boogie (-1)	Solomonic, Solomonic (US) 12", Solomonic lp, Island (UK) 112
Elec Boog B	Version	"
	Electro Boogie V/1	Solomonic (US) 12"
	Electro Boogie V/2	"
	Electro Boogie V/3	"
SM7 021 A	Electro Rap	Solomonic (UK), Solomonic 12", Solomonic (UK) 12"

PETER TOSH   August 23, 1983

Peter Tosh, vocal and percussion (-1); Constantine "Vision" Walker, harmony vocal and percussion; Winston Morgan, harmony vocal and percussion; Steve Golding, harmony vocal and guitar; Carlton "Santa" Davis, drums; George "Fully" Fullwood, bass; Donald Kingsey, guitar; Keith Sterling, keyboards; recorded live at the Greek Theatre, Los Angeles.

Creation	EMI CD 72435 36791 25
Buk-In-Ham Palace	"
Pick Myself Up	"
African	EMI lp ST-17126, EMI CD 72435 36791 25

Coming In Hot	EMI lp ST-17126, EMI CD 72435 36791 25
Not Gonna Give It Up	EMI CD 72435 36791 25
Rastafari Is (-1)	EMI lp ST-17126
" (full length)	EMI CD 72435 36791 25
Where You Gonna Run	"
(You Gotta Walk) Don't Look Back	"
Glass House	"
Equal Rights/Downpresser Man	EMI lp ST-17126
" (full length)	EMI CD 72435 36791 25
Peter's Rap	"
Bush Doctor	EMI lp ST-17126, EMI CD 72435 36791 25
Johnny B. Goode	" , "
Get Up Stand Up	" , "
Mama Africa	EMI CD 72435 36791 25

Note: Most of this concert is available on an EMI (Japan) video titled *Peter Tosh Live*.

PETER TOSH   September 1, 1983

Peter Tosh, vocal and guitar; Constantine "Vision" Walker, harmony vocal and percussion; Winston Morgan, harmony vocal and percussion; Steve Golding, harmony vocal and guitar; Carlton "Santa" Davis, drums; George "Fully" Fullwood, bass; Donald Kinsey, guitar; Keith Sterling, keyboards; recorded live on the David Letterman TV Show in New York City.

Equal Rights	unissued

JUDY MOWATT   circa: September 1983

Peter Tosh, vocal; Judy Mowatt, vocal; backing group is the One Vibe Band; recorded live in New York City.

One Love	unissued

Note: Peter walked on stage at this Judy Mowatt concert, and performed this one song with her.

PETER TOSH   circa: December 1983

Peter Tosh, vocal and percussion (-1); Constantine "Vision" Walker, harmony vocal and percussion; Winston Morgan, harmony vocal and percussion; Steve Golding, harmony vocal and guitar; Carlton "Santa" Davis, drums; George "Fully" Fullwood, bass; Donald Kinsey, guitar; Keith Sterling, keyboards; recorded live at the Dominion Theatre in London, England.

Unknown titles	Omni transcription disc

Note: Recorded by the BBC and broadcast on radio in January 1984. Issued on an Omni Magazine College Rock Concert vinyl transcription disc sent to radio stations only. There was no commercial release.

PETER TOSH   December 30, 1983

Peter Tosh, vocal and percussion (-1); Constantine "Vision" Walker, harmony vocal and percussion; Winston Morgan, harmony vocal and percussion; Steve Golding, harmony vocal and guitar; Carlton "Santa" Davis, drums; George "Fully" Fullwood, bass; Donald Kinsey, guitar; Keith Sterling, keyboards; recorded live at Reggae Superjam in Kingston, Jamaica.

Pick Myself Up	unissued
Wanted Dread & Alive	"
Hammer	"
Not Gonna Give It Up	"
Rastafari Is (-1)	"
Where You Gonna Run	"

Bob Marley at L'Hermitage Hotel in Hollywood in 1978, posing for *Soul* magazine – his first Black American magazine cover. Photo by Bruce Talamon.

    Medley: Jah Guide   unissued
       Stepping Razor   "
       Burial   "
       Legalize It   "
    Medley: Apartheid   "
       Can't Blame The Youth   "
       Them A, Fi Get A Beaten   "
    Glass House   "
    Legalize It   "
    Johnny B Good   "
    Get Up Stand Up   "
    Legalize It   "

Note: This was Peter's last live performance.

PETER TOSH   March 9, 1984

Peter Tosh, vocal, harmony vocal, guitar and keyboards; Ruddy Thomas, harmony vocal; Pam Hall, harmony vocal; Nadine Sutherland, harmony vocal; Cynthia Schloss, harmony vocal; June Lodge, harmony vocal; Carlton "Santa" Davis, drums; George "Fully" Fullwood, Gilbert "Gibby" Morrison, or Danny, bass; Steve Golding, guitar; Keith Sterling, keyboards; Tyrone Downie, keyboards; Uziah "Sticky" Thompson, percussion; Noel "Scully" Simms, percussion; unknown, drum machine; Dennis Thompson, engineer; recorded Dynamic Sounds Studio; twenty-four track; mixed at Music Mountain; Peter Tosh, production.

    Testify   unissued
    Testify   "
    Testify   Intel Diplo lp, EMI lp ELT-46700

BUNNY WAILER   circa: 1984

Bunny Wailer, vocal; Light Of Love, harmony vocals; Sly Dunbar, drums; Robbie Shakespeare, bass; Constantine "Vision" Walker, guitar; Keith Sterling, keyboards; Phillip Pearson, keyboards; Tyrone Downie, harmonica (-1); David Hamilton and Chris Stanley, engineers; recorded Tuff Gong Studio; twenty-four track; all tracks mixed at Tuff Gong except (-1) mixed at Right Track Recording Studio (US) by Francois Kervorkian and John Potokor; Bunny Wailer, production.

       Jump Jump (-1)   Solomonic, Solomonic 12", Solomonic (UK) SM 12-022
       Cool And Deadly   Solomonic SM lp 010
       Ally Worker   "
       Dance The Night Away   "
       Electric City   "
SM7 023A   Tears In Your Eyes   Solomonic (UK), Solomonic SM lp 010
SM 12-023-A   " (12" mix)   Solomonic (UK) SM 12-023
SM 12-023-A   Instrumental Mix   "
       Home Sweet Home   Solomonic SM lp 020
       Together   "

BUNNY WAILER   circa: 1984

Bunny Wailer, vocal; Light Of Love, harmony vocals; Sly Dunbar, drums; Robbie Shakespeare, bass; Constantine "Vision" Walker, guitar; Keith Sterling, keyboards; Philips Pearson, keyboards; Dean Fraser, alto sax; Junior "Chico" Chin, trumpet; Ronald "Nambo" Robinson, trombone; H. Thompson, percussion; David Hamilton and Chris Stanley, engineers; recorded Tuff Gong Studio; twenty-four track; Bunny Wailer, production.

    Stay With The Reggae   Solomonic SM lp 010
    Dance Hall Music   Solomonic, Solomonic 12", Solomonic (UK) SM 12-022

BUNNY WAILER   December 25, 1984

Bunny Wailer, vocal with unknown group; recorded live at the Reggae Consciousness Festival in Kingston, Jamaica.

Rastaman	unissued
Bright Soul	"
Love Fire	"
Amagideon (Armagedon)	"
Struggle	"
Battering Down Sentence	"
Dreamland	"
Medley: Walk The Proud Land	"
Rude Boy	"
Hypocrite	"
Medley: I'm The Toughest	"
Mellow Mood	"
Soul Rebel	"
Dancing Mood	"
Cool Runnings	"
Rock and Groove	"
Dance Rock	"
Rootsman Skanking	"
Ballroom Floor	"
Stay With The Reggae	"
Medley: Dance Hall Music	"
Cool and Deadly	"
Jump Jump	"

PETER TOSH   circa: June 1985

Peter Tosh, vocal, harmony vocal, and guitar; Carlton "Santa" Davis, drums; George "Fully" Fullwood, bass; Steve Golding, guitar; Tyrone Downie, keyboards; Keith Sterling, keyboards; Uziah "Sticky" Thompson, percussion; Noel "Scully" Simms, percussion; Dennis Thompson, engineer, Music Mountain Studio; twenty-four track; Peter Tosh, production.

Jah Love	unissued
Guava	"

PETER TOSH   June 4, 1985

Peter Tosh, vocal, harmony vocal, guitar, and keyboards; Carlton "Santa" Davis, drums; George "Fully" Fullwood; Gilbert "Gibby" Morrison, or Danny, bass; Steve Golding, guitar; Keith Sterling, keyboards; Tyrone Downie, keyboards; Uziah "Sticky" Thompson, percussion; Noel "Scully" Simms, percussion; Dennis Thompson, engineer; recorded Music Mountain Studio; twenty-four track; Peter Tosh, production.

No Nuclear War	unissued
Fight Apartheid	"

PETER TOSH   June 5, 1985

Peter Tosh, vocal, harmony vocal, guitar, and keyboards; Carlton "Santa" Davis, drums; George "Fully" Fullwood; Gilbert "Gibby" Morrison or Danny, bass; Steve Golding, guitar; Keith Sterling, keyboards; Tyrone Downie, keyboards; Uziah "Sticky" Thompson, percussion; Noel "Scully" Simms, percussion; Dennis Thompson, engineer; Music Mountain Studio; twenty-four track; Peter Tosh, production.

Babylon Queendom	unissued
Babylon Queendom	"
Fight Apartheid	"

PETER TOSH   June 7, 1985

Peter Tosh, vocal, harmony vocal, guitar, and keyboards; Carlton "Santa" Davis, drums; George "Fully" Fullwood, Gilbert "Gibby" Morrison, or Danny, bass; Steve Golding, guitar; Keith Sterling, keyboards; Tyrone Downie, keyboards; Uziah "Sticky" Thompson, percussion; Noel "Scully" Sims, percussion; Dennis Thompson, engineer; recorded Music Mountain Studio; twenty-four track; Peter Tosh, production.

        In My Song   unissued
        Nah Goa Jail   "

PETER TOSH   June 8, 1985

Peter Tosh, vocal, harmony vocal, guitar, and keyboards; Carlton "Santa" Davis, drums; George "Fully" Fullwood, Gilbert "Gibby" Morrison, or Danny, bass; Steve Golding, guitar; Keith Sterling, keyboards; Tyrone Downie, keyboards; Uziah "Sticky" Thompson, percussion; Noel "Scully" Simms, percussion; Dennis Thompson, engineer; recorded Music Mountain Studio; twenty-four track; Peter Tosh, production.

        No Nuclear War   unissued
        No Nuclear War   "
        Jah Man   "

PETER TOSH   June 10, 1985

Peter Tosh, vocal, harmony vocal, guitar, and keyboards; Ruddy Thomas, harmony vocal; Pam Hall, harmony vocal; Nadine Sutherland, harmony vocal; Cynthia Schloss, harmony vocal; June Lodge, harmony vocal; Carlton "Santa" Davis, drums; George "Fully" Fullwood, Gilbert "Gibby" Morrison, or Danny, bass; Steve Golding, guitar; unknown, guitar (-2); Keith Sterling, keyboards; Tyrone Downie, keyboards; Dean Fraser, tenor sax (-1); David Madden, trumpet (-1); Junior "Chico" Chin, trumpet (-1); Ronald "Nambo" Robinson, trombone (-1); Uziah "Sticky" Thompson, percussion; Noel "Scully" Simms, percussion; Dennis Thompson, engineer; recorded Music Mountain Studio; twenty-four track; Peter Tosh, production.

        Nah Goa Jail   unissued
        Nah Goa Jail   "
12-6156-B   Nah Goa Jail (-1)   Parlophone (UK) 12R6156, Intel Diplo lp,
                EMI lp ELT-46700
        No Nuclear War   unissued
        Fight Apartheid (-2)   Intel Diplo lp, EMI lp ELT-46700

PETER TOSH   **June 15, 1985**

Peter Tosh, vocal, harmony vocal, guitar, and keyboards; Ruddy Thomas, harmony vocal; Pam Hall, harmony vocal; Nadine Sutherland, harmony vocal; Cynthia Schloss, harmony vocal; June Lodge, harmony vocal; Carlton "Santa" Davis, drums; George "Fully" Fullwood, Gilbert "Gibby" Morrison, or Danny, bass; Steve Golding, guitar; Keith Sterling, keyboards; Tyrone Downie, keyboards; Uziah "Sticky" Thompson, percussion; Noel "Scully" Simms, percussion; Dennis Thompson, engineer; recorded Music Mountain Studio twenty-four track; Peter Tosh, production.

In My Song	unissued
In My Song	"
In My Song	Parlophone (UK) 12R6156, Intel Diplo lp, EMI lp ELT-4670

PETER TOSH   **June 16, 1985**

Peter Tosh, vocal, harmony vocal, guitar, and keyboards; Ruddy Thomas, harmony vocal; Pam Hall, harmony vocal; Nadine Sutherland, harmony vocal; Cynthia Schloss, harmony vocal; June Lodge, harmony vocal; Carlton "Santa" Davis, drums; George "Fully" Fullwood, Gilbert "Gibby" Morrison, or Danny, bass; Steve Golding, guitar; Keith Sterling, keyboards; Tyrone Downie, keyboards; Uziah "Sticky" Thompson, percussion; Noel "Scully" Simms, percussion; Dennis Thompson, engineer; recorded Music Mountain Studio; twenty-four track; Peter Tosh, production.

Jah Man	unissued
Jah Man	"
Jah Man	"

PETER TOSH   **June 19, 1985**

Peter Tosh, vocal, harmony vocal, guitar, and keyboards; Ruddy Thomas, harmony vocal; Pam Hall, harmony vocal; Nadine Sutherland, harmony vocal; Cynthia Schloss, harmony vocal; June Lodge, harmony vocal; Carlton "Santa" Davis, drums; George "Fully" Fullwood, Gilbert "Gibby" Morrison, or Danny, bass; Steve Golding, guitar; Keith Sterling, keyboards; Tyrone Downie, keyboards; Uziah "Sticky" Thompson, percussion; Noel "Scully" Simms, percussion; Dennis Thompson, engineer; recorded Music Mountain Studio; twenty-four track; Peter Tosh, production.

Lesson In My Life	unissued
Lesson In My Life	Intel Diplo lp, EMI lp ELT-46700

PETER TOSH   **June 21, 1985**

Peter Tosh, vocal, harmony vocal, guitar, and keyboards; Ruddy Thomas, harmony vocal; Pam Hall, harmony vocal; Nadine Sutherland, harmony vocal; Cynthia Schloss, harmony vocal; June Lodge, harmony vocal; Carlton "Santa" Davis, drums; George "Fully" Fullwood, Gilbert "Gibby" Morrison, or Danny, bass; Steve Golding, guitar; Keith Sterling, keyboards; Tyrone Downie, keyboards; Uziah "Sticky" Thompson, percussion; Noel "Scully" Simms, percussion; Dennis Thompson, engineer; recorded Music Mountain, twenty-four track; Peter Tosh, production.

Babylon Queendom	unissued
Babylon Queendom	"
Babylon Queendom	"

PETER TOSH   **June 24, 1985**

Peter Tosh, vocal, harmony vocal, guitar, and keyboards; Ruddy Thomas, harmony vocal; Pam Hall, harmony vocal; Nadine Sutherland, harmony vocal; Cynthia Schloss, harmony vocal; June Lodge, harmony vocal; Carlton "Santa" Davis, drums; George "Fully" Fullwood, Gilbert "Gibby" Morrison, or Danny, bass; Steve Golding, guitar; Keith Sterling, keyboards; Tyrone Downie, keyboards; Uziah "Sticky" Thompson, percussion; Noel "Scully" Simms, percussion; Dennis Thompson, engineer; recorded Music Mountain; twenty-four track; Peter Tosh, production.

	Come Together	unissued
	Come Together	"
12-6156-B	Come Together	Parlophone (UK) 12R6156, Intel Diplo lp, EMI lp ELT-46700

PETER TOSH   June 25, 1985

Peter Tosh, vocal, harmony vocal, guitar, and keyboards; Ruddy Thomas, harmony vocal; Pam Hall, harmony vocal; Nadine Sutherland, harmony vocal; Cynthia Schloss, harmony vocal; June Lodge, harmony vocal; Carlton "Santa" Davis, drums; Constantine "Vision" Walker, bass; Steve Golding, guitar; unknown, guitar (-1); Keith Sterling, keyboards; Tyrone Downie, keyboards; Dean Fraser, tenor sax; Dave Madden, trumpet; Junior "Chico" Chin, trumpet; Ronald "Nambo" Robinson, trombone; Uziah "Sticky" Thompson, percussion; Noel "Scully" Simms, percussion; Dennis Thompson, engineer; recorded Music Mountain Studio; twenty-four track; Peter Tosh, production.

No Nuclear War	unissued
No Nuclear War	"
No Nuclear War	"
No Nuclear War	Intel Diplo lp, EMI lp ELT-46700
" (single version)	EMI CD 72435 38852 29

PETER TOSH   circa: June 1985

Peter Tosh, vocal, harmony vocal, guitar and keyboards; Ruddy Thomas, harmony vocal; Pam Hall, harmony vocal; Nadine Sutherland, harmony vocal; Cynthia Schloss, harmony vocal; June Lodge, harmony vocal; Carlton "Santa" Davis, drums; George "Fully" Fullwood, Gilbert "Gibby" Morrison, or Danny, bass; Steve Golding, guitar; Keith Sterling, keyboards; Tyrone Downie, keyboards; Uziah "Sticky" Thompson, percussion; Noel "Scully" Simms, percussion; unknown drum machine; Dennis Thompson, engineer; recorded Music Mountain Studio; twenty-four track; Peter Tosh, production.

Vampire	Intel Diplo lp, EMI lp ELT-46700

PETER TOSH   July 10, 1985

Peter Tosh, vocal and guitar; Carlton "Santa" Davis, drums; George "Fully" Fullwood, bass; Gilbert "Gibby" Morrison, bass; Steve Golding, guitar; Keith Sterling, keyboards; Tyrone Downie, keyboards; Uziah "Sticky" Thompson, engineer; recorded Music Mountain Studio; twenty-four track; Peter Tosh, production.

Jah Man	unissued
Jah Man Version	"
Mystery Babylon	Columbia/Legacy CD CK 65921
Mystery Babylon Version	"

Note: "Mystery Babylon" is the same song as "Babylon Queendom."

BUNNY WAILER   circa: 1985

Bunny Wailer, vocal, harmony vocal, and percussion; Anthony "Style" Scott, drums; Errol "Flabba" Holt, bass; Eric "Bingy Bunny" Lamont, guitar; Dwight Pinkney, guitar; Wycliffe "Steely" Johnson, keyboards; Uziah "Sticky" Thompson, percussion; Sylvan Morris, engineer; recorded Dynamic Sounds Studio; twenty-four track; Bunny Wailer, production.

DSR 4531-A	Here In Jamaica		Solomonic, Solomonic lp, Shanachie lp 34059
DSR 5526-A	"	(12" mix)	Solomonic 12"
DSR 4532-B	Version		Solomonic
DSR 5527-B	"	(12" mix)	Solomonic 12"

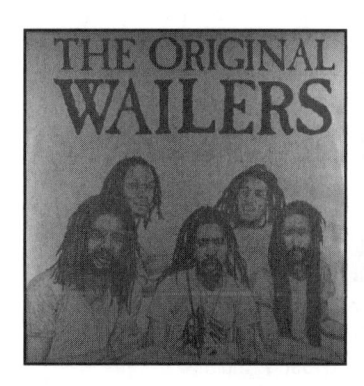

BUNNY WAILER
circa: 1985

Bunny Wailer, vocal, harmony vocal, and percussion; Anthony "Style" Scott, drums; Errol "Flabba" Holt, bass; Eric "Bingy Bunny" Lamont, guitar; Dwight Pinkney, guitar; Wycliffe "Steely" Johnson, keyboards; Sylvan Morris, engineer; Dynamic Sounds Studio; Bunny Wailer, production.

DSR 5435-A	Food	Solomonic, Solomonic lp, Shanachie lp 43059
	" (12" mix)	Solomonic 12", Solomonic (UK) 12"
DSR 5436-B	Version	Solomonic, Solomonic lp, Shanachie lp 43059
	" (12" mix)	Solomonic 12"

ORIGINAL WAILERS
circa: 1986

Bunny Wailer, vocal, harmony vocal, and percussion; Peter Tosh, harmony vocal and occasional lead (-1); Junior Braithwaite, harmony vocal and occasional lead (-1); Constantine "Vision" Walker, harmony vocal, guitar, and occasional lead (-1); Sly Dunbar, drums; Carlton "Santa" Davis, drums; Robbie Shakespeare, bass; Derrick Barnett, bass; Robbie Lyn, keyboards; Keith Sterling, keyboards; "Dizzy" Johnny Moore, trumpet (-2); Bobby Ellis, trumpet (-2); Barrington Bailey, trombone (-2); Harry T. Powell, percussion; Uziah "Sticky" Thompson, percussion; David Hamilton, Steven Stanley, and "Solgie" Hamilton, engineers; recorded and mixed at Tuff Gong Studio; twenty-four track; overdubs recorded at Channel One Studio; Bunny Wailer, production.

Together Again (-1)	Solomonic lp, RAS (US) lp 3501
" (early mix)	unissued
Nice Time (-1) (-2)	Tuff Gong 12" TRG 12 011, Solomonic lp, RAS lp (US) 3501
" (early mix)	unissued
" (early mix #2)	"
Dutch Pot	Solomonic lp, RAS (US) lp 3501
" (early mix)	unissued
Rescue Me (-2)	Solomonic lp, RAS (US) lp 3501
" (early mix)	unissued

Note: This was Peter Tosh's last recording session.

BUNNY WAILER
circa: 1986

Bunny Wailer, vocal, harmony vocal, and percussion; Psalms, harmony vocals; Anthony "Style" Scott, drums; unknown drum program; Errol "Flabba" Holt, bass; Eric "Bingy Bunny" Lamont, guitar; Dwight Pinkney, guitar; Wycliffe "Steely" Johnson, keyboards; Keith Sterling, keyboards; Sylvan Morris, engineer; recorded Dynamic Sounds Studio; twenty-four track; Bunny Wailer, production.

DSR 5548-A	Serious Thing	Solomonic
	" (12" mix)	Solomonic (UK) 12"
DSR 5549-B	Version	Solomonic

BUNNY WAILER   **circa: 1986**

Bunny Wailer, vocal, harmony vocal, and percussion; Anthony "Style" Scott, drums; Errol "Flabba" Holt, bass; Eric "Bingy Bunny" Lamont, guitar; Dwight Pinkney, guitar; Wycliffe "Steely" Johnson, keyboards; Keith Sterling, keyboards; Asher, keyboards; Uziah "Sticky" Thompson, percussion; Harry T. Powell, percussion; David Hamilton and "Solgie" Hamilton, engineers; recorded Channel One; sixteen track; Bunny Wailer, production.

SP-14-A	Rule Dance Hall	Solomonic, Solomonic lp, Shanachie (US) lp 43050
SP-14-B	Version	"
	Jolly Session	Solomonic lp, Shanachie (US) lp 43050
	Saturday Night	" , "
	Trash Ina We Bes	" ; "
	Put It On	" ; "
	Reggae In The U.S.A.	" , "
DSR 8815 DSRA	Haughty Tempo	Solomonic, Solomonic lp, Shanachie (US) lp 43050
DSR 8816 B	Version	"
	Camouflage	Solomonic lp, Shanachie (US) lp 43050
	Hot Foot Head	" , "
	Stir It Up	" , "
DSR 8286 A	Old Time Singting	Solomonic, Solomonic (UK), Solomonic lp, Shanachie (US) lp 43050
SM 12-023 AA	" (12" mix)	Solomonic (UK) 12" SM 12 023
DSR 8287 B	Version	Solomonic, Solomonic (UK)
SM 12-023 AA	Old Time Dub	Solomonic (UK) 12" SM 12 023
	Reasons	Solomonic lp, Shanachie (US) lp 43050

BUNNY WAILER   **July 12, 1986**

Bunny Wailer, vocal; Psalms, harmony vocal; Sly Dunbar, drums (-1); Anthony "Style" Scott, drums (-2); Robbie Shakespeare, bass (-1); Errol "Flabba" Holt, bass (-2); unknown guitar (-1); unknown guitar (-1); Eric "Bingy Bunny" Lamont, guitar (-2); Dwight Pinkney, guitar (-2); unknown keyboards (-1); Wycliffe "Steely" Johnson, keyboards (-2); Uziah "Sticky" Thompson, percussion; "Dizzy" Johnny Moore, trumpet (-3); Bobby Ellis, trumpet (-3); Barrington Bailey, trombone (-3); David Hamilton, engineer; recorded live at Long Beach University, California.

Speech	unissued
Dreamland (-1) (-3)	"
Love Fire (-1) (-3)	"
Bright Soul (-1) (-3)	"
Struggle (-1) (-3)	"
Rise And Shine (-1) (-3)	"
Rockers (-1) (-3)	"
The Old Dragon (-1)	"
Rastaman (-1) (-3)	"
Blackheart Man (-1) (-3)	"
Amagideon (Armagedon)(-1) (-3)	"
Battering Down Sentence (-1) (-3)	"
Fig Tree (-1) (-3)	"
Rock And Groove (-2) (-3)	"
Haughty Tempo (-2)	"
Jolly Session (-2)	"
Hot Foot Head (-2)	"
Camouflage (-2)	"
Rule Dance Hall (-2)	"
Rootsman Skanking (-2)	"
Dance Rock (-2) (-3)	"
Cool Runnings/Galong So (-2)	"
Old Time Singting (-2)	"
Good Good Rudie (-2) (-3)	"
Soul Rebel/Run For Cover (-2)	"

Hypocrite (-2) (-3)		unissued
I'm The Toughest (-2) (-3)		"
Crucial (-2)		"
Crazy Baldhead (-2)		"
No Woman No Cry (-2)		"

Note: This show was Bunny's first outside of Jamaica after he stopped touring with the Wailers.

BUNNY WAILER circa: late October 1986

Bunny Wailer, vocal and percussion (-1); Psalms, harmony vocals; Junior Braithwaite, vocal (-2); Constantine "Vision" Walker, vocal (-2); Anthony "Style" Scott, drums; Errol "Flabba" Holt, bass; Eric "Bingy Bunny" Lamont, guitar; Dwight Pinkney, guitar; Wycliffe "Steely" Johnson, keyboards; "Dizzy" Johnny Moore, trumpet (-3); Bobby Ellis, trumpet (-3); Barrington Bailey, trombone (-3); Uziah "Sticky" Thompson, percussion; David Hamilton, live film mix and recording engineer; recorded and filmed live at Madison Square Gardens, New York City.

The Old Dragon (-1)	Shanachie Video VHS 104
Blackheart Man (-3)	"
Dreamland (-3)	"
Love Fire (-3)	"
Struggle (-3)	"
Rise And Shine (-3)	"
Rockers (-3)	unissued
Dance Rock (-3)	Shanachie Video VHS 104
Rock 'N' Groove (-3)	"
Rootsman Skanking	"
Cool Runnings/Galong So	"
Ram Dancehall	"
Ballroom Floor (-3)	"
Walk The Proud Land	"
Rudie (-3)	"
I Stand Predominant (-3)	"
I'm The Toughest (-3)	"
Hypocrite (-3)	"
Together Again (-2)	"

BUNNY WAILER circa: 1987

Bunny Wailer, vocal, harmony vocal, and percussion; Anthony "Style" Scott, drums; unknown drum program; Errol "Flabba" Holt, bass; Eric "Bingy Bunny" Lamont, guitar; Dwight Pinkney, guitar; Wycliffe "Steely" Johnson, keyboards; David Hamilton and "Solgie" Hamilton, engineers; recorded Channel One Studio; sixteen track; Bunny Wailer, production.

SP-Botha-13-A	Botha	Solomonic
SP-13-B	Version	"

BUNNY WAILER circa: Summer 1988

Bunny Wailer, vocal; Psalms, harmony vocals; Carlton "Santa" Davis, drums; unknown bass; Earl "Chinna" Smith, guitar; unknown keyboards; unknown keyboards; "Dizzy" Johnny Moore, trumpet; Bobby Ellis, trumpet; Barrington Bailey, trombone; Harry T. Powell, percussion; Paul Special, engineer; recorded live at Fort Charles, Jamaica; Delilah Film, production.

Roots, Radics, Rockers & Reggae	unissued
Rise And Shine	"

Note: These selections were included in the film, *A Reggae Session*, broadcast by Cinemax.

BUNNY WAILER   circa: 1988

Bunny Wailer, vocal, harmony vocals, and percussion; Psalms, harmony vocals; Sly Dunbar, drums; Robbie Shakespeare, bass; Earl "Chinna" Smith, guitar; Stephen "Cat" Coore, guitar; Tony Asher, keyboards; Keith Sterling, keyboards; "Deadly" Headly Bennett, alto sax (-1); "Dizzy" Johnny Moore, trumpet (-1); Bobby Ellis, trumpet (-1); Barrington Bailey, trombone (-1); Uziah "Sticky" Thompson, percussion; Harry T. Powell, percussion; Sylvan Morris, engineer; recorded Dynamic Sounds Studio; twenty-four track; Karl Pitterson, mixing engineer; mixed at Mixing Lab Studio; Bunny Wailer, production.

	Didn't You Know	Solomonic lp, Shanachie (US) lp 43059
	" (alt. mix 1)	unissued
	" (alt. mix 2)	"
	" (alt. mix 3)	"
	" (alt. mix 4)	"
Baldhead Jesus A	Bald Head Jesus (-1)	Solomonic, Solomonic lp, Shanachie (US) lp 43059
Baldhead Jesus B	Version	"

BUNNY WAILER   circa: 1988

Bunny Wailer, vocal, harmony vocals, and percussion; Psalms, harmony vocal; Anthony "Style" Scott, drums; Earl "Flabba" Holt, bass; Eric "Bingy Bunny" Lamont, guitar; Dwight Pinkney, guitar; "Red Fox" Stewart, keyboards; "Deadly" Headly Bennett, alto sax; "Dizzy" Johnny Moore, trumpet; Bobby Ellis, trumpet; Barrington Bailey, trombone; Uziah "Sticky" Thompson, percussion; Harry T. Powell, percussion; Sylvan Morris, engineer; recorded Dynamic Sounds Studio; twenty-four track; Karl Pitterson, mixing engineer; mixed at Mixing Lab Studio; Bunny Wailer, production.

Rise And Shine   Solomonic lp, Shanachie (US) lp 43059

BUNNY WAILER   circa: 1988

Bunny Wailer, vocal, harmony vocal, and percussion; Psalms, harmony vocal; Carlton "Santa" Davis, drums; Daniel Thompson, bass; Earl "Chinna" Smith, guitar; Tony Asher, keyboards; Keith Sterling, keyboards; "Deadly" Headly Bennett, alto sax (-1); "Dizzy" Johnny Moore, trumpet (-1); Bobby Ellis, trumpet (-1); Barrington Bailey, trombone (-1); Uziah "Sticky" Thompson, percussion; Harry T. Powell, percussion; Sylvan Morris, engineer; recorded Dynamic Sounds Studio; Karl Pitterson, mixing engineer; mixing at Mixing Lab Studio; twenty-four track; Bunny Wailer, production.

Liberation (-1)   Solomonic lp, Shanachie (US) lp 43059
Botha The Mosquito (-1)   "   ,   "
Want To Come Home (1)   "   ,   "
Ready When You Ready (-1)   "   ,   "
"   (alt. mix 1)   unissued
"   (alt mix 2)   "
Dash Wey The Vial (-1)   Solomonic lp, Shanachie (US) lp 43059
Food (-1)   "   ,   "
"   (remix)   unissued
Serious Thing   Solomonic lp, Shanachie (US) lp 43059

        House Of Dread   unissued
        Child Of The Universe   "

BUNNY WAILER   circa: 1989

Bunny Wailer, vocal and harmony vocal; unknown drums; unknown bass; unknown guitar; unknown keyboards; unknown percussion; Sylvan Morris, engineer; recorded Dynamic Sounds Studio; twenty-four track; Bunny Wailer, production.

SM 45 029B	Sitting In The Park	Solomonic, Solomonic lp 013
SM 33.3 029B	Version/Acapella	"
	Family Affair	Solomonic lp 013
	Hit Back The Crack	"
	Just Be Nice	"

BUNNY WAILER   circa: 1989

Bunny Wailer, vocal, harmony vocal, and percussion; Psalms, harmony vocals; Chris Meredith, drums and drum machine; Danny Brownie, drums and drum machine; Robbie Shakespeare, bass; Danny Thompson, bass and guitar; Owen Stewart, guitar and keyboards; Harry T. Powell, percussion; Fatta, "Solgie" Hamilton, Carl, and David Rowe, engineers; recorded and mixed at Mixing Lab Studio; twenty-four track; Bunny Wailer, production.

	Sounds Clash	Solomonic lp 014
	Gumption	"
	Dog War	"
Warrior A	Warrior	Solomonic, Solomonic lp 014
Warrior Version B	Warrior Dub	"
	Don Man	Solomonic lp 014
DSR A side 1420	Reggae Burden	Solomonic, Solomonic lp 014
DSR B side 1421	Version	"
	See And Blind	Solomonic lp 014
	Pyaka (Bus Dem Shut)	"
	Never Grow Old	"
	Closer Together	"
	Wheel Yo Belly	Shanachie CD 43079
	Bad Boy Rap	unissued

    Note: Johnny Osbourne wrote "Warrior" and "See And Blind." Toots Hibbert wrote "Dog War" and "Never Grow Old." Curtis Mayfield wrote "Closer Together."

BUNNY WAILER   circa: October 1990

Bunny Wailer, vocal, harmony vocal, and percussion; Carl Ayton, drums; Chris Meredith, drums; Danny Thompson, bass; Owen Stewart, keyboards; Harry T. Powell, percussion; Junior, Carl, "Bulbie", and "Solgie" Hamilton, engineers; recorded and mixed at Mixing Lab Studio; twenty-four track; Bunny Wailer, production.

	Blackstone specials:	
	Young, Gifted And Black	unissued
	" (alt. mix)	"
	Never Conquer	"
	King Jammy's specials:	
	Keep On Running	unissued
	Hang Down Your Head	"
	Kilamanjaro special:	
	No Chuck It 'Pon Jaro	unissued
	Inner City specials:	
	Whip Them One By One	unissued
	Run For Cover	"

Exodus specials:
 Exodus   unissued
 Crucial   "
Gemini special:
 Who Laugh Last   unissued
Stone Love specials:
 I'm Still The King   unissued
 Big Special On His Hip   "
Black Cat specials:
 Keep On Moving   unissued
 Don Dadda   "
Four By Four special:
 Ram Dance Hall   unissued
Bodyguard special:
 I'm The Toughest   unissued
Wagatee special:
 Ram Dance Hall   unissued
Silver Hawk special:
 Burial   unissued
Addis special:
 Don Dadda   unissued

Note: These were recorded as sound system specials exclusively for the use of that system only. "Hang Down Your Head" is derived from the Kingston Trio's "Tom Dooley." "Big Special On His Hip" is derived from Marty Robbins' "Big Iron." "Never Conquer" was written by Jackie Mittoo and originally recorded by Delroy Wilson. "Young, Gifted And Black" was written by Simone and Irvine. "Who Laugh Last" was written by Peter Austin of the Clarendonians.

BUNNY WAILER   circa: 1990/1991

Bunny Wailer, vocal, harmony vocal, and percussion; Carl Ayton, drums; Chris Meredith, drums; Danny Thompson, bass; Owen Stewart, keyboards; Harry T. Powell, percussion; Junior, Carl, "Bulbie", and "Solgie" Hamilton, engineers; recorded and mixed at Mixing Lab Studio and Music Works Studio; twenty-four track; Bunny Wailer, production.

Sol DHFG A	Dance Ha Fi Gwan	Solomonic, Solomonic lp 2546
Sol DHFG Ver B	Version	"
	Still The King	Solomonic lp 2546
Don Dadda A	Don Dadda	Solomonic, Solomonic lp 2546
Don Dadda Version B	Version	"
SP 015-A	Dance Massive	Solomonic, Solomonic lp 2546
SP 015-B	Version	"
SOL RD A	Ram Dance	Solomonic, Solomonic lp 2546
SOL RD Ver B	Version	"
	Conscious Lyrics	Solomonic lp 2546
	Raggamuffin	"
	The Specialist	"
	Veteran	"
	Girls	"

BUNNY WAILER   circa: 1991

Bunny Wailer, vocal and harmony vocal; Carl Ayton, drums; Chris Meredith, drums; Danny Thompson, bass; Owen Stewart, keyboards; unknown engineer; recorded and mixed at the Mixing Lab Studio; twenty-four track; Bunny Wailer, production.

Love I Can Feel A	Love I Can Feel	Solomonic
Love I Can Feel B	Version	"
DSR A Side 2194	Walk 'N Talk	Solomonic
DSR B Side 2195	Version	"

Note: John Holt wrote "Love I Can Feel."

BUNNY WAILER   circa: 1992

Bunny Wailer, vocal and harmony vocal; Carl Ayton, drums; Chris Meredith, drums; Danny Thompson, bass; Owen Stewart, keyboards; unknown engineer; recorded and mixed at the Mixing Lab Studio; twenty-four track; Bunny Wailer, production.

DSR A830	Woman	Solomonic
DSR B800	Woman Dub	"
DSR A2192	Tribute To The Don	Solomonic
DSR B2193	Version	"

THE WAILERS   circa: 1993

Bunny Wailer, vocal and harmony vocal and percussion; Junior Braithwaite, vocal and harmony vocal; Constantine "Vision" Walker, vocal and harmony vocal; Andrew Tosh, vocal and harmony vocal; unknown drums; unknown drum machine; unknown bass; unknown keyboards; unknown engineer; unknown studio; twenty-four track; Bunny Wailer, production.

	Coolie Plum Tree (mix 1)	unissued
DSR B Side 6671	Coolie Plum Tree (mix 2)	Tuff Gong, RAS (US) lp 3501
	" (mix 3)	unissued
	" (mix 4)	"
	" (mix 5)	"
	" (mix 6)	"
	Coolie Plum Tree Version	"

THE WAILERS   circa: early 1994

Bunny Wailer, vocal and harmony vocal; Junior Braithwaite, harmony vocal; Constantine "Vision" Walker, harmony vocal and guitar; Andrew Tosh, harmony vocal; unknown drums; unknown bass; unknown keyboards; unknown horns; unknown engineers; unknown studio; twenty-four track; Bunny Wailer, production.

DSR A Side 6670	False Beneficiaries	Tuff Gong

BUNNY WAILER   circa: mid 1994

Bunny Wailer, vocal, harmony vocal, percussion, and keyboards; Carl Ayton, Sly Dunbar, Mikey "Boo" Richards, Anthony "Style" Scott, or Hugh Malcolm, drums (-1); Robbie Shakespeare, Daniel Thompson, Michael Fletcher, Aston "Family Man" Barrett, or Errol "Flabba" Holt, bass; Dwight Pinkney, Rudolph Bonitto, Winston "Bo Peep" Bowen, Junior Marvin, Owen "Dready" Reid, or "Gitsy" Willis, guitar; Keith Sterling, keyboards, percussion and computer programming; Mallory Williams, Lloyd "Obeah" Denton, Christopher Birch, Leroy Romance, or Tony Johnson, keyboards; "Dizzy" Johnny Moore, trumpet (-2); Bobby Ellis, trumpet (-2); Barrington Bailey, trombone (-2); Everton Gayle, horn (-2); Sylvan Morris, Lynford "Fatta" Marshall, Collin "Bulby" York, Chis Dailey, Ian "Fathead" McLean, Mikey Irish, Albert "Chemist" Thompson, David Hamilton or "Fatta" Brim, engineer; recorded at Mixing Lab, Dynamic Sounds, Music Works, I & I, or Aytonbridge Recording Studios; twenty-four track; Bunny Wailer, production.

Roots	RAS CD 3502
Chant Down Babylon	"
For Ever Loving Jah	"
Three Little Birds (-2)	"
Trench Town (-2)	"
Rastaman Vibration	"
Roots Rock Reggae (-2)	"
Johnny Was A Good Man	"
Want More	"
No More Trouble	"
Africa Unite (-2)	"
One Drop (-1)	"

Ambush	RAS CD 3502
Wake Up And Live (-2)	"
Can't Stop Them Now	"
Bad Card	"
Mi And Dem (We And Them)	"
Work (-2)	"
Rasta Dread (Natty Dread) (-2)	"
Bend Down Low (-1)	"
Talking Blues	"
Blackman Redemption	"
Sun Is Shining	"
Man To Man (Who The Cap Fit)	"
Stiff Neck Fool	"
Pimpers Paradise	"
Jump Nyahbinghi	"
Mix Up	"
Give Thanks And Praise	"
Trouble In The World	"
Zion Train	"
Rastaman Rides Again	"
Judge Not	"
Fancy Curls (-1)	"
Zimbabwe	"
Winepress (Babylon System)	"
Rat Race	"
Revolution	"
Top Rankin'	"
Rainbow Country	"
Simmer Down (-1)	"
Running Away	"
Guiltiness	"
Craven Choke Puppy (-2)	"
Natural Mystic	"
So Much Things To Say	"
Survivors (Survival) (-2)	"
One Love	"
Lively Up Yourself (-2)	"
Small Axe	"

Note: RAS CD contains opening and closing statements from Bunny Wailer.

BUNNY WAILER   circa: 1995

Bunny Wailer, vocal, harmony vocals, and percussion; unknown drums, unknown bass; unknown guitar; unknown keyboards; unknown horns (-1); unknown drum machine; unknown engineer; unknown studio; twenty-four track; Bunny Wailer, production.

Standing Ovation (-1)	unissued
Bear The Cross	"
Genetic Order (-1)	"
Reggae Rebel	"
Rockstone	"
Reggae Tree (-1)	"
Ghetto People	"
Easy Rude Boy (-1)	"
African Gypsy (-1)	"
What's New Pussycat	"
Rude Boys In The Hood (-1)	"
Rude Boy Rap	"

BUNNY WAILER circa: late 1990's

Bunny Wailer, vocal, harmony vocal, and percussion; Franklyn Francis, harmony vocal (-1); Big Dread, harmony vocal (-1); Abeja Livingston, harmony vocal (-1); Kadian Dixon, harmony vocal (-2); Leiba Hibbert, harmony vocal (-2); Shaddon Tucker, harmony vocal (-2); Ngeri Livingston, harmony vocal (-2); April Frye, harmony vocal (-2); Lloyd Knibbs, Hugh Malcolm, Carl Ayton or Owen Rennals, drums; Danny Thompson, Owen Rennals, Chris Meredith, or Lebert "Gibby" Morrison, bass; Ernest Ranglln, guitar; Rudolph Bonita, Danny Thompson, or Lebert "Gibby" Morrison, guitar; Keith Sterling, Earl Fitzsimmons, Chris Meredith, or Charmaine Bowman, keyboards; Dean Fraser, tenor or alto sax (-3); "Dizzy" Johnny Moore, trumpet (-3); unknown trombone (-5); Harry T. Powell, Bongo Herman, or Sky Juice, percussion; unknown scratch (-6); Sylvan Morris, engineer at Dynamic Sounds Studio or David Rowe at Anchor Records; Bunny Wailer, production.

        Standing Ovation (-2)   Solomonic/Tuff Gong CD
        Legends (-1, -3)   "
        Rockstone (-1)   "
        Against All Odds (-2, -5)   "
        Genetic Order (-1)   "
        The People's Cup   "
        Almighty Is A Rappa (-1, -6)   "
        Help Us Jah (-1)   "
        Bear The Cross (-2)   "
        Ethiopia (-2)   "
        Reggae Converts (-1, -3, -5)   "

Note: Solomonic/Tuff Gong CD is titled *Communication*.

BUNNY WAILER circa: 1999

Bunny Wailer, vocal, harmony vocal, and percussion; Franklyn Francis, harmony vocal; Big Dread, harmony vocal; Lloyd Knibbs, Hugh Malcolm, Carl Ayton, or Owen Rennals, drums; Danny Thompson, Owen Rennals, Chris Meredith, or Lebert "Gibby" Morrison, bass; Harry T. Powell, Bongo Herman, or Sky Juice, percussion; Sylvan Morris, engineer; Dynamic Sounds Studio; Bunny Wailer, production.

        Fiya Red   Solomonic/Tuff Gong CD

Note: Solomonic/Tuff Gong CD is titled *Communication*.

BUNNY WAILER circa: 1999

Bunny Wailer, vocal, harmony vocal, and percussion; Franklyn Francis, harmony vocal (-1); Big Dread, harmony vocal (-1); Kadian Dixon, harmony vocal (-2); Lieba Hibbert, harmony vocal (-2); Shaddon Tucker, harmony vocal (-2); April Frye, harmony vocal (-2); unknown child harmony (-3); Lloyd Knibbs, Hugh Malcolm, Carl Ayton, or Owen Rennals, drums; Danny Thompson, Owen Rennals, Chris Meredith, or Lebert "Gibby" Morrison, bass; Ernest Ranglin, guitar; Rudolph Bonita, Danny Thompson, or Lebert "Gibby" Morrison, guitar; Keith Sterling, Earl Fitzsimmon, or Chris Meredith, keyboards; Dean Fraser, tenor sax (-4); unknown alto sax (-5); "Dizzy" Johnny Moore, trumpet (-6); Rudolph Bonita, harmonica (-7); Harry T. Powell, Bongo Herman, or Sky Juice, percussion; unknown scratch (-8); unknown drum program (-9); Sylvan Morris, engineer at Dynamic Sounds Studio or David Rowe, engineer at Anchor Records; Bunny Wailer, production.

        Disarmament Speech   Solomonic/Tuff Gong CD
        Trigger Happy Kid (-1, -2, -3)   "
        Teeni Wappaz (-3, -8)   "
DSR 1911   Stand In Love (-2, -4, -5, -6, -7)   Solomonic 0029, Solomonic/Tuff Gong CD
DSR 1912   Stand In Version   "

Note: Solomonic/Tuff Gong CD is titled *Communication*.

BUNNY WAILER circa: 1999

Bunny Wailer, vocal, harmony vocal, and percussion; Ian "Haile" Maskel, bass and guitar; Patrick Ross, keyboards and drum programs; Bob Morse, engineer; Echo Sounds Studio; Bunny Wailer, production.

Side West	Millennium Rock (extended mix)	Solomonic 12", Solomonic/Tuff Gong CD
Side East	" (radio mix)	"
"	" (club mix)	"
"	" (rhythm version)	"

Note: Solomonic/Tuff Gong CD is titled *Communication*.

BUNNY WAILER   circa: 2003

Bunny Wailer, vocal and harmony vocal; unknown male harmony vocals; unknown drum programming; unknown bass; unknown guitar; unkown keyboards; unknown engineer and studio; Bunny Wailer, production.

World Peace	Solomonic CD
Total Destruction	"

Note: "World Peace" is based on a speech by Haile Selassie. "Total Distruction" is the Bob Marley song originally named "Real Situation." Solomonic CD is titled *World Peace*.

BUNNY WAILER   circa: 2004

Bunny Wailer, spoken word; unknown engineer; unknown studio; Bunny Wailer, production.

Introduction	Solomonic/Tuff Gong CD disc 1
Trench Town – Kingston 12, Birth Place Of The Wailers	"
Recruiting The Wailers	"
Preparation And Exposure	"
Auditioning	"
Wailers First Recording Session	"
Inheriting The Name Wailers	"
Challenging Times	"
Bratty's Migration To The USA	"
Wailers Frustration	"
First Concert Performance	"
The Trinity	"
Bob Migration To The USA	"
The Wedding Bells Tolled	"
Dreams Adoption To The Wailers	"
Rasta Shook Dem Up	"
The Guns Barked	"
Bob's Return From The USA	Solomonic/Tuff Gong CD disc 2
Coxsone Repressive System	"
The Wail 'N' Soul M Label	"
The Scanner	"
The Wailers Progress	"
Bunny's False Imprisonment	"
JAD The Scanners	"

Restoration of Wail 'N' Soul M	Solomonic/Tuff Gong CD disc 2
Wailers/Beverley's Combination	"
Introduction Of Tuff Gong	"
Skill's Appointment To Tuff Gong	"
Wailers/Upsetter Combination	"
Duppy Conqueror	"
Return Of JAD The Scanners	Solomonic/Tuff Gong CD disc 3
Wailers Tour With Johnny Nash	"
Wailers Clash With Johnny Nash	"
First Acquaintance With Blackwell	"
Wailers Return To Jamaica	"
Wailers Betrayed	"
Wailers/Island Combination	"
Wailers Catch A Fire Tour	"
The Wailers Split	

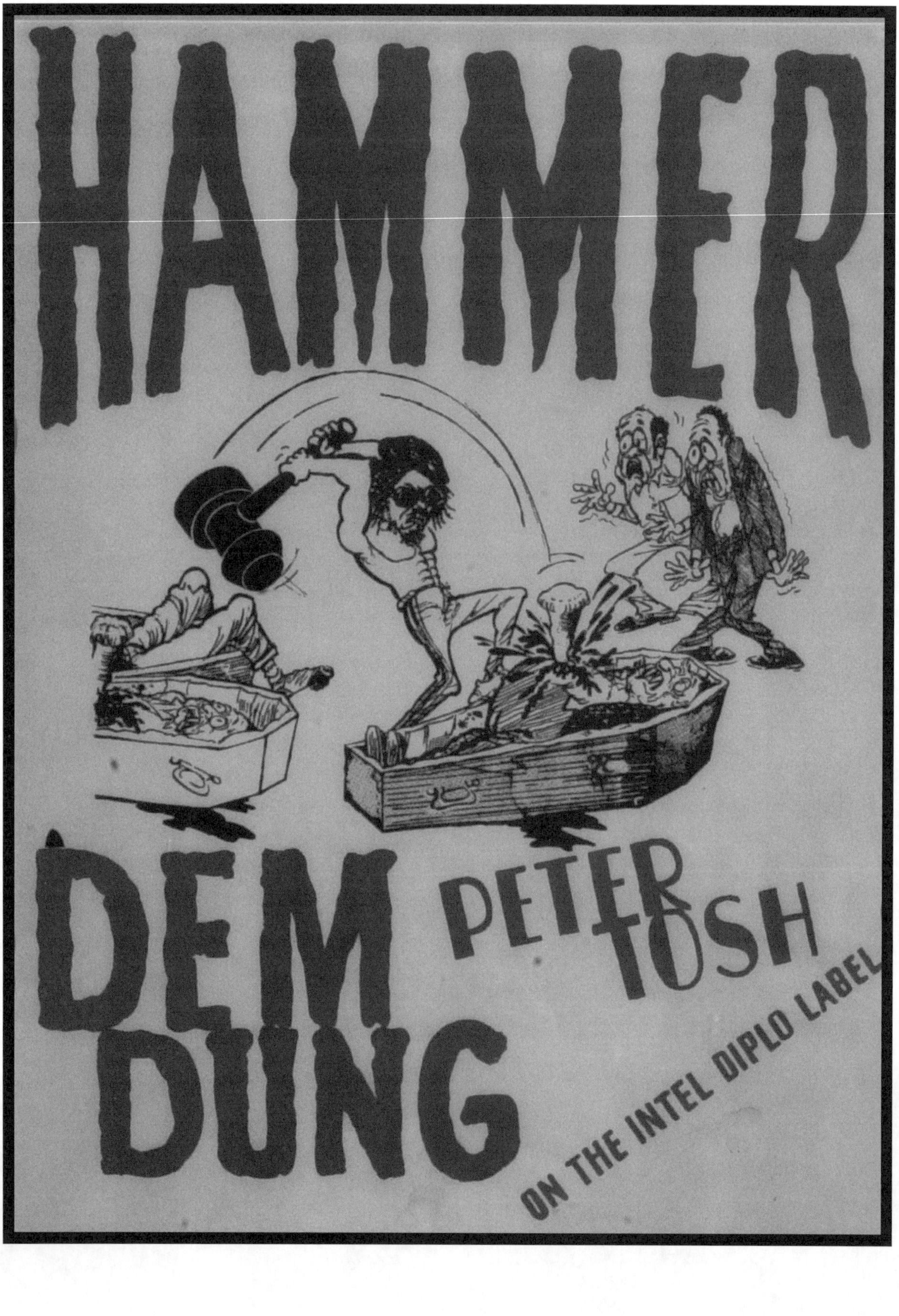
HAMMER
DEM DUNG
PETER TOSH
ON THE INTEL DIPLO LABEL

Chris Blackwell visits Roger Steffens' Reggae Archives in 2004 and holds Bob Marley's first two solo records, released on Blackwell's Island Records label in the UK in 1963. Photo by Roger Steffens.

Leroy Jodie Pierson, born in St. Louis in 1947, has been a professional blues guitarist/vocalist his entire adult life. He learned his craft first hand playing with legendary friends Son House, Fred McDowell, Johnny Shines, Henry Townsend, Yank Rachel, Rev. Robert Wilkins, and Mance Lipscomb. He has performed throughout America and has toured Africa, the Middle East, and Jamaica and has released albums on the Nighthawk and APO labels. In addition he has done studio production work on albums by St. Louisans Henry Townsend and Fontella Bass and Jamaican artists Justin Hinds, Junior Byles, the Ethiopians, the Gladiators, the Itals, and Culture. He has written the liner notes of over 60 albums for companies like Vanguard, Heartbeat, Columbia, Boogie Disease, Sony, Island, Nighthawk, JAD, and Tuff Gong. As a writing team, he and co-author Roger Steffens have annotated the entire Wailers catalog from 1964-1972. In St. Louis, he is also well known for his 14 years as a popular radio DJ promoting blues and reggae. He has been a dedicated Wailers collector since the late '70s.

Livication
To the memory of Justin Hinds, whose songs continue to provide strength and inspiration, and whose friendship will always be treasured.
–L.J.P.

Although best known for his numerous reggae involvements, Roger Steffens has made his living primarily as an actor since 1965. He made his film debut in 1976's *Rollercoaster*, and has had voice-over roles in *Forrest Gump, Wag the Dog, American President,* and hundreds of other film and television productions. His narrations have been featured at the Smithsonian Air and Space Museum, the Museum of Tolerance, the Getty, and dozens of other institutions. In addition, he narrated an Oscar-winning documentary, was the Audie-nominated voice of the most recent Bill Gates' book on tape, and for six years was the corporate voice for Time-Warner audio books. His interviews have ranged from Keith Richards and Ray Charles to Fela Kuti and Timothy Leary and countless reggae stars. A veteran of 26 months in Vietnam, he won a bronze star for his work with refugees, and lectured widely against the war upon his return to America in 1970. In the photo, Roger is shown doing field work for the discography behind the Tuff Gong offices at 56 Hope Road in Kingston, interviewing Scully "Zoot" Simms, the noted Jamaican percusionist, in 2001.

Livication
To my soul-mate and co-conspirator, Mary Higgins, who for thirty years has enabled me to pursue my obsession, and without whom none of this work would have been possible. My thanks and love for you are like the Wailers - never ending.
– R.S.

Born in Los Angeles, Geoff Gans is an award-winning graphic designer and musician with 25 years experience in album design, special project and marketing creation, and management. Gans began his career in publishing with the *LA Reader* and *The Beat* reggae magazine in the early '80s. During this period, he also began building his reputation for art and design work on the LA Indie Music scene. He segued to IRS Records in 1985, then joined Rhino Records, where he worked from 1989 to 1996 in the capacities of senior art director and later senior creative director, garnering five Grammy nominations.

Going independent in 1997, Geoff's knowledge, interests and expertise led to his involvement as a consultant/archivist/designer/art director for numerous music-driven film, radio and book projects. Since 1997, Geoff has also worked as personal art director to the Bob Dylan organization, with responsibility for all of his new album art, *Bootleg Series* releases, tour advertising, merchandising, and various book publications.

Geoff Gans with his prized "potato-head," Paul Whiteman 78 Westchester Ca., April 2005. Photo by Elisa Gans.

Cover design and book layout by Geoff Gans.

All record labels reproduced in this book are photographs of the original releases from the collection of Leroy Jodie Pierson.

All album covers and picture sleeve art reproduced in this book are photographs of the items from the collections of Roger Steffens and Leroy Jodie Pierson.

Contributing photographers, whose big-hearted generosity in sharing these pictures is gratefully acknowledged: Kate Simon, Bruce Talamon, Neville Garrick, Henry Eccleston, Peter Simon, Esther Anderson, and the authors.

Roger wishes to thank especially his friend, the inestimable graphic magician Geoff Gans, who, in the midst of months of painstaking, mind-numbing design and layout work, joined his fabulous wife Elisa in parenthood. We welcome Ella Gans into the world, and thank her father for his way-beyond-the-call-of-duty devotion to making this project transcend the ordinary with grace and precision.

The authors are grateful for the experienced hand of editor Brad San Martin, whose meticulous attention to detail and endless hours of proofreading helped insure the integrity of our text.

The authors also recommend an international rootzine called *Distant Drums* and its associated website, www.distantdrums.org.

Visit www.rounderbooks.com for to post your comments and emendations on this book's contents, and read regular updates from the authors.

This book is like an hourglass. Or more specifically, the center of an hourglass. The top is filled with grains of sand which represent the hundreds of people who have contributed to the discoveries and revelations herein. We think of this discography as the tiny choke point, spilling information out in a myriad of new connections.

Each of the persons named below is a precious part of the mass of information particles joining together to make this book a reality. Some have a grain or two, others big pinches, but all were necesary and all shared what they knew with us freely in a spirit of generosity and an abiding desire to keep the work of the Wailers alive for future fans. We heartically thank each of the following brethren and sistren, and so, we trust, will generations yet to come. Our gratitude to you is boundless.

R.S. & L.J.P.

Glen Adams
Karl Anthony
Olivier Albot
Elan Atias
Javier "Jah V" Aldohondo
Mark Alvarado
Al Anderson
Esther Anderson
Bob Andy
Wayne Auchaybur
Dominique Auffray
Kevin Aylmer
Ernie B
Bally and Yvonne Barton
Carly Barrett
Errol Barrett
George Barrett
Aston "Family Man" Barrett
Steve Barrow
Leggo Beast
John Bent
Big Youth
Dennis "Spliff Skankin" Bishop
Johnny Black
Pablov Black
Chris Blackwell
Adam Block
Bruno Blum
Klaus Boehmer
Cedella Booker
Adrian Boot

Junior Braithwaite
Cindy Breakspeare
Dave Brown
Ras John Bullock
Rabbit Bundrick
Carl from Randy's
Clark "Dagga DJ" Carmen
Geraldo Carvalho
Chili Charles
Phil Chen
Wayne Chen
Tony Chin
Greg Cockrell
Allan "Skill" Cole
Charlie Comer
Steven "Cat" Coore
Yvet Chrichton
Fikisha Cumbo
Sheila Curran
Lloyd Daley
Roger Dalke
Carlton "Santa" Davis
Stephen Davis
Kwame Dawes
Garth Dennis
Sanjay Dev
Dixie Diamond
Leonard Dillon
Sam Dion
Clement Dodd
Fred Donaldson

Tyrone Downie
Gael Doyen
DRO
"Sir Henry" Eccleston
Alton Ellis
Bobby Ellis
John Fitzmorris
Jeff Forester
Chuck Foster
George "Fully" Fullwood
Lars Fyledal
Viola Galloway
Geoff Gans
Neville Garrick
Carl Gayle
Dr. Alvaro Gaynicotche
Vivien Goldman
Kent Goodall
Mark Gorney
Kim Gottleib
Colby Graham
Leo Graham
Randall Grass
Cherry Green
Marcia Griffiths
Josh Harris
Earl Hayles
Joe Higgs
Justin Hinds
Gary "Doctor Dread" Himelfarb
Danny Holloway

Hank Holmes
Ray Hurford
Dermot Hussey
Jabba
Lee Jaffe
Jah Lloyd
Tomas Jardim
Winston Jarrett
"Jah Bill" Just
Paul Johnson
Frank Jones
Hedley Jones Jr. and Sr.
Joe Jurgensen
Dave Katz
Beverley Kelso
Brian Keyo
King Sporty
Donald Kinsey
Jacky Knafo
Jay "Boomshot" Langworthy
Greg Lawson
Elliott and Rene Leib
Bill Levenson
Colin Leslie
Lance Linares
Earl "Wya" Lindo
Glen Lockley
Kurt Mahoney
Bob Marley
Rita Marley
Jim Marshall
Junior Marvin
Winston "Pipe" Matthews
Charles Mendes
Herbie Miller
Jack Miller
Richard Miller
Ron Miller
Jim Milne
Charlie Morgan

Dizzy Johnny Moore
Pauline Morris
Sylvan Morris
Mossmon
Judy Mowatt
Tommy McCook
Lloyd "Bread" McDonald
Niney the Observer
Daniel Nelson
Eric Nelson
Seth Nelson
Jimmy Norman
Whitey Norton
Cory Nyberg
Michael Ochs
Adebayo Ojo
Thor Olsen
Seeco Patterson
Lee Perry
Sheila Pierson
Karl Pitterson
Mortimo Planno
Steve Radzi
Peter Ravheden
Tom Ray
Ras Michael
Penny Reel
David Rodigan
George Robinson
Dave Rosencrans
Jeff Roth
Hugh Roy
I Roy
Chris Salewicz
Carlos Santana
Keith Scott
Ivan Serra
Kirk Sherbourne
Kate Simon
Peter Simon

Danny Sims
CC Smith
Carlton Smith
Desmond "Dessie" Smith
Earl "Chinna" Smith
Dr. Matthew Smith
Ralph Smith
Roger Guenveur Smith
Warren Smith
Gary Steckles
Mary Steffens
Bob Steinhilber
Susan Stockstill
Jay Strausser
Roy Sweetland
Lowell Taubman
Dennis Thompson
Tom Threlkel
Mark Timmis
Dera Tompkins
Peter Tosh
Peter, Ton, and Wim van Arnhem
Carter van Pelt
Martha Velez
Joe Venneri
Amy Wachtel
Bunny Wailer
Constantine "Vision" Walker
Jeff Walker
Doug Wendt
Don Williams
Neville Willoughby
Chris Wilson
Delroy Wilson
Terry Wilson
Dr. Michael Witter

APPENDIX A: Album Title Index

Label/Cat#	Title	Artist
Anansi CD AN 0101-2	Soul Almighty	Bob Marley
BBC Transcription Disc CN 1813/S	Pop Spectacular	Bob Marley & The Wailers
Calla 2 CAS-1240	The Birth Of A Legend	Bob Marley & The Wailers
Columbia lp PC 34253	Legalize It	Peter Tosh
" lp PC 34670	Equal Rights	Peter Tosh
Columbia/Legacy CD CK 85478	Live & Dangerous Boston 1976	Peter Tosh
" CD CK 65921	Scrolls Of The Prophet: Best Of	Peter Tosh
" CD C3K 65064	Honorary Citizen	Peter Tosh
Cotillion lp SO 5228	Chances Are	Bob Marley
EMI ELT-46700	No Nuclear War	Peter Tosh
" RDC 2005	Mama Africa	Peter Tosh
" SO-17055	Wanted Dread & Alive	Peter Tosh
" ST-17126	Captured Live	Peter Tosh
Heartbeat CD HB 111/112	One Love At Studio One	Bob Marley & The Wailers
" CD HB 150	The Toughest	Peter Tosh
" CD HB 171	Simmer Down At Studio One	Bob Marley & The Wailers
" CD HB 172	The Wailing Wailers At Studio One	Bob Marley & The Wailers
" CD HB 191	Destiny: Rare Ska Sides From Studio One	Bob Marley & The Wailers
" CD HB 201	Wailers & Friends	Bob Marley & The Wailers
" CD HB 251	Climb The Ladder	Bob Marley & The Wailers
" CD HB 261	Greatest Hits At Studio One	Bob Marley & The Wailers
" CD HB 319	One Love At Studio One	Bob Marley & The Wailers
Island lp SW 9329	Catch A Fire	Wailers
" lp ILPS 9256	Burnin'	Wailers
" lp ILPS 9376	Live	Bob Marley & The Wailers
" lp ILPS 9383	Rastaman Vibration	Bob Marley & The Wailers
" lp ILPS 9415	Blackheart Man	Bunny Wailer
" lp DLPS 9498	Exodus	Bob Marley & The Wailers
" lp ILPS 9512	Protest	Bunny Wailer
" lp ILPS 9517	Kaya	Bob Marley & The Wailers
" lp ILPS 9542	Survival	Bob Marley & The Wailers
" lp ILPS 9596	Uprising	Bob Marley & The Wailers
" lp ISLD 11	Babylon By Bus	Bob Marley & The Wailers
" lp ISS 3	A Taste Of The Wailers	Bob Marley & The Wailers
" lp RSS 1	Record Shop Sampler	Bob Marley & The Wailers
" lp 90037-1	Natty Dread	Bob Marley & The Wailers
" lp 90085-1	Confrontation	Bob Marley & The Wailers
" lp 90169-1	Legend	Bob Marley & The Wailers
" lp 90520-1	Rebel Music	Bob Marley & The Wailers
JAD CD 1001-2	Soul Almighty: The Formative Years	Bob Marley
" CD 1002	The Complete Wailers 1967-1972 Part I	Bob Marley
" CD-1003	Black Progress: Formative Years Vol. 2	Bob Marley
" CD 1004	Complete Bob Marley & Wailers Part II	Bob Marley & The Wailers
" CD-1009	Live At The One Love Peace Concert	Peter Tosh
" CD-1012	I Am That I Am	Peter Tosh
" CD-1014	Live At The Jamaican World Music Festival	Peter Tosh
" CD 495250 2-PM 596	Complete Bob Marley & Wailers Part III	Bob Marley & The Wailers
" CD 533082 2	Jungle Dub	Bob Marley & The Wailers
" CD 537324 2-PM 580	Freedom Time	Bob Marley & The Wailers
" CD 537325 2-PM 580	Soul Adventurer	Bob Marley & The Wailers
" LP 542 222-1	Lonesome Feeling	Bob Marley & The Wailers
" CD B0003297-02	Original Cuts	Bob Marley & The Wailers
" CD B0003753-02	Fyah Fyah	Bob Marley & The Wailers
Jamaican Gold CD JMC 200 229	The Rarities Vol. 1	Bob Marley & The Wailers
" CD JMC 200 230	The Rarities Vol. 2	Bob Marley & The Wailers
" CD JMC 200 277	Rebel Revolution: The Extended Mixes	Bob Marley & The Wailers
Keytone lp KYT 719	Bamboo Reggae	Chris Hinze
Lagoon CD LG2-1040	The Upsetter Record Shop Part I	Bob Marley & The Wailers
Lagoon CD LG2-1044	The Upsetter Record Shop Part II	Bob Marley & The Wailers

Mango lp MLPS-9629	*Bunny Wailer Sings The Wailers*	Bunny Wailer
Mango lp MSTDA 1	*Countryman*	Various Artists
RAS CD 3501	*Hall Of Fame*	Bunny Wailer
" lp 3501	*The Never Ending Wailers*	Wailers
Rohit CD RRTG 7757	*All The Hits*	Bob Marley & The Wailers
Rolling Stones lp COC 39109	*Bush Doctor*	Peter Tosh
" lp CUN 39110	*Mystic Man*	Peter Tosh
" lp COC 39111	*Mystic Man*	Peter Tosh
Shanachie CD 43079	*Gumption*	Bunny Wailer
" CD 43095	*Dance Massive*	Bunny Wailer
" CD 45014	*Crucial! Roots Classics*	Bunny Wailer
Shanachie lp 43043	*Rootsman Skanking*	Bunny Wailer
" lp 43050	*Rule Dance Hall*	Bunny Wailer
" lp 43059	*Liberation*	Bunny Wailer
Solomonic lp 008	*Hook Line & Sinker*	Bunny Wailer
Solomonic lp 010	*Marketplace*	Bunny Wailer
Studio One lp SO 1106	*The Best Of Bob Marley & The Wailers*	Bob Marley & The Wailers
Trojan lp 183	*Creation Rockers Vol. 4*	Various Artists
" lp TRLS 221	*In The Beginning*	Bob Marley & The Wailers
Tuff Gong CD TGCBX 1	*Songs Of Freedom*	Bob Marley
" /Island CD B0000516-02	*Live At The Roxy*	Bob Marley & The Wailers
" /Island CD 314 548 635-2	*Catch A Fire: Deluxe Edition*	Bob Marley & The Wailers
" /Island CD 440 063 446-2	*Rastaman Vibration: Deluxe Edition*	Bob Marley & The Wailers
" /Island CD 314 586 408-2	*Exodus: Deluxe Edition*	Bob Marley & The Wailers
" /Island CD 314 586 714-2	*Legend: Deluxe Edition*	Bob Marley & The Wailers
" lp 101	*Catch A Fire*	Wailers
" lp 102	*Burnin'*	Wailers
" lp 422-848 243-1	*Talkin' Blues*	Bob Marley and The Wailers

APPENDIX B: Caymen Music Master Catalog

Below are listed songs that appear in the Caymen Music Master Catalog. Composition of all songs is credited to Bob Marley unless otherwise indicated by a different name appearing behind the title in parenthesis. There are several mistakes included such as the crediting of numerous Peter Tosh or Bunny Wailer songs to Bob. We have not corrected these mistakes. The catalogue includes numerous titles that have never been heard, but may well have been recorded in formal or informal sessions. Caymen Music was owned by Danny Sims.

A Lovely Day
A Song For You
A Toast To The People
African Herbsman
African Lady
All In One
All The Girls Are Ready
Baby Baby We've Got A Date
Back Out
Bailando Joda L Noche
Band Played On
Be Your Friend
Beautiful Baby
Beginnings
Bend Down Low
Black And White
Blue Flame
Blue Grass
Body Slang
Brain Washing
Brand New Second Hand
Burning And Looting
Can't You See

Caution
Celebrate Life
Chances Are
Cheer Up
Comma Comma
Common Mortal Man
Concrete Jungle
Corner Stone
Cotton Candy
Craven Choke Puppy
Cream Puff
Cry To Me
Curfew
Dance To The Reggae
Dancing Shoes
Do It Twice
Do You Feel The Same Way
Do You Remember
Don't Rock The Boat
Donna
Down In The Valley
Downpressor Man
Duppy Conqueror
Edge Of Life (Lee)

Elegant Donkey (McDonald)
Equal Rights
Essex
Everything's Got An Aura
Fall Together
Fanny Big Horn
Four Hundred Years
Freedom
Fussing And Fighting
Get Down
Get Up Stand Up
Gimme Just Another Try
Give a Smile
Go Tell It On The Mountain
Gonna Let You
Good Girls Culture
Goodbye You Hello Him
Guava Jelly
Hall Of Love
Hallelujah Time
Hammer
Hold Me Tight
How Good It Is
How Many Times

Hurting Inside
Hypocrite
I Am Going Home
I Am That I Am
I Don't Need Your Love
I Like Your Loving
I Made A Mistake
I Shot The Sheriff
I Want You
I'm A Rastaman
I'm Gonna Get You
I'm Gonna Put It On
I'm Leaving
I'm Still Waiting
I'm The Traveling
It Hurts To Be Alone
It's All Right
Jah Guide
Kaya
Keep On Dancing
Keep On Moving
Kings And Queens
Kinky Reggae
Las Flores Wechter
Lecion D Travest
Leroy
Let Him Go
Let's Be Friends
Let's Move And Groove Together
Little Lonely Girl (Norman)
Live Love Rejoice
Lively Up Yourself
Lonely Girl (Norman/Pyfrom)
Lonesome Feeling
Lonesome Track
Lord I'm Coming
Love
Love Ain't No Holiday (Jobson)
Love And Affection
Love I Get Ready
Loving You
Maga Dog
Magical Fountain
Make Me Love The Rain
Mango Coconut Sugar
Mellow Mood
Memphis
Midnight Ravers
Milk Shake & Potato Chips (Norman)
Mr. Brown
Muddy Water
My Cup
My Merry Go Round
Nice Time
Night Shift
Night Spots
No More Trouble
No Sympathy
No Water
No Woman No Cry

Nobody Knows (C. Dodd)
Nobody Knows The Trouble
On My Way
One Bad Habit
One Foundation
One Love
Ooh Baby You've Been Good
Pass It On
People In Love
Picking Up The Pieces
Positive Vibration
Pour Sugar On Me
Put It On
Quatrocientas Years
Rainbow Country
Rasta Man Chant
Reaction
Rebel's Hop
Redemption Song
Reggae On Broadway
Reggae The Night Away
Revolution
Riding High
Rock And Roll Junkie
Rock It Baby
Roots Rock Reggae
Rule This Land
Satisfy My Soul
Saturday Night
Screw Face
Season For Carnival (McDonald)
Selfish Lover
She's Gone
She's Older Now
Shout (Afrik S)
Si Tu Penses A Moi
Silver And Gold
Simmer Down
Slave Driver
Small Axe
So Jah Say
So Nice While It Lasted
Soon Come
Soul Almighty
Soul Brother Soul Captive
Soul Rebel
Soul Shake Down Party
South Carolina
Stand Alone
Standing In The Rain
Stay With Me
Steal Away
Stepping Razor
Stir It Up
Stop That Train (Tosh)
Sun Is Going Down
Sun Is Shining
Sunshine
Take Me Back
Tell It To The Mountains

Tell Me The World Is Changing
Thank You Jah
Thank You Lord
That's The Way We Get By
The Look In Your Eyes
The Very First Time
The World Is Changing (Norman)
There Are More Questions
There She Goes
This Train
Touch Me
Toughest
Travelling In Style
Treat You Right
Treat You Right (Norman)
Trench Town Rock
Trust Me
Try Me
Turn Your Lights
We Won
We're All A Like
Who Feels It
Who The Cap Fit
Why Must We Cry
Wisdom
Wishing Well
Yesterday's Children
You Can Do That To
You Can't Do That To Me (Norman)
You Got Soul
You Poured Sugar On Me

APPENDIX C: Additions and Corrections

This section lists recordings that we were unaware of until too late in the discography's preparation for inclusion in the main text.

BOB MARLEY   circa: 1968

Bob Marley, vocal, harmony vocal, and guitar; Rita Marley, harmony vocal; unknown percussion; informal demo.

           One Love, True Love   JAD CD B0003753-02

BOB MARLEY & THE WAILERS   circa: summer 1970

Bob Marley, vocal and guitar; Bunny Wailer, vocal and piano; Peter Tosh, vocal and organ; Hugh Malcom, drums; Lloyd Brevett, bass; Errol Thompson, engineer; recorded at Randy's Studio 17; four track; Wailers, production.

NL 824   Feel Alright   Tuff Gong

  Note: This recording is not an alternate take, but rather an alternate mix.

BOB MARLEY & THE WAILERS   circa: 1971

Bob Marley, vocal and guitar; Peter Tosh, harmony vocal and guitar; Bunny Wailer, harmony vocal; unknown drums; unknown bass; unknown tenor sax; unknown alto sax; unknown trombone; unknown engineer; unknown studio; Wailers, production.

        Pass It On   JAD CD B0003297-02
        Pass It On Version   "

  Note: Although this early version of the song shares the chorus with Bunny Wailer's later recordings, the verse lyrics are different.

BOB MARLEY   unknown date

Bob Marley, vocal and guitar; unknown male harmony; unknown percussion; informal recordings.

        Soul Rebel   unissued
        Wisdom   "
        Butterfly   "
        Lonely Day   "
        Down By The River   "
        Cry On   "
        Heat Of The Day   "

BOB MARLEY & THE WAILERS   circa: Aug./Sept. 1975

Bob Marley, guitar; Rita Marley, harmony vocal; Marcia Griffiths, harmony vocal; Judy Mowatt, harmony vocal; Carlton Barrett, drums; Aston "Family Man" Barrett, bass; Earl "Chinna" Smith, guitar; Danny Kinsey, guitar; Tyrone Downie, keyboards; Bernard "Touter"Harvey, keyboards; Alvin "Seeco" Patterson, percussion; Sylvan Morris, recording engineer; recorded at Harry J Studio; sixteen track; Alex Sadkin, mixing engineer; mixed at Criterion Studio, Miami by Aston "Family Man" Barrett and Chris Blackwell; Wailers, production.

AB 2891   Want More   blank label

  Note: This recording is not an alternate take, but rather an alternate mix with Bob's vocal deleted.

SONG TITLE	PAGE No.
007 Shanty Town	54
400 Years	44, 45, 62, 65, 71, 72, 91, 105, 128
400 Years (version)	45
A De Pon Dem	24
A Little Prayer	34
A Lovely Day	165
A Song For You	165
A Toast To The People	165
Adam And Eve	37
Africa Unite	115, 120, 153
African	93, 128, 135, 137, 138, 139
African Gypsy	154
African Herbsman	51, 165
African Herbsman Version	51
African Lady	165
African Version	93
Against All Odds	155
Ah-So	55
Ain't Nobody's Business	58
All Day All Night	67
All In One	48, 49, 165
All The Girls Are Ready	165
Ally Worker	142
Almighty Is A Rappa	155
Am-A-Do	79
Amagideon (Armagedon)	83, 143, 148
Ambush	116, 154
Ambush In Dub	116
Ambush In The Night	118, 120
Amen	4
Ammunition	56, 58
And I Love Her	12
Another Dance	15, 133
Anti-Apartheid	83
Apartheid	93, 142
Arab Oil Weapon	63
Arab's Oil Weapon	82
Arabs Oil Weapon	63
Arise Blackman	59
Armagedon	138
Armagedon (Dubd'sco)	83
Auditioning	156
Awake Rasta	59
Axe Man	42
Baby Baby Come Home	38
Baby Baby I Need You	25
Baby Baby We've Got A Date	165
Baby We've Got A Date	65
Babylon Feel This One	128
Babylon Queendom	91, 92, 117, 128, 136, 137, 138, 143, 145, 146
Babylon System	114, 116, 154
Babylon System Dub	116
Back Biter	56, 65
Back Biter Version	56
Back Out (Wailing Souls)	36
Back Out	38, 165
Back To School	137, 139
Bad Boy Rap	151
Bad Card	123, 124, 125, 154

SONG TITLE	PAGE No.
Bad Play (Bad Card)	125
Badder Ridim	139
Bailando Joda L Noche	165
Bald Head Jesus	150
Baldheaded Woman	133
Ballroom Floor	133, 139, 143, 149
Band Played On	165
Battering Down (Dubd'sco)	81
Battering Down Sentence	64, 81, 89, 138, 143, 148
Battle Axe	42
Be Your Friend	165
Bear The Cross	154, 155
Beard Man Ska	22
Beautiful Baby	165
Beggars Have No Choice	12
Beginnings	165
Belly Full	79, 83, 85, 90, 92, 99, 100, 111, 118, 120, 130
Bend Down Low	26, 31, 33, 49, 72, 73, 79, 83, 154, 165
Bend Down Low Version	79
Bide	63
Bide Up	62, 63
Big Iron	152
Big Special On His Hip	152
Birth Place Of The Wailers	156
Black And White	165
Black Candle	77
Black Dignity	55
Black On Black	63
Black Progress	36, 40, 164
Blackheart Man	85, 89, 138, 148, 149, 164
Blackman Redemption	114, 117, 118, 154
Bless You	22
Blowing In The Wind	25
Blue Flame	165
Blue Grass	165
Bob Marley Interviews	75
Bob Migration To The USA	156
Bob's Return From The USA	156
Boderation	139
Body Slang	165
Boney Dog	54
Botha	149
Botha The Mosquito	150
Brain Washing	165
Brainwashing	50
Brainwashing (version)	50
Brand New Second Hand	78, 165
Brand New Secondhand	49, 91, 138
Bratty's Migration To The USA	156
Bright Soul	99, 143, 148
Bring It Up	40
Buffalo Dub	127
Buffalo Soldier	127
Buffalo Soldier Instrumental	127
Buffalo Soldier Version	127
Buk-In-Ham Palace	139
Buk-In-Hamm Palace	113, 122, 128
Buk-In-Hamm Version	113
Bull Dog	54
Bullwhip	12

SONG TITLE	PAGE No.	SONG TITLE	PAGE No.
Bumbo Klaat	133, 134	Cotton Candy	165
Bunny's False Imprisonment	156	Could You Be Loved	115, 122, 123, 130
Burial	28, 75, 91, 105, 117, 126, 142, 152	Coxsone Repressive System	156
Burial - Dub	126	Craven Choke Puppy	60, 63, 154, 165
Burnin' & Lootin'	73, 83, 90, 103	Craven Version	60
Burnin' And Lootin'	70, 72, 73, 82, 97, 100, 103, 130	Crazy Bald Head,	130
		Crazy Baldhead	88, 92, 99, 101, 103, 111, 118, 120, 125, 130, 149
Burning And Looting	165		
Bus Dem Shut	27, 151	Crazy Baldhead Version	88
Bush Doctor	109, 111, 117, 128, 135, 138, 140	Cream Puff	165
		Creation	108, 138, 139
Business Man Version	58	Crimson Pirate	39
Butterfly	167	Crisis	95, 103, 111
Camouflage	148	Crisis Version	95
Can't Blame The Youth	67, 69, 73, 74, 75, 82, 89, 91, 92, 137, 138, 142	Crucial	125, 139, 149, 152
		Cry On	167
Can't Stop Them Now	154	Cry To Me	16, 19, 55, 86, 126, 165
Can't Take Your Slogans No More	122	Crying In The Chapel	34
Can't You See	24, 38, 103, 113, 165	Crystal Ball	113
Can't You See Instrumental	103	Curfew	165
Caution	38, 165	Curfew (Burnin' And Lootin')	70, 72, 73, 82, 97, 100, 103, 130
Cease Fire	125		
Celebrate Life	165	Cutting Razor	28
Challenging Times	156	Dana (Donna)	7, 10
Chances Are	29, 33, 164, 165	Dance Do The Reggae	62
Chant (Rasta Man Chant)	70	Dance Ha Fi Gwan	152
Chant Down Babylon	127, 128, 153	Dance Hall Music	142, 143
Chant I	70	Dance Massive	152
Chatterbox Version	44	Dance Rock	133, 138, 143, 148, 149
Cheer Up	38, 165	Dance The Night Away	142
Child Of The Universe	151	Dance To The Reggae	165
Choke	59, 60, 63	Dance With Me	7
Christmas Is Here	4	Dancing Mood	143
Climb The Ladder	3	Dancing Shoe - Dub	126
Closer Together	151	Dancing Shoes	23, 25, 126, 165
Cloud Nine	44	Dancing Version	25
Cold Blood	131	Dash Wey The Vial	150
Collie Man	137	Day The Dollar Die, The	113
Come By Here	25	Deh Pon Dem	24
Come Together	135, 146	Dem A Fi Get A Beatin'	28
Coming In From The Cold	123, 130	Dem Ha Fe Get A Beaten	109
Coming In Hot	132, 135, 136, 137, 138, 140	Dem Ha' Fi Get A Beatin'	28
		Destiny	1, 3, 4
Comma Comma	36, 55, 165	Dewdrops	55
Common Mortal Man	165	Diamond Baby	11, 12
Concrete	87	Dick Tracy	11
Concrete Jungle	58, 61, 64, 71, 72, 83, 97, 100, 111, 120, 123, 165	Didn't You Know	150
		Disarmament Speech	155
Concrete Jungle Version	58	Distant Drums	80
Conquering Lion	105	Distant Dub	80
Conqueror, The	139	Do It Right	12
Conqueror Version 3	43	Do It Twice	38, 165
Conscious Lyrics	152	Do The Boogaloo	25
Cool And Deadly	142, 143	Do You Feel The Same Way	165
Cool Runnings	134, 138, 143, 148, 149	Do You Feel The Same Way Too	13
Coolie Plum Tree	153	Do You Remember	1, 4, 165
Coolie Plum Tree Version	153	Do You Still Love Me?	1
Copasetic	49	Doctor Kildare	3
Corner Stone	44, 46, 165	Dog Teeth	60
Corner Stone Version	46	Dog War	151
Cornerstone	55	Don Dadda	152
		Don Man	151

SONG TITLE	PAGE No.
Don't Care What The People Say	19
Don't Cross The Nation	48, 49
Don't Cry Over Me	15
Don't Deceive Me	35
Don't Ever Leave Me	7, 8, 10
Don't Give Up	117
Don't Let The Sun Catch You Crying	43
Don't Look Back	23, 25, 109, 111, 128, 135 136, 137, 140
Don't Rock My Boat	28, 29, 53, 72
Don't Rock My Boat (version)	53
Don't Rock The Boat	165
Don't Space Out	109
Don't Want To Get Busted	103
Don't Want To See You Cry	25
Don't You Know	35
Donna 7,	165
Doppy Conqueror	43
Down By The River	167
Down In The Valley	165
Downpresser	49
Downpresser Man	19, 140
Downpresser Version	49
Downpressor Man	93, 165
Dracula	49
Dracula (Tosh)	92
Dracular	49
Dream Land (Dubd'sco)	51
Dreamland	25, 51, 89, 126, 138, 143, 148, 149
Dreamland Skank	51
Dreamland Version	51
Dreamland (version)	51
Dreams Adoption To The Wailers	156
Dub Feeling	39
Dub In Trenchtown	128
Dub Wise	106
Dubbing In Buk-In-Hamm	113
Duppy Conqueror	42, 43, 49, 70, 72, 73, 74, 156, 165
Duppy Conqueror V/4	43
Duppy Conqueror V/5	43
Dutch Pot	147
Earth's Rightful Ruler	36
Eastern Memphis	80
Easy Rude Boy	154
Easy Skanking	97, 103, 111
Easy Skanking Version	97
Edge Of Life (Lee)	165
Electric Boogie	139
Electro Boogie	139
Electric City	142
Electro Rap	139
Elegant Donkey (McDonald)	165
Equal Rights	93, 105, 140, 164, 165
Essex	165
Ethiopia	155
Ethiopian National Anthem	36
Everything's Got An Aura	165
Exodus	94, 99, 100, 101, 109, 111, 118, 120, 125, 130, 152

SONG TITLE	PAGE No.
Exodus Instrumental	94
Face Man	59
Fall Together	165
Fallin' In And Out Of Love	27
Falling Angel	99
Falling In & Out Of Love	29
Falling In And Out Of Love	27, 31
False Beneficiaries	153
Family Affair	151
Fancy Curls	154
Fanny Big Horn	165
Feel Alright	39, 167
Feel It	25
Feel No Way	131
Feel No Way Dub Mix One	131
Field Marshall	40
Fig Tree	85, 148
Fig Tree (Dubd'sco)	85
Fight Apartheid	143, 144
Fight On	113
Fight On (Instrumental)	113
Fighting Against Convictions	81
Fire Fire	28, 103
First Acquaintance With Blackwell	156
First Concert Performance	156
Fiya Red	155
Follow Bad Company	8
Follow Fashion Monkey	97
Follow Fashion Monkey Inst.	97
Food	147, 150
Fools Die	37, 103, 132
For Ever Loving Jah	153
Forever Loving Jah	122, 123, 124
Forever Loving Jah Version	124
Forsaken Friend	21
Four Hundred Years	165
Free Jah Children	106
Freedom	165
Freedom Time	26
Friends & Lovers	23
Funeral	28, 75
Fussing & Fighting	49, 50 165
Fussing & Fighting (version)	49
Galong So	133, 138, 148, 149
Gamblings	118
Genetic Order	154, 155
Get A Beaten	54
Get Down	165
Get Ready	26
Get Up Stand Up	69, 70, 71, 72, 73, 74, 75, 82, 83, 85, 90, 92, 93, 97, 99, 100, 101, 103, 105, 111, 117, 118, 120, 122, 125, 128, 136, 137, 139, 140, 142, 165
Ghetto People	154
Gimme Just Another Try	165
Girls	152
Give A Smile	165
Give Me A Ticket	37
Give Thanks And Praise	154
Give Thanks & Praises	124

SONG TITLE	PAGE No.
Glass House	135, 136, 140, 142
Go Jimmy Go	7
Go Tell It On The Mountain	38, 165
Gold Digger	36
Gonna Get You	35, 62
Gonna Let You	165
Good Girls Culture	165
Good Good Rudie	19, 148
Goodbye You Hello Him	165
Got To Leave This Place	63
Got To Move	106
Green Duck	39
Grinding Mill, The	7
Grooving Kingston	56
Grooving KNG. 12	56, 63
Guajara Ska	19, 21
Guava	58, 143
Guava Jelly	55, 58, 165
Guided Missile	87
Guiltiness	95, 99, 154
Guitar Solo	103
Guitar Solo #2	103
Gumption	151
Guns Barked, The	156
Habits	4
Hairy Mango	15
Hall Of Love	165
Hallelujah Time	69, 165
Hammer	28, 33, 34, 61, 91, 128, 140, 165
Hammer Dem Dung	91
Hand To Hand	7
Hang Down Your Head	151, 152
Harbour Shark	55
Haughty Tempo	148
He Who Feels It Knows It	22
Head Corner Stone	46
Heat Of The Day	167
Heathen, The	89, 96, 99, 101, 111, 118, 120, 130
Help Us Jah	155
Here Comes The Heart Aches	16
Here Comes The Judge	55
Here Comes The Sun	60
Here In Jamaica	146
Hey Happy People	46
High Tide Or Low Tide	64
Hit Back The Crack	151
Hold Me Tight	165
Hold On To This Feeling	40
Hold On To This Feeling Version	40
Home Sweet Home	142
Homeward Bound	39
Hook Line & Sinker	137, 165
Hooligan Ska	11, 12
Hooligans	4, 11, 12
Hoot Nanny Hoot	1, 4
Hot Dog	54
Hot Foot Head	148
House Of Dread	151
How Good It Is	165
How Many Times	1, 33, 34, 61, 165

SONG TITLE	PAGE No.
Hurting Inside	166
Hypocrite	26, 27, 126, 139, 143, 149, 166
Hypocrite - Dub	126
Hypocrites	26, 27, 118
Hypocrites Version	20
I Am Going Home	1, 3, 4, 166
I Am That I Am	93, 103, 164, 166
I Don't Need Your Love	1, 3, 166
I Know	87
I Know A Dub	105
I Know A Place	105
I Left My Sins	16
I Like It Like This	53
I Like Your Loving	166
I Made A Mistake	10, 11, 166
I Need You (Bob Marley)	10
I Need You (Bunny Wailer)	10, 25
I Need You So	25
I Shot The Sheriff	70, 82, 83, 89, 90, 99, 100, 111, 120, 126, 166
I Should Have Known Better	12
I Stand Predominant	25, 149
I Stand Predominate	126
I Stand Predominate - Dub	126
I Want Justice	8, 11
I Want You	166
I'm A Rastaman	166
I'm Gonna Get You	35, 166
I'm Gonna Put It On	8, 18, 49, 72, 73, 74, 166
I'm Hurting Inside	28, 55, 62
I'm Leaving	166
I'm Sorry For You Baby	23
I'm Still The King	152
I'm Still Waiting	14, 61, 166
I'm The Toughest	21, 109, 117, 126, 128, 135, 137, 138, 139, 143, 149, 152
I'm The Traveling	166
I'm Your Puppet	21
I've Got The Action	40
I've Got To Cry	40
I've Got To Go Back Home	22
Ice Water	12
If Ah-So	55
Igziabeher	90, 91, 105
Igziabeher (Let Jah Be Praised)	81
In My Song	144, 145
In The Iaah	50
In The Iwah	49, 50
Inheriting The Name Wailers	156
Innocent Blood	125
Instrumental	116
Introduction of Tuff Gong	156
Iration	78, 92
Iron Lion Zion	70
Is This Love	96, 109, 111, 120, 130
It Hurts To Be Alone	3, 8, 10, 35, 49, 61, 166
It May Sound Silly	75
It's All Right	166
It's Alright	45
It's Alright Version	45

SONG TITLE	PAGE No.	SONG TITLE	PAGE No.
It's Alright (version)	45	Leave My Business	58
Jack And Jill	15	Lecion D Travest	166
Jad The Scanners	156	Legalize It	77, 81, 89, 91, 103, 105, 122, 136, 137, 138, 142
Jah Guide	93, 103, 142, 166		
Jah Guide Me	131	Legends	155
Jah Is Mighty	46	Lemon Tree	24
Jah Live	87, 89, 92, 105	Leroy	166
Jah Love	143	Lesson In My Life	108, 145
Jah Man	91, 144, 145, 146	Let Him Go	19, 22, 108, 138, 166
Jah Man Version	146	Let The Children Dance	106
Jah Seh No	113	Let The Lord Be Seen In Me	15
Jailbreaker	122	Let The Lord Be Seen In You	15
Jailhouse	19	Let The Sun Shine On Me	54
Jamming	94, 96, 99, 101, 103, 105, 111, 118, 120 130	Let's Be Friends	166
		Let's Move And Groove Together	166
Jammins	134, 138	Letter, The	37
Jerico Skank	12	Liberation	150
Jerk, The	13	Lick Samba	60
Jerk All Night	16	Life Line	62, 63
Jerk In Time	23	Life Line Version	62, 63
Jerking Time	23	Lights In The Harbour	8
Johnny B Good	135, 136, 138, 140, 142	Linger You Linger	22
Johnny Too Bad	86, 97	Lion	60
Johnny Was	86	Lips Of The Righteous	37, 132
Johnny Was A Good Man	153	Little Boy Blue	16, 23
Jolly Session	148	Little Green Apples	39
Judge Not!	1, 154	Little Lonely Girl	166
Jumbie Jamboree	11, 12	Live	60
Jump Jump	142, 143	Live Love Rejoice	166
Jump Nyabinghi	127, 128	Lively Up Instrumental	103
Jump Nyahbinghi	154	Lively Up Yourself	60, 71, 72, 73, 74, 79, 83, 90, 99, 101, 111, 118, 125, 154, 166
Jump Them Outta Babylon	122		
Jungle Fever	123		
Just Be Nice	151	Lonely Day	167
Just In Time	16	Lonely Girl	35, 166
Kaya	48, 77, 97, 166	Lonesome Feeling	49, 164, 166
Kaya Skank	48	Lonesome Feelings	10, 35, 49
Kaya Version	48	Lonesome Track	16, 19, 166
Kaya (version)	48	Long Long Winter	48
Kaya (version 2)	48	Long Long Winter Version	48
Kayah Now	48	Look In Your Eyes, The	166
Keep On Dancing	166	Lord I'm Coming	166
Keep On Moving	50, 51, 92, 101, 126, 139, 152, 166	Lord Will Make A Way, The	28, 29
		Love	31, 166
Keep On Moving Dub	101	Love Ain't No Holiday (Jobson)	166
Keep On Moving – (Dub)	126	Love & Affection	8, 12, 49, 166
Keep On Moving Version	50, 101	Love Fire	100, 138, 143, 148, 149
Keep On Moving Version 2	101	Love Fire (Dubd'sco)	100
Keep On Running	151	Love I Can Feel	152
Keep On Skanking	77	Love I Get Ready	166
Ketchy Huby	78	Love Life	53
Ketchy Shuby	91	Love Light	53
Ketchy Shubby	78, 91, 92, 138	Love Light Version	53
Kings And Queens	166	Love Thy Neighbor	80
Kingston 12 Shuffle	56	Love Won't Be Mine This Way	8, 18
Kingston 12 Shuffle Version	56	Love's Version	100
Kinky Reggae	64, 65, 71, 72, 73, 74, 75, 83, 85, 109, 120, 166	Loving You	166
		Low Minded Hypocrite	8, 11
Knotty Dread	80, 83	Lyrical Satyrical I	27
Knotty Dread (Natty Dread)	79	Maga Dog	4, 12, 54, 60, 134, 166
Las Flores Wechter	166	Magical Fountain	166
Lay It On	22	Maingy Dog	54

172

SONG TITLE	PAGE No.	SONG TITLE	PAGE No.
Make Me Love The Rain	166	Never Had A Dream	43
Make Up	40	Nice Time	10, 26, 27, 31, 33, 49, 61, 83, 89, 147, 166
Making Love	24		
Mam To Man V/3	42, 43	Nice Time Version	26
Mama Africa	135, 140	Nicoteen	42, 43
Mama Africa Dub	135	Night Shift	86, 166
Man To Man (Lee Perry)	7	Night Spots	166
Man To Man	42, 43, 86	Nightfall Ruler	36
Man To Man (Who The Cap Fit)	154	No Chuck It 'Pon Jaro	151
Mango Coconut Sugar	166	No Faith	21
Mark Of The Beast	89, 91	No Mercy	67
Mark Of The Beast, The	69	No More Trouble	65, 71, 73, 74, 90, 92, 99, 100, 101, 111, 118, 120, 122, 130, 153, 166
Me No Go A Jail Fe Gang Jah	135		
Mellow Mood	26, 27, 33, 126, 143, 166		
Mellow Mood - Dub	126	No Nuclear War	143, 144, 146, 164
Mellow Mood Version	26	No Parshall	40
Memphis	50, 166	No Sound Boy No Cry	125
Memphis (version)	50	No Sympathy	46, 69, 78, 91, 166
Mi And Dem (We And Them)	154	No Sympathy Version	46
Midnight Raver	71	No Water	44, 45, 166
Midnight Ravers	61, 67, 73, 74, 83, 166	No Water Can Quench My Thirst	45
Milkshake & Potato Chips	35, 166	No Water Version	45
Mill Man, The	7	No Woman No Cry	80, 81, 83, 89, 90, 99, 100, 101, 111, 118, 120, 130, 139, 149, 166
Millenium Rock	156		
Mister Brown	49		
Misty Morning	95	Nobody Knows	7, 166
Mix Up	154	Nobody Knows The Trouble	166
Mix Up, Mix Up	117	North Scene Soundtrack	54
Monkey Speaks, The	137	Not Gonna Give It Up	134, 135, 136, 137, 138, 140
Moon Dust	39		
Mooving Skank	50, 51	Nothing But Love	132
Mooving Version	50	Ocean	11 19
More Axe	42	Oh Bumbo Klaat	133
More More Axe	42	Oh Lord I Got To Get There	62
Moses – The Prophets	108	Oh My Darling	10
Moses Children	97	Old Dragon, The	106, 138, 148, 149
Mr. Brown	166	Old Time Dub	148
Mr. Chatterbox	44	Old Time Singting	148
Mr. Talkative	3, 10	On Broadway	7
Muddy Water	166	On My Way	166
Mus' Get A Beatin'	28	Once Bitten	60
Music Gonna Teach	61	One Bad Habit	166
Music Gonna Teach Version	61	One By One	7
Music Lesson	61	One Cup Of Coffee	1
Musical Lesson	61	One Drop	115, 120, 153
Must Skank	62, 63	One Dub	115
My Cup	40, 166	One Foundation	69, 166
My Desire	40	One Love	13, 49, 89, 105, 140, 154, 164, 166
My Dream Island	51		
My Girl	15	One Love Version	13
My Merry Go Round	166	One Love, True Love	167
My Sympathy	45	One Love/People Get Ready	89, 96
Mystery Babylon	146	One More Chance	11
Mystery Babylon Version	146	Ooh Baby You've Been Good	166
Mystic Man	113, 136	Oppressed Song	69
Nah Goa Jail	144	Oppressed Song, The	83
Natty Dread	79, 80, 85, 99, 105, 154	Oppressor Man	19, 39
Natural Mystic	82, 95, 99, 105, 118, 120, 125, 130, 154	Pass It On	1, 63, 64, 69, 166, 167
		Pass It On Version	167
Natural Mystic Rhythm Track	82	Payaka	27
Never Conquer	151, 152	Peace Talk	106
Never Grow Old	151	Peace Talks	106

SONG TITLE	PAGE No.	SONG TITLE	PAGE No.
Peace Treaty	132	Reaction Version	46
People In Love	166	Ready When You Ready	150
People's Cup, The	155	Real Situation	124
Peter's Rap	140	Reasons	148
Pick Myself Up	103, 108, 117, 122, 138, 139, 140	Rebel Hop Version	46
		Rebel Music	78, 79, 90, 100, 109, 118
Picking Up The Pieces	166	Rebel Music (3 O'clock Road Block)	79
Picture On The Wall V/3	43	Rebel Version	45
Picture On The Wall V/4	43	Rebel's Hop	46, 166
Pimper's Paradise	122, 124, 154	Rebeloution	55
Place Of Peace	122	Record A New Song	122
Play Play Play	28	Recruiting Soldiers	113, 128
Playboy	3, 11, 12	Recruiting Soldiers (Version)	113
Pomps And Pride	122	Recruiting The Wailers	156
Poor Man Feel It, The	131	Red	58
Positive Vibration	86, 90, 92, 99, 100, 103, 105, 111, 118, 120, 125, 130, 166	Red Hot	132
		Red Red Red	58
		Redder Than Red	56, 58
Pound Get A Blow	28	Redemption Song	123, 124, 125, 130, 166
Pour Down The Sunshine	54	Reggae Burden	151
Pour Sugar On Me	166	Reggae Converts	155
Power & More Power	59	Reggae In The U.S.A.	148
Power Struggle	106	Reggae Mylitis	132, 135
Pray For Me	122	Reggae On Broadway	62, 166
Preparation And Exposure	156	Reggae Rebel	154
Punky Party Part Two	101	Reggae The Night Away	166
Punky Reggae Part Of Park One	101	Reggae Tree	154
Punky Reggae Party	101, 109	Reincarnated Soul	69
Punky Reggae Party Part One	101	Reincarnated Souls	85
Punky Reggae Version Part Two	101	Related To Life	63
Puss And Dog	130	Rescue Me	147
Pussy Galore	14	Restoration Of Wail 'N' Soul M	156
Pussy Man	14	Return Of Al Capone, The	39
Put It On	18, 33, 34, 48, 70, 148, 166	Return Of JAD The Scanners	156
		Reuben	55
Put It On Version	18	Revolution	78, 80, 154, 166
Put It On (version)	48	Rhythm	38, 39
Pyaka (Bus Dem Shut)	151	Ride Natty Ride	114, 115, 116, 120
Quatrocientas Years	166	Riding	133
Quit Trying	97	Riding High	50, 166
Raggamuffiin	152	Riding High (version)	50
Rainbow Country	81, 82, 154, 166	Right On	122
Rainbow Country Rhythm Track	82	Righteous Ruler	36
Ram Dance	152	Rightful Ruler	36
Ram Dance Hall	149, 152	Ringo's Ska	21
Rasta Dread (Natty Dread)	154	Rise & Shine	134
Rasta Man	83	Rise And Shine	148, 149, 150
Rasta Man (Dubd'sco)	83	Road Block	78, 79, 82, 83, 85, 92, 97, 111
Rasta Man Chant	70, 71, 72, 73, 74, 89, 92, 103, 166		
		Rock	114
Rasta Put It On	21	Rock 'N' Groove	149
Rasta Shook Dem Up	156	Rock And Groove	133, 138, 143, 148
Rasta Shook Them Up	21	Rock And Roll Junkie	166
Rastafari Is	132, 135, 136, 137, 138, 140	Rock In Time	114
		Rock It Babe	65
Rastaman	138, 143, 148	Rock It Baby	65, 166
Rastaman Live Up	114, 117, 118	Rock It Version	65
Rastaman Rides Again	154	Rock My Boat	53
Rastaman Vibration	153	Rock Steady	33
Rat Race	88, 90, 92, 109, 130, 154	Rock Sweet Rock	23
Ravers Version	67	Rock This Music	134
Reaction	44, 46, 166	Rock To The Rock	31

SONG TITLE	PAGE No.	SONG TITLE	PAGE No.
Rock With Me	132, 136	Secondhand Part Two	49
Rockers	114, 148, 149	See And Blind	151
Rocking Steady	31	Selassie	36
Rocking Steady Part 2	31	Selassie Is The Chapel	34
Rockstone	154, 155	Selassie Serenade	39
Rolling Stone	25	Selfish Lover	166
Romper Room	39	Send Me That Love	51
Root, Rock, Dub	86	Sentimental Journey	24
Roots 88,	153	Serious Thing	147, 150
Roots Man Skanking	134	Shame And Scandal	13
Roots Radics (Dubd'sco)	106	Shame And Scandal In The Family	13
Roots Rock Reggae	86, 90, 125, 153, 166	Shark	56
Roots Version	88	She Used To Call Me Da Da	128
Roots, Radics, Rockers And Reggae	106, 149	She's Gone	95, 166
Rootsman Skanking	138, 143, 148, 149	She's Older Now	166
Rub & Squeeze	18	Shocks Of Mighty	46
Rub-A-Dub-Style	124	Shotgun	14
Ruddie	19	Shout (Afrik S)	166
Ruddie Boy	19	Show Your Dreads On	122
Rude Boy	14, 72, 143	Si Tu Penses A Moi	166
Rude Boy Rap	154	Silver And Gold	130, 166
Rude Boy Ska	14	Simmer Down	1, 3, 49, 89, 137, 154, 166
Rude Boy Train	54		
Rude Boy Version	54	Simpleton	26
Rude Boys In The Hood	154	Sinner Man	19, 22, 39, 49
Rudie	19, 139, 149	Sitting In The Park	14, 151
Rudie Part Two	19	Ska Jam	14
Rudie Rudie	19	Ska Jerk	14
Rudie's Medley	54	Skanky Dog	54
Rule Dance Hall	148	Skill's Appointment To Tuff Gong	156
Rule Them Rudie	14	Slave Driver	62, 64, 71, 72, 73, 74, 82, 83, 118, 126, 166
Rule This Land	126, 166		
Rule This Land - Dub	126	Small Axe	42, 69, 70, 73, 154, 166
Rumors	122	Small Axe V/2	42
Rumours Of War	113	Smile Jamaica	92
Run For Cover	45, 139, 148, 151	Smile Jamaica Part One	90
Running Away	96, 99, 101, 103, 111, 118, 120, 125, 130, 154	Smile Jamaica Part Two	90
		So Jah Say	166
Running Away Dub	96	So Jah Seh	79, 80, 83, 89, 92
Russian Ska Fever	3	So Much Things To Say	97, 120, 154
Russians Are Coming, The	122	So Much Trouble	114, 120, 123
Samba	60	So Much Trouble Dub	116
Satisfy My Soul	59, 95, 166	So Much Trouble In World	116
Satisfy My Soul Babe	59	So Nice While It Lasted	166
Satisfy My Soul Jah Jah Dub	59	Solidarity	83
Satisfy My Soul Jah Jah	59	Solomonic Dub	134
Satisfy My Soul Jah Jah Version	59	Somewhere To Lay My Head	15
Satisfy My Soul Version	59	Soon Come	38, 109, 117, 166
Satta Massa Ganna	55	Sophisticated Psychedelication	38
Saturday Night	148, 166	Soul Almighty	31, 46, 164, 166
Say It Loud – I'm Black And I'm Proud	36	Soul Almighty Version	46
Sca-Balena	13	Soul Brother Soul Captive	166
Scanner, The	156	Soul Captives	38
Scanners, The	156	Soul Rebel	34, 44, 45, 103, 126, 139, 143, 148, 166, 167
Scheme Of Things	97		
Screw Face	56, 59, 166	Soul Rebel V/4	45
Screw Faces	56	Soul Rebels Version	45
Screw Faces Version	56	Soul Rocking Party	137, 139
Search For Love	62, 63	Soul Shake Down Party	35, 38, 166
Searching For Love	62, 63	Soul Shake Down Version	38
Season For Carnival (McDonald)	166	Soultown	53
Secondhand	49	Sound The Trumpet	4

SONG TITLE	PAGE No.
Sounds Clash	151
South Carolina	166
Specialist, The	152
Splish For My Splash	27, 29, 31
Stand Alone	49, 50, 166
Stand Alone (version)	50
Stand Firm	108
Stand In Love	155
Stand In Version	155
Standing In The Rain	166
Standing Ovation	154, 155
Staright To Rag-Jah-Rabbit Head	35
Stay With Me	35, 62, 166
Stay With The Reggae	142, 143
Steal Away	166
Steppin' Razor	91
Stepping Razor	28, 93, 105, 117, 128, 135, 137, 142, 166
Stick Up	36
Stiff Neck Fool	154
Stiff Necked Dub	128
Stiff Necked Fools	37, 128
Still The King	152
Stir It Up	27, 55, 61, 67, 71, 72, 73, 74, 111, 120, 148, 166
Stop That Train	65, 72, 73, 74, 103, 134, 166
Stop That Train (Instrumental)	65
Stop The Train	38, 71
Straight & Narrow Way	1, 3
Stranger On The Shore	27, 29, 31
Struggle	106, 138, 143, 148, 149
Sugar Sugar	37
Sun Is Going Down	166
Sun Is Shining	53, 97, 154, 166
Sun Is Shining Version	53, 97
Sun Is Shining V/2	53
Sun Is Shining V/3	53
Sun Valley	39
Sunday Morning	22
Sunshine	166
Survival	114, 115, 154
Survivors (Survival)	154
Swing Low Sweet Chariot	3
Swop Shop	137
Take Me Back	166
Talkin' Blues	78, 79
Talking Blues	79, 83, 85, 154
Talking Blues (Version)	79
Tears In Your Eyes	142
Teenager In Love	8, 12
Teeni Wappaz	155
Tell It To The Mountains	166
Tell Me The World Is Changing	166
Tell Them Lord	4
Ten Commandments Of Love	18
Terror	1
Testify	142
Thank You Jah	166
Thank You Lord	26, 27, 37, 166
Thank You Lord Version	26
That Ain't Right	23

SONG TITLE	PAGE No.
That's The Way We Get By	166
That's What They Will Do	131
The Lord Will Make A Way	28, 29
Them A, Fi Get A Beaten	54, 55, 137, 138, 142
Them Belly Full	90, 120
Them Belly Full (But We Hungry)	79
Them Have To Get A Beating	55
Theme From Rockers	114
There Are More Questions	166
There She Goes	10, 33, 34, 166
This Train	16, 27, 37, 55, 85, 166
This Train Is Bound For Glory	16, 27
Three Little Birds	97, 153
Three Little Birds Dub	97
Till Your Well Runs Dry	77
Time To Cry	24
Time To Turn	24
Time Will Tell	95, 103, 130
To The Rescue	53
Togawar Game	125
Together	142
Together Again	5, 61, 147, 149
Tom Dooley	152
Too Much Rats	131
Top Rankin'	116, 154
Top Rankin' Dub	116
Total Destruction	156
Touch Me	34, 35, 166
Tough Rock Soft Stones	109
Toughest	166
Toughest, The	21, 54, 109
Toughest - Dub	126
Toughest Version	109
Train Is Coming, The	25
Trash Ina We Bes	148
Travelling In Style	166
Tread-O	35
Tread-O Version	35
Treat Me Good	24, 33
Treat You Right	34, 35, 166
Trench Town	127, 128, 153, 156, 166
Trench Town - Kingston 12	156
Trench Town Rock	56, 63, 83, 85, 89, 90, 92, 100, 105, 166
Tribulation	99
Tribute To The Don	153
Trigger Happy Kid	155
Trinity, The	156
Trod On	64
Trouble Dub	36
Trouble In The World	154
Trouble Is On The Road Again	137
Trouble On The Road Again	36
True Confessions	8, 10
True Love	44
Trust Me	166
Try Me	40, 166
Try Me Version	40
Trying To Keep A Good Man Down	10
Turn Me Loose	48, 77
Turn Me Loose (Pipe & The Pipers)	56
Turn Your Lights	166

SONG TITLE	PAGE No.
Turn Your Lights Down Low	96
Unity	134
Unjust, The	4
Uprising Theme	123
Vampire	92, 146
Version Of Cup	40
Version Rebel Am I	80
Very First Time, The	166
Veteran	152
Vexation	122
Vision Land	51
Voo Doo Moon	24
Vow, The	10, 11
Wages Of Love	16, 19
Wages Of Love Rehearsal	16
Wail 'N' Soul M Label, The	156
Wailers Betrayed	157
Wailers Catch A Fire Tour	157
Wailers Clash With Johnny Nash	156
Wailers First Recording Session	156
Wailers Frustration	156
Wailers Progress, The	156
Wailers Return To Jamaica	156
Wailers Split, The	157
Wailers Tour With Johnny Nash	156
Wailers/Beverley's Combination	156
Wailers/Island Combination	157
Wailers/Upsetter Combination	156
Waiting In Vain	94, 95, 103
Waiting In Vain Dub	95
Wake Up And Live	116, 118, 120, 154
Wake Up And Live Version	116
Walk 'N Talk	152
Walk The Proud Land	67, 73, 126, 143, 149
Walk The Proud Land - Dub	126
Walking Razor	28
Want Love True Love	27
Want More	86, 90, 92, 103, 153, 167
Want To Come Home	150
Wanted Children	97
Wanted Dread & Alive	131, 140, 164
War	87, 90, 92, 99, 100, 101, 105, 111, 118, 120, 122, 130
Warrior	151
Warrior Dub	151
We And Dem	122
We And Them	124, 154
We Can Make It	60
We Can Make It Uptight	60
We Won	166
We're All A Like	166
Wedding Bells Tolled, The	156
Wellbread	75
What A Confusion	43
What Am I Supposed To Do	25
What Goes Around Comes Around	29, 31
What You Gonna Do	75, 90
What's New Pussy Cat	8, 13
What's New Pussycat	154
Whatcha Gonna Do	91
Wheel Yo Belly	151

SONG TITLE	PAGE No.
When The Well Runs Dry	23
Where Is My Mother	15, 16
Where Sammy's Gone	3
Where Will I Find	8, 13
Where You Gonna Run	135, 140
Where's The Girl For Me	11, 12
Whip Them One By One	151
White Christmas	15
White Liver Mabel	55
Who Colt The Dub	105
Who Colt The Game	105
Who Feels It	97, 166
Who Feels It Knows It	22
Who Is Mister Brown	49
Who Is Mr. Brown	92
Who Laugh Last	152
Who The Cap Fit	43, 86, 103, 118, 154, 166
Whose Mr. Brown	49
Why Must I Cry	77, 91
Why Must We Cry	166
Why Should I	61
Wicker Man	131
Winepress (Babylon System)	154
Wings Of A Dove	7, 27
Wirly Girly	114
Wisdom	37, 132, 166, 167
Wishing Well	166
Woman	153
Woman Dub	153
Women Wine And Money	12
Work	87, 122, 124, 130, 154
World Is Changing, The	34, 35, 166
World Peace	156
Worly Girly	114
WXFM Radio ID	103
Ya Ya	16
Yesterday's Children	166
You Can Do That To	166
You Can't Blame The Youth	73
You Can't Do That To Me	35, 166
You Can't Fool Me Again	35
You Can't Get Away	55
You Got Soul	166
You Pour Sugar On Me	37
You Poured Sugar On Me	166
You Say I Have No Feelings	29, 31
Young, Gifted And Black	151, 152
Your Love	3, 12
Zigzag	42, 43
Zimbabwe	115, 118, 120, 125, 130, 154
Zimbabwe Version	115
Zimmerman	19
Zion Express	124
Zion Train	122, 123, 124, 130, 154